how t

Yo

Degree

Course

A survey of degree courses in British Universities and Colleges

by

BRIAN HEAP

TROTMAN

This edition published in 1996 in
Great Britain by
Trotman and Company Limited
12 Hill Rise, Richmond, Surrey TW10 6UA

© Brian Heap and Trotman and Company Limited

British Library Cataloguing in Publication Data
A catalogue record for this book is available from the
British Library

ISBN 0-85660-286-8

Typeset by Page Bros (Norwich) Limited
Printed and bound in Great Britain

Contents

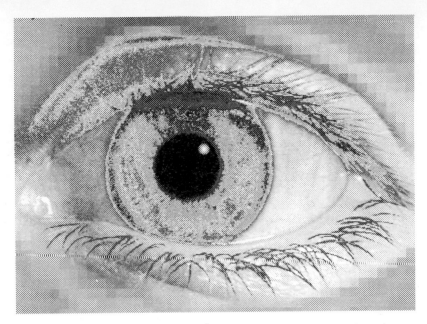

As one of the world's leading firms of accountants and business advisers, we are proud of our ability to take a broader business view whilst focusing on our clients' individual needs.

Likewise, as a graduate, you will soon discover the broader picture and appreciate the sheer number and variety of opportunities available to you when you join us.

"A broader vision"

We are proud of our position as one of the leading innovators in what is an increasingly challenging global business. Each and every individual is important to this success, which is why our priority is to encourage and nurture your potential.

You will gain valuable experience and have the opportunity to specialise in one of the following business sectors:

Audit & Accountancy • Tax • Public Sector
Computer Audit & Security • Corporate Recovery

Whilst gaining a professional qualification is very important, we also know through experience that the exposure you will have to the international business world will be of equal importance. Working with like-minded colleagues, we offer you the chance to develop your skills in a challenging andstimulating environment.

If you are now ready to broaden your vision of a career with KPMG, write for your own copy of our brochure to David Miller, National Graduate Recruitment Partner, 8 Salisbury Square, Blackfriars, London EC4Y 8BB.

KPMG

SPONSOR'S INTRODUCTION

KPMG is the UK practice of one of the world's leading accountancy and management consultancy firms with over 800 offices in 131 countries worldwide.

Each year KPMG recruits approximately 600 graduates into its 39 UK offices. Whilst the majority of graduates pursue careers in audit and accountancy, an increasing proportion are looking for careers in tax, corporate recovery and corporate finance.

KPMG employs graduates from all degree disciplines and therefore we know that your choice of course will have a major part in shaping your future career.

We are pleased to be associated with this book offering information and guidance for anyone considering higher education as the next stage in their career development.

David Miller
National Graduate Recruitment Partner

Get reading!!

Right now, you're facing some of the most important decisions you'll ever make - but with Ford, we make sure that whether you decide to go on to higher education or embark on your career now, you're opening doors rather than closing them.

That's because we offer opportunities to suit you whatever your decision - if you go to university, you could enrol on our sponsorship programme, or you might opt instead for an Apprenticeship or a Ford Undergraduate scheme. Either way, you won't be giving up the chance to study for further qualifications.

ENGINEERING & SYSTEMS SPONSORSHIP

For school leavers who plan to read either an Engineering or a Systems/Information Technology degree at one of a number of approved higher education institutions.

PURCHASING & LOGISTICS UNDERGRADUATE SCHEME

Whilst working at Ford you will work towards a BA (Hons) degree in Business Studies through a part-time/day release course.

MANAGEMENT ACCOUNTANCY TRAINEE SCHEME

You will study part-time towards full membership of the Chartered Institute of Management Accountants.

We also offer **Engineering Apprenticeships** for 16-19 year olds where you can gain a BTEC qualification and NVQIII, and you may even be given the opportunity to progress onto a Ford sponsored degree.

For specific details of the entry requirements for each scheme, please write for an information pack to us at College Recruitment, Room 1/360, Ford Motor Company Limited, Eagle Way, Brentwood, Essex CM13 3BW.

These opportunities are open to both young men and women regardless of ethnic origin in line with Ford's equal opportunities policy.

ABOUT THIS BOOK

Each year over 250,000 students leave schools and colleges to embark on degree courses in universities and colleges throughout the UK. Unfortunately, each year about 40,000 of them drop out, simply because they chose the wrong course.

Perhaps this is hardly surprising in view of the fact that there are over 750 degree subjects and 70,000 course combinations on offer. Despite the mass of information in circulation, however, it is impossible for any student to maintain a memory bank of courses which might be relevant to his or her interests, abilities and aspirations, or to remember how courses differ between one university and another. In addition, lack of career knowledge across the choice of over 400 occupations also makes it difficult to compare careers with degree course choices.

So what are the questions which applicants need to ask? What does a degree course really involve? How do courses in the same subject but at different universities differ? What are the distinguishing features between courses? Is it better to choose your favourite school subject and study it to degree level or to try for a vocational course?

You will find the answers to these questions in this book.

This new updated fifth edition of *How To Choose Your Degree Course* is not a compendium of all degree courses but aims to provide a quick and easy reference source to all the major university single honours degree courses offered in the UK. It outlines what is involved in a study of the subject and how the courses may vary from one institution to another - the differences in course structure, and some of the options which can be taken. The range of course titles will thus enable the reader to build up a broad understanding of course content and titles which are similar in many university courses.

No one book however can give you all the answers but *How To Choose Your Degree Course*, prospectuses, visits to Open Days at various institutions and discussions with staff and students involved in courses can all help you to make sure that your three, four or five years in higher education could be the most exciting and fulfilling of your life.

I am grateful to the Higher Education Funding Council (England) for permission to use information on some of the courses.

Good Luck!

Brian Heap, June 1996

N.B. Because of constant changes in the funding of university courses readers are reminded that some established courses are being withdrawn and new courses are taking their place. The content of courses too may alter. You are, therefore, **advised** to check prospectuses and contact admissions officers at the institutions for up-to-date information on any recent changes.

CHAPTER 1
CHOOSING YOUR DEGREE
COURSE

HIGHER EDUCATION OR NOT?

Why do you want to go on to higher education? If you are taking A/AS-levels GNVQs or other examinations next year this is an important question to ask. Higher education is but one of two options you have. The other is employment, and perhaps it is important to remember that higher education is not necessarily the best option for everyone. It is, however, one which is appropriate for many and therefore should not be rejected lightly. Higher education will not only open many doors and give you opportunities for work and leisure which would never be possible in a nine-to-five job, but it leads very often and quite accidentally into careers you have never previously considered.

Most courses in higher education lead to a degree or a diploma and, for either, you will have to make a subject choice. This can be difficult because universities and colleges offer over 700 degree subjects.

There are three main options when choosing your course:

Choosing a course similar or the same as one (or more) of your A-level subjects

Choosing a course related to an interest outside the school curriculum eg Anthropology, American Studies, Archaeology

Choosing a course in preparation for a future career eg Medicine, Engineering.

CHOOSING YOUR COURSE

Degree/Diploma Course Choice by A-level Subject
The A-level subject choice is a reasonably safe option. You are already familiar with the subject and what it involves and you can possibly look forward to studying it to a much greater depth over the next few years. If the long term career prospects concern you, don't worry - a degree course isn't necessarily a training for a job. If you are taking science subjects then these can naturally lead on to a range of scientific careers although many scientists follow non science careers such as law, and accountancy. If you are taking arts or social science subjects remember that the training for most non scientific careers starts once you have got your degree.

But let's go a stage further:

A-level subjects do not stand on their own, in isolation. Each subject you are taking is one of a much larger 'family'. Each school subject has many similarities with subjects which can be offered in degree and diploma courses with a variety of names which you might not have considered. So before you decide finally on taking an A-level subject to degree level read through the following tables. Here you will find some examples of degree courses with similarities to the A-level subjects you might be taking.

(a) A-LEVEL SUBJECTS AND RELATED DEGREE/ DIPLOMA COURSES

Accountancy (Principal of Accounts)
Accountancy
Accounting
Actuarial Science
Agricultural
    Economics
Banking
Business
    Administration
Business Economics
*Business Studies
Commerce
Economics
Estate Management
Finance
Financial Services
Financial Analysis
Financial Economics
* Hotel (Hospitality)
    Management
Industrial Economics
Insurance
Investment
Land Economics
Management Science
Managerial Sciences
Marketing
Quantity Surveying
Retail Management
Valuation

Ancient History
Ancient Civilisation
Ancient Greek
Ancient History
Ancient
    Mediterranean
    Studies
Anglo-Saxon
Anthropology
Archaeology
Art (Islamic)

Biblical Studies
Byzantine Studies
Celtic Studies
Classical Archaeology
Classical Studies
*Classical Civilisation
East Mediterranean
    History
Greek Archaeology
Greek (Ancient)
Greek and Roman
    Studies
Heritage Management
History
History of
    Architecture
History of Art
History of Religions
Islamic Art and
    Archaeology
Jewish History
Middle Eastern
    Civilisation/
    Cultures
Religious Studies
Roman Archaeology
Roman Studies

Archaeology
Anthropology
Archaeology
Byzantine Studies
Celtic Studies
Classical Civilisation
Classical Studies
Combined Studies
Conservation of
    Buildings
Conservation
    (Restoration)
Earth Science
East Mediterranean
    History

Environmental
    Science
Geology
Greek Archaeology
Greek and Roman
    Studies
History of
    Architecture
History of Art
History of Design
Islamic Art and
    Archaeology
Maritime History
Middle Eastern
    Studies
Nautical Archaeology
Roman Archaeology

Art and Design
Advertising
    (Copywriting,
    Design)
Advertising
    (Photography)
Advertising
    (Management)
Animation
Applied Arts
Archaeology
Architecture
Art (Islamic)
Art teaching
Bookbinding
Ceramic Design
Combined Studies
Communication
    Studies
Conservation
    (Archaeological)
Conservation
    (Building)
Conservation
    (Restoration)
Costume Design

Creative Arts
Design Crafts
Designs for Media
Embroidery
Fashion Designs
Fashion Promotions
Film Studies
Fine Arts
Fine Arts Restoration
Floral Design
Furniture Design
Garden Design
Gemology
Glass Design
Graphic Arts
Graphic Designs
Heritage Management
History of
    Architecture
History of Art
History of Design
History of Film
Illustration
Industrial Design
Interior Design
Landscape
    Architecture
Media Studies
Model-making
Photography
Print Design
Product Design
Sculpture
Silversmithing, Gold
    and Jewellery
TV Studies
Textile Design
Theatre Design
Typography
Valuation (Fine Arts)
Visual Arts
Visual
    Communications
Visual Studies

Biology
Agricultural
    Biochemistry
Agricultural Biology
Agricultural
    Biotechnology
Agricultural Botany

Agricultural Zoology
Agriculture
Agroforestry
Agronomy
Anatomy
Animal Behaviour
Animal Biology
Animal Ecology
Animal Management
Animal Nutrition
Animal Physiology
Animal Production
Animal Science
Anthropology
Applied Biology
Applied Ecology
Applied Plant Biology
Applied Zoology
Aquatic Biology
Aquaculture
Arboriculture
Bacteriology
Behavourial Biology
Behavourial Studies
Bio Organic
    Chemistry
Bioanalytical Science
Biochemical
    Engineering
Biochemistry
Biogeochemistry
Biological Chemistry
Biological Sciences
Biology
Biology teaching
Biomolecular
    Chemistry
Biophysics
Bioprocess
    Engineering
Biosciences
Biosciences (Medical)
Biotechnology
Botany
Brewing and Distilling
Cell Biology
Childhood Studies
Combined Studies
Consumer Sciences
Consumer Studies
Cosmetic Science

Countryside
    Management
Crop Protection
Crop Science
Dental Laboratory
    Practice
Dental Technology
Dentistry
Developmental
    Psychology
Dietetics
Domestic Animal
    Science
Domestic Science
Earth Resources
Earth Science
Earth Studies
Ecology
Environmental
    Biochemistry
Environmental
    Biology
Environmental Health
Environmental
    Landscape
    Management
Environmental
    Planning
Environmental
    Protection
Environmental
    Science
Environmental
    Studies
Environmental
    Toxicology
Equine Studies
European Food
    Studies
European Health
    Sciences
Exercise and Health
Farm Management
Fisheries Science
Fisheries Technology
Floristry
Food Bioprocessing
Food Economics
Food Engineering
Food Management
Food Manufacturing
Food Marketing

Food Production
Food Quality
Food Technology
Forensic Science
Forest Products
 (Wood)
 Technology
Forestry
Forest Management
Garden Designs
General Science
Genetics
Golf Course Studies
Health Administration
Health and Fitness
Health and
 Community
 Studies
Health and Safety
Health Care
Health Promotion
Health Psychology
Health Sciences
Health Studies
Health Services
Horse Studies
Horticulture
Human Biology
Human
 Communication
Human Ecology
Human Ergonomics
Human Evolution
Human Geography
Human Life Sciences
Human Movement
 Studies
Human Nutrition
Human Physiology
Human Psychology
Human Sciences
Immunology
Land Management
Landscape
 Architecture
Landscape Design
Learning Disabilities
Life Sciences
Marine Biology
Marine Botany
Marine Environment
Marine Resources

Marine Zoology
Medical Biosciences
Medical Electronics
Medical Microbiology
Medical Physics
Medicinal and
 Cosmetic
 Products
Medicinal Chemistry
Medicine
Medicine (Herbal)
Microbiology
Midwifery
Molecular Biology
Molecular Genetics
Molecular Pathology
Molecular Sciences
Natural Resources
 Sciences
Neuroscience
Nursing
Nutrition
Nutritional
 Biochemistry
Occupational Health
Occupational Therapy
Ocean Science
Oceanography
Ophthalmics
Optometry
Orthoptics
Osteopathy
Paper Science
Parasitology
Pathology
Pharmaceutical
 Chemistry
Pharmacology
Pharmacy
Physical Education
 (teaching)
Physical Geography
Physiology
Physiotherapy
Plant Biology
 Ecology
 Science
Podiatry
Polymer Science
Population Biology
Poultry Production
Process Biochemistry

Prosthetics and
 Orthotics
Psychology
Psychosocial Science
Public Health
Radiography
Recreation Studies
Rural Environmental
 Studies
Rural Resources
Social Anthropology
Social Care
Social Psychology
Social Work
Soil Science
Speech Therapy
Sports Science
Toxicology
Turf Science
Underwater Studies
Veterinary Science
Wood Science
Zoology

Business Studies
Accountancy
Administration
Advertising
American Business
 Studies
Arts Management
Banking
Building Management
Business
 Administration
 Analysis
 Computing
 Decision Analysis
 Economics
 French
 Information Systems
 Information
 Technology
 Law
 Mathematics
 Studies
 Studies (with
 German)
 Studies (Welsh)
Combined Studies
Commerce
Consumer Studies

Countryside Management
Decision Management
Distribution Management
Economics
Estate Management
European Accountancy and Finance
European Business Administration
European Business Economics
European Land Management
European Marketing
European Tourism
Farm Management
Financial Services
Food Marketing
Health Administration
Heritage Management
Hospitality Management
＊Hotel Management
Industrial Relations
Institutional Management
International Business Economics
International Hotel Management
International Marketing
International Tourism Management
International Transport
Land Economy
Land Management
Leisure Management
Management Science
Management Studies
Marketing
Operational Research
Organisation Studies
Print Management
Property Management
Public Administration
Publishing
Purchasing

Quality Management
Quantity Surveying
Retail Management
Risk Management
Rural Economics
Rural Resource Management
Social Administration
Stage Management
Surveying
Telecommunications Management
Transport Management
Tourism Management
Urban Estate Management

Chemistry
Agricultural Biochemistry
Agricultural Biology
Agricultural Chemistry
Agriculture
Analytical Chemistry
Animal Nutrition
Animal Sciences
Applied Chemistry
Bacteriology
Biochemical Engineering
Biochemistry
Biological Chemistry
Biological Sciences
Biomedical Science
Biotechnology
Botany
Brewing and Distilling
Cell Biology
Ceramic Science
Chemical Physics
Chemical Technology
Chemistry
Chemistry of Food
Chemistry teaching
Colour Chemistry
Combined Studies
Computational Chemistry
Computer-Aided Chemistry

Cosmetic Science
Dentistry
Dyeing and Dyestuffs Technology
Engineering
(Chemical)
(Fire)
(Food)
(Fuel and Energy)
(Nuclear)
(Petroleum)
Environmental Biochemistry
Environmental Biology
Environmental Chemistry
Environmental Toxicology
Fisheries Science
Food Science
Forensic Science
Fuel Science
General Science
Genetics
Geochemistry
Geoscience
Glass Technology
Health Sciences
Horticulture
Human Biology
Human Nutrition
Human Physiology
Human Sciences
Immunology
Life Sciences
Marine Chemistry
Materials Science
Medical Laboratory Science
Medical Microbiology
Medicinal and Cosmetic Products
Medicinal Chemistry
Medicine
Mineral Exploitation
Mineral Processing
Molecular Biology
Molecular Genetics
Molecular Pathology
Molecular Sciences

Natural Sciences
Neuroscience
Nursing
Nutrition
Ocean Science
Paper Science
Parasitology
Petroleum Geology
Pharmaceutical
    Chemistry
Pharmacology
Pharmacy
Plant Science
Polymer Science
Process Biochemistry
Soil Science
Sports Science
Textile Chemistry
Toxicology
Zoology

Classical Studies in
Greek and Latin
Ancient Civilisations
Ancient Greek
Ancient History
Ancient
    Mediterranean
    Studies
Archaeology
Biblical Studies
Classical Civilisation
Classical Studies
Greek
Greek Archaeology
History (Greek and
    Roman Studies)
History of Art
History of
    Architecture
Latin
Middle Eastern
    Ancient
    Civilisation
Roman Archaeology
Roman Studies

Computer Science
Artificial Intelligence
Business Computing
Business Information
    Systems

Business Information
    Technology
Cognitive Science
Combined Studies
Computational
    Chemistry
Computational
    Linguistics
Computational
    Physics
Computational
    Science
Computational and
    Experimental
    Mathematics
Computer Aided
    Chemistry
Computer Aided
    Design
Computer Aided
    Engineering
Computer Animation
Computer Studies
Decision Systems
Engineering
    (Computer
    Systems)
Engineering (Control
    and Systems)
Engineering
    (Information
    Systems)
Engineering
    (Software)
Information Science
Information Systems
Intelligent Systems
Robotics

Design and
Technology
Architecture
Art and Design
Building
Ceramic Design
Combined Studies
Dental Technology
Design Crafts
Design and
    Technology
    Teaching
Design History

Furniture Design
Industrial Design
Interior Design
Jewellery
Landscape
    Architecture
Product Design
Prosthetics and
    Orthotics
Silversmithing Gold
    and Jewellery
Technical Illustration

Economics
Accountancy
Actuarial Science
Administrative
    Science
Agricultural
    Economics
American
    Management
    Science
Applied Mathematics
Applied Statistics
Banking
Business Studies
Business
    Administration
Business Analysis
Business Economics
Business Information
    Systems
Business Studies
City and Regional
    Planning
Combined Studies
Commerce
Decision Management
Decision Mathematics
Development Studies
Economics
Economics teaching
Economic and Social
    History
Environmental
    Economies
European Business
    Administration
European Land
    Management
European Marketing

European Planning
European Politics
European Studies
Farm Management
Finance
Financial Services
Food Marketing
Geography
Government
Human Resource
   Economics
Human Resource
   Management
Land Economics
Library Studies
Management Science
Mathematical
   Economics
Mathematical
   Statistics
Mathematics
Mathematics
   (Applied)
Money, Banking and
   Finance
Operational Research
Planning
Politics
Quantity Surveying
Resources Science
Social Sciences
Social Studies
Social History
Sociology
Statistics

Electronics
Astronautics
Audio-Visual
   Production
Audiotechnology
Avionic Systems
Broadcasting
Computer Science
Control Systems
Digital Systems
Electroacoustics
Electronic Design
Electronic Media
Electronic Music
Engineering
   (Aeronautical)

Engineering
   (Aerospace
   Systems)
Engineering
   (Computer
   Systems)
Engineering
   (Electronic)
Engineering
   (Information)
Engineering
   (Mechatronic)
Engineering (Physics)
Engineering
   (Software)
Engineering (Systems)
Engineering (Tele-
   communications)
Intelligent Systems
Laser Systems
Media Studies
Medical Electronics
Microelectronics
Music Technology
Optoelectronic
   Engineering
Planetary Physics
Power Systems
Signal Processing

English
Advertising
   (Copywriting)
American Studies
Anglo Saxon
Arts (Combined)
   (General)
Broadcast Media
Broadcasting Studies
Communications
   Studies
Contemporary
   Writing
Creative Writing
Cultural Studies
Drama
English
English as a Foreign
   Language
English Literature
English Teaching
Information Science

Journalism
Library Studies
Linguistics
Literary Studies
Literature
Media Studies
Publishing
Scottish Literature
Theatre Studies
TV Studies

Environmental
Science
Agriculture
Agroforestry
Animal Science
Architecture
Biology
Botany
Chemistry
City and Regional
   Planning
Combined Studies
Conservation
Countryside
   Management
Crop Science
Development Studies
Earth Resources and
   Management
Ecology
Economics
Estate Surveying
European Planning
Forestry
Garden Design
Geography
Geology
Heritage Management
Horticulture
Land Management
Landscape
   Architecture
Leisure Management
Marine Environment
Oceanography
Population Studies
Recreational Land
   Management
Rural Resources
Surveying

Town and Country
 Planning
Topographic Science
Underwater Studies
Urban Estate
 Management
Urban Studies

Geography
African Studies
Afro Asian Studies
Agriculture
Agroforestry
Anthropology
Applied Ecology
Applied Geology
Archaeology
Canadian Studies
Caribbean Studies
Cartography
City and Regional
 Planning
Combined Studies
Countryside
 Management
Development Studies
East Asian Studies
Earth Sciences
Ecology
Economics
Environmental
 Studies
Estate Management
Estate Surveying
European Land
 Management
European Planning
Fishery Science
Food Marketing
Geochemistry
Geographical
 Information
 Systems
Geography
Geography teaching
Geology
Geophysics
Geoscience
Government
Human Geography
Land Economy
Land Management

Land Surveying
Landscape
 Architecture
Marine Resources and
 Management
Maritime Studies
Meteorology
Mineral Surveying
Mining Geology
Nautical Studies
Oceanography
Planning
Politics
Population Studies
Recreational Land
 Management
Rural Resources
 Management
Strategic Studies
Surveying and
 Mapping
Surveying (Estate)
Surveying (Minerals)
Surveying
 (Valuations)
Topographic Science
Town and Country
 Planning
Transport
Travel & Tourism
Underwater Studies
Urban Estate
 Management
Urban Studies

Geology
Agriculture
Applied Ecology
Archaeology
Astronomy
Chemistry
Combined Studies
Earth Science
Ecology
Environmental
 Science
Geochemistry
Geographical
 Information
 Systems
Geography

Geological
 Engineering
Geology
Geomorphology
Geophysical Science
Geotechnics
Human Geography
Hydrography
Meteorology
Mineral Surveying
Mining Engineering
Mining Geology
Natural Resources
Ocean Science
Offshore Engineering
Petroleum Geology
Physics
Rural Resources
Soil Science
Surveying
Topographic Science

*Geometrical and
Mechanical Drawing*
Architecture
Art
Art and Design
Building Design
Cartography
Design Crafts
Design and
 Technology
Engineering (Civil)
Engineering (Design)
Engineering
 (Mechanical)
Engineering Surveying
Furniture Design
Garden Design
Graphic Design
Industrial Design
Interior Design
Landscape
 Architecture
Model making
Naval Architecture
Print Design
Product Design
Surveying and
 Mapping Science
Surveying (Building)
Technical Illustration

Theatre Design
Topographic Science

***Government and
Politics***
Administration
African Studies
Afro-Asian Studies
Agricultural
    Economics
American Studies
Anthropology
Applied Social
    Sciences/Studies
Asian Studies
Banking
Broadcasting Studies
Business Economics
Business Law
Business Studies
Canadian Studies
Caribbean Studies
Chinese Studies
City and Regional
    Planning
Combined Studies
Commerce
Communication
    Studies
Community Studies
Consumer Sciences/
    Studies
Defence and Security
    Studies
Development Studies
Earth Resources and
    Management
Economics
Education (Not
    teaching)
Environmental Policy
Environmental
    Protection
Environmental
    Studies
European Business
    Economics
European Community
    Studies
European Politics
European Social
    Policy

European Studies
Financial Economics
French Law
French Studies
German Law
German Studies
Government
Health Administration
History
Housing Management
Human Organisation
Industrial Relations
International
    Agriculture
International Business
    Economics
International Finance
International History
International
    Marketing
International Politics
International
    Relations
International Studies
Investment
Italian Studies
Japanese Studies
Labour Studies
Law
Natural Resources
Peace Studies
Peace and War
    Studies
Politics
Political Economy
Philosophy
Public Policy and
    Administration
Public Sector
    Economics
Race Studies
Scandinavian Studies
Social Administration
Social Anthropology
Social Care
Social Ethics
Social History
Social Policy
Social Research
Social Work
Sociology
Strategic Planning

Town Planning
Urban Studies
Welfare and Social
    Policy
Youth and
    Community Work

History
African Studies
American Studies
Ancient Civilisations
Ancient History
Anglo Saxon
Anthropology
Archaeology
Biblical Studies
Byzantine Studies
Canadian Studies
Chinese History
Church History
Classical Civilisation
Classical Studies
Classics
Combined Studies
Conservation
    (Building)
Conservation
    (Restoration)
Criminal Justice
Cultural Studies
Divinity
East Mediterranean
    History
Economic History
European History
Film History
History
History of
    Architecture
History of Art
History of Design
History of Ideas
History of Science
History Teaching
International History
International
    Relations
Irish Studies
Islamic Art and
    Archaeology
Italian Studies
Jewish History

Latin American
   Studies
Law
Medieval Studies
Near and Middle
   Eastern Studies
Peace Studies
Politics
Religious Studies
Scottish History
Social History
Social Sciences
Social Studies
Sociology
Strategic Studies
Victorian Studies
War Studies
Welsh History

History of Art
Advertising
Anthropology
Archaeology
Architecture History
Art and Design
Art History
Arts Management
Church History
Combined Studies
Conservation
   (Archaeological)
Conservation
   (Buildings)
Conservation
   (Restoration)
Costume Designs
Crafts (Printmaking)
Film History
Fine Art Valuation
Furniture Restoration
Heritage Management
History
Victorian Studies

Home Economics
*This subject area also
involves courses
concerned with food and
drink and the consumer.*
Advertising
Administration
Animal Nutrition

Applied Consumer
   Studies
Behavioural Science
Biological Sciences
Biology
Brewing and Distilling
Business Studies
Catering Science
Chemistry
Chemistry of Food
Communications
   Studies
Community Studies
Consumer Product
   Design
Consumer Sciences
Consumer Studies
Dietetics
Environmental
   Studies
Fashion
Food (Economics)
Food (Bioprocessing)
Food (Manufacturing)
Food (Marketing &
   Management)
Food (Production)
Food (Quality)
Food (Technology)
Health and
   Community
   Studies
Health and Safety
Health Care
Health Services
Home Economics
Home Economics
   Teaching
Hospitality (Hotel)
   Management
Housing Studies
Human Biology
Human Nutrition
Human Psychology
Human Sciences
Industrial Design
International Hotel
   Management
Leisure Studies
Marketing
Media Studies

Medicinal and
   Cosmetic
   Products
Nursing
Nutrition
Psychology
Retail Management
Secretarial
   Administration
Social Administration
Social Policy
Social Studies
Sociology
Textile Arts
Women's Health
Women's Studies
Youth and
   Community Work

Languages
*Students of modern (or
ancient) languages,
frequently choose the
same languages to study
to degree level. It should
be noted, however, that
the ability to speak and
write in a range of
foreign languages can be
an important asset when
applying for jobs. It is
therefore suggested that
those students with an
interest and ability in
languages should look
beyond their 'A' level
subjects and extend their
skills into new
languages.*
African Languages
Akkadian
Ancient Greek
Anglo Saxon
Asian Languages
Assyriology
Bantu
Bengali Studies
Breton
Bulgarian
Burmese Studies
Celtic
Chinese

Combined Studies
Communication
   Studies
Czech & Slovak
Danish
Dutch
East European Studies
Egyptian
European Studies
   (French)
European Studies
   (German)
European Studies
   (Italian)
European Studies
   (Russian)
European Studies
   (Spanish)
European Tourism
Finnish
French
French Law
French Teaching
Gaelic
German
German Law
German Teaching
Greek (Modern)
Hausa
Hebrew
Hindu
Hispanic Studies
Hungarian
Indonesian
International Hotel
   Management
International Studies
Interpreting and
   Translating
Iranian
Irish
Italian
Italian Law
Italian Teaching
Japanese
Korean
Languages for
   Business
Latin
Latin-American
   Studies
Linguistics

Literature
Marathi
Modern Languages
Nepali Studies
Norse
Norwegian
Oriental Languages
Pakistan Studies
Persian
Polish
Portuguese
Romanian
Russian
Russian Teaching
Sanskrit
Scandinavian Studies
Serbo-Croat
Sinhalese
Slavonic Studies
South Asian Studies
Spanish
Spanish Law
Spanish Teaching
Swedish
Tamil
Turkish
Urdu
Vietnamese Studies
Welsh

Law
American Legal
   Systems
Business Law
European Community
   Studies
European Law
Government
History
International History
International
   Relations
Legal Studies
Legislative Studies
Police Studies
Politics
Property Management
Public Administration
Social Administration
Social Policy
Strategic Studies
Urban Studies

Mathematics (and Statistics)
Accountancy
Acoustical
   Engineering
Actuarial Science
Applied Mathematics
Applied Statistics
Architecture
Astrophysics
Automotive
   Engineering
Banking
Building
Business Computing
Business Economics
Business Information
   Systems
Business Studies
Cognitive Science
Combined Studies
Commerce
Computer Science
Decision Systems
Economics
Engineering
   (Aeronautical)
Engineering
   (Aerospace
   Systems)
Engineering
   (Avionics)
Engineering (Civil)
Engineering
   (Communications)
Engineering
   (Computer
   Systems)
Engineering (Control
   Systems)
Engineering
   (Electrical)
Engineering
   (Electronic)
Engineering (Marine)
Engineering
   Mathematical
Engineering
   (Mechanical)
Engineering (Mining)
Engineering Physics

Engineering
  (Software)
Engineering (Systems)
Environmental
  Engineering
Ergonomics
European Business
  Economics
Financial Analysis
Financial Services
Industrial
  Mathematics
Information Science
Insurance
Integrated
  Engineering
Intelligent Systems
Investment
Management Science
Mathematics (Pure
  and Applied)
Mathematics and
  Statistics
Mathematics
  Teaching
Naval Architecture
Offshore Engineering
Operational Research
Opto electronics
Probability and
  Statistics
Quantity Surveying
Risk Management
  (Financial)
Robotics and
  Cybernetics
Ship Science
Statistics
Surveying
Systems Analysis
Systems Modelling

Media Studies
Advertising
Art
Art and Design
Arts Management
Audio-Visual
  Production
Band Studies
Broadcasting

Communications
  Studies
Design (Advertising)
Drama
Electronic Music
Ethnic Studies
Film Studies
Human Organisations
Human Psychology
Jazz Studies
Journalism
Leisure Studies
Marketing
Media Studies
Media and Theatre
  Studies
Music
Music Technology
Politics
TV Studies
Visual Arts
Visual Performance

Music
Acoustics
Band Musicianship
Book Publishing
Broadcasting
Combined Studies
Creative Music
  Technology
Dance
Drama
Electronic Music
Ethnomusicology
Jazz Studies
Media Studies
Media Production
Music
Music Teaching
Performance Arts
Stage Management
Theatre Studies

Philosophy
Ancient Civilisation
Cognitive Science
Conflict Resolution
Divinity
Economics
Educational Studies
  (Not teaching)

European Philosophy
Government
History
History of Ideas
History of Religions
History and
  Philosophy of
  Science
Law
Peace Studies
Philosophy
Philosophy of Science
Politics
Psychology
Religious Studies
Social Ethics
Theology
Women's Studies

Physics
Acoustics
Aerodynamics
Air Transport
  Engineering
Applied Physics
Architecture
Astronautics
Astronomy
Astrophysics
Automotive
  Engineering
Biophysics
Broadcasting
  (Electronics)
Building
Ceramic Science
Chemical Physics
Combined Studies
Computer Science
Cybernetics
Digital Systems
  Engineering
Electro acoustics
Engineering
  (Aeronautical)
Engineering
  (Aerospace
  Systems)
Engineering
  (Agricultural)
Engineering
  (Avionics)

Engineering
  (Communications)
Engineering
  (Computer
  Systems)
Engineering
  (Electrical)
Engineering (Electro-
  mechanical)
Engineering
  (Electronics)
Engineering
  (Mechanical)
Engineering (Nuclear)
Engineering Physics
Engineering
  (Software)
Engineering (Systems)
Engineering (Tele-
  communications)
Fire Engineering
Fuel and Energy
  Engineering
Geophysics
Glass Technology
Horology
Hydrography
Information
  Engineering
Laser Systems
Materials Science
Mechatronic
  Engineering
Metallurgy
Meteorology
Microelectronics
Minerology
Mining Engineering
Naval Architecture
Oceanography
Offshore Engineering
Ophthalmic Optics
Physics
Physics Teaching
Planetary Physics
Prosthetics and
  Orthotics
Robotics
Radiography
Ship Science
Signal Processing

Solid State Electronics
Technology

Psychology
Advertising
Animal Behaviour
Anthropology
Artificial Intelligence
Behavioural Science
Business Studies
Childhood Studies
Christian Ministry
Clinical Psychology
Cognitive Science
Combined Studies
Community Studies
Counselling
Criminology
Criminal Justice
Drama
Education
Educational
  Psychology
Gender Studies
Health Administration
Health and Fitness
Health Psychology
Hotel (Hospitality)
  Management
Human Biology
Human-Computer
  Interaction
Human Evolution
Human Geography
Human Life Science
Human Organisations
Human Psychology
Human Resource
  Management
Industrial Relations
Journalism
Life Sciences
Management
Medicine
Neuroscience
Nursing
Occupational
  Psychology
Occupational Therapy
Organisational
  Behaviour
Psycholinguistics

Psychology
Psychosocial Science
Public Health
Public Policy
Public Relations
Robotics
Social Administration
Social Care
Social Ethics
Social Policy
Social Psychology
Social Work
Sociology
Speech Therapy
Tourism
Town Planning
Urban Studies
Women's Studies
Zoology

Public Affairs
Administration
Arts Management
Banking
Business Studies
City and Regional
  Planning
Community Studies
Education
Estate Surveying
European Planning
European Politics
European Social
  Policy
Government
Health and
  Community
  Studies
Housing
Human Organisation
Human Resource
  Management
Industrial Relations
International
  Relations
Land Management
Law
Leisure Management
Marketing
Organisation Studies
Police Studies
Politics

Public Administration
Public Health
Public Policy
Public Relations
Public Sector
  Economics
Public Services
Social Administration
Social Care
Social Policy
Social Work
Sport and Health
Tourism
Town and Country
  Planning
Transport
Urban Studies
Women's Health
Youth and
  Community Work

Religious Studies
Anthropology
Applied Theological
  Studies
Behavioural Studies
Biblical Studies
Christian Studies
Church History
Combined Studies
Comparative Religion
Divinity
Education
Ethnic Studies
Health and
  Community
  Studies
Hebrew
History
History of Religions
Human Psychology
Jewish Studies
Philosophy
Psychology
Psychosocial Sciences
Religious Studies
Religious Studies
  Teaching
Social Administration
Social Anthropology
Social Ethics
Social Policy

Sociology
Theology

*Science, Technology
and Society*
Agriculture
Agricultural Sciences
Animal Science
Astronomy
Biology
Botany
Biotechnology
Building
Chemistry
Computer Science
Conservation
Ecology
Engineering
Environmental
  Science
Food Studies
Forestry
General Engineering
General Science
Human Sciences
Marine Resources
Materials Science
Nutrition
Ocean Science
Technology (Building)
  (Chemical)
  (Fisheries)
  (Food)
  (Geological)
  (Leather)
  (Marine)
  (Polymers)

Sociology
Administration
Anthropology
Behavioural Studies
Broadcasting
Business Studies
City and Regional
  Planning
Combined Courses
Communication
  Studies
Consumer Studies
Development Studies
Economics

Economic and Social
  History
Environmental
  Science
Geography
Government
History
Industrial Relations
Management Studies
Organisation Studies
Police Studies
Politics
Psychology
Public Administration
Social Administration
Social Policy
Social Work
Sociology
Town and Country
  Planning
Urban Studies

Textiles
Art and Design
Carpet Design
Clothing Engineering
Consumer Studies
Costume Design
Fashion Design
Footwear Design
History of Art
History of Design
Home Economics
Industrial Design
Interior Design
Knitwear
Textile Design
Textile Economics
Textile Management
Textile Marketing
Textile Technology
Visual Arts

Theatre Studies
Advertising
Arts Management
Broadcasting
Classical Civilisation
Communication
  Studies
Dance
Drama

Education
English Literature
Film Studies
Leisure Studies
Literature
Media Studies
Performance Arts
Stage Management
Theatre Design
Theatre Studies

TV Studies

Welsh
Celtic Civilisation
Celtic Studies
Communication
   Studies
Drama
Education
History

Irish Studies
Literature
Media Studies
Performance Arts
Welsh
Welsh (Drama)
   (History)
   (Literature)
   (Teaching)

(b) CHOOSING A COURSE BY WAY OF A CAREER GROUP

It is possible, however, that you may be one of those people who want to know where you are going and wish to follow a course which leads to a job. This is fine if you have given a lot of time to considering careers and in particular your chosen career. This doesn't simply mean reading about a career or hearing that a certain occupation 'is a good job': you should also be visiting places of work and taking to people in the job, getting their views and impressions and gaining some work experience.

Like school subjects, careers also belong in families in which there are other careers with many similarities. Firstly it's important to remember that all careers fall into six main groups. As a start to making a career choice try to include yourself in one or more of the following groups and the appropriate degree courses.

Scientific careers
(some appropriate
degree courses
Agricultural
   bacteriology
   biochemistry
   botany
   zoology
Agricultural sciences
Agriculture
Analysis of science
   and technology
Anatomy
Animal biology
   nutrition
   physiology
   sciences
Anthropology
Astronomy
Astrophysics
Bacteriology
Biochemistry
Biological sciences
Biology

(animal)
(applied)
(cell)
(development)
(environmental)
(human)
(marine)
(molecular)
(plant)
Biomedical sciences
Biophysics
Botany
   (agricultural)
   (horticultural)
   (marine)
Brewing
Cell biology
Chemical education
   physics
   process technology
Chemistry
   (agricultural)
   (applied)
   (biological)

(colour)
(industrial)
(marine)
(petrochemical)
(polymer)
(textile)
Colour chemistry
Computation
Computer science
   courses
Computer systems
Computing
   mathematics
Crystalline state
Data processing
Dentistry
Development biology
Domestic animal
   science
Dietetics
Earth sciences
Ecology
Environmental
   chemistry

control
science
Food science
Forestry
Fuel science
Genetics
Geochemistry
Geography
Geology
Geophysics
Health and life
  sciences
Home economics
Horticulture
Human biology
  ecology
  sciences
Life sciences
Marine biology
  sciences
Materials science
Mathematics
  (actuarial)
  (Computing)
  (engineering)
Medicine
Metallurgy
Meteorology
Microbiology
Mineral sciences
Mineralogy
Molecular biology
  sciences
Nautical studies
Neuroscience
Nursing
Nutrition
Oceanography
Operational research
Ophthalmic optics
Optometry
Paper science
Petrology
Pharmacy
Physical sciences
Physics
  (applied)
  (chemical)
  (marine)
  (mathematical)
  (theoretical)
Physiology

Plant
  biology
  physiology
  sciences
Polymer chemistry
Polymer science
Psychology
  (experimental)
Radiation physics
Rural resources
  courses
Rural science
Toxicology
Veterinary science
Virology
Wood science
Zoology
  (agricultural)
  (applied)

*Scientific careers
dealing with people
(some appropriate
degree courses)*
Chiropody (podiatry)
Chiropractic
Communication
  studies
Dentistry
Dietetics
Educational studies
Environmental health
Health and life
  sciences
Home and community
  studies
Home economics
Human psychology
Librarianship
Medicine
Nursing
Occupational therapy
Ophthalmic studies
Pharmacy
Physiotherapy
Podiatry
Physics (teaching)
Prosthetics/Orthotics
Psychology
Teaching courses
Veterinary science

*Technical,
constructional
practical careers
(some appropriate
degree courses)*
Aeronautical
  engineering
Architecture (naval)
Automotive
  engineering
Biochemical
  engineering
Building courses
Ceramics
Chemical engineering
Civil engineering
Colour chemistry
Computer courses
Control engineering
Control systems
Cybernetics
Data processing
Design engineering
Electrical engineering
Electro-mechanical
  engineering
Electronic
  communication
Electronic engineering
Electronics
Engineering science
Ergonomics
Forestry Fuel
  engineering
Gas engineering
Glass technology
Manufacturing
  engineering
Marine engineering
Maritime studies
Metallurgy
  engineering
Minerals engineering
Minerals exploitation
Mining
Mining engineering
Naval architecture
Nuclear engineering
Paper science
Petroleum engineering
Physics
Polymer engineering

Production
  engineering
Quantity surveying
Resource science
Ship science
Speech therapy
Structural engineering
Surveying
  Estate management
  Land economics
System analysis
Systems engineering
Telecommunications
  engineering
Textile engineering
Transport
  management
Typography

*Office-based careers
(some appropriate
degree courses)*
Accountancy
Actuarial mathematics
Administration
Administrative studies
Architecture
Art
Banking
Behavioural science
Business courses
Commerce
Computer science
  courses
Design engineering
Dietetics
Economics
  (agricultural)
  (mathematical)
Estate management
Financial services

Food marketing
Graphics
Hospitality
  management
Hotel and catering
  administration
Industrial relations
Insurance
Land economy
Land use
Landscape
  architecture
Landscape design
Law
Leisure/recreation
  studies
Librarianship
Library and
  information
  studies
Marketing
Meteorology
Nutrition
Psychology
Public administration
Secretarial studies
Social administration
Surveying
Teaching
Textile courses
Town and country
  planning
Transport
  management

*Careers requiring
artistic and other
talents (some
appropriate degree
courses)*
Architecture

Architectural studies
Art
Drama
Fine art
Interior design
Landscape
  architecture
Music
Textile design
Typography and
  graphic
  communications

*Mobile and active
careers (some
appropriate degree
courses)*
Agriculture
Business studies
  courses
Civil engineering
Drama
Engineering
Environmental health
Estate management
Forestry
Golf course
  management
Horticulture
Journalism
Marine engineering
Meteorology
Mining engineering
Nursing
Physical education
Recreational studies
Surveying
Sports studies courses
Veterinary science

(c) CHOOSING A COURSE BY WAY OF A CAREER

If you have decided on a specific career, check out the other careers in the same job families. There are degree courses appropriate to each of those listed in the following tables.

Accountancy
Accounts executive -
  advertising
Actuarial science

Banking
Business studies
Insurance

Actuarial Science
Accountancy
Banking
Insurance

Agriculture
Agricultural
  engineering
Agricultural sciences
Animal sciences
Ecology
Environmental science
Estate management
Food science
Forestry
General practice
  surveying
Horticulture
Rural environment
  studies

Animal sciences
Agriculture
Agricultural sciences
Biochemistry
Biological sciences
Veterinary science
Zoology

Archaeology
Anthropology
History
History of art and
  architecture

Architecture
Building
Building services
  engineering
Civil engineering
Landscape
  architecture
Surveying
Town and country
  planning

Art
Advertising
Architecture
Education
Industrial design
Interior design
Landscape
  architecture
Printing
Scientific illustration

Three dimensional
  design
Visual studies courses

Astronomy
Astrophysics
Mathematics
Physics

Audiology
Nursing
Occupational therapy
Orthoptics
Speech therapy
Teaching the deaf

Banking/Insurance
Accountancy
Business studies
Economics
Insurance

*Biological Sciences/
Biology*
Agricultural sciences
Agriculture
Bacteriology
Biochemistry
Biology
Botany
Ecology
Environmental health
Environmental science
Forestry
Genetics
Medicine
Microbiology
Physiotherapy
Scientific illustration
  and photography
Speech therapy

Book Publishing
Advertising
Business studies
Printing
Typographical
  communication

Brewing
Biochemistry
Chemistry
Food science

Building
Architecture
Building surveying
Civil engineering
Estate management
General practice
  surveying
Land surveying
Municipal engineering
Quantity surveying
Structural engineering

Business Studies
Accountancy
Accounts executive -
  advertising
Banking
Economics
Export
Housing management
Industrial relations
Insurance
Marketing
Operational research
Personnel work
Public relations
Purchasing and supply
Retailing and
  distribution
Travel agency work
Tourism

Cartography
Geography
Land surveying
Tourism (via business
  studies)
Travel agency work

Catering Science
Baking technology
Dietetics
Food science
Home economics
Nutrition

Ceramics
Materials science -
  metallurgy
Physics

Chemistry
Agriculture
Biochemistry
Botany
Ceramics
Chemical engineering
Colour chemistry
Environmental science
Geochemistry
Pharmacology
Pharmacy
All technologies (eg
    food, paper,
    polymer, plastics,
    materials science)

Clothing Studies
Business studies
Dress design
Textiles

Computer Studies
Business studies
Mathematics
Micro-electronics
Electronic engineering
Telecommunications

Construction
Building
Civil engineering
Municipal engineering
Structural engineering

Dance
Drama
Human movement
    studies
Physical education
Theatre studies

Dentistry
Biochemistry
Medicine
Nursing
Ophthalmic/optic
Orthoptics
Pharmacy
Speech therapy

Drama
Dance

Human movement
    studies
Theatre management
Theatre studies

Education
Psychology
Social work
Speech therapy
Youth and community
    work

**Educational
Broadcasting**
Broadcasting
Communications
    studies
Film and TV studies
Journalism
Media studies

Engineering
Computer studies
Engineering -
    chemical
Civil
Control
Electrical
Mechanical
Nuclear
Telecommunications
Mathematics
Patent work
Physics
Technical illustration

Estate Management
Building Civil
    engineering
Economics
Forestry
Housing
Quantity surveying
Rural environmental
    studies
Town and country
    planning
Urban land economics

Fishery Sciences
Biological sciences
Maritime studies
Nautical studies

**Food and
Accommodation
Studies**
Dietetics
Home economics
Hotel and institutional
    management
Housing management
Nutrition

**Food Science and
Technology**
Biochemistry
Chemistry
Dietetics
Home economics
Nutrition

Footwear Design
Fashion design

Forestry
Applied biology
Biological sciences
Botany
Ecology
Environmental science
Forest products
    technology
Furniture design
Plant biology
Wood science

Furniture Design
Forest products
    technology
Furniture production
Three dimensional
    design

Geology
Chemistry
Earth sciences
Engineering (civil,
    mining)
Environmental science
Geochemistry
Geography
Land surveying
Metallurgy

Graphic Design
Advertising
Scientific illustration
Photography
Printing
Technical illustration

Health and Safety
Environmental health
Health studies
Nursing
Occupational health

Home Economics
Dietetics
Domestic science
Environmental health
Food science
Food technology
Housing management
Housing studies
Institutional
   management
Nutrition

Horticulture
Agriculture
Botany
Landscape
   architecture
Plant biology

**Hotel and Catering
Administration**
Cookery
Food science
Food technology
Health and safety
Travel and tourism

Housing
Architecture
General practice
   surveying
Social administration
Social policy
Town and country
   planning

Industrial Design
Engineering
Ergonomics

Technical illustration
Three dimensional
   design

Industrial Relations
Behavioural science
Business studies
Production
   engineering

Information Science
Computer science
Information
   processing
Information systems
Librarianship
Systems analysis

**Institutional
Management**
Food and home
   economics
Hotel and catering
   administration
Housing management

Interior Design
Architecture
Exhibition design
Furniture design
Textile design
Three dimensional
   design

Landscape
Architecture
Environmental science
Horticulture
Town and country
   planning

Law
Business studies
Government
History
International history
Land management
Politics

**Leisure and
Recreational Studies**
Dance

Drama
Human movement
   studies
Music Physical
   education
Social work
Sports science
Theatre studies
Travel and tourism
Youth and community
   work

Librarianship
Information science
Publishing

Maritime Studies
Marine biology
Marine engineering
Marine studies
Nautical studies
Naval architecture
Oceanography
Offshore engineering

Marketing
Business studies
Operational research
Packaging
Travel and tourism

**Materials Science -
Metallurgy**
Applied chemistry
Applied physics
Chemistry
Design (mechanical
   and production)
Engineering
Geology
Geophysics
Glass technology
Materials technology
Mineral exploitation
Physics
Polymer science

Mathematics
Accountancy
Banking
Business studies
Computer studies

Economics
Education
Engineering
Operational research
Physics
Quantity surveying

Medicine
Anatomy
Biochemistry
Biological sciences
Dentistry
Medical social work
Nursing
Orthoptics
Pathobiology
Pharmacy
Physiotherapy
Social work

Micro-electronics
Computer studies
Electrical-electronic
    engineering
Telecommunications

Mineral Processing
Chemistry
Earth sciences
Engineering
    (chemical, mining)
Environmental science
Geology
Soil science

Music
Drama
Performing arts
Theatre studies

Nautical Studies
Hydrographic
    surveying
Marine engineering
Maritime studies
Naval architecture
Oceanography
Offshore engineering

Naval Architecture
Hydrographic
    surveying

Engineering (marine,
    offshore)
Maritime studies

Nursing
Anatomy
Audiology
Biochemistry
Biological sciences
Biology
Dentistry
Education
Environmental health
    and community
    studies
Medical social work
Nursery nursing
Occupational therapy
Orthoptics
Physiotherapy
Psychology
Radiography
Social administration

Nutrition
Food science and
    technology
Home economics
Nursing

Occupational Therapy
Art
Audiology
Mental nursing
Nursing
Orthoptics
Physiotherapy
Psychology
Speech therapy

Ophthalmic Optics
Applied physics
Orthoptics
Physics

Packaging
Graphic design
Printing

Photography/Film/TV
Audio/video systems

Communication
    studies (some
    courses)
Educational
    broadcasting
Documentary films
Graphic art
Industrial
    photography
Medical photography
Press photography
Photo-journalism
Scriptwriting

Physical Education
Human movement
    studies
Leisure and recreation
    management
Physiological
    measurement/
    medical physics
Sport and recreational
    studies
Sports science
Youth and community
    work

Physics
Applied physics
Astronomy
Astrophysics
Engineering (civil,
    electrical,
    mechanical)
Ophthalmic optics

Physiotherapy
Audiology
Chiropractic
Nursing
Orthoptics
Osteopathy
Physical education

Polymer Science
Applied chemistry
Chemistry
Materials science
Plastics and rubber
    technology

Printing
Advertising
Graphic design
Typographic design
and
communication

**Production
Technology**
Engineering
(mechanical,
production)
Materials science

**Property and
Valuation
Management**
Architecture
Estate management
Quantity surveying
Urban land economics

Psychology
Applied social studies
Education
Occupational therapy
Psychology (clinical,
educational,
occupational)
Social administration
Social policy
Social work

Public Administration
Applied social studies
Business studies
Social administration
Youth and community
work

Quantity Surveying
Architecture
Building
Civil engineering
Surveying (building,
land and
valuation)

Radiography
Audiology
Biological sciences
Medical photography
Nursing
Orthoptics
Photography
Physiotherapy

Secretarial Studies
Bi-lingual secretarial
studies
Business studies
Secretarial studies

**Silversmithing/
Jewellery**
Three dimensional
design

**Social Science/Social
Studies**
Anthropology
Journalism
Religious studies
Politics and
government
Social administration
Sociology
Town and country
planning
Youth and community
work
Welfare work

Speech Therapy
Audiology
Education
Nursing
Occupational therapy
Psychology
Radiography

Statistics
Business studies
Economics
Mathematics

Operational research

Textile Design
Art
Clothing studies
Fashion design
Textile management
Wool technology

Theatre Design
Drama
Interior design
Leisure and
recreational
studies
Theatre management
Theatre studies

**Three Dimensional
Design**
Architecture
Industrial design
Interior design
Theatre design

**Town and Country
Planning**
Architecture
Environmental science
Estate management
Geography
Leisure and
recreational
management
Planning studies
Statistics
Transport
management

Veterinary Science
Agricultural sciences
Agriculture
Animal sciences
Medicine
Pharmacology
Pharmacy
Zoology

TYPES OF COURSES

Having decided on the subject or subjects to study, the next stage is to consider the main types of courses and how the teaching is organised within different institutions. The main options to consider are:

- **Single honours**

One subject is studied within which special subjects are often available, varying from one institution to another. Some of these special subjects are optional, some compulsory.

- **Joint honours**

This involves the study of two separate but equal subjects which can be related or indeed unrelated (eg German and Maths; English and Classical Studies).

- **Combined honours**

This can involve the study of two, three or more closely related subjects or a selection from a range (eg General Studies, Combined Arts).

- **Major and minor**

This involves the study of two subjects, the 'major' option naturally taking more time than the minor option. These courses are usually entitled for example French with Business Studies in which French is major and Business Studies minor.

- **Modular courses**

These courses consist of 'modules', in a variety of subjects. Students choose a 'pathway' through the degree course by making a personal choice of modules. This type of course offers considerable flexibility in subject choice.

- **CATS**

This means Credit Accumulation and Transfer Scheme in which students gain 'credits' for study at certain levels (eg certificates, diplomas and professional qualifications). Students can then add more 'credits' by further study, leading to a degree.

- **Sandwich courses**

This involves alternating periods of study and related work experience which makes the course longer than the usual three years. The work experience can count towards a professional qualification and can make a graduate more marketable generally. Many firms employ the graduates who have worked with them on sandwich placement on a full-time basis when they have completed the course. Another type of sandwich arrangement is **sponsorship**, in which you become a paid employee of a firm for your periods of work experience. After completing your course you return to work for that firm. These sponsorships are competitive and an A-level potential of at least CCC is expected from applicants. Full details of sponsorships are published annually in the COIC book *Sponsorships*. But there are some important points to consider if you are looking for sponsorship. Are there sponsorships available for your choice of degree subject? Do you want a higher education course of study which is linked to an employer? Are there any particular universities, polytechnics or colleges designated by the employer for the sandwich course of your choice? You need to weigh up the advantages and the disadvantages.

Sandwich courses - the advantages

a) Security of industrial placement and vacation work.

b) Financial benefits - grant supplement and salary during work periods.

c) Relevance of the work you have done on your course to practical experience with the firm.

d) Personal development gained through work experience and team work in employment.

e) A knowledge of working situations in a particular employment area.

f) Opportunities to work in different areas of the sponsoring organisation, perhaps in different locations.

g) Likelihood of full-time employment with the sponsor.

Sandwich courses - the disadvantages

a) Moral obligation to work for the sponsor - even if you find you don't like the organisation.

b) Breaks in academic study may be unsettling.

c) Limitations on choice of course options.

d) Course content may not link with practical experience.

e) Restricted industrial experience.

f) Shorter vacations.

GENERAL AND COURSE REQUIREMENTS

Choosing a subject to study for a degree or diploma is not quite the same as the choice of A-level subjects which you made two or three years ago. There are additional factors to consider which relate to the way in which each institution selects applicants, and the standards of entry set by various departments. Once you have chosen a subject, therefore, you cannot assume that you will be qualified to study it at every institution and you must check the general requirements of the university concerned.

Difficulties in meeting the general requirements often arise from three subjects: English, a modern language, and mathematics or a science subject. Some universities insist on Grade C or above in GCSE in these subjects, irrespective of the course you want to follow.

After checking the general requirements, the next step is to check the course requirements for your chosen institutions. These can also vary: for example, for Architecture, Bath University requires English language, Glasgow University requires English language or English literature, and Edinburgh University asks for physics but will accept chemistry as an alternative. (All details of the general and course requirements are found in prospectuses.)

FINALLY.... when choosing your course, it is important to remember that one course is not better than another - it is just different. The best course for you is the one which best suits **you**. The same approach also applies to the institutions you choose. Each will differ a great deal, for example in their location (town or deep in the countryside), in the facilities they offer, in the ways they organise their courses and their teaching.

Differences between the selection procedures and the offers made in the same subject at the different institutions are described in *The Complete Degree Course Offers* (see **Booklist**.)

After provisionally choosing your courses read the prospectuses again carefully to be sure that you understand what is included during the three, four or more years of study for each. Each institution varies in its course content even though the course titles may be the same. Courses differ in several ways, for example, in their:

- subject options (minor courses of study alongside the main subject)
- methods of assessment (eg unseen examinations, continuous assessment, project work, dissertations)
- contact time with tutors
- lectures
- practicals
- library and laboratory facilities
- amount of free study time available

These are useful points of comparison between courses in different institutions when you are making final course choices.

CHAPTER 2
COURSE PROFILES

This section gives details of the major courses offered by universities and colleges at degree level throughout the UK. Higher National Diplomas (HND) courses are not listed in these tables but it can be assumed that new universities offering a subject at degree level will also offer HND courses. Transfers are possible from HND to degree courses, subject to satisfactory academic progress at the end of the course and in some cases at the end of the first year of diploma studies. Transfers are sometimes possible between degree courses offered in the same university faculty.

Many degree courses in any one subject are similar in content in year one. In years two and three, options can vary and these options provide the applicant with the distinctive 'course menu'. It is this 'menu' which applicants should consider carefully when making their initial short list of courses they wish to follow.

Because of the many thousands of courses and course combinations offered it is not possible to describe every course. In each subject table, therefore, the aim has been **to give a selection of the types of courses available**. The descriptions given provide the reader with a background of how courses differ between institutions in both subject and content, although it must be stressed that each university will offer several combinations of courses in each subject area. Many of the course descriptions have been provided by admissions tutors and department heads.

Because of constant course changes, often brought about by staff movement, the reader is advised to obtain up-to-date prospectuses before making final course decisions.

Under some subject headings the research rating of universities is published. These ratings are based on assessments made by the Higher Educations Funding Council (England). Universities listed have achieved the top ratings of 5 and 4 which refers to research undertaken at international and national levels. It must be stressed, however, that there is no direct link between research rating and the teaching quality at undergraduate level.

ACCOUNTANCY
(See also **Banking/Financial Services**)

- **Special subject requirements:** A-level mathematics often 'required' or 'preferred'. GCSE (grades A–C) mathematics essential.

- **Subject information:** All courses offer financial management and accountancy training. Students should note that a degree in Accounting is not the only method of qualifying as an accountant. In addition to degree courses applicants should note that many institutions offer Foundation Courses which provide opportunities to move directly into degree courses. Accountancy courses are not necessarily intended for those wishing to become accountants since it provides an excellent training for any career in business.

Most of these courses will give graduates exemptions from the examinations of the various professional accounting bodies. Applicants should check with universities before applying since these examinations are essential for those wishing to qualify as accountants.

Aberdeen (*Accountancy*) Accountancy at levels 1, 2 and 3 covers the practice of accountancy in modern society, financial reporting, management accountancy, taxation, and the use of computers in business. There are also eleven joint courses in arts and social science subjects and an MA course.

Abertay Dundee A broad vocational degree in accounting. The course includes information technology, industrial studies and the opportunity to continue (or begin) a language (Spanish, German, French or Russian).

Aberystwyth (*Accounting and Finance*) The course covers an introduction to financial accounting or an introduction to management accounting and business. Languages option including Welsh. There are also eleven joint courses offered covering arts, social science and science subjects.

Bangor (*Accounting and Finance*) The course offers training in accounting skills (including 'hands-on' computer experience). In addition, students are encouraged to develop an understanding of relevant theories and the role of accounting in organisations and society. An emphasis is placed on financial theory and decision-making techniques, providing integration with neighbouring economics and banking disciplines. (*Euro Financial Management*) A four year double qualification with specialist degrees in France, Belgium and Germany. A course is also offered in Banking, Insurance and Finance with language options possible as well as ten joint courses in modern languages, economics and mathematics.

Belfast (*Accounting*) The degree is intended to provide an academic education in accounting and an introduction to professional studies. Students with second class Honours degrees and above gain exemption from Parts I and II of the ICA in Ireland. Accounting is offered as a major Honours subject coupled with a minor in economics or politics or as a minor subject with majors in economics, business studies or politics or as a general degree with economics and commercial law, and transfers are possible up to the end of Year 2. There are also courses in Finance involving investment decisions, company finance and management of stock. Joint courses are also offered with Law and Languages.

Birmingham (*Accounting*) The degree emphasises the study of accounting and finance throughout the three years of the course. The course includes economics, industrial relations, law, information technology and marketing. Some courses are taught in conjunction with local large firms of practising accountants. There is also an accounting course with French.

Brighton (*Accounting and Finance*) There is an emphasis on seminar work, problem-solving and core-study material. The first year course includes behavioural science and computer studies, Years 2 and 3 each being divided into two semesters. The main features of this course are: the wide range of options in finance as well as accountancy; options of one year's placement in profession or commerce; the emphasis upon applications of computers, and on European and international awareness, and the extensive use of case studies and student-centred learning to link the 'real world' with your academic studies. Accounting with Law and an international accounting course are also offered with French, German and Spanish.

Bristol Courses are offered in Economics and Accounting (three year full time) and a four year course which includes a year in Europe.

Bristol UWE (*Accounting and Finance*) This vocational course (three year or four year sandwich alternatives) provides a sound basis for careers in other fields of management. The first year course includes electives from a wide range of subjects, with a range of options available in the third year including business languages. A financial services course is also offered.

Buckingham (*Accounting and Financial Management*) The two-year course (starting in January) with a common preliminary programme for the first two terms provides options in accounting and financial management or economics or insurance. This leads to more advanced studies, granting exemptions from foundation examinations of all the leading accountancy bodies. Accounting can also be taken with economics, insurance and computer science. Tutorial groups are small - not exceeding eight students.

Cardiff (*Accountancy*) The course covers all aspects of accountancy in addition to providing supporting courses in relevant areas of financial and management accountancy, economics, business studies and law. Courses with management, economics and modern languages are also offered.

Central England (*Accountancy*) Students take eight core subjects in each year in addition to project work with an option to change to other business studies courses after Year 1. Core subjects in accountancy include law, computer studies, financial management and taxation, with options in the second and third years in behavioural aspects, international accounting and languages. A course in financial services offers options to specialise in banking, insurance, investments or foreign languages. There are also ten joint courses.

Central Lancashire (*Accounting*) The course focuses on a study of the current practice, problems and developments in accounting and the practical applications of computers. Distinguishing features of the course include: an integrated approach to the teaching of computing; an information technology course in Year 2; a case study approach to the teaching of law, with simulated meetings; a choice of certain options in Year 3. There is an accountancy option in the combined honours programme.(*Financial Services*) This course will be of interest to anyone aiming for banking, insurance or broking.

City A three year (full time) course is offered in Economics and accounting.

De Montfort Two accounting courses (one with a vocational emphasis) are offered in the combined studies programme in addition to a systems accounting and decision management course, covering marketing, business mathematics, accountancy in industry and commerce.

Derby (*Accountancy*) Accounting is offered as a major, joint or minor subject within a modular scheme.

Dundee (*Accountancy*) The course emphasises analytical and conceptual issues and does not deal at length with procedural matters. Specialisms include business finance, management information systems, management or accountancy. Chemistry, computer science and mathematics can also be offered with accountancy.

East Anglia (*Accountancy; Computerised Accountancy*) Both courses combine the traditional approach to accountancy with a special emphasis on computing and management control. Core subjects are taken in Years 1 and 2; in Year 3 students choose from a wide range of courses. There is also a European language course and courses combining with business finance, law and economics.

East London (*Accounting and Finance*) The three year course provides a business education covering law, management accountancy, taxation and computing. Over 35 joint courses are also offered in a very wide range of subjects to suit all tastes.

Edinburgh Three joint courses are offered covering business or economics or law with accounting.

Essex (*Accounting and Financial Management*) First-year students take courses in economics, accountancy, and computer applications or mathematics and politics, sociology, computer applications or philosophy. The degree offers specialised studies in accountancy, commercial law and financial management. There are options in auditing and public accountancy, international accountancy and business strategy.

Exeter (*Accountancy Studies*) The single Honours course in accountancy has a vocational emphasis. Students reading other degrees in the Faculty of Social Studies may also take an accountancy paper in Part I or II. A four year course is also offered with European study.

Glamorgan (*Accounting and Finance*) This is a three year full time or four year thick sandwich course which includes a third year in a commercial or industrial placement. Options exist in European languages, marketing, European business and international financial management. Accounting can also be taken as a joint degree with computing or combined with a European language.

Glasgow (*Accountancy*) This degree centres on accounting and financial management. Economics, law and quantitative methods are some of the subjects studied in the third year along with several other options. Full-time and sandwich courses are offered.

Glasgow Caledonian (*Accountancy*) Three or four year courses are offered with two options from public sector or management accounting, international finance and financial reporting. A financial services course is also offered.

Greenwich (*Accountancy and Finance*) After a foundation course in accounting, business and information technology, students proceed to international accountancy and auditing, business strategy and international business and marketing.

Heriot-Watt (*Accountancy and Finance*) An ordinary (three year) and Honours (four year) course, offered in accountancy and finance. (Year 1 is common with Accountancy and Information Management). Students take one elective class each year from 30 elective subjects which include several modern languages. Accountancy is also offered as a joint course with French, German or Spanish.

Hertfordshire (*Accounting and Management Information Systems*) International accounting, financial and treasury management and company law are final year subjects in this accounting course. A three year accounting course is also offered.

Huddersfield (*Accountancy Studies*) The first year course consists of basic accounting and a study of the legal, social and economic environment. In the second and third years there is an emphasis on the use of financial information in business planning, control and decision-making, insolvency and employee relations. A course is also offered with management.

Hull (*Accounting*) In the first year students take accounting with two compulsory courses in economics, statistics and maths for economists, plus a fifth choice selected from a range of options. Financial accounting, management accounting and the principles of economics are taken in the second year. The course emphasis lies in finance, accounting and computing. A joint course with economics is also available.

Humberside (*Accountancy and Finance*) A three year full-time course with Year 3 options including taxation and finance law and international business finance. A four year sandwich course includes European accountancy with placements in France and Germany in Year 3.

Kent (*Accounting*) This course provides a training in the wider aspects of accounting and is not specially directed towards an expertise in accounting practice. Accountancy is taught as an application of the social sciences. First year studies include business law, statistics and economics. Part II covers decision-making in the public and private sectors, and industrial relations. There are also over twelve joint courses with accountancy.

Kingston (*Accounting and Finance*) The course provides a study in depth of accounting and financial management including company law, accounting and revenue law and taxation. The core subject in Year 1 is legal and financial strategy. Option choices include marketing, languages, international accountancy and computer systems. A joint course with law is also offered.

Lancaster (*Accounting and Finance*) Students wishing to major in this subject also take a Part I course in economics and a third course which could include a language or a science subject. All single major students also take a two year minor course which may include business law, marketing, industrial relations or organisational psychology. The free ninth unit course also enables students to choose an additional subject from a considerable range of options. Seven joint courses are also offered.

Leeds (*Accounting and Finance*) The course covers the main aspects of financial and management accounting, economics, taxation and business finance. Computer science, information systems and operational research are also offered with accounting.

Leeds Metropolitan (*Accounting and Finance*) This is a three year full-time or four year sandwich course in Accounting and Finance with placements occupying the third year. Second year options include French or German. This degree provides an academic foundation for a career in accounting or finance in either public or private sector organisations. There is also a three year course in European Finance and Accounting, with Spanish, German, Italian or French options.

Liverpool (*Accounting*) The courses in Accounting and in Management Economics and Accounting (joint Honours) have a common core of economics, mathematics and statistics with degree courses in Economics and Business Studies. Students take additional subjects according to their chosen specialism. Computer science can also be taken with accounting.

Liverpool John Moores (*Accounting and Finance*) Law and computing are taken throughout this three year course. Options include auditing, taxation systems and public sector accounting. This course has a common foundation year with other courses in the Business School, and transfers are possible up to the end of the first year.

London Guildhall (*Accountancy*) This is a multidisciplinary scheme permitting candidates to choose special Honours degrees or combinations of fields of studies in the Modular programme. The course in Accountancy includes a study of law and economics together with a considerable amount of mathematics, computing and statistics. A financial services course is also offered covering banking, insurance and investment.

London (LSE) (*Accounting and Finance*) The course covers managerial and financial accountancy. Other subjects such as anthropology, geography, history, psychology can be taken in Year 1.

Loughborough (*Accounting Financial Management*) This four year sandwich course provides a broad educational base for a career in management. Various aspects of management are studied in depth. Economics is also offered with accountancy.

Luton Over 60 subjects are offered jointly with accounting.

Manchester (*Accounting and Finance*) Subjects include financial management, investments, law and economics.

Manchester Metropolitan (*Accounting and Finance*) This is a full-time course in Accounting and Finance with an emphasis in management accountancy and options in banking and insurance. Three European courses are also offered in France, Germany and Spain. (*Financial Services*) This course has an emphasis on interpersonal communication and presentation skills.

Middlesex (*Accounting and Finance*) Modules are offered in taxation management and international accountancy. There is also a multidisciplinary course in which accounting is offered.

Napier (*Accounting*) The degree involves extensive use of microcomputers in each year, enabling students to become familiar with information technology in the commercial world. A financial services degree is also offered.

Newcastle (*Accounting and Financial Analysis*) Economics and law are included in the first year course, with additional options in the second and third years. This course and the course in Economics and Accounting together provide the opportunity to offer flexible combinations of business-related subjects either with the intention of proceeding to professional training in accountancy or a more flexible preparation for an industrial or commercial management career. Eight joint courses with accounting are offered in addition to the combined studies programme.

North London (*Accounting/Finance*) The course in accounting is biased towards the quantitative aspects of economic and business analysis and decision-making. French, German or Spanish may be taken as a minor subject. A combined IIonours programme with accounting and finance is also offered.

Northumbria (*Accountancy*) This is a three year full-time Accountancy course which includes options in human behaviour in business organisations, the accountant in management, the accountant in the public sector and international accounting and finance. A course with information systems is also offered.

Nottingham A course is offered in industrial economics with accounting.

Nottingham (Trent) (*Accounting and Finance*) This is offered as a three year full-time or four year sandwich course with industrial placement in Year 3 and option to transfer to Business Studies. Languages, human resource management and marketing are offered as minor subjects. A financial services course is also offered.

Oxford Brookes Over forty subjects are offered with accountancy and finance in the modular programme.

Paisley (*Accounting*) This can be taken as a three year full-time course with two option streams in Finance or International Accounting or as a four or five year sandwich option with business information technology.

Plymouth (*Accounting and Finance*) The course provides a broad overview of business, a detailed study of the accounting function and an understanding of business information systems. It thus provides students with a sound preparation for a career in accounting and finance, whether in business or in professional practice and covers marketing, manpower and operations.

Portsmouth (*Accounting*) This is a three year full-time or a four year sandwich course in Accounting. Part I covers the first two years; Part II includes the sandwich year and two operational studies. The course has a computer option route in the second and fourth years and a European studies route involving a year abroad in France, Germany, Holland or Spain.

Reading Accounting is offered with economics.

Robert Gordon (*Accounting and Finance*) There is a common first year with the BA Business Studies (with options to transfer at the end of the year). Specialist options include advertising, financial accountancy and taxation.

Salford (*Finance and Accounting*) The degree has a leaning towards management and financial accounting, and sends a good proportion of its graduates into industry in addition to the more usual destination of the chartered profession.

Sheffield (*Accounting and Financial Management*) First year students take an introductory course together with two other subjects and a course in statistical methods. In the second and third year students take a number of core courses, some of which are options. Managerial analysis is taken in the third year by students working in groups. There are also four joint courses with accounting and financial management.

Sheffield Hallam (*Accounting and Management Control*) This is a three year full-time of four year sandwich course, with the third year spent on industrial placement. The first year offers a broad study allowing students in Year 2 to specialise in accountancy, administration and law. There is also a degree in Financial Services which includes French or German and an optional placement. A combined studies programme with accountancy is also offered.

Southampton Nine joint courses are offered with accounting.

South Bank (*Accounting and Finance*) Covers financial and management accounting, law, economics, auditing, taxation, financial institutions, and offers exemption from Levels 1 and 2 of the ACCA examinations. There are also three joint courses with computing, mathematics and management.

Staffordshire (*Accounting and Finance*) Single or joint courses are offered and some free electives can be taken from other programmes in the university.

Sterling (*Accountancy*) This subject can be taken as a major, minor or subsidiary course in Part I. Part II courses lead to the General degree or the Honours degree. There is also a degree course in Financial Studies and eleven joint Honours combinations.

Strathclyde (*Accounting*) Financial accounting and finance are taken in Years 1 and 2 followed by management topics and options in Year 3. Six specialisms are offered in Year 1. A course in mathematics, statistics and accounting is also offered. Over fifteen joint courses are also available in Accounting with other subjects offered within the Business School and also with a Modern language.

Sunderland Accounting is combined with business or computing or mathematics.

Teesside (*Accounting and Finance*) This is part of the modular business scheme in which students take eight subjects (common to all business degrees) and progress to their special degree subject in Years 2 and 3. The course includes an optional work placement at the Year 3 stage.

Thames Valley (*Accounting and Finance*) This is a three year full-time course which has a common first year with the one year foundation course. A range of options is offered in the second year. Accounting Studies Europe offers an international emphasis. Law and management studies can also be taken with accounting.

Ulster (*Accountancy with Specialisms*) The course provides a firm foundation in accounting and other related subjects. It is recognised by the professional accountancy bodies and exemptions are gained from their examinations. Final year options include auditing and financial management and two from Business Policy, Information Systems Design, Public Sector Accounting or Economics or Finance.

Warwick (*Accounting and Financial Analysis*) The first year is largely common with the Management Sciences course, and provides a broad base for the study of accountancy. A choice of three specialist subjects is made in Year 3 from a list of financial topics and includes a choice of one non-finance subject. One of the largest business schools in the U.K.

Wolverhampton Accounting is offered as a specialist route in addition to a four year sandwich in accounting and finance and a modular degree scheme with accounting.

• **Top research universities**
London (LSE), Manchester, Bristol, Essex, Exeter, Leeds, Thames Valley, Edinburgh, Strathclyde, Aberystwyth, Warwick.

• **Colleges and Institutes of Higher Education offering degree courses**
Bolton (Inst), Cheltenham and Gloucester (Inst) (*Financial Services*), Farnborough (Coll), Gwent (Coll), Nene (Coll), Southampton (Inst), Suffolk (Coll), Swansea (Inst).

• **Other courses to be considered**
Actuarial studies, banking, business studies, economics, insurance and quantity surveying, mathematics, applied mathematics, statistics.

ACTUARIAL SCIENCE

• **Special subject requirements:** A-level mathematics and one other subject. Most institutions will require Grade A or B GCSE mathematics.

• **Subject information:** This is reputed to be one of the highest paid careers in finance, and so naturally attracts a number of applicants! Training as an actuary, however, is extremely demanding and must not be under-estimated. An alternative route for actuarial work would be a Mathematics degree course. See also under **Accountancy** and **Banking**.

Courses usually offer full exemptions from some of the examinations of the Institute and Faculty of Actuaries which lead to professional qualifications.

City (*Actuarial Science*) The course covers mathematics, statistics and financial studies.

Heriot-Watt (*Actuarial Mathematics and Statistics*) Covers Life Office procedures, pension funds and risk theory.

Kent (*Actuarial Science*) A strong mathematical background is required for a course which covers economics, computing, probability and inference, mortality, operational research and life contingencies.

London (LSE) (*Actuarial Science*) Covers statistics, mathematical methods, investigations and life contingencies. Options are offered in statistics, mathematics, economics, sociology, social psychology and population studies.

Southampton Actuarial Science is offered jointly with either economics or mathematics.

Swansea (*Actuarial Science*) Three and four year courses are offered including a year abroad in the latter. The first year is largely common with other degree schemes in the Business School. Part 2 is approximately 50 per cent actuarial and 50 per cent financial maths, life insurance and management, whilst in Part 3 a wide range of specialist modules is on offer.

• **Other courses to be considered**
Accountancy, financial services, banking, insurance, economics, mathematics, applied mathematics, statistics, business studies.

AFRICAN STUDIES

• **Special subject requirements:** usually GCSE (grades A–C) mathematics.

• **Subject information:** African Studies is often combined with Caribbean Studies and can involve geography, history, popular culture, political science and sociology.

Birmingham (*African Studies*) This can be taken as a main or subsidiary subject. The course covers African history focusing on West Africa through its history, culture and social sciences. African Studies can also be taken as part of the General Honours course and in over 12 joint courses.

North London (*Caribbean Studies*) This is offered in the Combined Honours programme and as a joint course with social research or tourism studies.

London (SOAS) (*African Studies*) There are different approaches offered by way of geographical region (African Studies) or its language and culture including an African Language or by way of African languages - Amharic Studies (Ethiopia), Hausa Studies (Nigeria), Swahili Studies (East Africa). In each case the language is supported by studies covering social anthropology, history, law, linguistics, art and archaeology.

London (UC) An African language is offered with French.

Sussex (*African and Asian Studies*) Ten joint courses are offered including international relations, social psychology, social anthropology, geography, history, politics and modern languages.

• **Top research universities**
Aberystwyth, Bristol, Edinburgh, Essex, Exeter, Leeds, London (LSE), Manchester, Strathclyde, Thames Valley.

- **Colleges and Institutes of Higher Education offering degree courses**
Edge Hill (Coll) offers courses in Asian and African Studies as a minor subject combined with applied social science, community and race relations, geography or history.

- **Other courses to be considered**
Anthropology, international relations, politics.

AGRICULTURAL COURSES
(See also **Forestry and Horticulture**)

- **Special subject requirements:** 2–3 A-levels including chemistry and 1–2 other subjects from mathematics/science, except for Agric Econ/Agric/ Food Marketing for which GCSE (grades A–C) mathematics is the only requirement. Practical experience for Agriculture courses required for entry to Aberystwyth, Bangor, Newcastle, Nottingham. Check entry requirements for other courses.

- **Subject information:** Farming, biochemical applications to plants and animals and agricultural surveying are just some of the specialisms within Agriculture courses; for some agricultural courses practical experience is required. There has also been a recent expansion in agribusiness studies courses.

  Profiles of Degree courses offered at Colleges of Agriculture are also listed below.

Aberdeen (*Agriculture*) The following courses lead to the BSc (Agriculture): (1) Agriculture Economics (2) Animal Science (3) Crop Science (4) General Agriculture (three year and four year courses). There are common courses for all students in the first and second years, with the choice of options leading to the different courses beginning in the third year. Associated courses in Countryside and Environmental Management, Ecology, Biological Sciences, Soil Science and Forestry are also offered.

Aberystwyth (*Rural Resource Management*) This degree covers environmental management, rural communities and planning, rural economics and business, temperate agriculture and organic farming. Module options in conservation, forestry, agroforestry and overseas rural development are also available. The Welsh Institute of Rural Studies also offers degrees in Countryside Management, Agriculture, Agricultural Sciences, Agribusiness and Marketing, Rural Economy and Equine Science. This is a major centre for rural studies and research.

Askham Bryan (C Ag) (*Land Management*) Entry is by way of a HND in Agriculture or Horticulture. (*Business Studies*) Entry is by way of a HND in Business Studies.

Bangor (*World Agriculture*) The degree scheme in World Agriculture, with its opportunities to study both temperate and tropical agriculture, and to combine these with forestry, agroforestry and other land uses, is unique in the UK. The three year course is based on a modular structure, with access to a wide range of general land use topics, modules covering the scientific basis of agricultural production, crop and animal husbandry. The School of Agricultural and Forest Sciences also offers degrees in

Environmental Science, Forestry, Agroforestry and Rural Resource Management.

Belfast (*Agriculture/Agricultural Science*) Specialisms are offered in agricultural chemistry, animal nutrition, environmental management and soil and plant nutrition and microbiology.

Bournemouth (*Land Based Enterprise*) Two options exist in agriculture and retail aspects or agriculture and tourism.

Cirencester (Royal Ag. Coll.) (*Crop Production Ecology and Management*) The course aims to provide an appropriate applied training to meet the increasing demands of crop production and includes biotechnology, business management, tropical crops, land, water and finance. Exchanges with Germany, Holland and France exist. (*International Agriculture, Land and Business Management*) Includes a study of French, German or Spanish. Year 3 options include marketing, finance and personnel. (*Agriculture and Land Management*) Options exist in livestock production systems, dry land farming, aquaculture and fish farming, conservation and horse management. (*Rural Land Management*) This course gives full exemption from the RICS written exams for the Rural Practice Division and covers economics, management, valuations, law and buildings. International Agricultural and Equine Business Management, International Agribusiness Management and Rural Estate Management are also available.

Coventry (*Recreation in the Countryside*) This is a four year sandwich course with placements in appropriate organisations in Year 3. The course is modular and includes geography, business and planning.

Cranfield (*Agricultural Technology and Management*) In this four year sandwich course particular emphasis is placed on the requirements and techniques needed for the effective management of soil, water, machinery and human resources; the business aspects of farm and allied enterprises; the planning, development and management of complex systems to produce profitable products; and financial management. There is a European language option and work experience available. There are also courses on the environment involving ecological resources, landscape technology and engineering, planning and environmental pollution, forestry and woodland management and business studies.

De Montfort Courses are offered in Equine Science, Forestry, Landscape Ecology, Animal Science, Crop Production and Crop Protection, Environmental Studies/Biology and Rural Land Management.

East Anglia (*Development Studies*) This is a very broad subject touching on topics such as agricultural production systems, environmental management and planning, resource development and conservation, natural resources, economics, sociology and politics. The focus extends to world problems.

Edinburgh (*Agriculture*) Four year courses are offered in Agriculture and Agricultural Science with specialisms in animal science, crop and soil science and agricultural microbiology. It is possible to transfer from Biological Science to Agriculture up to the end of the second year. There are also degree courses in Forestry and in Agriculture, Forestry and Rural

Economy. The latter relates agriculture and forestry to wildlife ecology, freshwater fisheries, water resources, game management and rural recreation.

Glasgow (*Agricultural Science*) Courses are also offered in Agricultural Botany, Agricultural Economics and Agricultural, Food and Environmental Chemistry.

Harper Adams (Coll. Ag.) (*Agriculture*) A common first year for all, followed by a choice of degree from (1)Agriculture/Agricultural Marketing (2) Animal Science (3) Crop Management (4) Land and Farm Management (*Agricultural Food Marketing*) A common first semester with agriculture students - European language option. (*Agricultural Engineering*) A 4 year course with placement in Year 3 for one semester. The course covers engineering, animal production, business organisation and finance. (*Rural Enterprise/Land Management*) Industrial placement takes place in Year 3. The course includes farm and woodland management, crop production, farm management, marketing, business organisation, valuation and taxation. (*Rural Environmental Protection*) In addition to crop and animal production the course covers woodland and countryside management and wildlife conservation.

Humberside (*Agriculture - Countryside Management*) This course is taken at Bishop Burton College of Agriculture and covers ecology, biology, earth sciences and soil science, habitat studies, botanical and zoological sciences, landscape form, landscape history, environmental issues and countryside issues. Options in business studies and ornithology.

Liverpool John Moores (*Countryside Management*) Habitat investigation, environmental hazards, leisure studies and wildlife conservation are covered in this course which is offered at major or minor levels or as a joint course with other subjects. French and German are possible. The core study of applied ecology is set against the socio-economic background necessary for the understanding of countryside issues.

London (Wye) (*Agriculture*) The course carries an emphasis on animal and crop production, management and marketing. (*Countryside Management*) This course covers forestry and farm management, amenity land management, environmental pollution and policies, hydrology and water resources. (*Agricultural Business Management*) The course gives an agricultural bias by way of crop and livestock production, land and estate management, human resource management and marketing. Other courses include Agriculture and the Environment, Animal Agriculture, Equine Science, Horticulture, Horticultural Business Management and Plant Sciences.

Newcastle (*Agriculture*) The wide range of courses on offer includes: Agriculture (with options in agronomy, animal production science, farm business management, rural resource management); Agricultural Biotechnology, Agri-Business Management and Marketing, Animal Science, Ecological Resource Management, Food Marketing and Rural Economics.

Nottingham (*Agriculture*) Pre-university practical experience desirable. Students in the Faculty of Agricultural Science (course taught at the

Sutton Bonington campus) follow the same foundation course in the first and second terms, covering agriculture, biochemistry, biology and physical science. Six streams are chosen for third, fourth and fifth terms, giving flexibility of choice (agriculture, horticulture, plant science, animal science, food science, environmental biology). In Agriculture, three subjects are chosen from a range of eight options in the sixth, seventh, eighth and ninth terms. Degree courses are also offered in Agricultural Biochemistry, Plant and Crop Science, Animal Science, Biotechnology in Agriculture, each of these courses being offered with European Studies.

Plymouth (*Agriculture*) This is a four year modular course run at Seale Hayne College, and has two industrial training periods. Topics covered include animal and crop production management, and communication studies (which involves a study of French). There is a common course structure which allows students to transfer between courses covering agriculture, food quality and production, countryside management, environment, rural estate and resource management.

Reading (*Agriculture*) The course is divided into three parts: Part I (two terms) includes agriculture, crop production, animal production, plant and soil science and agricultural economics. Part II (three terms) includes crop physiology, crop protection, plant breeding and animal breeding. Part III (four terms) offers a choice of one of six options. This is a very wide ranging modular course structure with fairly common terms 1 and 2 allowing a change of degree. Courses offered include crop science, horticulture, landscape management, rural resource management and agricultural botany, some of these with European Studies.

Scottish Agricultural College (*Rural Resource Management*) This course aims to bring together scientific, land based and business skills to the problems arising from pressures in the rural environment. Also available are courses in Rural Business Management, Horticulture (with Horti-cultural Management), Environmental Protection and Management, Food Production and Land Use and Food Production Manufacturing and Marketing.

Sheffield Hallam (*Countryside Recreation Management*) The course covers all aspects of recreation and leisure in society, finance, business studies and a language option (French, German, Italian or Spanish).

Writtle (Coll. Ag.) (*Rural Resource Development*) Core modules include science and the environment, information technology, environmental law and electives in nature conservancy and valuations. Specialisations include countryside and leisure development, wildlife and landscape conservation and rural estate development. (*Leisure Management*) Final degree path-ways in heritage management, rural tourism, countryside recreations and leisure management. Other courses include Agriculture, Agriculture (Business Management), Agriculture (Science), Rural Business Manage-ment, Rural Environmental Management, Equine Studies and Agricul-tural Engineering.

• Top research universities
Newcastle, Nottingham, London (Wye), Reading, Aberdeen, Stirling.

- **Colleges and Institutes of Higher Education offering degree courses**
Cheltenham & Glos (CHE) (Global Forest Resources), Buckinghamshire (Coll), New (Coll) (Urban Woodland Management), Trinity (Coll) Carmarthen (Rural Environment)

- **Other courses to be considered**
Animal sciences, biology, biochemistry, biological science, botany, chemistry, conservation management, crop science, ecology, environmental sciences, estate management, food science and technology, forestry, horticulture, land surveying, plant science, veterinary science and zoology.

AMERICAN STUDIES

- **Special subject requirements:** A-level history and English are required for some course; GCSE (grade A–C) in mathematics and a language for others.

- **Subject information:** American literature and history represent the core of most courses, with a year in the USA.

Aberystwyth (*American Studies*) Part I includes the history of the USA and an introduction to American literature, government and politics. Part II includes five core courses covering history, literature and politics, the American revolution and also two optional courses. Over 12 joint courses are also offered with American Studies.

Belfast (*American Studies*) Students follow a course in English and modern history in Year 1 and thereafter study American economic history, literature and politics.

Birmingham (*American Studies*) Specialist studies on this history and literature course include Latin America and Canada. Option study in Canada. Nine joint courses are also offered.

Central Lancashire (*American Studies*) This is a three year course with the opportunity to study in the USA. Literature and history are studied; also film, music, architecture and popular culture. It is also offered as part of the Combined Honours programme.

De Montfort American Studies is offered as part of the Combined and joint arts courses.

Derby American Studies is offered in the Modular Scheme.

Dundee (*American Studies*) Five main themes: geography, economic expansion, the Americanisation process and democracy and the welfare state. Over 12 joint courses are also offered with American Studies which can also be taken in the Arts and Social Sciences and Combined Honours programme.

East Anglia (*English and American Literature*) The preliminary programme (two terms) covers literature, history and philosophy or linguistics plus options. The Final Honours programme is chosen at the end of the second term. There is a wide choice of Honours programmes covering English and American literature, history, drama, film studies, linguistics and philosophy. (*American Studies*) Emphasis on modern American cultural studies.

Edinburgh (*American Studies*) The course covers the history, literature, languages, culture, institutions and society of the American continent (Canada, USA, Central America and Latin America).

Essex (*United States Studies*) The history, literature, culture, social and political structure of the United States are covered in this course. The third year of this four year course is spent in the US. It is also possible to take a degree in Government, History, Literature or Sociology specialising in the United States, or optional courses on American topics in the School of Comparative Studies and in the School of Social Studies.

Exeter (*American and Commonwealth Arts*) This is a four year course with the third year spent in the US or Canada. The emphasis is not only on literature, but on all the arts, including film, photography, painting and popular music. It covers the US and comparable developments in areas of the Commonwealth.

Glamorgan (*American Studies*) This is offered as part of the Humanities programme.

Greenwich (*American Studies*) Part I covers a broad study of the USA and the political, social and cultural themes, with a parallel study of Europe and Britain in the 19th and 20th century. Part II focuses on aspects of American life such as writing, drama, the working class, Jazz and Black Theology.

Hull (*American Studies*) All students study American history and literature, politics and society. Special Honours students select one ancillary subject from a wide range on offer. The course lasts four years (involving Year 3 in the USA).

Keele (*American Studies*) History, geography, politics are covered in this joint course which includes one semester in the USA or Canada. There are over 50 subjects offered jointly with American Studies.

Kent (*American Studies*) American Studies is offered as a multidisciplinary course with a bias in history or literature or politics and government and can also be studied with English literature. The course lasts four years with Year 3 in the United States.

Lancaster (*American Studies*) The three-year course covers American history and literature. Year 2 is spent in the USA.

Leicester (*American Studies*) American history and politics to 1945 with a supplementary subject taken in Year 1. The subject can also be studied within the Combined Arts programme with other subjects.

Liverpool John Moores (*American Studies*) This is offered as a joint course with a choice of over 15 other subjects.

London (King's) United States Studies is offered jointly with Latin American Studies.

Manchester (*American Studies*) Spanish, Latin American Studies and English literature can be taken with American Studies which covers history, government, literature and society.

Manchester Metropolitan American Studies is offered as part of an extensive Combined Studies or Humanities Studies programme.

Manchester (UMIST) American Business Studies is offered with International Management.

Middlesex American Studies is part of the multidisciplinary programme with a large range of subjects and covers history, politics and literature. It can be taken as a major or minor subject.

Nottingham (*American Studies*) The course includes American history, literature, thought and culture. Single Honours students devote two-thirds of the course to American Studies and the remainder to a subsidiary course outside the department. There are option modules on Canada and Year 2 can be taken in Canada or the USA. There are also joint courses with history, philosophy or English studies.

Reading (*American Studies*) This course is taught in three departments (English with Film and Drama, Politics and History). Students spend a period of their studies in the USA.

Sheffield (*American Studies*) The course covers American history from the Revolution to the present day and American literature from the colonial period to the first half of the nineteenth century. During the first year students also take a third arts or social science subject, eg politics, geography, economics or a language.

Staffordshire (*American Studies*) Modules are offered in history, film, literature and the Spanish language. It can also be taken as a joint course with a choice of over 24 other subjects.

Sunderland American Studies is a joint course offered with eleven other subjects.

Sussex (*American Studies*) The subject may be studied with an emphasis on history, literature or social aspects. All students take interdisciplinary courses within the School of English and American Studies. This is a four year course with a year spent at a university in the USA. It is also possible to combine North American Studies with 29 other subjects.

Swansea (*American Studies*) In Year 2 American Studies is taken with two other subjects from English, history, geography, politics, philosophy, Hispanic Studies or Welsh.

Thames Valley American Studies is part of the university's Humanities programme.

Ulster American Studies is taken as part of Modern Studies in the Humanities programme.

Warwick (*Comparative American Studies*) First year students do two courses on themes and problems in North America, Latin America and the Caribbean, and a beginner's course in Spanish. Second year students choose four options of which one must relate to North America and one to

Latin America and two should be either historical or literary. Third year courses are chosen from a range of options in this multidisciplinary course which covers politics, history, literature and film studies.

Wolverhampton American Studies is taken as part of an extensive Humanities scheme.

● **Top research universities**
Manchester, Nottingham, Keele, East Anglia, Sussex.

● **Colleges and Institutes of Higher Education offering degree courses**
Brunel (Univ Coll), Canterbury (Chr.Ch.Coll), King Alfred's (Coll), Liverpool (IHE), Nene (Coll), Ripon/York St. John (Coll).

● **Other courses to be considered**
English literature, government, history, international history, international relations, Latin-American relations, Spanish-American studies and politics.

ANATOMICAL SCIENCE/ANATOMY

● **Special subject requirements:** 2–3 A-levels in science/mathematics subjects; chemistry sometimes 'required' or 'preferred'.

● **Subject information:** Anatomical Science/Anatomy is a highly specialised scientific study covering the biological sciences and a variety of research techniques. The subject is an excellent basis for careers in neuroscience, molecular endocrinology, oral biology or skeletal tissue research. Anatomy also forms part of some biological and medical science courses.

Belfast (*Anatomy*) A number of course options exist at Level 1 which may enable successful students to transfer to other degree courses in the Faculty of Science.

Bristol (*Anatomical Science*) Anatomy occupies one third of the curriculum which includes seminars on neurobiology, biology, anthropology and computing.

Cambridge Anatomy is offered as part of the Natural Sciences programme.

Cardiff (*Anatomical Sciences*) Part I covers anatomy, biochemistry and physiology. Parts II and III focus entirely on anatomy (human and microscopic), developmental, cell and tissue biology and neuroscience.

Dundee (*Anatomical Sciences*) Anatomy teaching commences in the second year at the end of which students opt for a Single Honours degree in Anatomical Sciences or a Joint Honours degree in Anatomy and Physiology.

Edinburgh (*Anatomy*) Human anatomy is offered as a third year course leading to Honours specialisation in Year Four.

Glasgow (*Anatomy*) Anatomy when taken at level 2 can lead to a two year Honours degree. It is also offered as part of the Science Ordinary course.

Liverpool Anatomy is taken either with Human Biology or as part of the Combined Studies programme.

London (UC) Anatomy is offered with Development Biology.

Manchester (*Anatomical Sciences*) This is offered as a three year or four year sandwich course or with a modern language.

Sheffield This three year course is offered with Cell Biology. There is also a Foundation Year course with Cell Science.

● **Top research universities**
Birmingham, Cambridge, Oxford, Liverpool.

● **Other courses to be considered**
Biological sciences, biology, genetics, microbiology, neuroscience and physiology.

ANIMAL SCIENCES

● **Special subject requirements:** 2–3 A-levels from science/mathematics subjects; chemistry usually required.

● **Subject information:** A popular course choice for those who fail to obtain a place in Veterinary Science. Courses cover a biological study of animals, reproduction and nutrition. Horse Studies has also become popular in recent years, particularly at HND level.

Aberdeen (*Animal Science*) Core subjects include chemistry, biochemistry, biology and ecology at levels 1 and 2. Animal production, breeding, nutrition and feeding are studied at levels 3 and 4.

Bangor (*Animal Management*) The course covers farming, nutrition, breeding and disease control.

Bristol (*Equine Science*) Anatomy, biochemistry and physiology are studied in Year 2 with equine science and animal subjects. The university has an international reputation with a self-contained Equine Sports Medicine Centre and the only high-speed equine treadmill in the UK.

Coventry (*Equine Studies*) This is a four year course (at Warwickshire College) with a Year 3 industrial placement, which covers management for the industry (stud farms, feed manufacturers) and equine veterinary research.

Humberside Courses are offered in Equine Management, Equine Science and Technology and Equine and Business Technology.

Lancaster A course is offered in Biochemistry with Animal Physiology.

Leeds (*Animal Science*) A course is also offered in Animal Nutrition and Physiology which includes biochemistry, applied zoology and genetics in Year 1 and similar in Year 2 with the inclusion of animal nutrition.

London (Wye) (*Animal Sciences*) Biology, chemistry, physiology, animal breeding and production are included in this course.

Newcastle (*Animal Science*) The course involves physiology, biochemistry, nutrition and reproduction and the health and welfare of livestock. Studies also cover the environmental concerns over the production of meat and other animal products. There is also a course in Domestic Animal Science.

Nottingham (*Animal Science*) Specialist topics include animal production, physiology and nutrition and environmental science (plants and animals). This is also offered with European Studies on a four year course.

Reading (*Animal Science*) The course focuses on the reproduction, lactation and nutrition of farm animals with applications in biology and immunology to animal production.

Scottish Agricultural College (*Applied Plant and Animal Science*) This course integrates biological, chemical and physical sciences into agricultural practice and business management. Agriculture is also offered.

Sheffield A course is offered in Animal and Plant Biology.

York A three year full-time or four year sandwich course are offered in Animal Physiology.

• **Colleges and Institutes of Higher Education offering degree courses**
Cheltenham and Gloucester (Coll), the Royal Agricultural, the Scottish Agricultural, the Welsh Agricultural and Writtle Agricultural Colleges.

• **Other courses to be considered**
Agriculture, agricultural sciences, veterinary science, zoology.

ANTHROPOLOGY AND SOCIAL ANTHROPOLOGY

• **Special subject requirements:** none.

• **Subject information:** The study will include some biology, some history and a study of the cultures, rituals and beliefs of mankind (ancient and modern) with extensions into art, kinship, family, religion, political and legal structures.

Belfast (*Social Anthropology*) This course can be taken as a single Honours course, a joint or combined Honours course or a major/minor course. The course (a comparative study of society and culture) compares societies around the world. Topics covered include economics, relationships, politics, religious systems, modes of livelihood, perception and belief, marriage and the organisation of public life.

Brunel Social Anthropology is offered as a four year thin sandwich course with either Sociology or Communications.

Cambridge (*Archaeology and Anthropology*) The areas of study cover the social, cultural evolution and variation of mankind by way of archaeology, biological anthropology and social anthropology.

Durham (*Anthropology*) Teaching and research is offered in social and biological anthropology (no previous knowledge is assumed). The former covers social institutions and cultures, with specialised studies in family, kinship, art, religion, ritual and political and legal structures. Biological anthropology involves the evolution of the species and ecology. It is also offered as a joint subject with Archaeology, Arabic, Psychology or Geography and also as part of the course in Natural Sciences or the Combined Social Sciences Course.

East Anglia Anthropology is offered with Archaeology and Art History.

East London (*Anthropology*) Depending on the student's choice in this modular course the object may be either a specialised or joint degree with another subject. The course covers the anthropology of South Asia, archaeology and animal behaviour. Anthropology is also offered as a joint course with over 30 other subjects.

Edinburgh (*Social Anthropology*) Human perceptions of the supernatural, witchcraft, magic and the systems of belief are covered in this course. The content also includes religion, family, marriage and gender.

Hull Anthropology is offered with Psychology or Sociology and Gender Studies. Social Anthropology is offered jointly with Sociology and Development Studies.

London (Goldsmiths') (*Anthropology*) A range of specialist studies includes anthropological aspects of food, health, complex societies, European integration, art, sex, gender and psychological perspectives. There is also a unique course with Communication Studies which includes media studies and advertising. (This is not a practical course).

London (LSE) (*Social Anthropology*) A course on the introduction to social anthropology should be taken by students embarking on Part I to obviate the necessity of taking it in Year 2. Part II courses cover Years 2 and 3 in which a special subject is chosen for study.

London (SOAS) (*Social Anthropology*) First year students take introductory courses in social anthropology and social theory, and study the ethnography of a selected area of Africa or Asia. In the second year, they take a theory of anthropology course, a course in the history, geography, politics or language of their region of interest, and several optional courses including art, music, medical anthropology, food, religion, power and society. In the final year there is one obligatory course and a range of options. Social Anthropology may be combined with several other disciplines including ethnic minorities in Britain.

London (UC) (*Anthropology*) The department is unusual in covering all three branches of anthropology: biological, social, and material culture. Students study all three branches for the first two years, after which they may choose to specialise in one field or to combine courses from two or three branches. Several joint Honours are offered.

Manchester (*Social Anthropology*) This course follows a similar pattern and covers the same topics on other courses in this field with departmental interests covering Africa and the Far East.

Oxford Anthropology is combined with archaeology.

Oxford Brookes Anthropology is offered with forty other subjects.

St Andrews (*Social Anthropology*) During the first two years introductory courses in social anthropology are studied, together with three other subjects. Topics covered in the third and fourth years include gender studies, communities in Britain, hunting and gathering societies, and literacy and semiotics.

Sussex (*Social Anthropology*) The course is offered as a subject with the Schools of African and Asian Studies, Cultural and Community Studies and Social Sciences.

Swansea (*Social Anthropology*) In the first year students take social anthropology, sociology and four other courses in the Faculty of Economic and Social Studies. In the second and third years they take five compulsory courses in social anthropology plus introduction to social theory and two options selected from a range including minority Americans, deviance, complex societies, and the anthropology of development. Combined Honours courses are available.

- **Top research universities**
Cambridge, London (LSE), London (SOAS), London (UC), Manchester, Oxford, Brunel, Durham, Kent, Sussex, Edinburgh.

- **Other courses to be considered**
History, psychology, religious studies, sociology and archaeology.

ARABIC

- **Special subject requirements:** A-level in a language sometime preferred.

- **Subject information:** Linguists may wish to extend their interest into a different language form, although in this subject interest in the Middle Eastern cultures must also predominate. Such courses, however, should never be underestimated as they involve considerable study.

Cambridge (*Arabic*) The course is offered as part of the Oriental Studies Tripos in which one or two languages may be studied. In addition to the language the Tripos covers the history, literature, religion, philosophy, politics and archaeology of the area.

Durham (*Arabic*) Emphasis on written and spoken Arabic with cultural and Islamic studies. Seven joint courses are also offered and the subject is also part of the Social Sciences Combined course in Islamic Studies.

Edinburgh (*Arabic*) The course covers modern standard Arabic and classical Arabic, Islamic history and Arabic literature. There are also 10 joint courses with Arabic which is also offered in the General degree.

Exeter (*Arab Studies*) Emphasis on Classical Arabic language and literature, history (1258–1600), philosophy, art and architecture. Students spend Year 2 in Egypt or Jordan. Arabic is also offered with Islamic Studies, French or Spanish.

Leeds (*Arabic*) The course concentrates on language as a tool for research, literature and history. Year 1 includes a subsidiary subject. Year 2 is spent in Egypt.

Glasgow (*Arabic*) The course covers Modern Standard Arabic with some work on classical Arabic. A high degree of linguistic ability is required of applicants.

London (SOAS) (*Classical and Modern Arabic*) An intensive language course occupies the first two years along with modern and classical literature. Up to two course units outside these subjects may also be taken.

Oxford (*Oriental Studies*) The course covers history, cultural studies, language, literature and Arabic with Islamic Art, Archaeology or Modern Middle Eastern Studies.

St Andrews Arabic is offered as a joint subject with 24 other subjects and is also offered as part of the General Degree of MA.

Salford Arabic is studied as a joint subject with modern languages.

Westminster Arabic is offered with seven other language subjects.

● **Top research universities**
Birmingham, Cambridge.

● **Other courses to be considered**
Alternative courses will depend on the student's preferences towards other languages or courses in Middle Eastern or African Studies.

ARCHAEOLOGY

● **Special subject requirements:** Latin and Greek occasionally 'required' or 'preferred' at A-level. GCSE (grade A–C) language required.

● **Subject information:** It would be unusual for an applicant to pursue this degree course without having been involved in some basic fieldwork. Studies can cover European, Greek, Roman or African spheres.

Bangor Archaeology is offered with history or Welsh history. There is also a course in Nautical Archaeology.

Birmingham (*Archaeology*) A study of archaeological materials, excavation and surveying. Options in British, Mediterranean and European archaeology.

Belfast (*Archaeology*) This course is a study of European prehistory and history from the Middle Ages. Special attention is given to the British Isles and Europe, and Ireland's setting therein. There are also several joint courses offered.

Bournemouth (*Archaeology*) Emphasis on practical archaeology. There is a strong vocational emphasis which includes financial, personnel and management skills. At least four weeks archaeological experience is necessary prior to applying for this course.

Bradford (*Archaeological Sciences*) A scientific approach to archaeology is taken in the course which covers British and European history and scientific methods of investigation (science A-levels are not required). In the final year specialism is possible in a study of the biological or physical sciences in archaeology, plus a further option. The course also includes applications of modern computing methods in archaeology.

Bristol (*Ancient Mediterranean Studies*) The course carries an emphasis on archaeology, ancient history and art. (*Archaeology*) A bias towards the Mediterranean - Iberia to the Middle East. There is extensive fieldwork in the UK and European sites. The course focuses on strong practical training.

Cambridge (*Archaeology and Anthropology*) A study of evolution, behaviour, cultural and social life. Part 1 covers Archaeology, Biological and Social Anthropology. In Part 2 (2 years) a specialism is chosen from the Part 1 subjects.

Cardiff (*Archaeology*) The course focuses primarily on British and European archaeology and involves 'hands on' experience in various archaeological techniques such as drawing, surveying and excavation. For students with an appropriate science background particularly in chemistry, there is also a degree course in Archaeological Conservation.

East London (*Archaeology and Anthropology*) This is a modular course with compulsory modules and free choice units from other subject areas in the university.

Durham (*Archaeology*) The first year of the course consists of a general introduction to the history and nature of archaeology for the prehistoric Roman and early medieval periods. Single Honours students also take an ancillary subject in the first year. The second year course covers both scientific and practical techniques. Archaeology is also offered as a joint course and in the Social Sciences combined programme.

East Anglia Archaeology can be studied alongside Anthropology and Art History whilst Landscape Archaeology is offered as a minor subject with joint studies in History and English.

Edinburgh (*Archaeology*) The course covers pre-history and early history in Scotland and Europe, and the history of ancient and early Middle Eastern civilisation. This is an academic course with opportunities for practical training, the use of microprocessors, computing and the processing of air-photographs. (*Environmental Archaeology*) The course combines a study of environmental biology and archaeology.

Exeter (*Archaeology*) The archaeology of Western Europe with special reference to the British Isles from the origins of humankind to the Middle Ages is the focus of this course, which carries a strong emphasis on practical work with excavations, surveying and draughtsmanship. Options include wetlands archaeology and security and defence in the Ancient and Medieval World. There are combined courses in Archaeology with History and Ancient History.

Glasgow (*Archaeology*) This is offered in the Faculties of Science, Arts or Social Science, the choice being dependent on the other subject students wish to study. The course covers a commitment to British archaeology from the earliest times to AD 1000 and later to European and Mediterranean areas. There is an emphasis on practical and scientific aspects of the study. There are also over 40 joint courses combining archaeology with other subjects.

Lampeter (*Archaeology*) Palaeolithic to modern cultures. There are particular strengths in landscape, prehistoric and environmental archaeology.

Leicester (*Archaeology*) In this BA course one additional subject is taken in Years 1 and 2 from biology, chemistry, computer science, geography, geology, physics, maths and sociology. Two options are taken in Year 2 and three options in Year 3. The study covers Europe, Western Asia, Africa, Australasia and the Americas and archaeological methodology. An ERASMUS exchange allows for some students to study in Denmark, France or Italy. Archaeology is also offered as a joint subject or in the Combined Arts or Sciences programmes.

Liverpool (*Archaeology*) The Arts course covers the ancient civilisation of the Eastern Mediterranean, Africa, Europe and the Near East. There is also a degree course for students with A-levels in the sciences emphasising scientific techniques. Archaeology also features in the combined arts, science or social science programmes.

London (King's) (*Classical Archaeology*) The course unit structure allows great flexibility but all students undertake some study of Latin or Greek.

London (SOAS) Archaeology is offered under six specialisms combined with the History of Art.

London (UC) (*Archaeology*) Six courses are offered in Arts, Science, Classical, Western Asiatic, Egyptian and Medieval Archaeology. There is also a degree in Archaeological Conservation. The course in Classical Archaeology lasts four years with the first two having an emphasis on the study of ancient history and a language. The third and fourth years specialise in the archaeology of Greece with options in Roman archaeology; Medieval Archaeology reviews British archaeology covering Anglo-Saxon and post-Conquest periods, Celtic Britain, Ireland and the Vikings.

Newcastle (*Archaeology*) A broad course from early prehistory to the industrial revolution. It involves a comprehensive practical training including fieldwork, excavation, museum work, computing etc. There is also a joint course offered with archaeology and Ancient History and with other subjects in the Combined Studies programme.

Nottingham (*Archaeology*) Part I (two years) covers the methods used by archaeologists, and a study of the development of civilisation in Britain and Europe over 11,000 years. Part II (third year) follows specialist studies in prehistoric, Roman, Medieval or European regional archaeology as well as historical buildings, numismatics and mathematical and computer applications in archaeology. Excavation takes place during vacation periods. Subsidiary language study is possible and six joint Honours courses are available.

Oxford (*Archaeology and Anthropology*) The course covers world archaeology and introduces anthropological theory. Topics include human evolution and ecology, social analysis and interpretation, cultural representations and beliefs and urbanisation. The geographical areas cover the Aegean, Middle East, Maritime South East Asia, S. America, Africa and the Islamic world.

Reading (*Archaeology*) There are two topics in the First University Examination: instruction in techniques of excavation and the theory, methodology and interpretation of archaeology. Seven remaining subjects cover British and European archaeology and archaeology and science. Archaeology can also be taken with several other subjects.

Sheffield (*Archaeological Science*) The course provides opportunities for single Honours students to bias their studies towards prehistoric archaeology or Roman or medieval archaeology at the beginning of the second year. Option courses are offered in the second and third years. Anthropology and environmental studies are central elements in the teaching programme. There are also two courses combined with prehistory and three with landscape design, geography or geology.

Southampton (*Archaeology*) A general introduction in the first year is followed by five themes in the second year: subsistence and survival, emergence of complex societies, art and society, archaeology, and history and scientific methods. Options are available in the third year, ranging from Saxon England and Roman Spain to computers in archaeology.

Warwick A course is offered in Classical Archaeology with Ancient History.

York (*Archaeology*) The course is concerned both with archaeological method (including a significant practical element) and theory (with special courses on the interpretation of archaeological data). One main course is taken each term based on single themes covering Europe from the Bronze Age onwards. There are opportunities to study a foreign language. The department has particular strengths in medieval history and medieval archaeology.

• **Top research universities**
Cambridge, London (UC), Oxford, Reading, Sheffield, Southampton, Durham, Belfast, Edinburgh.

• **Colleges and Institutes of Higher Education offering degree courses**
King Alfred's (Coll), Winchester and Trinity Carmarthen (Coll).

• **Other courses to be considered**
Ancient history, anthropology, classical studies, classics, geology, history, history of architecture, art and design, medieval history, prehistory and social anthropology.

ARCHITECTURE

• **Special subject requirements:** One A-level from mathematics or physics occasionally required. English language and mathematics GCSE (grades A–C) necessary.

• **Subject information:** Institutions offering architecture have very similar courses. An awareness of the relationship between people and the built environment is necessary, plus the ability to create and to express oneself in terms of drawings, paintings etc. Most architecture schools will expect to see a portfolio of art work, particularly drawings of buildings or parts of buildings.

Bath (*Architectural Studies*) For the BSc in Architectural Studies, the first year is spent in university, and the summer terms of years two, three and four spent in training. The course leads on to the Bachelor of Architecture degree but admission is not automatic as the minimum requirement is a second class Honours degree - second division. Bath has a joint School of Architecture and Building Engineering and has a common first year course for all civil engineering, building and architecture students. Teaching rating 'excellent'.

Brighton (*Architectural Design*) Architectural design dominates the course, which provides a balance between environmental needs, technology and creative design. The course also includes landscape design and a European language. The BA (Hons) degree is followed by a two year diploma course.

Belfast (*Architecture*) This is a standard architectural course leading to a BSc degree and to subsequent professional training as a qualified architect.

Cambridge (*Architecture*) Parts I and II provide a basic training in architecture, through design and studio exercises with the history of European architecture. After taking the degree, students normally take a further two year course leading to the Diploma in Architecture (giving exemptions from the RIBA Part II examination).

Cardiff (*Architectural Studies*) This is a two-tier scheme of study, first leading to a BSc in Architectural Studies in three years followed by two years of study (including one year in practice) for the BArch degree. Visual communication, interior design, town planning and landscape design are included throughout the BSc course and opportunities exist for a specialist study in the BArch degree. There is a focus on design creativity integrated with technological and environmental concerns of modern architectural practice. The School of Architecture works in close liaison with the Town Planning Department in the fields of urban design, housing and landscape.

Central England (*Architecture*) The School is one of the largest in the country and draws strength from its association with the Departments of Planning, Landscape and Construction, and Surveying. A postgraduate diploma course gives complete exemptions from RIBA examinations. Architecture can also be studied with an emphasis on urban design, conservation or regeneration.

De Montfort (*Architecture*) The course is taken at Leicester and Milton Keynes. The 3 year course is followed by one year of practical study followed by a further 2 years to the graduate diploma.

Dundee (*Architecture*) This five year course comprises three years leading to the BSc (Arch) followed by BArch (Hons) after a further two years. A year of practical experience may be taken between the third and fourth years. ERASMUS links with Europe. Architecture and Urban Studies is also offered.

East London (*Architecture*) Environmental design, history, construction, conservation, law, the building industry and urban studies are topics covered in this standard architecture course. The course is suitable for students with an arts-based background.

Edinburgh (*Architecture*) Two main courses are covered in Years 1 and 2 in design and architectural science. Architecture history is added in Year 3 with two other courses chosen from the Faculties of Social Science or

Arts. There is also a study of Architectural History offered in the Social Science programme.

Greenwich (*Architecture*) This is a design-based course with strong visual studies and computing input. Teaching rating 'excellent'.

Heriot-Watt (*Architecture*) The School of Architecture has a reputation for a studio-based course focusing on architecture and the environment. This four year course leading to the BArch is followed by a one year course for the diploma of Architecture. A year of practical experience usually precedes entry to the Diploma course. There are scholarships and endowments for organised group travel.

Huddersfield (*Architectural Studies (International) Design*) Design, design technology, communication and context of design are the four main subject areas. Unique in the UK, this course of 3 years only is designed specifically to apply the principles of design on a worldwide basis. The course in Architecture runs parallel for Year 1 after which students decide their course route.

Humberside (*Architecture*) Project based design teaching covering technical, professional, human and social aspects and historical studies.

Kent Institute of Art and Design (*Architecture*) A two-term introductory course is followed by lectures and seminars in historical and technical subjects, leading to the BA at the end of the third year. Optional studies in graphic design, painting, sculpture and photography are also available. The Diploma in Architecture occupies the fourth and fifth years prior to which the student spends a year out in practical training.

Kingston (*Architecture*) The course has design as its principal core element. A particular feature of the course is the use of continuous assessment. The degree aims to give students an awareness of the social and practical problems which face an architect, and the skill and knowledge necessary to begin to tackle these problems. Pathways are offered including computer applications, architectural psychology, building economics and conservation.

Leeds Metropolitan (*Architecture*) Architectural design is the main feature of the course which is linked with building, design management, urban and landscape design and environmental control. Interior design and a study of Third World housing is also included. The graduate diploma course follows the three year BA (Hons) course.

Liverpool (*Architecture*) There is a strong emphasis on design having close links with building, civil engineering and civic design areas.

Liverpool John Moores (*Architectural Studies*) This is a standard course in architecture preparing students for graduation and professional qualifications.

London (UC) (*Architecture*) This three year course for a BSc degree provides a very broad academic education for those who are concerned with planning, design and management of the built environment.

Manchester (*Architecture*) The three year BA course leads on to the two year study for the Bachelor of Architecture degree. The course is predominantly design-based.

Manchester Metropolitan (*Architecture*) This is a three year full time or four year sandwich course with design projects supported by studies in technical and administrative skills. Postgraduate studies lasting two years lead to the Graduate Diploma in Architecture.

Middlesex (*Architecture*) This is a three year full time or four year sandwich course leading to professional qualifications after appropriate professional experience.

Newcastle (*Architectural Studies*) This three year course covers the theory and history of architecture, building technology, studio design projects and environmental design. It is followed by a year's practical training leading on to a two year course of advanced architectural design for the BArch degree. The course presents a realistic view of the environment of architecture and encourages students to develop a personal philosophy of design that responds to it. The course is strongly biased towards project work. History of Architecture can also be studied as part of the Combined Studies programme. Teaching rating 'excellent'.

North London (*Architecture*) Full and part-time courses are offered with good design studio accommodation.

Nottingham (*Architecture*) A three year BA (Hons) course in Architecture and Environmental Design is followed by two years to the BArch degree. A year of practical experience follows the BA course. The course is planned around project work investigating a wide variety of building problems and achieves a balance between art and technology and stresses the integration of technical work with projects but is without a strong scientific bias. Teaching rating 'excellent'. (*Architectural Studies*) The first two years are identical to the BA Architecture course. In Year 3 the student chooses three specialised pieces of work to reflect his or her own interests. (Does not lead to professional recognition.)

Oxford Brookes (*Architectural Studies*) A three year project-based course is supported by environmental and construction technologies, social sciences, history and philosophy. The Graduate Diploma Course of two years follows with a year of practical experience.

Plymouth (*Architecture*) A standard course of 3 years full time duration followed by practical experience and two years of study leading to a diploma.

Portsmouth (*Architecture*) Teaching is based on design projects (60 percent of the course). The first year covers drawing techniques, user studies, planning and circulation, and environmental comfort. The second and third year studies focus on three themes: the house, urban residential and commercial buildings, and a public building – supported by history, drawing, computer-aided design, computing and construction.

Robert Gordon (*Architecture*) In addition to this course it is also possible to take Architecture with Languages and an exchange in Europe.

Sheffield (*Architecture*) At the end of the second year students decide whether to take the traditional BA degree or to opt for a new course which leads on to professional qualifications in both architecture and planning. There are several options open to those who take the standard BA degree which, combined with practical experience, lead to exemptions from RIBA examinations. Work experience advised before application.

South Bank (*Architecture*) The course includes design, environmental science, history of architecture and 'the profession of architecture'.

Strathclyde (*Architectural Studies*) The course has two parts (1) Foundation Studies - a 2 year modular course covering theory and practice and (2) Graduation Studies - another 2 year modular course allowing specialisations and leading to the BSc degree.

Westminster (*Architecture*) The course is largely based on design project work and covers a study of architectural form and the physical, social and psychological needs of the user.

● **Top research universities**
Cardiff

● **Other courses to be considered**
Building, building surveying, civil engineering, estate management, land surveying, landscape architecture, quantity surveying, and town and country planning.

ART (HISTORY/DESIGN)

Art courses leading to degree qualifications in Art can be divided into two main groups:

(1) Degree courses for which two A-level passes and five GCSE subjects at grade C or above are required as a minimum qualification in universities, colleges and institutes of higher education for students applying through UCAS. (See table below.)

(2) Art and Design degree courses (specialist practical art courses) are also offered in universities, colleges and schools of art, for which applications are submitted through the Art and Design Admissions Registry (ADAR). Entry to these courses is normally through a Foundation course in Art for which A-level passes may not be necessary if applicants have a minimum of five subjects at GCSE grade C or above. Specialisms include Graphic Design, Fine Art, Textiles/Fashion, Three Dimensional Design, Furniture Design, Interior Design, Silversmithing, Industrial Design, Carpet Design and Theatre Design.

● **Special subject requirements:** Modern language or art or an art portfolio may be required at A-level for some courses: GCSE Grades A–C in a modern language is usually required.

Aberdeen (*History of Art*) A broad study of painting, sculpture, architecture, decorative and industrial arts.

Aberystwyth (*Art*) A very comprehensive studio programme of practical art is offered in painting, photography, printmaking and book illustration. Art History can also be taken in over 12 joint combinations.

Anglia (Poly Univ) (*Art History*) This is a three year full-time course, or four years with a language (French, German, Italian or Spanish). Modules include photography and 'the English Country Home'. There is also a course in Studio Art and Art History and several joint courses. There are also several courses in Graphic Arts for which application is made through UCAS.

Birmingham The History of Art is offered in combination with over 20 other subjects.

Bournemouth Several design courses are offered (application through UCAS), including Computer Visualisation and Animation, Interior, Product, Furniture and Creative Advertising Design.

Brighton (*History of Design*) The course covers all aspects of design (industrial, interior, graphic, fashion, engineering and environmental) from 1700 to the present day. Courses are also offered in the History of Decorative Arts and Crafts and Visual Cultures. There is also a Design and Technology Education course with Qualified Teacher Status.

Bristol (*History of Art*) The course covers British and European Art from the classical period to the present day.

Bristol UWE Secondary teaching Design and Technology courses are offered - 2 year and 4 year full-time programmes. Primary teaching art courses are also available, also Art in a Social Context and Community Arts.

Buckingham (*History of Art and Heritage Management*) This is a two year full-time degree course involving European Art and Architecture, furniture and the decorative arts plus a language (French, German, Italian or Spanish).

Cambridge (*History of Art*) This course focuses on a history of the visual arts and architecture in Western Europe from the Middle Ages. The History of Art Tripos is a Part II option only and taken after Part I of another Tripos (for example, Modern Languages, Archaeology and Anthropology, Theology, Philosophy, History and English). Homerton College also offers Art with Education.

Central England (*Art and Design*) A three year practical course in design, media and management is offered. Students write their own art and design based course. Art (Theory and Practice) is also available.

Central Lancashire (*Design History*) There are two defined routes: Design History with either Film and Media Studies or with Museum and Heritage Studies and Visual Studies, which covers visual phenomena in society combined with Art History. Design History, Visual Studies and Design Studies and Creative Design for Fashion can also be taken with Combined Honours programmes.

Coventry (*Art and Craft*) A multidisciplinary practical course covers ceramics, metal, textiles or specialisation in one area. Practical work is supported by modules relating to historical, contemporary and professional practice.

De Montfort (*History of Art and Design*) The course covers art and design from the mid-eighteenth century to the present day and embraces architecture, painting, design, film, photography and museum studies. In the second year students spend six weeks on a placement in a museum, gallery, film or TV studio, or an auction house. There is also a History of Film course. History of Art and Design can also be taken as part of the Combined Arts or Joint Arts and Humanities programme. There are also a number of practical design courses on offer through UCAS covering graphics, fashion and textiles, knitwear, multi-media and 3D design. Conservation and Restoration is also available.

Derby (*Visual Cultures*) The course covers the History of Art, Design, Film and Photography. Practical design courses offered cover the Applied Arts, graphics and photography.

East Anglia (*History of Art*) Students follow a coherent programme built around two separate periods in the history of art, selected from a wide variety of subjects which range from antiquity to the present day. Areas covered include Asia, Africa, Oceania and the Americas. Special subjects which can be taken with a project include graphic satire and popular journalism and the Spectacle of the City.

East London (*Art History/Design/Film*) Students choose their pathway in Art History, Design History, Architecture History, Art and Psychoanalysis and Film History. (*Design*) The course leads to one of four degrees (Illustration, Photography, Textile Design and Surface Decor or Visual Communications) in combination with Art and Design and Film History or other non-Art subjects. Both courses are also offered with over 30 other subject options.

Edinburgh (*Fine Art/History of Art*) The MA (Hons) History of Art is offered as a specialist study without any practical work. The MA (Hons) Fine Art takes five years which combines the history of art and practical art with (in Years 1 and 2) a second subject. There is also a course in Architectural History and eleven joint courses with Art History.

Essex (*Art History and Theory*) This is a non-practical course. The first year includes art and a course on the European Enlightenment, and three options. The second year covers Tuscany from 1300 to 1500, nineteenth century art or Pre-Columbian art and architecture, the interpretation of the visual arts, Russian art, industrial design and fine arts in England. There is also a course in Art History and Theory and Music which includes music practicals and two Art History options. Several joint courses are also offered.

Glamorgan The course in Creative Arts includes visual arts, creative writing, theatre, media and drama. Product Design courses are also offered in addition to Design options on the Combined or Joint Honours programmes.

Glasgow (*History of Art*) The course covers classical European, medieval, modern and Scottish art. Reading knowledge of a European language is an advantage. Over 30 joint courses are also offered.

Greenwich Design and Technology and also Industrial Design are offered.

Heriot-Watt Textile Design is offered free standing or as part of the Combined Science course.

Humberside Applications are submitted through UCAS for the Interior Design course.

Keele Visual Arts is offered on 44 joint courses.

Kent The History of Art is offered in over 15 joint courses.

Lancaster (*Visual Arts*) In Part I Visual Arts is taken with two other subjects and consists of practical studio work and theory. Practical work covers drawing, painting, sculpture and three dimensional work. In the second and third years students choose from graphic design, painting, sculpture or three dimensional work and certain technical specialisms, for example, screen printing, welding, ceramics, woodwork. Theoretical studies cover twentieth century art and other options, eg photography and architecture. There is also a course in Visual Culture covering Modernism and two other subjects plus a language course. (*Creative Arts*) This covers a choice of subjects from theatre studies, music and visual arts with practical studies.

Leeds (*Fine Art*) This is a four year course focusing on the history of art and studio work. (*Fine and Decorative Arts*) This is a four year course covering history of art and architecture in Europe and America. Studio work optional in the first year. (*History of Art*) This is a three year course, covering history of art and architecture in Europe and America. Options in the history of photography and cinematography are available in the third year. A course in Textile Design is also offered.

Leeds Metropolitan (*History and Theory of Art and Design*) The course covers art history, painting, sculpture, photography, furnishings, films and TV. Design and Technology (Secondary education) is also offered.

Leicester (*History of Art*) This is a three year course with two additional subjects studied, one in the first and second year and one in the first year only. The course covers the history of European art from the Renaissance to modern times - mainly painting, but with sections dealing with architecture and sculpture. Part of the first semester of the final year is spent in Italy. (*History of Art (European Union)*) Students transfer to this course from History of Art course. The History of Art can also be studied as part of the Combined Arts and Combined Science programme.

Liverpool There are two combined programmes (Social and Arts) in which the History of Art and Architecture are offered.

Liverpool John Moores Eight joint courses are offered with Visual Studies which involves drawing, media and visual language. Art, Design and Technology courses leading to Primary and Secondary teaching are also available.

London (Courtauld) (*History of Art*) A general first year foundation leads to a choice of a special period of study (European art 1200–1350, the sixteenth century, or 1848–1925) in the next four terms. Students then choose a special subject for the final two terms which could cover art, architecture or sculpture.

London (Goldsmiths') (*Fine Art(Studio Practice)*) Studio work and art history are studied in equal proportions. Specialist historical options include cinema, photography, Eastern art, and primitivism. (*Fine Art and Art History*) This course is specifically aimed at students from overseas for whom English is not their first language. Art History theory and studio practice are combined. There are also courses in Textiles and in Art Education leading to Primary education and Design and Technology (Secondary education).

London (SOAS) (*History of Art*) The course is divided between European and non-European art and can be combined with Archaeology with several specialisms.

London (UC) (*History of Art*) The first year of this covers the history of art from antiquity to the present day with the techniques of art and architecture. The second and third years offer a choice of historical periods. Students also take courses in anthropology, history or philosophy.

London Guildhall (*Design Studies*) The course has two pathways, Design Studies or Design Management.

Loughborough History of Art and Design is offered with English.

Luton (*Visual Arts*) Several joint courses in animation are offered, also design courses in graphics, interior, industrial and product design.

Manchester (*History of Art and Architecture*) A study of Western Art followed by specialisms in Greek and European Art and Architecture.

Manchester Metropolitan (*History of Design*) This course is 75 per cent academic and 25 per cent practical. (No previous graphical experience necessary.) Both areas cover communication arts (graphics, printing, photography, film). Three-dimensional design (ceramics, furniture, metal, glass) and textile design (print, weave, embroidery, fashion) are also included in the course. Design and Technology courses are also offered.

Middlesex (*History of Art, Design and Film*) This specialist programme is based on the Modular Degree Scheme's Art History set. It allows students to plan their own programmes, covering particular aspects of the history of art and design from the Italian Renaissance to the present as well as film and television studies. The flexibility of the scheme allows students to combine art history with work from other subject areas which are relevant, including history, communications and women's studies. Several design courses are also offered including Design and Technology/Video Games, and also with three pathways in Software Engineering, Visual and Narrative Design or Music and Sound for games.

Napier Applied Arts, Graphic Communications Management and Interior Design are offered.

Newcastle (*Fine Art*) This is a four year course in the history of European art and architecture, with studio work in painting, sculpture or design. It incorporates a foundation course in the first year. At the end of Year 3 students have a choice of options with an emphasis either on practical work or Art History. The History of Art is offered as part of the Combined Studies (BA) programme.

Northumbria (*History of Modern Art, Design and Film*) The course focuses on the history of European and American art from 1770 to the present day covering (1) painting and sculpture (2) architecture, design (3) film (4) social history. One day each week is spent on practical work or conservation studies. Art History is also combined with Fine Art, Design Information Studies and Women's Cultures. Design and Technology is also offered.

Nottingham (*Art History*) The course covers architecture, painting and sculpture from the Renaissance in Italy, Northern Europe and England. Practical work is available but not compulsory.

Nottingham Trent There is a course in Design and Technology (Secondary teaching). A course in Creative Arts covers music, the visual arts, performance and dance.

Oxford (*Fine Art*) This is a three year course, with practical work taking place in the Ruskin School. Full-time study is made of drawing, painting, printmaking, sculpture, history of art and anatomy. Specialist studies in painting or printmaking start in the second year.

Oxford Brookes Over 30 subjects are offered with the History of Art. Fine Art is offered with over 40 other subjects.

Plymouth Art History is offered jointly with nine other subjects including Design Arts which is also offered at the Primary level. Art and Design is also offered with several separate subjects.

Reading (*Art*) A four year practical course is offered with opportunities for painting with construction, painting with paint, and sculpture with multi-media art and group projects. (*History of Art and Architecture*) is a seven-term course following the First University Examination, which covers a major and minor area in the history of painting, sculpture and the history of architecture. History of Art is also offered with nine other subjects. A practical design course is also offered in Typography and Graphic Communication.

St Andrews (*Art History*) This is a very comprehensive course covering the history of European painting, sculpture, architecture and graphic art forms from the Middle Ages to 1800. Several specialised topics are also available including landscape and design, domestic architecture in Britain, British furniture design and American post-war painting.

Sheffield Hallam (*History of Art, Design and Film*) Three subjects are linked in the first year, students opting for two of them in the second year and one in the third year. The course draws mainly on nineteenth and twentieth century material. First hand experience of works of art and design is supported by a programme of study visits. Art is also offered as part of the Combined Studies.

Staffordshire (*History of Design and the Visual Arts*) The course includes history of design, architecture, painting, sculpture and social history. All first year students select six options (1) history of ceramics and glass (2) graphic design (3) architecture of the industrial society (4) history of painting and sculpture (5) film studies (6) history of fashion. Two of these options are selected in Year 2 and one in Year 3. All first and second year students take practical courses relevant to their options. Visual Arts is also offered with 20 other courses and Design Studies with eight subjects.

Sussex (*History of Art*) The course involves a study of architecture, painting, sculpture and photography. The degree does not include studio work, but many students practise some from of art in their own time. Art History is offered in the Schools of Cultural and Community Studies, the School of English and American Studies, and the School of European Studies.

Teesside (*History of Design*) The course covers the period from the mid-seventeenth century to the present day, with an emphasis on the history of architecture.

Thames Valley History of Art is offered as part of the Humanities programme.

Warwick (*History of Art*) A broad course is offered dealing with the history of European art and architecture. Topics include specific areas such as artistic media and techniques, the English home, and wide areas of study such as art in Florence, Flanders, France and twentieth century architecture. There is also a language course in Italian.

Wolverhampton History of Art and Design is offered as part of the Modular Degree Scheme.

York (*History of Art*) After an introductory course in Term 1, in Terms 2, 3 and 4 there is one course in Art History and two in English Art. In all there are 18 courses offered from Early Christian Art to the present day.

* **Top research universities**
Bournemouth, Brighton, Brunel, Coventry, London (Gold), (Royal College of Art) (Univ Coll), Northumbria, Reading (Typography), Wimbledon (CA).

* **Colleges and Institutes of Higher Education offering degree courses (UCAS Scheme)**
Bangor Normal (Coll), Bath (Coll), Bishop Grosseteste (Coll), Blackburn (Coll), Bolton (Inst), Bradford/Ilkley (Coll), Bretton Hall (Coll), Buckinghamshire (Coll), Canterbury Chr. Ch. (Coll), Central School/Speech Drama, Cardiff (Inst), Cheltenham/Glos (Coll), Chester (Coll), Chichester (Inst), Colchester (Inst), Croydon (Coll), Cumbria (Coll) (Graphic Design), Edge Hill (Coll), Falmouth (Sch of Art), Gwent (Coll), Kent (Inst), Kidderminster (Coll), King Alfred's (Coll), Liverpool (Inst), London (Inst), Loughborough (Coll), La Sainte Union, Nene (Coll), Newman (Coll), Norfolk (Inst), Ravensbourne (Coll), Ripon/York St. John (Coll), Roehampton (Inst), Rose Bruford (Coll), Scarborough (Univ Coll), Salford (UC), St. Mark/St. John (Coll), Southampton (Inst), Stockport (Coll), Suffolk (Coll), Surrey (Coll A D), Swansea (Inst), Westhill (Coll), West Herts (Coll), Wimbledon (Sch A D), Winchester (School of Art), Worcester (Coll). Applications for other courses are submitted through the ADAR scheme.

• **Other courses to be considered**
All practical art and design courses. Architecture, archaeology, classical civilisation, communication studies, film studies and landscape architecture.

ASTRONOMY/ASTROPHYSICS

• **Special subject requirements:** 2–3 A-levels from science subjects; mathematics and physics important.

• **Subject information:** These courses have a mathematics and physics emphasis. Applicants, however, should also realise that subject-related careers on graduation are limited. Astrophysics courses involve both physics and astronomy and are more difficult than single honours; students weak in mathematics and physics should avoid them.

Belfast Physics is offered with Astrophysics.

Birmingham (*Physics with Astrophysics*) This course is appropriate for those with an interest in astronomy and astrophysics who wish to combine this with a training in basic physics.

Bristol Physics is offered with Astrophysics.

Cardiff (*Astrophysics*) Applied mathematics and astronomy are available as second and third year subjects. Pure maths, applied maths and physics are recommended Part I subjects.

Central Lancashire (*Astrophysics*) Practical observations are made with Britain's largest optical telescope. The course has a common first year with Observational Astronomy and Instrumentation. Completion of the course leads to graduate fellowship of the Institute of Physics.

Edinburgh (*Astrophysics*) The first two years of this course are largely similar to those for physics students. In the third and fourth years the work is divided between astronomy and physics.

Glasgow (*Astronomy/Physics*) Courses cover the universe and the methods used in assessing distances, motions and nature of celestial objects. Later studies examine the modern developments in the study of the universe. The course in Astronomy and Mathematics covers the same ground in Astronomy subjects.

Hertfordshire (*Astronomy*) This is offered within the university's Combined Modular Scheme with an industrial placement option prior to the final year as with the Astrophysics course. There is a well-equipped teaching observatory.

Keele (*Astrophysics*) The subject is taken with 29 other subjects and includes two subsidiary courses in Astronomy.

Kent (*Physics with Astrophysics*) The course provides a broad understanding of basic physics and an opportunity for a detailed study of the physics of the cosmos. There is also a course which includes a year in Europe.

Leeds (*Physics with Astrophysics*) The first year is similar to that of the Physics course which means that transfers between the Physics and the

Physics with Astrophysics courses can be arranged up to the end of the first year.

Leicester Courses are offered in Mathematics or Physics with Astronomy, Physics with Astrophysics and Physics with Space Science Technology, which includes solar physics and space flight dynamics.

Liverpool John Moores (*Astrophysics*) The course involves physics, mathematics, computing astrophysics and communication skills in Year 1, and in Year 2 focuses on the detection and analysis of light. Year 3 is centred around 'The Multi-frequency Observatory' - a modular course. Some observational work is carried out at Jodrell Bank and at La Laguna University in Tenerife.

London (King's) A course is offered in Physics with Astrophysics.

London (QMW) (*Astrophysics*) A physics programme is accompanied by specialised topics such as stellar and galactic structure and cosmology. (*Astronomy*) Physics and the principles and techniques of astronomy have equal emphasis in the first two years. Options in physics and observation and interpretational astronomy are offered in the third year. It is possible to study either subject as part of a joint Honours degree with Mathematics.

London (RH) (*Physics with Astrophysics*) This is a single Honours course with the optional topic of astrophysics, a theoretical study of astronomy.

London (UC) (*Astronomy*) The first year provides an introduction to the theory and practice of astronomy with maths and physics. Astrophysics, spectroscopy and astronomical methods follow in the second year, with a variety of courses and observational astronomy in the third year. The degree course in Astronomy and Physics comprises a selection of subjects from both these specialist fields. There is also a degree course in Astrophysics.

Manchester (*Physics and Astrophysics*) A physics course with specialist studies in astrophysics.

Manchester (UMIST) Astrophysics can be taken as a third year option in courses with physics, computational physics and physics with Environmental Science.

Newcastle (*Astronomy and Astrophysics*) A training is given in applied maths and physics. In the first year maths, physics and another science subject are studied and students may defer choice of degree until then. Second and third years introduce astronomy and astrophysics, computing, electronics and nuclear physics.

Plymouth Astronomy is offered as a minor pathway in combination with major subjects.

Sheffield Astronomy is offered with Chemistry, Mathematics or Physics.

Southampton Courses are offered in Physics with Astronomy or Space Science.

St Andrews (*Astronomy and Astrophysics*) Single and joint Honours courses are offered in the Faculty of Science. The first and third years introduce the subjects and later provide advanced instruction in all the modern practical and technical aspects of the subjects. A study of maths and physics predominates in the second year. Astronomy and Astrophysics can also be taken in the Faculty of Arts as a joint Honours course with Logic and Philosophy of Science, Mathematics or Electronics.

Sussex (*Physics with Astrophysics*) Students taking the Astrophysics minor option spend about a quarter of their time on this subject, and undertake a third year project on a topic in Astrophysics.

York (*Physics with Astrophysics*) Courses on planetary science and stellar physics are taken in Year 2 and observational astronomy in Year 3.

● **Other courses to be considered**
Computer science, electronics, geology, geophysics, materials science, mathematics, meteorology, mineral sciences, oceanography, ophthalmic optics, applied physics or physics.

BANKING AND FINANCE (including Insurance)

● **Special subject requirements:** GCSE (grades A–C) in mathematics.

● **Subject information:** These are specialised courses leading to a career in banking. Major banks offer sponsorships. Most courses follow a similar menu.

Bangor (*Banking, Insurance and Finance*) This course is taken with two other subjects in Part I, for example accountancy and finance, mathematics or languages. It can be taken as a single Honours course in the second and third years or as a joint course in Banking or Insurance with Mathematics or Banking and Insurance with Modern Languages (two from French, German, Italian and Russian), one year being spent abroad. Sponsorship is available from two major banks and a building society.

Belfast (*Finance*) The course covers capital investment decisions, management of stock, debtors, company and international finance. Year 3 is a placement year in a financial institution.

Birmingham (*Money, Banking, Finance*) The course offers a study of the UK financial system and a sound grounding in law, accountancy, finance and economics. It is also offered with French, German or Spanish.

Bournemouth (*Financial Services*) A four-year sandwich course covering accounting, banking, financial management, insurance, marketing, building societies, money markets, business strategy and information technology. The third year is spent in a financial services firm. There is also a European language option.

Brighton (*Accounting and Finance*) See under **Accountancy**.

Bristol UWE (*Financial Services*) The course offers topics in financial planning, international finance, insurance, banking and risk management. There is also a course in Accountancy and Finance.

Buckingham (*Accounting and Financial Management*) See under **Accountancy**.

Cardiff (*Banking and Finance*) An economics based course which includes a training relevant to the practice of banking. Optional courses include accounting, management or a foreign language. Four year courses with French, German, Italian or Spanish are also offered.

Central England Banking and International Finance are offered with Accountancy and Business Administration.

Central Lancashire (*Financial Services*) The course is aimed at those contemplating a career in banking and finance and leads to some exemptions from professional examinations.

City (*Banking and International Finance*) Economics, statistics, computer programming and introductions to law and accounting are studies with banking and international finance in the first year. There are options in two subjects to be chosen in the second and third years, with examinations at the end of each year. (*Insurance and Investment*) A unique course which includes international insurance and investment policies in Europe, North America and Japan.

Dundee (*Finance*) Courses are offered in Financial Economics which can also be taken with eight other subjects.

Essex (*Accounting and Financial Management*) See under **Accountancy**.

Glasgow Caledonian (*Financial Services*) Options on this course include Business Management, social security, languages, insurance, banking, building societies, international banking and underwriting. There is also a course in Risk Management relating to insurance with topics involving fire, employee injury, pollution, and computer fraud.

Heriot-Watt (*Accountancy and Finance*) See under **Accountancy**.

Humberside (*Accountancy and Finance*) See under **Accountancy**.

London Guildhall (*Financial Services*) The course covers banking, insurance, investment and financial aspects of the European Community. This degree can be taken by way of single Honours or as a joint degree or as a minor subject. Courses in Insurance and Banking Studies are offered subject to approval.

London (LSE) (*Accounting and Finance*) See under **Accountancy**.

Loughborough (*Banking and Finance*) Three and four year courses are offered, covering managerial, financial, legal and economic aspects of banking and finance. Optional subjects include French, German, computing, personnel work, marketing and economic history. Candidates for the three year course must have at least one year's experience in a financial institution. The four year course includes one year of practical experience in banking. A course is also offered in Accounting and Financial Management. See under Accountancy.

Manchester (*Accounting and Finance*) See under **Accountancy**.

Manchester Metropolitan (*Financial Services*) A course with options in banking and insurance.

Middlesex (*Money, Banking and Finance*) The course includes accounting, economics, financial systems and markets and international finance. It can be taken as part of a combined course or as a major or minor subject.

Napier Financial Studies can be taken with mathematics.

Nottingham Insurance is offered with Industrial Economics.

Portsmouth (*Financial Services*) A four year sandwich course covering building society and banking operations and the marketing of financial services. There are options to study in France, Germany, Holland or Spain.

Salford (*Finance and Accounting*) See under **Accountancy**.

Sheffield Hallam (*Financial Services*) A four year sandwich course. Core subjects include economics, business accounts, international finance, financial and management accounting, quantitative analysis, information systems, financial institutions, law and marketing. Language options available in French or German with a voluntary placement year.

South Bank (*Accountancy and Finance*) See under **Accountancy**.

Stirling (*Financial Studies*) Advanced units on this course include management of business finance, external reporting, international finance, security markets and financial analysis. The subject can also be followed combined with thirteen others including Japanese.

Strathclyde Finance is offered with mathematics and statistics.

Ulster (*Banking and Finance*) Economics, accounting, law, business organisation and management and banking are the main components of this course. (NB: The major Northern Ireland banks impose restrictions on the employment of personnel over the age of 21.)

Warwick (*Accounting and Financial Analysis*) See under **Accountancy**.

Wolverhampton (*Financial Services*) A four year sandwich course which covers accounting, economics, UK and European financial institutions and marketing. Language options in French, German, Spanish, Russian or Italian are available and some students opt for a placement year in Europe.

• Colleges and Institutes of Higher Education offering degree courses
Cheltenham and Gloucester (Coll) - Financial Services can be studied in combination with nineteen other subjects; Gwent (Coll) - Finance is offered with Business or Accounting; NESCOT - Financial Services is offered with Mathematics; Salford (Univ Coll) offers business with finance; Suffolk (Coll) offers two business courses with options in Insurance or Financial Services.

• Other courses to be considered
Actuarial studies, accounting, business studies, economics and retail management.

BIOCHEMISTRY

- **Special subject requirements:** 2–3 A-levels from mathematics/science subjects. Chemistry often essential; physics sometimes preferred.

- **Subject information:** Many subjects can be covered in these courses, eg medical biochemistry, plant and animal physiology, microbiology, biophysics. Different courses will suit different students; check your prospectuses carefully.

Aberdeen (*Biochemistry*) There is no level 1 course available (entry is by Molecular Biology). After introductory studies, level 3 and 4 courses cover molecular aspects of biotechnology and immunology with options in the latter which can lead to Honours in Biochemistry (Immunology). A course is also available in parasitology.

Aberystwyth (*Biochemistry*) Study in Part I also includes a chemistry, biological or a mathematical course. The second and third year Biochemistry is taken with modules in chemistry and biology and medical biochemistry in Year 3. There are opportunities for some students to study in Europe. A degree course in Environmental Biochemistry is also offered with short employment opportunities during the course.

Bangor (*Biochemistry*) The course covers biochemistry in a broad and physiological context. It extends from the characteristics and interactions of micro-organisms to the functions of higher plants and animals. Molecular biology has a high and increasing profile within it and recent developments include the introduction of biotechnology courses. Thus biochemistry, biophysics, biotechnology, immunology and genetics are explored over a wider range than is often the case in departments with, for example, a specific bias toward clinical biochemistry. ERASMUS links with European institutions.

Bath (*Biochemistry*) This is a sandwich course. Biochemistry is taken with chemistry and cell biology in the first year, together with plant and animal physiology and microbiology. Genetics and statistics are taken in the second year and a range of options in the fourth year including biotechnology and clinical biochemistry. The department has a range of training placements in Europe and the USA.

Belfast (*Biochemistry*) In the first year subjects include chemistry plus three from physics, mathematics, statistics, computer science, botany or zoology. After level 1 students decide which special degree programme they wish to follow from biochemistry, biological science, environmental biology, genetics, microbiology, plant science or zoology.

Birmingham (*Biochemistry*) Transfers are possible in Year 1 between biochemistry, medical biochemistry, biochemistry with biotechnology or molecular and cell biology.

Bradford (*Biomedical Sciences*) A common programme is followed by all students taking Biomedical Sciences. In the final year you specialise in one of the five major options namely metabolic biochemistry (the study of the body's biochemical responses), cellular pathology, microbiology, nutrition and food policy or pharmacology. An option exists to take a year out in industry after Year 2.

Bristol (*Biochemistry*) Flexibility is a keynote in the Faculty of Science. Choice of subjects in Years 1 and 2 can give either a Biological or Physical bias to the course. At the end of the first year students may transfer to Honours courses in Chemistry, Microbiology or Physiology. Biochemistry students can specialise in biology, biotechnology, medical biochemistry or plant biochemistry. (Half Bristol's students proceed to higher degrees.)

Brunel (*Applied Biochemistry; Medical Biochemistry*) These are offered as four year (sandwich) or three year full-time degree courses. Academic content, in addition to biochemistry and chemistry, includes courses in cell biology, microbiology, physiology and biotechnology. Options in the final year include cell biology, environmental ecotoxicology, biochemistry of disease, cancer genetics, human molecular genetics, pharmacology and toxicology. Transfer to Applied Biology is possible at the end of Year 1.

Cambridge (*Biochemistry*) This is offered as part of the course in Natural Sciences. In the second year, intending biochemists usually take biochemistry, molecular biology, molecular cell biology and chemistry, with more specialised options in the third year. See also **Chemistry**.

Cardiff (*Biochemistry*) The first two years provide a broad scientific base centred on biochemistry but also including aspects of genetics, microbiology and physiology. A four year course including a year in industry is available. At Cardiff, Biochemistry can also be offered with Medical Biochemistry, Molecular Biology, Chemistry or Physiology.

Central Lancashire (*Applied Biochemistry*) This three year course includes animal, food and microbiological biochemistry. A language option is also available. Biochemistry is also offered as part of the Combined Honours programme.

Coventry (*Biochemical Science*) Three year full-time or four year sandwich courses are offered, the latter with Year 3 in professional training or industry. A range of options is available in the final years. There is also a European option with concurrent language study in all years from French, German, Italian or Spanish from zero. An admissions newsletter BIOLINK is available on request.

Dundee (*Biochemistry*) The department has an international reputation and the highest possible rating for research in the UK, with particular strengths in enzymology, neurobiochemistry, molecular genetics and cancer research. Three science courses are taken in Year 1 from a choice of 62 courses. The final choice is made at the end of Year 2. Biochemistry is offered as a Second Science subject. In Third Science, topics include biochemistry of enzymes, membranes and cells and biochemistry of gene expression. Single Honours biochemistry students normally read both Third Science courses and go on to selected areas of specialism. Joint courses are offered with Chemistry, Pharmacology or Physiology.

Durham (*Molecular Biology and Biochemistry*) First year students take courses in botany, zoology and chemistry, going on to specialist areas which include genetics, virology and immunology.

East Anglia (*Biochemistry*) Chemistry and biology are taken in the first year, allowing students to transfer to degree courses in Biological or Chemical Sciences. In the second year biochemistry and molecular biology are taken with a selection from microbiology, physiology, protein engineering and biotechnology. In the third year students make a selection from a range of subjects. Biochemistry can also be taken with a year in Europe or the USA.

East London (*Biochemistry*) A modular degree involving cell and molecular biology, genetics, medical and plant biotechnology. There is the opportunity to switch between courses in Life Sciences (your specialist course on entry is not binding). A very large number of subjects varying from Art and Design, through Media Studies to Womens Studies can be taken with Biochemistry.

Edinburgh (*Biochemistry*) There is a common first year for all students entering courses in the School of Biology, which includes biology, chemistry, introductory physics and maths. In the second year students follow a half-course in biology and three other half-courses from eight subjects. The biochemistry specialism begins in the third year.

Essex (*Biochemistry*) Students take a course in Biosciences in Year 1 which leads to a degree course in biochemistry in Years 2 and 3. At the end of the first year it is also possible to take Biological and Medicinal Chemistry. This is the application of chemical principles and methods to the study of biological systems. Linked with Medicinal Chemistry, the course provides a good grounding in chemistry and in modern developments in this field. Full-time and sandwich courses are available.

Exeter A course is offered in Biological and Medicinal Chemistry designed for graduates who wish to take advantage of new opportunities in the rapidly expanding field of biotechnology.

Glasgow (*Biochemistry*) Biochemistry and molecular biology are studied in the first and second years, with specialisation in the third year. A fourth year is required for the Honours degree. There is also a parallel degree course in Medical Biochemistry.

Greenwich (*Biochemistry*) The course covers animal and plant biochemistry and biotechnology. This is a three year full-time or four year sandwich course in which genetics, protein biochemistry and biochemical methods are offered in Year 2. There is also a European Studies option.

Heriot-Watt (*Biochemistry*) The first year course covers biology, chemistry, physics, maths and statistics. An option in the second year is taken from a range of courses in non-scientific subjects. In the third year, in addition to biochemistry, options include computer science, marine biology, microbiology and chemical engineering. A research project is undertaken in the final year. The first two years of all courses in Biological Science are common allowing freedom to transfer up to Year 2.

Hertfordshire (*Applied Biology (Biochemistry)*) The degree in Applied Biology provides a common base for all subject options. In Year 2 two subject areas may be studied from a choice of seven, including biochemistry, or alternatively three subjects. Year 3 occupies work experience in industry or research and specialisation in biochemistry takes place in Year 4.

Huddersfield (*Biochemistry*) A modular course of three or four years (which includes a year in employment) and the final year with research into a major study of selected specialisms.

Keele (*Biochemistry*) The course carries an emphasis on human and agricultural biochemistry. Biochemistry can be taken in combination with a choice from over thirty other subjects. Those combining Biochemistry with Biology, Chemistry, Computer Science, Electronics, Geology and Physics may specialise in Biochemistry in their final year.

Kent (*Biochemistry*) A common core of subjects is taken in the first five terms when specialist studies in biochemistry follow. There is an option of a one year sandwich placement in industry, hospitals or government, and bursaries of up to £1,000 are available to selected students. Biochemistry can also be combined with biotechnology, neuroscience and medical biosciences and there is also a year in Europe option.

Kingston (*Biochemistry*) The course covers chemistry, physiology and computing with other modules in the biology of disease, microbiology, pharmacology, immunology and medical chemistry.

Lancaster (*Biochemistry*) Biological sciences, chemistry and one other subject are taken in the first year. Biochemistry, chemistry and biological sciences follow in the second year, with more advanced biochemistry topics being introduced in the third year including immunology, pharmacology, genetics, animal physiology and microbiology.

Leeds (*Biochemistry*) A modular programme within the School of Biological Sciences gives great flexibility of choice. Specialisms at level 3 include plant and medical options. Over twelve other science subjects can be taken with biochemistry.

Leicester (*Biological Sciences (Biochemistry)*) A common first year for ten subject areas provides flexibility for applicants to delay a final choice or specialisation which takes place in the second and third years.

Liverpool (*Biochemistry*) This course has common first and second years for students leading to one of the sixteen specialist subjects in the final year. In biochemistry there is a bias towards nucleic acid biochemistry and molecular biology. The work includes a study of insects, plants and bacteria and includes a study of microbial biochemistry and aspects of human biochemistry.

Liverpool John Moores (*Applied Biochemistry*) This is a three year full-time or four year sandwich course with Year 3 spent in industry. It investigates biological problems at the molecular level, enhances understanding of the biochemical workings of living organisms, the chemical basis of reproduction and heredity, and the nature of disease.

London (Imp) (*Biochemistry*) The department offers: three year courses in Biochemisty, Biotechnology, and Biochemistry with Management; four year courses in Biochemistry with Management and/or a Year in Industry, Biotechnology with a Year in Industry, Chemistry and Biochemistry, Chemistry and Biotechnology: and five year courses in Chemistry and Biochemistry, or Chemistry and Biotechnology, with a Year In Industry. All courses lead to the award of the BSc degree.

London (King's) (*Biochemistry*) The subject is studied in Year 1 in the context of cell biology with courses in biochemistry, chemistry, physiology, microbiology and statistics. Optional courses are available in Years 2 and 3. There is a degree course in Medical Biochemistry, as well as several joint Honours possibilities.

London (QMW) (*Biochemistry*) After a common first year in biological science, specialist topics are introduced in the second year with reference to animals, plants and microbes. Project work is a component of third year studies. A joint degree course in Chemistry with Biochemistry is offered.

London (RH) (*Biochemistry*) Students following courses in biochemistry, cell biology, medical biochemistry and biotechnology follow a common first year programme. When final degree options are made students cover basic biochemistry, cell biology, microbiology and chemistry and may also take computer science, life sciences and statistics among a number of additional subjects. In the third year, specialist subjects include parasite biochemistry, drug metabolism and plant and animal biochemistry. (*Medical Biochemistry*) This course includes physiology and a hospital experience course in the summer vacation of the second year. Specialist courses include nutrition, birth control, disease and pollution. There are also courses in Biochemistry for Management and Plant Biochemistry.

London (UC) (*Biochemistry*) Biochemistry students take chemistry, genes to organisms, cellular and molecular biology and microbiology in their first year, with experimental biochemistry. As most of the first year is common with other biological sciences programmes, transfer is usually then possible. Molecular biology, metabolic biochemistry, physical biochemistry and chemistry (organic and physical) make up the second year. In the final year students choose from a range of advanced courses and undertake a research project.

London (Wye) (*Biochemistry*) An agricultural bias is given to this course with third year options in plant cell physiology, biotechnology and chemical pesticides.

Manchester (*Biochemistry*) There is a modular course structure which allows for early transfer within the School of Biological Sciences. Students choose second and final year modules in keeping with their career aspirations.

Manchester (UMIST) (*Biochemistry*) Courses are offered in Biochemistry, Biochemistry with Clinical Biochemistry, Biochemistry with Applied Molecular Biology and Biochemistry with German. All have a common first two years, with transfer possible after entry. Courses offered open the door to a study of biotechnology. In the third year some students take advanced biochemistry and either clinical biochemistry or applied molecular biology. The course is biased towards a thorough practical understanding of the subjects through project work.

Newcastle (*Biochemistry*) This degree shares a common first year with Genetics and Molecular Biology.

North London (*Biochemistry*) A general science course theme permits a variety of choice in subjects with over 33 options at single Honours, major, joint or minor level.

Northumbria A course is offered in Chemistry with Biochemistry.

Nottingham (*Biochemistry and Biological Chemistry*) In the first year students take biochemistry, chemistry and a third subject, usually physiology and pharmacology or physics and maths. In the second and third years the teaching is shared equally between the departments of Biochemistry and Chemistry leading to specialisms in pharmaceutical and agrochemical science, enzyme technology and toxicology. There is also a degree course in Nutritional Biochemistry which allows for specialisation in either Animal or Human Nutrition. Biochemistry may also be studied with Genetics.

Oxford (*Biochemistry*) This is a four year course in which biochemistry, chemistry and biology are offered in the first year. Physiology and microbiology and related areas of genetics and immunology occupy the remaining parts of the course.

Reading (*Physiology and Biochemistry*) A range of science subjects is chosen in the first year followed by a specialised subject choice at single or combined levels from over 20 options.

St Andrews (*Biochemistry*) This subject can be studied as a single Honours degree or as a joint course with Chemistry, Microbiology or Biotechnology. It also forms part of several degree courses in Biology.

Salford (*Biochemical Sciences*) The course is offered in the School of Biological Sciences with modules in biological science and biochemical science being shared. A final degree decision is made at the end of the first year.

Sheffield (*Biochemistry*) In the School of Biological Sciences six course units are taken from anatomy and cell biology, biochemistry, botany, chemistry, genetics, microbiology, physiology and zoology in the first year. Second year studies are divided equally between biochemistry and a subsidiary subject of the student's choice (usually chemistry, physiology or microbiology). The third year is devoted exclusively to biochemistry.

Southampton (*Biochemistry*) This course includes molecular biology, pharmacology and physiology. The structure of the School of Biological Sciences is extremely flexible and allows students to transfer between various single and combined degrees in the second and third years.

Staffordshire Biochemistry is offered with Microbiology, Physiology or Chemistry.

Stirling (*Biochemistry*) Biology and chemistry are taken in semesters 1 and 2 with subsidiary courses. Biochemistry is studied from semester 3. The Department's main interests are in developmental biochemistry, plant biochemistry and the biochemistry of brain and nerve tissue.

Strathclyde (*Biochemistry*) This is a four year course, the first two years in the Faculty of Science are largely common to all students in the biological sciences and transfers are usually possible. Special topics are offered in the final two years, one major option being pharmacology. Honours degree courses are also offered in Biochemistry and either Pharmacology or Immunology. Most students in the Department of Bioscience and

Biotechnology can defer their ultimate choice of Honours degree until the end of Year 2.

Surrey Four degree courses are available: Biochemistry, Biochemistry (Medical), Biochemistry (Toxicology) and Molecular Biology. All are common for the first two years allowing interchange up to the end of the second year. These are four year courses, with the third year consisting of professional training away from the university. In the fourth year Biochemistry students select three options from a wide range of modules.

Sussex (*Biochemistry*) Biochemistry is offered in the Schools of Biological or Chemistry and Molecular Sciences. The distinctive feature of the course is the availability of biology as well as biochemistry components. Biochemistry may be combined with a number of subjects, including European Studies, which involves a year abroad in France, Germany or Spain.

Swansea (*Biochemistry*) In the first year the course prepares the student for Levels 2 and 3, or it stands as a one year course leading on to such courses as Biological Sciences or Chemistry and transfers are possible. A detailed study of the biochemistry of plants, animals and micro-organisms occupies Levels 2 and 3. Chemistry and biology are taught in the first and second years of the course.

Ulster (*Applied Biochemical Sciences*) After a broad scientific course in Years 1 and 2, industrial placement follows in Year 3, and biochemistry and a small business project and a research project lead to graduation in Year 4.

Warwick (*Biochemistry*) A common first year in the Department of Biological Science allows entrants to biochemistry the option to transfer to degree courses in Microbiology and Virology, Microbiology, Virology and Biological Sciences at the end of the first year.

Wolverhampton (*Biochemistry*) This is a three year full-time or four year sandwich course taught on the flexible modular system.

York (*Biochemistry*) Biochemistry and Chemistry students are taught together for the first part of the course. In the remaining two parts, biochemistry specialisms include major practical courses in microbiology and biophysical techniques and biology as well as a range of selected optional subjects. The aim of this course is to study metabolic, genetic and physiological aspects of biology which can be understood at the molecular level. This aim entails continued study of chemistry (for four terms) and broadly-based coverage of biology. Weekly tutorials for all students, in groups of four, are a distinctive and effective feature. There is an optional sandwich year.

• Top research universities
Cambridge, Oxford, Dundee, Glasgow, Bath, Birmingham, Bristol, Leeds, Leicester, Manchester, London (Imp).

• Colleges and Institutes of Higher Education offering degree courses
Halton (Coll), NESCOT, North East Wales (Inst), Norwich City (Coll), Stockport (Coll).

• **Other courses to be considered**
Agricultural sciences, agriculture, biological sciences, botany, brewing, chemistry, food science, geochemistry, geological sciences, materials science, medicine, microbiology, nutrition, pharmacology and pharmacy.

BIOLOGICAL SCIENCES

• **Special subject requirements:** 2–3 A-levels from mathematics/science subjects. Chemistry usually essential; GCSE (grades A–C) in mathematics/science subjects.

• **Subject information:** In many universities the Department or School of Biological Sciences will offer a modular programme covering subjects such as biochemistry, botany, biotechnology, genetics, physiology and zoology. This type of programme usually offers a common first year for all students allowing them to make a final choice of single or joint degree course in Year 2. In other universities Biological Science is offered as a single named subject.

Aberdeen (*Biological Sciences of Agriculture*) Students take several biological and chemistry subjects at level 1 and animal biology, soil science and crop biology at level 2. At levels 3 and 4 students choose five subjects from two groups which cover agricultural, animal and food topics.

Anglia (Poly Univ) (*Biological Sciences*) A range of courses, including Microbiology, Environmental Biology and Biomedical Sciences, is offered at the Cambridge campus.

Bangor (*Biological Sciences*) Modular courses are offered covering biology and biochemistry, animal and plant biology and applied zoology.

Belfast (*Biological Sciences*) In the School of Biology and Biochemistry six courses are studied at level 1. Specialisms follow in levels 2 and 3. Careful selection in the first two years can enable the student to retain substantial freedom of choice.

Birmingham (*Biological Sciences*) Students choose from six specialist fields - Biological Sciences, Animal Biology, Biotechnology, Environmental Biology, Genetics, Microbiology, Physiology or Plant Biology.

Bradford (*Biomedical Sciences*) Subjects studied in the first two years include biochemistry, mammalian physiology, microbiology, pharmacology and cell biology and pathology. In the third year, options are offered in cellular pathology, metabolic biochemistry, microbiology, nutrition and food science, pharmacology and toxicology. It is possible to have a year of professional experience between the second and final year.

Bristol UWE (*Applied Biological Sciences*) The course is a broad study of biological sciences. Placement takes place in Year 3. Options are available in the final year which include medical microbiology, immunology, clinical biochemistry, physiology, pharmacology, genetics and plant sciences. There is also a course in Biomedical Sciences with a sandwich year in NHS laboratories.

Cambridge (*Biological Sciences with Education*) This is a four year BEd offered at Homerton College as part of the Education Tripos leading to teaching in the Primary sector (lower primary 4–8 or junior 7–11). A three year BA is also offered without an integrated teacher training element.

Durham (*Biological Sciences*) Students read botany and zoology as part of their first year programme. Final options are chosen in Year 3. Year 1 consists of biology, genetics, biochemistry, animal and plant biology and ecology. Students then choose Honours in Biological Science, Molecular Biology and Biochemistry or Natural Sciences.

East Anglia (*Biological Sciences*) Courses are taught on a science course unit system allowing students to choose biology or other units appropriate for their specialisation. The preliminary programme covers the first year and provides a broad coverage of the biological sciences and leads on to the Honours programme in Years 2 and 3. Third year specialist programmes include biochemistry, genetics, plant biology, ecology, animal physiology, microbiology and zoology. In the School of Biological Sciences degrees in Biophysics, Ecology, Genetics and Microbiology as well as Biological Sciences can be taken as four year courses, in which the third year will be spent in the USA, Germany or France.

East London Biological Sciences is offered with over 30 subjects in addition to which there is a three subject degree scheme. The course involves applied biology, biomarketing and management and medical biophysics. Separate courses are also offered in Infectious Diseases, Applied Ecology and Wildlife Conservation.

Edinburgh (*Biological Sciences*) It is possible to transfer from Biological Science to Agriculture up to the end of the second year. Honours specialisations include Bacteriology, Biochemistry, Botany, Genetics, Immunology, Microbiology, Molecular Biology, Neurosciences, Pharmacology, Physiology, Psychology, Zoology.

Essex (*Biological Sciences*) There are two first year options, Biosciences I and II. By taking Biosciences I you can then proceed to three degree schemes, Environmental Biology, Cell Biology or Biological Sciences. In the second year biological scientists take compulsory courses in physiology and biology and in the third year take six courses from a choice of 18 subjects covering ecology, genetics, zoology, physiology and biochemistry.

Exeter (*Biological Sciences*) A broad course provides a background to genetics and physiology, biochemistry, freshwater ecology and zoology and leads on to the second year in which students choose ten from eighteen courses. Four courses - each lasting half a term - form the third year specialisms. An ancillary subject is taken in the first year, chosen from chemistry, geography, geology, psychology and information technology.

Glasgow Caledonian (*Applied Biosciences*) Honours options are offered in Biology, Microbiology, Physiological Science or Biomedical Sciences. Year 3 topics include molecular biology and immunology, pharmacology, virology and haematology and cell pathology.

Heriot-Watt (*Biological Sciences*) Biology, chemistry and physics are taken in Years 1 and 2 with options in marine biology and microbiology in the third year. A course in Brewing and Distilling is also offered.

Keele (*Biological Sciences*) The Department of Biological Sciences offers courses in Biochemistry, Biology and Biomedical Sciences which are offered as separate subjects.

Lancaster (*Biological Sciences*) There is flexibility to spend as little as one third or as much as two thirds of the first year on your main subject. There are options to move to Biochemistry or Ecology degrees after Year 1. Specialisms in Biological Sciences include animal and plant physiology, biochemistry, genetics and ecology. A course is also offered with a year in the USA or Canada.

Leicester (*Biological Sciences*) In the first year Biological Sciences are taken with a supplementary subject from chemistry, geography, geology, psychology, pure maths, statistics or economics. Students may graduate following specialisation in physiology, biochemistry, genetics, microbiology, cell/molecular biology, plant sciences, environmental biology or zoology.

Liverpool John Moores A range of three year courses (with optional placement years) is offered, focusing on different aspects of the interaction between humans and the natural environment. These include Biophysics, Applied Ecology, Environmental Science, Environmental Science and Policy, Applied Microbiology and Applied Plant Science.

London (QMW) (*Biological Sciences*) Course units are offered leading to degrees in Biology, Freshwater Biology, Genetics, Ecology, Biochemistry, Microbiology and Zoology.

Manchester Metropolitan (*Applied Biological Science*) Core units of genetics, ecology, biochemistry and physiology in the first year are followed by second year options including a six month industrial placement. The final year allows a wide choice of units such as physiology and health, environmental toxicology, conservation biology, cellular pathology and agricultural microbiology. Degrees in Biomedical Science and Environmental Health are also available.

Napier (*Biological Sciences*) This three or four year course allows students to draw on modules from the four specialised full-time degrees offered by the department: Applied Microbiology and Biotechnology, Biomedical Sciences, Environmental Biology and Health Studies.

Newcastle (*Biological Sciences*) See **Biology** for details.

North London (*Biological Sciences*) This course permits considerable flexibility of choice of subjects at single Honours, major, joint or minor levels. There is also a European language option.

Northumbria (*Biomedical Sciences*) This three year full-time or four year sandwich course is available as a single Honours (including an optional year abroad) or combined with Chemistry. It is CBSM approved and IBMS accredited.

Oxford (*Biological Sciences*) The Honour School of Biological Sciences covers pure and applied biology, botany and zoology. The essence of this course is flexibility and the choice exists in specialising in plant studies, animal studies or a combination of both.

Plymouth (*Biological Sciences*) A modular course covering ecology, plant science, microbial and cellular biology, human and marine biology. Specialisations can be delayed and there is an optional year in industry and the opportunity to study a foreign language. Each area may be studied as a specialist degree or combined with other subjects.

Reading (*Biological Sciences*) The degree contains two main options (a) Biology, Microbiology and Zoology (b) Animals and microbes. In both options, which cover Years 1 and 2, specialisation is delayed until the final year choice of one of the three main disciplines studied.

Robert Gordon (*Applied Biosciences & Chemistry*) This is a very flexible course with the option of an industrial placement after Year 2.

Salford (*Biological Sciences*) The course has an applied biology emphasis and has a common first year with Biochemical Science (which has a biochemistry emphasis). The final choice of course is made at the end of Year 1. Year 3 can be spent in industry.

Sheffield (*Biological Sciences*) Modules covering all the subjects offered in the School of Biological Sciences are taken by all students. Other university subjects can also be studied. Students make a choice of single or joint degree in Year 2.

Strathclyde (*Biological Sciences*) The course allows students to delay their choice of specialisation. In the third year the students commence their special subject for graduation, leading to a pass degree at the end of the year or an Honours degree at the end of the fourth year.

Sunderland (*Biological Sciences*) Four separate course are offered in Biological Sciences, Environmental Biology, Biomedical Sciences and Applied Microbiology, with an optional sandwich year and a wide range of specialist studies such as brewing and winemaking, wildlife conservation, haematology and enzyme technology respectively.

Sussex (*Biological Sciences*) The School of Biological Sciences offers sixteen major degrees. A preliminary course is taken in the first two terms covering four or five chosen subjects. During the following four terms most students also follow a non-science course.

Swansea (*Biological Sciences*) The deferred choice course allows students to defer their choice of degree specialisation until the end of the first year, whilst the alternative course (C102) allows students to specialise in two areas of biological sciences, eg botany, biochemistry, environmental biology, marine biology, genetics or zoology. There is also a four year course in which a language is taken (French, German, Spanish or Italian) and Year 3 is spent in the relevant European country.

Ulster (*Biological Sciences*) A broad first year course allows students to proceed to one of three Honours options (biotechnology, human biology and applied ecological sciences).

Warwick (*Biological Sciences*) This is a flexible course with the opportunity to transfer to the degree courses in Microbiology and Virology. In the third year the Biological Science course focuses on genetics, medicine, agriculture and industry.

Wolverhampton (*Biological Science*) This is a full-time (three years) or sandwich course (four years). The course enables students to specialise in specific areas of biotechnology, biomedical sciences, applied animal biology, microbiology, biochemistry and ecology, or to develop a broad programme of studies.

● **Top research universities**
Birmingham, Bristol, Dundee, Durham, East Anglia, Edinburgh, Kent, Leicester, London (Imp), Nottingham, St Andrews, Sheffield, Sussex, UMIST, Warwick.

● **Colleges and Institutes of Higher Education offering degree courses**
Canterbury (Chr.Ch.Coll), Chester (Coll), Halton (Coll), King Alfred's (Coll), La Sainte Union (Coll), NESCOT, North East Wales (Coll), St Martin's (Coll), Suffolk (Coll), Worcester (Coll).

● **Other courses to be considered**
Agriculture, bacteriology, biochemistry, botany, dentistry, ecology, environmental sciences, forestry, medicine, pharmacology, pharmacy, speech science.

BIOLOGY
(Refer also to the **Biological Sciences table**)

● **Special subject requirements:** 2–3 A-levels from mathematics/science subjects. Chemistry usually essential. GCSE Grades A–C in mathematics/science subjects.

● **Subject information:** These courses usually are more specialised than Biological Sciences with such options as aquatic biology, human biology, animal and plant biology. Many of these options are also offered on Applied Biology courses.

Aberdeen (*Biology*) A degree course is offered leading to specialisations in Biology, Cell Biology, Ecology and Environmental Science. There is also an Aquaculture course covering all aspects of fish farming.

Abertay Dundee Joint courses are offered in Biology and Chemistry, Computing, Economics, Psychology and Management. Biotechnology is also offered.

Aberystwyth (*Biology*) The course will be of interest for those wishing to study molecular, cellular and physiological aspects of biology across the boundaries of botany, microbiology and zoology. Third year options cover immunology, animal sciences, biotechnology and physiology. There is also a course in Biometry covering the interplay between mathematics, statistics and Biology and courses in Aquatic Biology and Applied Plant Biology.

Anglia (Poly Univ) Fourteen subjects are offered on joint courses with Biology, whilst Environmental Biology (offered on the Combined Science programme) covers ecology, population and genetics.

Aston (*Applied and Human Biology*) This course emphasises human biology, reflecting the relevance of biology to medicine and the intimate association of man with the environment. The programme builds from a broad biological foundation into a selection of specialist options in biomedical sciences by way of a modular system, including immunology, medical biochemistry, pharmacology and microbiology.

Bangor (*Biology*) Biology, biochemistry, soil science and earth sciences are taken in the first year leading to single Honours Biology in the second and third years. Topics covered include freshwater, terrestrial and aquatic biology, evolution and marine and animal behaviour. Degree courses are also offered in Applied Animal Biology which includes applied and marine biology.

Bath (*Biology*) The degree schemes in Biology (non-sandwich) and Applied Biology (four-year sandwich course) have identical academic content during the first two years of a broadly based foundation followed by specialisation. The choice between the sandwich or non-sandwich pattern can be deferred until the latter part of the first year. Sandwich placements in Belgium, France, Finland or Switzerland are possible.

Belfast (*Environmental Biology*) A broad course covering natural and human environments. The course includes physiology and genetics.

Bradford (*Biomedical Science*) A modular course with the first two years providing a broad basis in subjects allied to medicine. Specialisation takes place in the final year (eg biochemistry, pathology, microbiology, pharmacology, toxicology and nutrition.) There is also an option to take a year out.

Brighton (*Applied Biology*) Core units are taken in Years 1 and 2. Optional units include biochemical techniques, microbiology, public health and pollution.

Bristol (*Biology*) Students may follow a broad course or specialise in Years 2 and 3. Units are offered in botany, zoology, microbiology, psychology, physiology, geology and geography. Changes are possible between Biology, Botany, Zoology and joint courses.

Brunel (*Applied Biology; Medical Biology*) There are four year thin/thick sandwich courses (including two placements of six months or one of one year) or three year full-time courses. In the early years a framework of biochemistry and genetics supports specialist subjects and it is possible to change to Applied/Medical Biochemistry after the first semester. In the final year students select four options from plant productivity, crop plant development, environmental ecotoxicology, cancer genetics, human molecular genetics, immunology and parasitology, medical microbiology, cell biology, biochemistry of disease, pharmacology and toxicology. A project is undertaken in association with one of the research groups.

Cardiff (*Pure and Applied Biology*) There is a common first year for Pure and Applied Biology which covers cells, microbes, physiology, evolution, ecology, biological chemistry, maths, statistics and computing. Students then choose their special study in Year 2 leading to a degree in Applied Biology, Biology, Biotechnology, Ecology, Environmental Management, Microbiology or Zoology. This is a three year full-time or four year sandwich course.

Central Lancashire (*Applied Biology*) After Year 1, students select from a wide range of options from biochemistry, microbiology, ecology, physiology, plant science or nutrition.

Coventry (*Applied Biology*) This is a three year full-time or four year sandwich course with placements at home and abroad in the third year. Final year options include biotechnology, biology, conservation and genetics. It can also include a year in Europe which is supported by studies in French or German. A course in Medical Instrumentation offers modules in clinical physiology and physics application in medicine.

De Montfort (*Applied Biology*) After a broad first year which includes toxicology and environmental biology, students choose specialist subjects in Year 2. Courses in Biology, Biomedical Science and Biotechnology are also offered.

Derby (*Biology*) Students choose a minimum of three biology modules in Year 1 plus a module of common skills and a complementary module from one other subject area, eg environmental studies, geology, chemistry or geography. Increasing numbers of biology modules are taken in Years 2 and 3.

Dundee (*Biology*) Students take a range of subjects in the first and second science courses. They then proceed to an Honours course in Biology, with modules available in botany, ecology, microbiology and zoology in the Department of Biological Sciences.

Durham (*Biology (Natural Sciences)*) All departments in the Faculty of Science offer Main, Double Main, Main and Subsidiary or Subsidiary units which lead to Single or Joint Honours degrees. The first year course in Biology includes genetics, biochemistry, animal and plant biology, physiology, ecology and behaviour. Further core subjects are taken in Year 2 and in Year 3 a modular scheme allows for considerable specialisation.

East Anglia (*Cell Biology*) This is one of the degree options in the School of Biological Sciences in which the Honours programme with specialisation occupies Years 2 and 3.

East London (*Applied Biology*) This is offered with Biological Sciences as a three year full-time or four year sandwich course.

Edinburgh (*Molecular Biology*) The course covers genetic engineering, medicinal, agricultural and industrial applications.

Exeter Biology is offered with Geography and also as part of the Primary and Secondary Education course.

Essex (*Biology*) After a common first year, degree programmes are offered in Environmental Biology, Biological Science, Molecular Biology or Biochemistry.

Glamorgan (*Biology*) This three year full-time or four year sandwich course considers living organisms, their structure and survival mechanisms. Core modules include genetics, plant and animal diversity, and physiological ecology. Biology can be studied as part of a Combined programme.

Glasgow Degrees in the Faculty of Science follow a very flexible course structure allowing late decisions on all specialist subjects. All students take three subjects in their first year from a choice of eighteen. Named degree subjects include Anatomy, Animal Developmental Biology, Aquatic Bioscience, Cell Biology, Genetics, Microbiology, Molecular Biology, Neuroscience, Physiology, Parasitology and Immunology. There is also a course in Aquatic Bioscience.

Greenwich (*Applied Biology*) Units cover biochemistry, cell biology, genetics, animal and plant physiology, microbiology and ecology. In Year 3 there are options in biotechnology, pharmacology and muscle physiology.

Heriot-Watt (*Applied Marine Biology*) This is a four year course. The first year course in chemistry, physics, biology, maths and statistics leads on to biology, chemistry and a non-science option in the second year. Marine Biology continues in Years 3 and 4 along with marine technology and microbiology. Diving science is a fourth year option.

Hertfordshire (*Applied Biology*) After a foundation course students choose one of the following - Agricultural Botany, Biochemistry, Biotechnology, Microbiology, Molecular Biology, Pharmacology and Physiology.

Huddersfield (*Molecular Biology*) This is a scientific course with a language strand and optional work experience in Year 3. Final year options include immunology, medical biology and DNA technology.

Hull (*Biology*) After Year 1 it is possible to change to degrees in Molecular Biology and Biotechnology, Environmental Biology, Aquatic Biology with a Fisheries option, Environmental Biology and Geography or Biology and Education.

Keele (*Biology*) Biology may be taken in combination with over thirty subjects. The Biology course offers modules in cell biology and biochemistry, behaviour and ecology, genetics, and plant and animal physiology.

Kingston (*Applied Biology*) The course includes biochemistry, pharmacology, physiology, biology, genetics, clinical chemistry and medical microbiology.

Leeds (*Applied Biology*) This is a new course covering biological topics of economic and social importance including the pharmacology of parasites, pesticide biochemistry and environmental conservation. Students can choose to specialise in biochemical or environmental concerns in the first two years, with a range of options in the final year.

Leeds Metropolitan (*Human Biology*) After a broad introduction covering two semesters, students proceed to five main themes of study - the ages of man (conception to old age), the environment, nutrition, health and disease and behaviour and work.

Liverpool (*Applied Biology*) This four-year Life Sciences Unit scheme provides flexibility by enabling students to select a range of units related to the choice of degree. Applied biology is also offered on a four year sandwich course - students specialising in one of: plant science, environmental biology, genetics, marine biology or zoology.

Liverpool John Moores (*Applied Biology*) The first year gives a foundation in biology and associated subjects, including chemistry and computing. A wide range of modules is offered.

London (King's) (*Cell Biology, Biology and Molecular Biology*) These are offered in the School of Life Sciences. First year courses are largely common for all students with specialist options following thereafter.

London (Imp) (*Biology*) The department offers: three year courses in Biology, Biology with Management, Biology with Microbiology, Ecology, Microbiology, Parasitology, Plant Science and Zoology; and four year courses in Applied Biology, and Biology with a Year in Europe. All courses lead to the award of the BSc degree.

London (QMW) (*Biology*) The School of Biological Sciences is organised on a course unit system in which students choose units appropriate to the degree which they wish to follow in Year 2. Specialisms include ecology or aquatic biology or biochemistry or genetics.

London (RH) (*Biology*) The Life Sciences department offers a range of Biology courses including Environmental Biology, Geography and Biochemistry. Course units in Year 1 depend on the degree stream to be taken: Biology, Botany, Environmental Biology, Plant Biology or Zoology or a range of combined courses.

London (Wye) (*Biology*) Options in this course include animal breeding, plant/insect relations, environmental physiology and animal behaviour. Other courses include Biochemistry, Animal Sciences and Plant Sciences.

London (UC) (*Biology*) This course provides a broad and flexible programme for students interested in biology and acts as an entry route for those who decide to transfer to more specialised degrees (such as microbiology, immunology, biochemistry, ecology, zoology) at the end of Year 1. After first year courses in chemistry, cellular and molecular biology, microbiology, genetics and whole organism biology, students may concentrate on their chosen areas.

Loughborough (*Human Biology*) Three and four year courses (the latter with industrial placement) are offered. A range of options in the final year includes human behaviour, ecology, occupational health, psychology, ergonomics and information technology.

Luton (*Biology*) After Year 1 specialisms follow in animal physiology, biotechnology, plant physiology and ecology. Biology, Biochemistry, Biotechnology, Environmental Biology, Health Science, Human Biology and Plant Biology are offered as major, joint and minor awards.

Manchester (*Biology*) This is a broad course with specialisation following in Years 2 and 3. Three year full-time and four year sandwich courses are offered. It is also possible to take Biology with a Modern Language. The modular course structure gives flexibility and easy transfer within the School of Biological Sciences.

Manchester Metropolitan (*Applied Biology*) The second year of this course provides the opportunity for a six-month industrial placement followed by a wide choice of biological topics in Year 3. There are also BSc and MSc courses in Biomedical Science. Biology is also offered in the combined studies scheme.

Newcastle (*Molecular Biology*) The wide range of Biology degrees offered includes: Animal Science (with options in domesticated animal science, entomology and pest management and wildlife biology): Applied Biology (with options involving biochemistry, microbiology and biotechnology); Environmental Biology, Genetics, Molecular Biology, Marine Biology, Medical Microbiology, Plant Science and Zoology. Under a Biological Sciences deferred choice scheme, students can choose their final degree at the end of the first year.

North London (*Applied Biology*) Depending on the results of the first year course, students may have the opportunity to transfer in Year 2 to degrees in biochemistry, biological sciences, ecological sciences, food and nutritional sciences and microbiology.

Nottingham (*Biology*) In the first year, in addition to Biology other subjects are available: biochemistry, botany, chemistry, genetics, geology, psychology and zoology. Second year students attend field courses in either marine biology, terrestrial zoology, population genetics or botany. All students take set modules in semesters 1 and 2 in addition to other course units in biological sciences. In the third year students choose four options from options including animal science, plant science, genetics and microbiology.

Nottingham Trent (*Applied Biology*) This course offers four main themes - biomedical science, crop protection, environmental biology and micro-biology and biotechnology.

Oxford Biology is taken as part of the course in Biological Sciences.

Oxford Brookes (*Environmental Biology*) Modules are offered in country-side planning, soil science, animal behaviour, nutrition, climate and wildlife resource management. Courses are also offered in Cell Biology and Human Biology.

Paisley (*Biology*) This is offered as BSc (3 year), BSc (Honours) (4 year) and BSc (Honours) sandwich (5 year) courses. After a broad introduction students can then specialise in Biochemistry (microbiology and biochem-istry) or environmental biology.

Portsmouth (*Biology*) After a common first three semesters students choose one of the elective streams in either cellular and molecular biology or environmental systems and population biology leading to a range of named degrees.

St Andrews (*Biology*) After a broad first year students can specialise in one of several specialist studies which cover Animal Biology, Biology, Cell Biology, Experimental Pathology, Marine and Environmental Biology, Plant and Environmental Biology, and Physiology.

Salford Applied Biology is offered with Mathematics, Chemistry, Computer Science or Geography.

Sheffield Hallam (*Applied Biology*) The course involves analytical science, management studies and biotechnology with two main options from diagnostic procedures, pharmacology, exercise physiology and public health microbiology.

Southampton (*Biology*) Courses offered by the department are based on a unit structure with a common first year after which students can specialise in such fields as biology, applied biology, plant science and zoology.

South Bank (*Applied Biology*) This is a three year full-time or four year sandwich course which studies processes at the level of cell, tissue and organism, together with the nature of life itself. Courses are also offered in Human Biology, Conservation, Microbiology and Biochemistry.

Staffordshire (*Applied Biology*) All students take core modules at level 1 with transfers possible to joint Honours courses at the end of this stage. A selection of modules in Year 2 leads to Applied Biology or Biochemistry options.

Stirling (*Biology*) Biology may be taken to minor, subsidiary or major level in Part I. After an introductory course, students can proceed to one of four specialist areas: animal physiology, plant biology, ecology and marine and freshwater biology.

Strathclyde (*Mathematical Biology*) The course covers mathematics and statistics at the outset leading on to more advanced mathematical modelling and biological material. Project work takes place with the Department of Bioscience and Biotechnology.

Sunderland (*Biology*) Biology is available as part of the Combined Programme Scheme, and can be combined with nine other subjects. Modules of study cover three main areas: environmental biology, microbiology and biotechnology, and biomedical sciences. Additional topics include molecular biology, immunology, medical microbiology and pollution.

Sussex (*Biology*) Cellular biochemistry, evolution, physiology and the behaviour of animals are studied in the first two terms along with maths and chemistry. This is followed during the next four terms with a study of major areas of biology, and at the end of the second year students choose four options from a range of subjects.

Swansea (*Biology*) First year students take two other subjects in the biological sciences as well as biology, or they may take botany, zoology and one other subject from geography, psychology, mathematical methods or chemistry. In the second year course work covers genetics, biochemistry, cell and molecular biology, plant and animal biology. There is also a research project. The final year is devoted to a specialised area.

Wolverhampton (*Biology*) The subject may be combined with other subjects as a minor, joint or major subject with other scientific or technological subjects, or in the modular scheme with an extensive list of other subjects.

York (*Biology*) Part I (five terms) is common to degree programmes in Biology, Applied and Environmental Biology, Cell Biology, Ecology, Genetics and Animal Physiology. Transfers are possible between courses during this time. Specialist options then follow in Part II (terms 6–9). An optional year is available in research or industry and there is a one year exchange scheme with students in the USA and Canada. (*Applied Environmental Biology*) The course involves conservation of natural resources, control of pollution, environmental disease and human nutrition.

- **Top research universities**
London (Imp), London (UC), Sussex, Warwick, Edinburgh, Birmingham, Bristol, Durham, East Anglia, Kent, Leicester, UMIST, Nottingham, Sheffield, York, Dundee, St Andrews.

- **Colleges and Institutes of Higher Education offering degree courses**
Bath (Coll), Bolton (Inst), Canterbury (Chr.Ch.Coll), Cardiff (Inst), Chester (Coll), Edge Hill (Coll), Nene (Coll), NESCOT, Norwich City (Coll), Roehampton (Inst), Scottish Agricultural (Coll), Scarborough (Univ Coll), St Mary's (Univ Coll), Stockport (Coll), Suffolk (Coll).

- **Other courses to be considered**
Agriculture, bacteriology, biochemistry. botany, dentistry, ecology, environmental health, environmental science, forestry, medicine, microbiology, pharmacology, pharmacy and speech science.

BIOTECHNOLOGY

- **Special subject requirements:** 2–3 A-levels in mathematics/science subjects; GCSE mathematics at grades A–C.

- **Subject information:** This is an interdisciplinary subject which can cover specialisms in agriculture, biochemistry, microbiology, genetics, chemical engineering, biophysics etc. (Courses in these named subjects should also be explored.)

Aberdeen (*Biotechnology*) Degrees are offered with a specialism in applied molecular biology and agricultural biotechnology.

Abertay Dundee (*Biotechnology*) Courses are offered in environmental, medical, microbial, plant and animal biotechnology.

Birmingham (*Biotechnology*) The subject is offered as part of the degree course in Biological Sciences.

Cardiff (*Biotechnology*) The course covers agricultural and environmental topics but also covers aspects of medicine. There are seven biological degrees all served by the same broadly based first year.

De Montfort (*Biotechnology*) This is a four year sandwich course with options in cell biology, microbiology, genetics and process technology.

Glamorgan (*Biotechnology*) This three year full-time or four year sandwich course provides a basis for understanding biological processes of industrial significance. Options include foreign languages and work placements in the food or biological waste disposal industries. It can also be studied as part of the Combined programmes.

Hertfordshire (*Biotechnology*) Final year courses cover biochemistry, microbiology and molecular biology plus applied aspects such as industrial enzymology, fermentation and process technology.

Leeds (*Biotechnology*) The course offers advanced studies in fermentation science, medical aspects of biotechnology and computer modelling of protein structure and drug design.

Liverpool (*Microbial Biotechnology*) Twelve weeks are spent in industry on this course which focuses on microbiology.

Liverpool John Moores (*Biotechnology*) The course covers aspects of manufacturing techniques in agriculture and medicine placing emphasis on the manipulation of microorganisms and plants.

London (Imp) (*Biotechnology*) See **Biology**.

London (King's) (*Biotechnology*) Final year options cover biotechnology related to plants and molecular biology.

London (UC) (*Biotechnology*) Chemistry, cellular and molecular biology, microbiology, biological engineering and experimental biochemistry are studied in the first year. These strands carry on into Years 2 and 3, and a final year research project is undertaken in one of these main areas.

Manchester Biotechnology is offered as a joint degree with either biochemistry or microbiology, following a broadly based first year. Three year full-time and four year sandwich courses are offered.

Napier (*Applied Microbiology and Biotechnology*) This three or four year course is about biological systems, their functions and how they can be manipulated. Study of genetics engineering, fermentation technology and environmental microbiology is included, as well as pure and applied aspects of immunology.

Nottingham (*Biotechnology*) The emphasis is on agricultural aspects.

Paisley (*Biology*) Biotechnology specialisms in microbiology and biochemistry.

Reading (*Biotechnology*) The final year of the course covers industrial microbiology (fermentation, molecular biology, applied genetics and water and waste treatment), biochemical processes relating largely to food processes and industrial management.

Sheffield Biotechnology is offered with microbiology.

South Bank (*Biotechnology*) This is a three year full-time or four year sandwich course with an industrial emphasis. After a general first year, students choose units from metabolic biochemistry and molecular genetics to physiology and enzymology.

Strathclyde (*Biotechnology*) The course covers microbiology and molecular biology. Most students in the department can defer their ultimate choice of Honours degree until the end of Year 2.

Sussex (*Biotechnology*) The course has a focus on molecular biology and genetics.

Swansea (*Process Biotechnology*) Areas covered include pharmacology, the food, dairy and beverage industries.

Teesside (*Process Biotechnology*) The course prepares students for careers in fermentation, healthcare, food, brewing and environmental chemistry areas.

Westminster (*Biotechnology*) The bias is towards medical, food and agricultural biotechnology.

Wolverhampton Biotechnology is offered as a single subject degree, or as part of the Applied Sciences and Modular degree schemes programmes. There is a bias towards microbial and plant biotechnology.

- **Colleges and Institutes of Higher Education offering degree courses**
NESCOT, Suffolk (Coll).

- **Other courses to be considered**
Biological science subjects, agriculture, microbiology, genetics.

BOTANY
(See also **Biological Sciences**)

- **Special subject requirements:** 2–3 A-levels in mathematics/science subjects.

- **Subject information:** Botany is also sometimes referred to as Plant Science in which final year studies lead to specialised studies of plant physiology or broader areas of ecology or environmental aspects. Biological Science courses also may offer botany as an optional study.

Aberdeen (*Plant Science*) No previous knowledge of botany is required for this course. Subjects covered include aspects of zoology, genetics and microbiology. Plant ecology, tropical ecology and plant/animal interaction are offered at level 4.

Aberystwyth (*Botany*) First year students take Part I of the Biological Sciences foundation course (see **Biological Sciences**). Second and third year courses include ecology, plant-soil relations, genetics and evolution of land flora, plant physiology and floral biology. Third year students make a choice of specialism from eight options.

Bangor (*Botany with Marine Biology*) This course emphasises marine aspects of botany with several marine biology modules being taken in Year two.

Belfast (*Plant Science*) This is mainly a physiological, molecular and ecological study.

Bristol (*Botany*) A foundation study is made on this course for all the applied disciplines, for example, forestry, horticulture, water management, pharmacology. Botany is taken with zoology in the first year plus one other course taken for the first two years. Units can be taken in zoology, microbiology, geography, geology, physiology and psychology. Transfers are possible with Biology or Zoology or joint Honours courses up to the end of Year 2.

Cambridge (*Natural Science*) Botany is taken as part of the course in Natural Sciences starting as an option in the second year.

Dundee (*Botany*) Botany is offered as a Second Science course with an emphasis on cell biology, whole plant structure and genetics. Advanced studies follow in the third and fourth years which include agricultural and economic botany, plant breeding ecology and plant pathology.

East Anglia (*Plant Biology*) This is a third year specialist programme and part of the degree in Biological Sciences. The plant biology programme includes courses in molecular biology, biochemistry, physiology, pathology, genetic manipulation of plants and ecology. The flexible programme enables students to give extra emphasis to important areas of plant biology in which Norwich is particular strong.

Edinburgh (*Botany*) Various programmes of study under the Biological Sciences heading are offered with optional courses leading to a specialisation in the third and fourth years which include physiology, ecology and evolution.

Glasgow (*Botany*) First year students take the Biology course, followed by applied botany, environmental plant science and molecular plant science in the second year. The Honours course pays special attention to plant physiology and biochemistry, the study of fungi (mycology) and ecology, and four option courses are taken.

Lancaster Biochemistry is offered with Plant Physiology.

Leeds (*Molecular Plant Biology*) The School of Biological Sciences offers the course which provides a broad first year course in general biology leading to specialisation at level 3.

Leicester (*Plant Science*) The course is offered within the School of Biological Sciences, course units being chosen appropriate to the final Honours degree.

Liverpool (*Plant Science*) The course is studied as part of the Life Sciences group of subjects which initially also includes Biology, Genetics and Zoology. In the final year a wide range of units is offered including freshwater and marine botany, plant microbiology and biotechnology.

London (Imp) (*Plant Science*) A common first year is offered leading to degrees in Biology, Microbiology, Plant Science and Zoology. In Year 1 students wishing to study Plant Science follow a route which includes plant forms and physiology, genetics, evolution and ecology, pollutants and the effects of environmental damage, photosynthesis, plant/animal respiration, biological timekeeping, ageing, plant and animal water balance/electrophysiology, neurochemistry, endocrinology, animal defence mechanisms.

London (RH) (*Plant Biology*) Broad courses are available in the Biology Department with the chance to specialise in applied plant biology (plant pathology, breeding and genetics) or botany and microbiology.

London (Wye) (*Plant Sciences*) The course covers physiology, insect relations, virology, biochemistry and biotechnology.

Manchester (*Plant Science*) The course covers all aspects of botany including reproduction, evolution and environmental aspects. First year courses are common for other biological sciences.

Newcastle (*Plant Biology*) The Plant Biology course emphasises the place of plants in global ecology and human society. (*Biology of Plants and Animals*) First year students choose from a wide range of biological subjects covering the interactions between plants and animals.

Nottingham (*Plant Life Science*) The course covers the biology of plants and micro-organisms, conservation and biotechnology. The course in Plant Science offers specialisms in plant physiology and pathology.

Oxford (*Plant Sciences*) The first two terms of this Biological Science course are spent doing a preliminary course in biology. The subsequent years provide considerable flexibility and choice in specialising in plant or animal studies or some combination of both.

Plymouth Plant Sciences is offered jointly with twelve other subjects.

Reading (*Botany*) In the first two terms students take botany and two other subjects. A research project occupies the final year, with a choice of advanced courses which include genetic engineering, plant anatomy, physiology, biochemistry and botanical conservation.

St Andrews (*Plant and Environmental Biology*) After two years studying a range of courses in the biological sciences, students may go on to specialise. The third year is spent on environments, population biology and adaptive physiology. These lead into specialised options such as symbiosis, genetics, community ecology and applied plant breeding, and a research project is undertaken.

Sheffield (*Plant Sciences*) In the first year the student chooses either biological sciences or biology plus two complementary subjects. In the second year a study of botany is combined with one from biochemistry, genetics, geography, geology, microbiology or zoology. The third year is devoted entirely to plant science.

Swansea (*Botany*) This is offered as part of the Biological Sciences course in which two main biological disciplines are studied. Botany can be taken with genetics, zoology or microbiology.

● **Other courses to be considered**
Agriculture, biochemistry, horticulture, forestry and landscape architecture.

BUILDING (including **Architectural Engineering, Building Services Engineering**)
See also **Surveying (Building)**

● **Special subject requirements:** 2–3 A-levels from mathematics/physics/chemistry.

● **Subject information:** These courses involve the techniques and management methods employed in the building industry. This subject also covers Civil and Structural Engineering and Architecture.

Abertay Dundee Building courses are offered in Built Environment, Building Services, Engineering, Construction Management, Building

Maintenance Management, Building Engineering and Management and Building Surveying.

Anglia (Poly Univ) There are several courses offered in Building Technology, Building Management and Design, three and four year sandwich courses are on offer. The courses are based at Chelmsford.

Belfast (*Architectural Engineering*) This is a three year course covering aspects of building engineering and services and involving the departments of Civil Engineering, Architecture and Planning.

Bournemouth (*Heritage Conservation*) The course combines elements of material science, environmental science, building conservation and archaeology with a study of cultural resource management. A wide variety of third year options allows specialisation to suit individual tastes.

Brighton (*Building Engineering and Management*) The course focuses on three main areas of building studies - performance, production and business. Honours students are selected at the end of the second year and industrial placement occupies the third year. There is also a course in Building Surveying.

Bristol UWE (*Building Engineering and Management*) This is a four year sandwich course preparing students who have appropriate design and business skills to take a leading role in the industry. There is the opportunity to specialise in either structural or environmental engineering in the final year. There is also a course in Construction Management offering European placements.

Central England (*Building Surveying*) The course covers construction, surveying, building surveying, management and law. There is also a degree course in Building Services Engineering.

Central Lancashire (*Building Management*) Building Management concerns the study of construction technologies and management disciplines with reference to the design, construction and aftercare of buildings. Building managers are involved at each stage of the building process as managers and leaders of the design team and as managers of the construction process. There is also a course in Building Surveying.

Coventry (*Building Surveying*) This course aims to educate graduates for professional careers in building surveying which involve advising on the planning, construction, maintenance and repair of all types of commercial and residential property. The course may be studied over three academic years, or extended to a four years by including either a year of study in Europe or a professional training year. Accreditation by the Royal Institution of Chartered Surveyors is in progress. There are also courses in Building Structures, Building Services Engineering and Building Management with European studies.

De Montfort (*Construction Technology and Management*) Supervised industrial placement occupies part of this course. Elective routes in the final year allow students to specialise in an area of their choice. There is also a course in Building Surveying.

Glamorgan (*Building Technology and Management*) This three year full-time or four year sandwich course leads to full exemption from all written exams of CIB, ABE and BIAT. There are opportunities to spend one semester in another European country.

Glasgow Caledonian (*Building Surveying*) This is a four year sandwich course involving building, valuation and management. Building Control and Building Engineering and Management are also offered.

Greenwich (*Building Surveying*) This is a three year full-time or four year sandwich course which has a common first year with Estate Management and Quantity Surveying. (Transfers are possible).

Heriot-Watt (*Building*) This is a four year course covering all aspects of building. The course also includes valuation and quantity surveying, economics, technology, law, business studies and management. Other degree courses offered include Building Surveying and Building Economics and Quantity Surveying.

Hertfordshire (*Construction Management*) Technology, planning, design and construction are the main themes of this course. The Building Services Engineering course covers architecture, engineering studies (mechanical, electrical/electronic, public health, illuminations, acoustics) and environmental studies.

Huddersfield (*Building Conservation*) The course is primarily concerned with the preservation of buildings of architectural or historic merit. In addition to historic aspects the course also involves building surveying and science and planning legislation.

Kingston Courses are offered associated with Building in the School of Surveying, ie Building and Quantity Surveying, Construction Economics and Property Studies.

Leeds Metropolitan (*Building Studies*) Basic studies of this course include European studies. Special studies include environmental science and services engineering, systems management, construction engineering and financial management. Students spend Year 3 in industry; optional placements take place in UK and Europe. There is also a building surveying course.

Liverpool (*Building Management and Technology*) The course covers building construction engineering or building services engineering (a shortage area for graduates) with a common first year for both areas and students specialising in the second year. An optional year in industry may follow Year 2. Subjects include acoustics, lighting and thermal services. There is also a degree course in Building Services and Environmental Engineering.

Liverpool John Moores (*Building*) This four year course involves construction management, construction technology, materials science, environmental science, surveying, economics and legal studies and information technology. There is an opportunity for a year's placement in industry.

London (UC) (*Construction Management*) The first term is common to architecture, planning and construction management after which the degree course leads to specialisation in chosen topics. Completion gives some CIOB exemptions.

Loughborough (*Construction Engineering Management*) This course is fully sponsored by ten major UK construction companies. All students on the course are sponsored. The main themes cover management, law, economics and finance, engineering and building services.

Luton (*Construction Management*) This course covers building technology and management, building economics, law and computing. There is also a building surveying course involving European business (French, German, Italian, Spanish languages), economics and management and courses in Architecture and Built Environment.

Manchester (UMIST) (*Construction Management*) The course encompasses aspects of management, science and technology. Emphasis is placed on communication skills. In the Building Technology degree the emphasis lies in materials, performance and science as applied to construction situations. A degree course is also offered in Building Services Engineering, specialising in heating, ventilation and other mechanical services in buildings.

Middlesex (*Construction Engineering and Management*) The course covers topics common to both business studies and civil engineering.

Napier The university offers several courses including Building Control, Architectural Technology, Building Engineering and Management, Building Surveying, Quantity Surveying, Estate Management and Planning and Development Surveying. All have a common first year allowing students to choose their specialisation in Year 2.

Northumbria (*Building Management*) The course covers the whole spectrum of activities from the design to the final completion of a building project including technology, design, economics and finance. (*Building Services Engineering*) The course is split equally between theoretical studies, applied studies (heating, lighting and air-conditioning) and project work, with an emphasis on computer-aided design. This is a four year sandwich course, including an optional European route. A course in Built Environment is also offered.

Nottingham (*Building Services Engineering*) The course contains 50 per cent architecture and 50 per cent engineering modules. There are extensive links with leading companies in the industry and excellent research and test facilities.

Nottingham Trent Courses are offered in Construction Management, Building, Residential Development and Architectural Technology which cover the design, construction, production and conservation of buildings within a European and environmental framework.

Oxford Brookes (*Building*) Technology, management, design, construction and the maintenance of buildings form the core of this four year sandwich course.

Paisley (*Construction Management*) The course covers the mechanics of structures and mathematics in Year 1, leading on to land surveying, design, law and economics, marketing and management. Industrial training takes place after Easter in each of the Years 2 and 3. Civil engineering, planning and development follow in Year 4.

Portsmouth (*Construction Management*) (See Quantity Surveying).

Reading (*Building Construction and Management*) The first year is common with the courses in Quantity Surveying and Building Surveying. The course will appeal to students interested in building and civil engineering but who do not wish to undertake a highly mathematical and theoretical course concentrating mainly upon design. There is a course in Building Services Engineering.

Robert Gordon (*Building Surveying*) The first 3 semesters of this BSc are common with Quantity Surveying, Architectural Technology and Construction Management, and transfers are possible between the four courses.

Sheffield Hallam (*Construction*) The main themes of the course are housing development, commercial and industrial medium rise structures and multi-storey schemes. There is an optional study of a European language. Year 3 is in industry. Other courses offered include Architectural Technology and Environmental Management.

Salford (*Construction Management*) This is a four year scheme with two six month placements in industry covering financial management, law and construction.

South Bank (*Construction Management*) The course offers an opportunity to study in Australia and international projects involve subsidised four day visits to a European city (previously Amsterdam, Barcelona and Berlin).

Staffordshire (*Building Surveying*) This course shares a common first year with the Property and Constrcution Management programme. It covers the refurbishment and adaptation of existing buildings, structural surveys and building management.

Strathclyde (*Building Design Engineering*) The course leads to professional recognition of the Royal Institute of British Architects (Part 1) or the Institute of Civil and Structural Engineers (Parts 1 and 2), covering architecture, civil engineering, building science and environmental engineering.

Ulster (*Building Engineering and Management*) A four year course with Year 3 in industry. The course focuses on technology and management and includes design, law and finance.

Westminster (*Construction Management*) There are two major themes: (a) building management; (b) construction technology and science, with the option to specialise in Year 2. The course is taught on the modular system, allowing the maximum level of flexibility. Two industrial placements are included in the four year course with two compulsory field visits. All students take French, German or Spanish.

Wolverhampton (*Building Management*) This is a broad-based course covering all the major topics required by a building engineer, with law, computing, management and language options.

• **Colleges and Institutes of Higher Education offering degree courses**
Barnsley (Coll), Bolton (Inst), Buckinghamshire (Coll), Nene (Coll), NESCOT, North East Wales (Inst), Southampton (Inst), Suffolk (Coll), Swansea (Inst).

• **Other courses to be considered**
Architecture, building services engineering, building surveying, civil engineering, quantity surveying, valuation surveying, estate management, land economics.

BUSINESS COURSES

• **Special subject requirements:** GCSE (grades A–C) English and mathematics. Some university courses require mathematics at A-level.

• **Subject information:** This is a very large subject area which may consist of courses in general topics (Business Studies or Business Administration), Management Science courses, which tend to have a mathematics emphasis, and more specialised fields which are covered by courses in advertising, consumer science, company and public administration, financial services (see under banking), industrial relations, organisation studies, retail management and travel and tourism.

At HND level many institutions offer Business Study courses with specialist streams as follows: accountancy, advertising, broadcasting/media, business administration, company secretaryship, computer studies, distribution, European business and marketing, fashion, food, health, horticulture, journalism, languages, law, leisure, marketing, media, personnel, printing, publicity, purchasing and tourism.

Aberdeen Over 20 joint courses are offered with Management Studies.

Abertay Dundee (*Retail Management*) Sandwich course with two 6 month placements. Strong commitment needed.

Aberystwyth (*Business Studies*) Final year options in accountancy, economics, marketing and public administration. There are also seven joint courses with business studies.

Anglia (Poly Univ) (*Business Studies*) A four year sandwich course. Core courses in each year provide a sound framework in business studies. The modular system allows students to combine this with a range of associated disciplines or to focus on one area. Over 30 joint courses are also offered including some which are combined with languages and also two European Business programmes with the option to study in Germany (Berlin) for a dual English and German award.

Aston (*Managerial and Administrative Studies*) French, German and Spanish options are available in Years 2 and 4. Specialisms include finance and accountancy, legal studies, personnel and marketing. Aston is also one of the few universities offering specialist degrees in Transport Management. There are also over 15 joint courses with Business Administration including International Business Courses (France or Germany).

Bangor A joint course in Business Studies and computer studies is offered and also European Financial Management. This is the main centre for European financial studies with links with the principal European banking schools.

Bath (*Business Administration*) This is a blend of practical experience and academic study in a four year sandwich course. First year core subjects include business economics, behaviour in organisations, accounting and some computing statistics and law. The course continues with specialisms in finance, employee relations and marketing. Language options include Mandarin Chinese for beginners. Two courses are also offered in International Management with a Foreign language (French or German). ('Excellent' teaching rating.)

Belfast (*Industrial Management*) The course is partially taught in the Schools of Mechanical and Process Engineering, Finance and Information and Modern Languages. Business Administration joint courses are also offered with languages (French, German, Italian, Russian or Spanish).

Birmingham (*Commerce*) This is a multi-disciplinary course with core subjects in business economics and accounts and third year options in investment, banking and marketing. A four year degree is offered with French, German, Italian or Spanish. 16 courses in Management or Commerce are also offered jointly with a range of subjects including a choice of five languages (French, German, Spanish, Italian or Portuguese).

Bournemouth (*Business Studies*) This is a four year sandwich course with fourth year options in accounting, financial services, manpower studies, business computing and marketing. (Public Relations) Covers consumer advertising, public affairs, and European public relations. (Advertising) Management, copywriting, art direction and account planning are the main topics on this course. Courses are also offered covering other management subjects including Retail Management (preference given to applicants with retail experience).

Bradford (*Business and Management Studies*) This is a broad course for two years and includes accounting, law, economics, computing and behavioural science. There are over 50 modules offered on this course including the opportunity to study a foreign language. An industrial or commercial year of practical training is optional in the third year. There is also a Managerial Studies course with Spanish which includes a year abroad. This long established Business School also offers several joint courses including International Management with French, German or Spanish.

Brighton (*Business Studies*) This is a sandwich course with a full-time placements officer, and very successful record of placing students in industry/commerce. There is increasing emphasis on international business with a language option in Years 1 and 2 and information technology throughout the course. There is a choice of specialist options in the final year from marketing, finance, employment studies and materials management. Brighton also offers a degree course in European Business with Technology with a six-month placement in Italy. Over 10 joint courses are also offered including European Business and Tourism courses.

Bristol UWE (*Business Studies*) This is a four year course with industrial placement in the third year.Special fourth year options in business policy finance, marketing, employee relations and production. Bristol also offers an International Business Studies course with languages from French, German and Spanish.

Brunel (*Management Studies*) The course covers management, economics and organisational behaviour and offers various popular options such as marketing, personnel or market research in Year 3. Over 25 joint courses are also offered which, in addition to law, cover many technological fields.

Buckingham (*Business Studies*) A two year course with compulsory core subjects in economics, statistics, accounting and computing. These lead on to more advanced courses in which one modern language must be studied. The university also offers several joint courses including European Business Management programmes with French, German or Spanish.

Cardiff The Business School offers six specialist first degrees covering Accounting, Banking, Economics, Business Economics, Business Administration and Business Studies which can be combined with Japanese language and an optional placement in Japan. Six joint courses are also offered five of which include languages (French, German, Spanish, Italian and Japanese). Cardiff also offers specialised degrees in International Transport and also Maritime Studies.

Central England (*Business Studies*) The main focus is on business problem-solving within the European framework. There is also a large number of joint courses which cover Management and Business Administration.

Central Lancashire (*Business Studies*) In Part I, which extends over six terms, students follow a broad programme in marketing, human resource management, law, accounting and finance, decision modelling and possibly a language. The third year is spent on an industrial placement. In Part II, the final year, there is one compulsory course and four options chosen from a wide range. Business Public Relations and Management Sciences also feature in Combined Honours Programmes.

City (*Management and Systems*) This is a three or four year course which offers a study of management systems and decision-making. It covers behavioural science, international relations, economics, financial management and decision analysis. Teaching rating 'excellent'. The Business Studies course offers finance, marketing and language options in Year 3.

Coventry (*Business Studies*) This is a sandwich course with two six-month periods of business placement, possibly abroad. The first two years are common with European Business Studies course focusing on French, German or Spanish. There is also a degree in Business Administration with majors available in accounting, marketing, business computing or tourism.

Cranfield Management courses involving agriculture and the environment are offered by this university.

De Montfort (*Business Studies*) This four year course aims to provide advanced general education in business combined with practical work experience and a measure of specialisation in the final year. Several options are available in Year 2 including computing and languages and there is also a European Business stream. Several joint courses with science subjects are offered and also an Arts Management course.

Derby (*Business Administration*) Full time and sandwich courses are offered. Marketing or Personnel Management options are available in Year 4 and optional language courses are arranged in French, German or Spanish.

Dundee Over fifteen joint courses are offered with Management which is also offered as part of the Arts, Social Science and Combined Honours programme.

Durham Management Studies is offered as part of the Social Sciences Combined programme and also as a joint course with Chinese or Japanese.

East Anglia Management Studies and Business Studies are offered jointly with nine subjects including Danish.

East London (*Business Studies*) Students on all courses in this subject follow the same course units with the option to follow a pathway in Accountancy, Human Resource Management, Marketing or Languages. There are over 30 joint courses offered with Business Studies.

Edinburgh (*Business Studies*) All students cover the basic management subjects, single Honours B.Com students studying at least one year of Accountancy and Economics. There are also eighteen courses with Business Studies.

Essex European Business Studies is offered with Chemistry on three year full-time or four year sandwich courses.

Glamorgan (*Business Studies*) The first year of the course is common with the Accounting and Finance degree allowing transfers at the end of the year. Industrial placement occupies Year 3. Specialisms in accounting, marketing or European studies. Joint and combined courses are also offered in Business Studies and European Business.

Glasgow (*Management Studies*) The course covers operations business systems, marketing, economics and finance. Management Studies is also offered on joint courses with 46 other arts and social science courses at Honours level whilst ordinary degrees are also offered.

Glasgow Caledonian (*Business Studies*) This is a broad-based course in business education covering accountancy, economics and law. Options include industrial relations, personnel management, information systems development, financial administration, law and marketing. This is a sandwich course with a separate diploma for successful completion of Year 3. A wide range of business courses are on offer including Retail

Management, European Business Studies (with Spanish, French or German language), International Travel and Risk Management.

Greenwich (*Business Studies*) The modular sandwich degree course is based on two semesters each year with a final Honours choice made in semester 4. There is a language option (French, German or Spanish) as well as 40 other specialist options. (*Business and Marketing Communication*) This has a special emphasis on advertising, public relations, direct marketing, and market research. Several joint courses are also offered with scientific and technological subjects.

Heriot-Watt (*Business Organisation*) This is a three year Ordinary degree course or a four year Honours degree course. A broad-based course, it includes accounting, marketing, organisational behaviour and personnel studies. Courses in International Business are also offered with German, Spanish and Russian and there are courses available in the Combined Arts and Science programmes.

Hertfordshire (*Business Studies*) Ordinary degree students follow a general course. At the end of Year 2 Honours students can take options in accounting, languages, marketing, management science or personnel administration. The third year of this four year course is spent on a professional placement. Over 20 joint courses with Business are offered in addition to a European Business Studies sandwich course with French, German, or Spanish.

Huddersfield (*Business Studies*) A standard business education course which can also be taken with a language on a three year full-time or four year sandwich course or jointly with Accountancy or Technology.

Hull (*Management Sciences*) Three degrees are offered. The BA course covers the analysis and management of organisations. The BSc degrees offer an emphasis in mathematical methods or operations analysis and include computing and statistics. Degrees in Business Studies are offered with a choice of five languages. Several joint courses with languages are also offered (French, German, Dutch, Italian, Scandinavian Studies or Spanish).

Humberside (*Business Studies*) The course covers marketing, personnel management and accountancy. Courses are also offered in European Business Studies with languages (French, German, Spanish) and in European Marketing and International Business all of which are four year sandwich courses.

Keele Over seventy joint courses are available chosen from Management Science, Human Resource Management or Business Administration options.

Kent (*Management Science*) Students take course units in management, economics, accounting, statistics, and computing. Additional courses can be taken in social sciences, eg industrial relations and behavioural science. In addition ten joint courses with Management Science are available and there are also European Management Science courses, focusing on France or Germany.

Kingston (*Business Studies*) The department has a top teaching rating and offers a range of business topics and a foreign language in the first five terms, with later specialisation in marketing, finance, multinational business, manpower and purchasing. Those students following the European programme take part in a two term exchange in Year 3 in France, Italy, Germany or Spain. There are also several joint courses with Business Administration including a Business Studies course with a European programme in France, Germany, Italy and Spain.

Lancaster (*Management*) The School of Management is offering a BBA Bachelor of Business Administration. This is a four year course with the third year being spent in employment, which includes accounting and finance, economics, marketing and operations management. There are also modern language options in French, German, Italian and Spanish. Marketing can also be taken as a specialist study within the Management Sciences course, the other option being Operational Research which is a branch of business related to problem-solving covering management, computer programming and statistics. Joint courses are also available in Organisation Studies and Management Science.

Leeds (*Management Studies*) One of the larger Business Schools in the UK with a strong focus on applied economics and human aspects of business. The first two years concentrate on the major disciplines of management: economics, accounting, psychology, sociology and information science. The third year offers a core course in business policy, and students select optional courses covering the major areas of business, eg marketing, personnel management, international management. Over 20 joint courses are also offered across a range of arts and science subjects and a specialist degree in Textile Management.

Leeds Metropolitan (*Business Studies*) This is a four year 'thin' sandwich which includes two periods of paid industrial training. Core studies include the basic business disciplines followed by functional specialisms. There are options in French or German for post A-level students and German, Italian, Spanish options *ab initio*, quantitative methods, and organisational behaviour. Students taking the language options spend their first placement abroad and their third year in a Business School in France or Germany. Courses are also offered in Tourism Management, Consumer Studies and Public Relations.

Liverpool Several joint courses in Management are offered with Mathematics or Engineering.

Liverpool John Moores (*Business Studies*) This is a broad course with final year options in finance, purchasing, marketing and personnel work. Industrial placement takes place in the third year. (*International Business Studies*) Business Studies with French, German, Japanese or Spanish. There is also an interesting range of joint courses with Business covering such diverse areas as product design, law, sports science and Food and Nutrition.

London Guildhall (*Business Administration*) Three year full-time and four year sandwich courses are offered in Business which include banking and corporate finance. There is also a European Business course and Modular programmes.

London (Imp) Ten joint courses are offered with Management and a range of scientific and technological options. The department has a top teaching rating.

London (King's) (*Business Management*) Taught in the School of Physical Sciences the course focuses particularly on management in scientific professional and human areas of business, industry and the public sector. Joint courses are also offered with several scientific subjects.

London (LSE) (*Management*) After a broad first year students take courses in accountancy, finance, economics, management science, law and international marketing. Management is also offered with French or German and there is also a course in Industrial Relations.

London (QMW) Joint courses with Business are offered in eleven subject combinations in science, engineering and languages.

London (RH) (*Management Studies*) Subsidiary subjects are offered in French, German, Italian, mathematics, economic history, economics, sociology, public administration and social policy. Twenty seven subjects can also be taken with Management Studies.

London (SOAS) Management is offered with an Asian or African language.

London (UC) Management Studies can be taken with several other subjects.

London (Wye) Business Studies programmes are linked with Agriculture, Horticulture or the Food Industry.

Loughborough The university offers a variety of management courses including Management Sciences, European Business, Retail Management and Transport Management covering air, rail and sea transport, town planning and financial management.

Luton Business Administration is a single Honours course of 3 years but business subjects are offered with other subjects in over 250 combinations.

Manchester Business and Management are offered with a small number of scientific and technological subjects.

Manchester Metropolitan (*Business*) There is a strong vocational emphasis to this course with a management development stream. There is a language studies option (French, German, Spanish or Italian) on this broad-based course. Students spend a term at an academic institution in Europe and the third year in an industrial placement. (*Retail Marketing*) The course includes two periods of work experience. Applicants must have had work experience in retailing.

Manchester (UMIST) (*Management Science*) This course covers economics, accounting, psychology, social statistics and mathematics. There is a wide range of third year options covering various elements of management activity, for example, production, marketing, finance, personnel and business policy. There are also several joint courses including International Management with American Business, French or German.

Middlesex (*Business Studies*) A four year sandwich course with options in marketing and finance. (*European Management*) There is an alternative degree scheme operated in conjunction with the Ecole Internationale des Affaires in Marseilles, France, leading to qualifications at both institutions.

Napier (*Business Studies*) Full-time and sandwich courses are offered with final year options covering business policy, economics, financial analysis and human resources management. (*Commerce*) The emphasis is on the management of information technology.

Newcastle (*Business Management*) A vocationally oriented degree programme covering accounting, marketing and business strategy with a foreign modern language also offered. European and International Business Management courses are also available and several related to agricultural business activities.

North London A wide range of business courses is offered including Combined Honours courses covering Business, Business Economics, International Business (focusing on French or German), Business Operations and Arts and Entertainment Management.

Northumbria (*Business Studies*) A broad-based course is offered with industrial placements. The four main options cover finance, management services, manpower, and marketing. (*Secretarial and Business Administration*) Secretarial studies, business information and organisation with one optional subject from international business or a modern language (French, German, Spanish or Russian). Four week placements follow the first and second years of the course. The department has a top teaching rating. (*Travel and Tourism Management*) This is a new degree course offered with an optional language. Placements are arranged with the leading travel and tourist organisations in Year 3. Business administration is also offered with science and engineering subjects and courses in the Combined Honours programme.

Nottingham Management Studies can be taken with languages (French, German, Portuguese or Spanish) and also with Chemistry, Mathematics or Computer Science.

Nottingham Trent (*Business Studies*) Alternate six month periods are spent in industry in the first three years. Final year students select two option subjects from finance, marketing, personnel, computing or operations management. Flexible course structure with opportunities to transfer. European Business Studies (with French, German or Spanish) and programmes of Interfaculty Combined Studies with Business Administration or Industrial Management (designed as a basis for management careers in both manufacturing and service-based industries) are also available.

Oxford Management is offered with Economics, Engineering and Economics and Metallurgy and Economics.

Oxford Brookes (*Business Studies*) On this course there are pathways in human resource management, information systems, finance and accountancy and marketing. Over 200 joint courses are offered involving management subjects.

Paisley (*Business and Management*) A broad business course covering major management topics and including a language (French, German or Spanish) in Year 1 which can be continued through the course. There is an optional sandwich year.

Plymouth (*Business Studies*) Finance, marketing and personnel and one unusual option in 'The Business of Perfumery' amongst others are offered. Year 3 is spent in practical supervised experience. Business Studies may be combined with French, German, Italian or Spanish, and there is a degree course in International Business and several joint courses with Maritime Business. For these courses the sandwich year will be spent abroad.

Portsmouth (*Business Studies*) Business placement takes place during the third year. In the final year business analysis and planning are taken, plus four options from twelve covering accounting, personnel, marketing and information systems and technology, travel and tourism. Language options (French, German and Spanish) and opportunities for work or study abroad are available with the European Business programme.

Reading (*Management and Business Administration*) A three year degree course which includes economics and accounting and optional courses in marketing or strategic management and business policy.

Robert Gordon (*Business Studies*) Business is offered as a three year full-time or four year sandwich course. After Year 1 it is possible to transfer to Accountancy and Finance, Commerce in Business, Computing or Business Administration (European Business). Year 3 placements take place in France or Germany. Consumer Production Management is offered. Other courses include food, textiles, financial services, nutrition, retail and distribution. There is also a degree course in publishing.

Salford (*Business and Management Studies*) On this course specialisms are offered in marketing, general management, finance or personnel management. Courses are also offered in Business Operations and Control (which has a strong mathematical bias) and European Business.

Sheffield (*Business Studies*) The first year course covers economics, maths and statistics. Courses in management organisation and economics are taken in the second year with marketing finance, accounting and labour law. In the third year students take five options including retailing, industrial relations, enterpriseship and small businesses. Business Studies is also offered with French, German, Japanese, Russian, Spanish or Korean Studies.

Sheffield Hallam (*Business Studies*) This is a four year sandwich course. French or German may be studied in all years with two terms spent abroad for the European Business option. Other options in the final year include finance, marketing, employment studies and government. (*International Business*) This course focuses on a study of business coupled with a study of language (choice of four). Options include marketing, tourism, and industrial relations. The business school offers opportunities for second language training in French, German, Italian, Japanese, Portuguese and Spanish.

Southampton (*Management Sciences*) This is a single Honours degree with specialisation in areas such as European Studies and Accounting.

South Bank (*Business Studies*) The first year covers accounting, business studies, computing, law, economics and a language: French or German. The second year concentrates on business studies, computing, marketing and human resource development and two out of ten options. The third year is spent in an industrial or commercial attachment. Final year students take corporate management and planning, and choose from a range of options. The course in Product Management offers specialist studies in Applied Resources. Joint courses with a range of subjects including Accounting and Modern Languages are also available.

St Andrews (*Management (Arts); Management Sciences (Science)*) These courses are offered in the Faculties of Arts and Sciences as single or joint Honours courses of four years. There is a focus on analytical methods of decision-making in business organisations, management, business policy and information technology. A very wide range of joint courses is also available.

Staffordshire (*Business Studies*) This is a modular course, the choice of modules (including languages) determining the final choice of specialisms which include accountancy and finance, international business, accountancy and marketing. A wide range of joint courses can be taken ranging from Design Studies to International Relations.

Stirling (*Business Studies*) This may be taken to major, subsidiary or minor levels in Part I. Twenty-eight options are offered in Part II including accountancy, management science, marketing, retail studies, European business, taxation and personnel management. Students on courses in the School of Management combine business with a foreign language (French, German, Spanish or Japanese). Over forty joint courses are also offered covering Business Studies and Human Resource Management.

Strathclyde (*Business*) The Strathclyde Business School offers a BA course with principal subjects offered to single Honours level, eg Accounting, Administration, Economics, Industrial Relations, Marketing, International Business and Modern Languages.

Sunderland (*Business Studies*) The foundation course lasts until half-way through the second year of this four year course, when students may begin to specialise in marketing, finance, systems, human resource management or European business through their choice of electives. The third year is spent on an industrial or commercial placement. Joint courses with Business Studies as well as a European Business course are also available with options in French, German or Spanish.

Surrey (*Retail Management*) In this sandwich course with placement in Year 3 there are options in Fashion, Homeware, Food and Nutrition Management and International Retailing. Business courses are also offered with Mathematics and Physics.

Sussex Over ten joint courses are offered with Mathematics, Engineering and Science courses.

Swansea (*Business Studies; Management Science*) In the first year core subjects in computing, accountancy and statistics are taken, leading to specialist topics in the third year. The university also offers courses in European Business (France, Germany, Italy or Spain) and also American Business Studies courses.

Teesside (*Business Studies*) Emphasis is placed on small and medium-sized firms. Main subjects in the first two years are economics, accountancy, law, computer applications in business, marketing and people at work. Industrial placement occupies Year 3 and specialised options are provided in the fourth year. Courses are also offered in Human Resource Management and Business Studies (Europe) (France, Germany or Spain).

Thames Valley (*Business Studies*) This is a thin sandwich course of four years which includes industrial training, psychology or modern languages (French, German, Spanish). The languages can be taken in the third year.

Ulster (*Business Studies*) The four year course offers disciplines relevant to the business world, with elective choices in the fourth year taken from personnel, marketing, finance, production and small businesses. Year 3 is spent in work experience. Courses are also offered in European Business Studies and Business Studies with Japanese.

Warwick (*Management Science*) Basic subjects are taken in the first two years and with core subjects in Year 2 covering organisational behaviour, economics and quantitative methods. The International Business course recruits by way of French, German or Italian streams. Several joint courses are also offered with science and engineering subjects. The department has a top teaching rating.

Westminster (*Business Studies*) A four year sandwich course with optional languages and major areas of study in marketing, accounting and international business. European Land Management is also offered with French, German, Italian or Spanish.

Wolverhampton (*Business Studies*) A general business course with in-depth study of specialist areas - accounting, information management and human resource management. Supervised work placement takes place in Year 3. There is also a European language option. Modular courses are also offered which include Business and a European Business programme is also available.

York Business management courses are offered which include Information Technology and languages and also with Physics.

● **Top research universities**
Bradford, Lancaster, London (LSE), UMIST, Warwick, Strathclyde, City, Southampton, Cardiff.

● **Colleges and Institutes of Higher Education offering degree courses**
Askham Bryan (Coll), Bangor Normal (Coll), Barnsley (Coll), Bath (Coll), Bedford (Coll), Bishop Grosseteste (Coll), Bolton (Inst), Bradford and Ilkley (Comm Coll), Brunel (Univ Coll), Bucks (Coll), Canterbury (Chr.Ch.Coll), Cardiff (Inst), Cheltenham and Gloucester (Coll), Colchester (Inst), Dartington (Coll), Doncaster (Coll), Edge Hill (Coll),

European Business School, Farnborough (Coll), Gwent (Coll), Harper Adams (Coll), King Alfred's (Coll), Leeds (Trinity & All Saints Coll), London (Inst), Matthew Boulton (Coll), Nene (Coll), Newman (Coll), North East Wales (Inst), Northern (Coll), Norwich City (Coll), Queen Margaret (Coll), Ripon/York St. Johns (Coll), Roehampton (Inst), Royal Agricultural (Coll), Scottish Agricultural (Coll), Salford (Univ Coll), Scarborough (Univ Coll), Southampton (Inst), Stockport (Coll), Suffolk (Coll), Swansea (Inst), Warrington (Coll Inst), West Herts (Coll), Worcester (Coll), Writtle (Coll).

- **Other courses to be considered**
Accountancy, banking, economics and insurance, in addition to the alternative courses listed under 'subject information' at the beginning of this table.

CHEMISTRY

- **Special subject requirements:** 2–3 A-levels from mathematics/science subjects. Chemistry 'required' or 'preferred' in most cases.

- **Subject information:** There is a considerable shortage of applicants for this subject which has very many career applications. These include oceanography (marine chemistry), agriculture and environmental work, colour chemistry, medical chemistry, pharmacy, pharmacology and polymer science. Refer to tables covering these subjects.

Aberdeen (*Chemistry*) Two courses are offered, one for students wishing to proceed to further studies in physical, organic and inorganic chemistry, the other being a broader course mainly for students interested in biology or the applied sciences. Level 3 allows for specialisation including environmental and industrial chemistry. Chemistry is also offered with languages (French, German or Spanish).

Abertay Dundee (*Applied Chemistry*) This is a flexible course with options in Year 3 and 4 allowing specialisations in Chemistry with Business Management, Materials Chemistry, Environmental Chemistry, Pharmaceutical Chemistry, Analytical Chemistry, Accounting, Economics or a European language.

Anglia (**Poly Univ**) (*Chemistry*) A three year full-time course based in Cambridge covering organic, inorganic and physical chemistry. Specialisations include archaeological, polymer and environmental chemistry. Chemistry is offered with languages (French, German, Italian or Spanish) and courses include Chemistry in Society and Medicinal Chemistry.

Aston (*Chemistry; Applied Chemistry*) The course involves organic, inorganic and physical chemistry, computer-based studies, learning aids, business skills and economics. The emphasis throughout is on the applications of chemistry to industry and commerce. There is extensive laboratory work. Sandwich and full-time courses are possible and the opportunity to transfer to the degree course in Chemical Engineering is a feature of these courses.

Bangor (*Chemistry*) Year 1 is modular with students choosing 12 modules. Emphasis throughout centres on small group tutorials. Major subject choices can be changed at the end of Year 1. Courses with European Experience are also offered. (*Marine Chemistry*) This course is run jointly by the School of Ocean Sciences and the Department of Chemistry. Aspects of chemistry with particular relevance to the ocean as a chemical system are studied. This involves the natural organic and inorganic components of the sea and the assessment of pollution problems in estuaries and coastal waters. A top quality rating department.

Bath (*Chemistry*) Part I covers the first two years after which students either can take a year's industrial training before starting Part II or proceed directly to Part II. The final decision can be made at the end of the second year. Chemistry is taken with ancillary maths in the first year with options in biochemistry, physics, languages (French, German, Italian), education or chemical engineering. The second year includes computing with a range of special topics following in Part II including advanced analytical chemistry, petrochemicals and polymer chemistry. Students can also take a four year course which includes a Certificate in Education. Chemistry can also be studied with a period abroad and also as part of a Natural Sciences programme.

Belfast (*Chemistry*) The course is designed to provide a basic understanding of all the major aspects of chemistry, allowing some degree of choice in the final year of study. It is also possible to combine chemistry with Computer Science and chemistry with a study in Europe (France, Germany or Spain).

Birmingham (*Chemistry*) First year students also take a course chosen from physics, biological sciences, geological sciences, or computer science. Final year options include those with an environmental chemistry bias. Courses are offered with a year in industry or a year in Europe.

Bradford (*Chemistry and Chemical Technology*) The course consists of four equal components - inorganic, physical and organic chemistry, and chemical technology, ie applications and processing of chemicals. Subsidiary subjects studied are computing and mathematics. The third term of the final year is a full-time research project. Options are available in polymers, dye stuffs and chemical engineering. Chemistry is also offered as part of several joint courses including Management and Pharmaceutical and Forensic Science.

Brighton Chemistry is offered as part of several joint courses.

Bristol (*Chemistry*) Chemistry is taken in Year 1 with two other subjects from: biochemistry, physics, geology, maths, or computer methods. In Year 2, chemistry is taken with one other from: environmental chemistry, chemistry and industry, computer methods, biochemistry. The third year involves a research project. Special emphasis in Years 2 and 3 on synthetic and bio-organic chemistry, organometallic chemistry and surface and colloid polymer chemistry. A top quality rating department.

Bristol UWE (*Applied Chemical Sciences*) This is a three year full-time or four year sandwich course with five final year options including environmental monitoring and pollution control. Chemistry is also available in the Combined Sciences programme.

Brunel (*Chemistry; Applied Chemistry; Medicinal and Environmental Chemistry; Chemistry with Management*) The first foundation semester is common to all courses allowing students to change their degree specialisation. In addition to the three year full-time mode, the last three can be can be taken as four year sandwich courses, providing valuable experience in the application of the subject. Enhanced schemes leading to the MChem are available.

Cambridge Chemistry is offered as part of the Natural Sciences programme in which first year scientists choose three sciences from the Biology of Cells, Biology of Organisms, Chemistry, Materials and Mineral Sciences, Geology, Physics and Physiology depending on their objectives. The course is designed for those who wish to specialise in chemistry and also for those whose interests lie in subjects such as geology, biochemistry and pharmacology. A top quality rating department.

Cardiff (*Chemistry; Applied Chemistry; Industrial Chemistry*) All courses have the same academic content in Year 1. Transfer between courses is possible within the first year. Medicinal chemistry, polymer science and technology are specialisms in the Chemistry course. Applied and Industrial Chemistry focuses on applied aspects including catalysis, polymer chemistry and industrial processes. A top quality rating department.

Central Lancashire (*Chemistry; Applied Chemistry*) Study in Europe is possible with language options in French, German and Spanish. There are also courses in Biological Chemistry, Chemistry and International Business and a four year BSc in Chemistry. There is also a Combined Honours programme with Chemistry.

Coventry (*Applied Chemistry*) Three subjects are taken in Year 1. Decisions on a choice of single subject or combined course are delayed until the end of the first year. The second and final years offer a selection of areas of special interest and a year of professional training provides first-hand experience of the chemical industry. In Year 2 French or German can be studied from a GCSE base. There is also a course focusing on Pharmaceutical Chemistry and over 12 joint courses including Applied Chemistry and Management.

De Montfort (*Applied Chemistry*) This is a four year sandwich course. Topics include environmental, pharmaceutical, polymer and biological chemistry and information technology. Chemistry is also offered as part of the Combined Sciences programme and with Business Studies.

Derby (*Chemistry*) A modular course with an opportunity to study analytical and/or environmental chemistry.

Dundee (*Chemistry*) This is offered as a single Honours subject, as half of a combined course in Biological or Medical Chemistry or jointly with other science subjects and also with accountancy and economics.

Durham (*Chemistry*) The first year Honours course may be accompanied by a wide range of subsidiary courses including computing, electronics, biology, business studies, history and philosophy of science etc. If a suitable first year course is chosen, then a subsequent Honours course can include chemistry as part of a joint Honours course (Zoology or Physics and Chemistry of Materials) or as part of the Natural Sciences course (with Biology, Maths, Physics, etc.). Common first year courses provide maximum flexibility. The third year course includes optional theory courses and an optional research project. A top quality rating department.

East Anglia (*Chemistry; Chemistry/USA; Chemistry/Europe*) The flexibility in the choice of units in the chemistry course enables a range of scientific areas to be studied. Therefore the overall content of the degree programme depends to a large extent on the interests and strengths of an individual student. The Chemistry/USA course extends over three years with the second year spent at the University of Massachusetts, Amherst. Courses studied in the USA count fully towards the degree classification. For the Chemistry/Europe course students study at a university in Denmark, France, Germany or The Netherlands during the third year of their course. In addition to participating in undergraduate teaching programmes, students are encouraged to develop their knowledge of the cultural and social life of their host country.

Edinburgh (*Chemistry; Environmental Chemistry*) A wide range of additional subjects can be taken in the Chemistry course. Environmental chemistry covers topics which include the natural environment, natural resources, and chemistry in relation to man's activities. A top quality rating department.

Essex (*Chemistry*) Six degree schemes are offered including biochemistry offered jointly with the Department of Biology. First year courses are designed so that there is a choice of at least two degree schemes at the end of the year. Courses including European Business Studies or Environmental and Industrial Chemistry are also available.

Exeter (*Chemistry*) Three year and four year courses are planned on the unit course system which provides a considerable flexibility and wide range of options. First year lectures are supplemented by courses in mathematics and another subject. Chemistry is offered with European Study, Industrial Experience and Law.

Glamorgan (*Chemistry*) Core modules include maths, computing, inorganic and analytical chemistry with specialisms in Years 3 and 4 in pharmaceutical, agrochemistry and food chemistry. The study of a foreign language can be continued throughout the course. Several joint courses are offered along with Combined Science and Combined Studies programmes.

Glasgow (*Chemistry*) This is a broad course which provides a basis of the principles of chemical science in the early years and leads to special topics at Honours level in the fourth year. There are also courses with specialisms in computer applications and medical chemistry. A top quality rating department.

Glasgow Caledonian Courses are offered with Information Technology and Instrumentation.

Greenwich (*Applied Chemistry*) Specialist courses include biochemistry, microbiology, biotechnology, materials science, and chemistry in medicine and agriculture. Year 3 is spent in industrial placement, or in work and study in another EC country. There is also a course in Applied

Geochemistry with environmental and oil exploration options. There are also courses in Pharmaceutical Chemistry and joint courses with Business Management and European Studies.

Heriot-Watt (*Chemistry*) Chemistry, maths and physics are taken in the first year of the three year course to Ordinary level or four years to Honours level. Optional subjects on this course include computer science, physics and accountancy and finance. Courses in Colour Chemistry and Chemistry with Polymers are also on offer in addition to the Combined Science programme.

Hertfordshire (*Chemistry*) A foundation year provides a basic grounding followed by pure chemistry in Year 2 and professional training in Year 3. Specialised areas include analytical chemistry, chemical technology and medicinal chemistry. Chemistry is also offered in the Modular Scheme and with over 30 joint courses.

Huddersfield (*Chemistry*) A modular course with options in Year 2 leading to biochemistry or chemical technology. Fourth year options include chemical engineering and management.

Hull (*Chemistry*) Basic chemistry is offered in the first four semesters followed by a choice of options. To obtain a degree in Chemistry with Bio-organic Chemistry and Toxicology students follow final year options in medicinal chemistry and toxicology. In addition a study of toxicology and forensic science leads to the degree in Chemistry with Analytical Chemistry and Toxicology. Topics include the natural environment, natural resources, and chemistry in relation to man's activities. Chemistry with French or German is also offered.

Keele (*Chemistry*) This can be taken in combination with 20 other subjects including arts subjects and three languages. Students taking some of these combinations may take single Honours chemistry in the final year. The Chemistry course covers the main areas of chemistry with a selection of options in the final year.

Kent (*Chemistry*) A number of chemistry courses are offered including Chemistry with Environmental Science, Business Studies or Management Science which include a year in Europe. Part I contains common core subjects and enables students to make final decisions on Part II courses at the end of the first year. The final year contains a range of options.

Kingston (*Applied Chemistry*) Industrial placement takes place throughout Year 3. The second year contains options in life sciences or petrochemicals. The final year contains major options in medical chemistry or polymer chemistry and minor options in computers and laboratory automation or chemistry and society. Courses focusing on Medical Chemistry and Chemistry with Business are also available.

Lancaster (*Chemistry; Chemistry with Polymer Science*) Students taking these courses follow alternative Part I schemes. The latter course will have special appeal for those aiming for a career in the plastics and rubber industries. In the Chemistry USA course students spend the second year at a university in the USA. There is also a course with modern languages (French, German, Italian or Spanish). Several joint courses are also offered in addition to a wide choice on the Combined Science programme.

Leeds (*Chemistry; Medicinal Chemistry; Chemistry with Analytical Chemistry*) These three single subject courses have the same academic standing and a common first year; they are offered at BSc and MChem level and may be coupled with a year abroad or in industry. Leeds also offers a Colour Chemistry degree. The course provides both a general degree in applied chemistry, and specialised training in all aspects of dye chemistry, textile, paint and ink technology, photochemistry and spectroscopy, and carries professional recognition as a chemistry degree. A wide range of joint courses are also offered. A top quality rating department.

Leeds Metropolitan A course in Applied Chemistry is offered with Business Studies. Modules include food chemistry, financial management, international marketing and employee relations.

Leicester (*Chemistry*) Students in Chemistry study a supplementary subject in the first year from a choice of other science subjects and astronomy, economics, geology and computing. In Year 2 a course in computing for chemists is offered whilst third year courses cover options in physical, organic and inorganic chemistry. Chemistry can also be taken with a placement in Europe or in the USA. A top quality rating department.

Liverpool (*Chemistry*) In the first year chemistry can be taken with physics or mathematics or life sciences. Additional options in the second year include materials science, oceanography, computer science, biochemistry or pharmacology. There are also degree courses in Chemistry and Oceanography or Pharmacology and a new degree course in Chemistry with Industrial Chemistry or a European language.

Liverpool John Moores (*Applied Chemistry*) Three year degrees (with optional sandwich placement years) are offered in Applied Chemistry, Environmental Chemical Analysis and Industrial Chemistry, exploring the principles and applications of modern chemistry.

London (Imp) (*Chemistry*) The department offers: three year courses in Chemistry and Chemistry with Management; four year courses in Chemistry, and Chemistry with Biotechnology, Biochemistry, Medicinal Chemistry, a Year in Europe or in Industry, or Management and a Year in Industry; and a selection of five year BSc and MSci courses.

London (King's) (*Chemistry*) All courses contain a central core of chemistry and a wide range of complementary courses are offered. Transfer from single to joint Honours is possible. A range of other chemistry degree courses is also offered including Biological Chemistry, Chemistry with Analytical Chemistry and Chemistry with a Year in Europe.

London (QMW) (*Chemistry*) In the first year a supporting subject is taken with chemistry such as computer science, maths or physics or a subject involving the applications of chemistry such as biochemistry or geology. Integrated and flexible schemes allow students to specialise in chemistry, biological chemistry, environmental chemistry and other options.

London (UC) (*Chemistry; Chemical Physics; Medicinal Chemistry*) Chemistry students take a course in maths and two other courses from a range of science subjects and also computer science, psychology, statistics and languages. The course in Chemical Physics provides an emphasis in maths and physics whilst the Medicinal Chemistry course includes biology, pharmacology, physiology and biochemistry. Chemistry can also be studied with mathematics, management studies, materials science or a European language with 75% of the course chemistry and 25% the elected option. All courses may be taken as three year BSc or a four year MSc.

Loughborough (*Chemistry*) There are several courses offered including chemistry with Analytical Chemistry, Polymer Chemistry/Technology, Medicinal and Pharmaceutical Chemistry and Physical Education and Sports Science. All have three or four year options except the Sports Science course.

Manchester (*Chemistry*) The department was one of only a few to be rated 'excellent' following the Teaching Quality Assessment Audit. Nine courses are offered, including Medicinal Chemistry and Patent Law, and opportunities to study for a year in industry or Europe.

Manchester Metropolitan (*Chemical Science*) Transfers are possible to the Applied Chemistry or Chemistry degrees. In Applied Chemistry it is possible to take a year in industry in the UK or Europe.

Manchester (UMIST) (*Chemistry*) Five topics are covered in the first two years - chemistry, industrial chemistry, chemical physics, polymer chemistry and analytical chemistry. There is a common two year core chemistry course for all students before specialising in the third year. The distinguishing features of Chemistry at UMIST are the range of courses open to students and the industrial relevance given to the subjects. Several courses are also offered in various Chemistry specialisms such as Environmental, Industrial and Medicinal Chemistry.

Napier (*Applied Chemistry*) A three year full-time or four year sandwich course specialising in polymer science and technology or analytical science and technology in Years 3 and 4.

Newcastle (*Chemistry*) Chemistry is taken with two other subjects in the first year and a wide range of topics is offered in the final year. Transfers are possible to Chemistry with Applied Chemistry and Medical Chemistry. Newcastle also offers a preliminary year for those without certain A-level and GCSE subjects. An optional industrial year is possible.

North London (*Chemistry*) There is a sandwich placement in this course occupying most of the third year. Final year specialisms include agricultural, medicinal, environmental and pollution chemistry. Chemistry is also offered as a component on the BSc modular degree.

Northumbria (*Applied Chemistry*) This is a three year full-time or four year sandwich course with the industrial training period in Year 3 or a European route. A short course in production management is offered in the fourth year. Major options include biochemistry, chemical engineering, environmental chemistry and food science.

Nottingham (*Chemistry*) This is a modular course with options in a wide range of subjects (scientific and non-scientific) in all years and the opportunity to transfer to the MSc (4 year) course at the end of the second year. (*Chemistry and Molecular Physics*) Foundation modules in chemistry, physics and mathematics lead to specialisms covering inorganic and quantum chemistry, electro chemistry, medical imaging electronics and lasers. A top quality rating department.

Nottingham Trent *(Applied Chemistry)* This is a sandwich course with main studied chosen from analytical chemistry, applied surface chemistry or applied organic chemistry. French and German options. A top quality rating department.

Oxford *(Chemistry)* This is a four year course, with the fourth year spent doing research. All undergraduates attend a brief course in computing and their time is divided equally between chemistry lectures, practical work and preparation for tutorials and classes. A top quality rating department.

Oxford Brookes *(Environmental Chemistry)* The central theme of this course is the chemical nature of biogeochemical cycling processes and how these affect and control the environment. The course covers fundamental aspects of chemical reactions, bonding, and energy transfer, atmospheric chemistry and pollution measurement and control. *(Biological Chemistry)* The behaviour of molecules in living systems is the main theme, while molecular genetics, the molecular basis of disease, pharmacology and toxicology are also covered.

Paisley *(Chemistry)* In addition to a broad study of organic, inorganic and physical chemistry, students choose two other science subjects in Year 1 and may continue with one of them in Year 2. Optional industrial placement takes place in Year 3.

Plymouth *(Applied Chemistry)* The first two years provide a comprehensive grounding in the subject. Areas of specialisation include modern material and porous media (oil bearing rocks, paper coatings etc). Chemistry may be read as a major or minor subject in the Combined Honours scheme and a large number of joint courses are also offered.

Portsmouth *(Applied Chemistry)* This is a sandwich degree course in which study of 'pure' chemistry is completed in Years 1 and 2, thereby allowing Year 4 (after the industrial training year) to be devoted to the study of Applied Chemistry. Options include analytical chemistry, corrosion/ electrochemistry (unique to undergraduate courses) and fuels and energy. A full-time research project concludes the course. There is also a joint Honours programme with Chemistry.

Reading *(Chemistry)* In Part I students take three units of chemistry and three from a wide selection of other units. In terms 3, 4 and 5 Chemistry students spend two-third of their time on chemistry and one-third on a subsidiary subject. Thereafter, their whole time is spent on chemistry, with equal emphasis on inorganic, organic and physical chemistry throughout most of the course, but with some specialisation in the third year. Courses with a year in Europe are also offered and also several joint courses.

Robert Gordon *(Applied Chemistry)* From the basis of inorganic, physical and organic chemistry a wide range of applied topics can be studied with analytical chemistry a major integrating theme. A top quality rating department.

Salford (*Chemistry*) 12 chemistry courses are offered including full-time and sandwich options. Foreign languages can be studied. In the Chemistry course, considerable flexibility exists in Years 1 and 2 in the choice of ancillary subjects. Training periods are possible in Belgium, France, Germany and Switzerland (practical language tuition available). For Chemistry/USA the second year is spent in Ohio and with Chemistry/France the third year in Lyons (GCSE (Grades A–C) French required: French language tuition is given in the first and second years).

Sheffield (*Chemistry*) During the first year a complementary subject is followed from a very wide range of subjects. A subsidiary subject is also taken in the second year which can include a modern language. The third year course is entirely devoted to chemistry; joint courses with Chemistry can also be taken. The course structure adopts a modular approach linked to examinations which permit students to proceed at different rates through the course depending upon background and ability.

Sheffield Hallam (*Applied Chemistry*) This is a sandwich degree course. In the final year up to one third of the chemistry studies can be replaced by industrial studies (operational planning and marketing). Options include biomedical studies (genetics, quality and safety and pharmacology), European languages and environmental chemistry. Chemistry is also offered with Combined Studies, Management and Environmental Science.

Southampton (*Chemistry*) The first year course includes maths for chemists, oceanography and computer science. In the second year chemistry is combined with oceanography and biology. Chemistry occupies the whole of the final year. Over 20 joint courses with Chemistry are offered. A top quality rating department.

St Andrews (*Chemistry*) Basic studies occupy the first and second years, certain subjects being obligatory in the Second Science course for those taking the joint Honours course in Chemistry with Pharmacology (chemistry and physiology). There is also a degree in Geochemistry. A top quality rating department.

Staffordshire (*Applied and Analytical Chemistry*) This course focuses on applied aspects of chemistry such as the development of new commercial materials and the use of analytical skills. Options in the second and third years include mathematics, polymers, pharmaceutical and toxicological chemistry. Chemistry, Environmental Chemistry and several joint Honours degrees are also offered.

Stirling (*Chemistry*) This course is offered to General Degree level with specialisation in atmospheric, water and soil chemistry in Year 3. Students wishing to proceed to Honours level transfer to another Scottish university at the end of Year 2.

Strathclyde (*Chemistry; Applied Chemistry*) All students take the same course in the first three years after which there is an industrial placement of 5 or 12 months duration. The choice between degrees in Chemistry and Applied Chemistry is then made. There is also a course in Forensic and Analytical Chemistry. A top quality rating department.

Sunderland (*Chemical and Pharmaceutical Science*) A comprehensive understanding of pharmaceutical and chemical science is developed through extensive study of chemical and biological analysis. Emphasis is placed on the scrutiny of pharmaceuticals, together with drug design and formulation. Final year specialisms include drug development, medical chemistry, forensic analysis, environmental analysis and food analysis. An optional sandwich year is available. Chemistry can also be studied in the Combined Programme with a choice of nine other subjects, covering everything from basic atomic structure to kinetics and spectroscopic techniques.

Surrey (*Chemistry*) The main areas are covered in the first year which also includes computing and management studies. Ninety per cent of entrants take the four year course with one year of industrial training, mostly in Europe, Canada, Australia and New Zealand. An exchange scheme in the USA can replace Year 2. Industrial chemistry is studied in all years. For those taking the alternative degree in Computer-Aided Chemistry, half the course is occupied with computing. Industrial placement takes place in the third year. Major and minor options occupy the final year. A strong feature of this course are the specially equipped computer applications laboratories supported by industrial sponsors. Chemistry for Europe (France or Germany) is designed to produce bilingual chemists and involves intensive courses in the language and professional training in the appropriate country. Courses are also offered in Chemistry with Management Studies, Analytical and Environmental Chemistry and Chemistry with a PGCE.

Sussex (*Chemistry*) All students take the preliminary course (terms 1 and 2), then follow courses in chemistry or in joint combinations which include languages, management science and polymer science. Chemistry can also be offered with a Minor in European Studies (French, German, Italian or Spanish) and with North American and Management Studies.

Swansea (*Chemistry*) This subject can be studied jointly with Analytical Science in Europe, Japan, the USA, or a year in industry. Biomedical Chemistry, Environmental Chemistry are also options, and there are also 20 joint courses with chemistry. There is an industrially sponsored scholarship scheme.

Teesside (*Chemistry*) The course includes a three month external placement towards the end of the second year. The course in Manufacturing Chemistry provides graduates with qualifications in chemistry and chemical engineering. Other chemical and biotechnological sciences can be studied in the modular science scheme.

Ulster Chemistry can be studied with Biology.

Warwick (*Chemistry*) Considerable flexibility exists for first year students to transfer from one Chemistry course to another in the second and third years. Chemistry may be combined with several subjects including medicinal chemistry, business studies, psychology and industrial environmental chemistry.

Wolverhampton (*Applied Chemistry*) This is a modular course involving organic, physical and inorganic chemistry complemented by modules on analytical and industrial chemistry, polymers and water science. Chemistry is also offered on the Applied Sciences and Modular degree schemes.

York (*Chemistry*) All students, irrespective of their choice of Chemistry degree course, follow the same first year (Part I) course which includes some maths, computing and biochemistry. Part II includes more advanced chemistry studies and a choice of modules which allows students to specialise in mainstream Chemistry, Chemistry Management and Industry, Chemistry Resources and the Environment or Chemistry, Life Systems and Pharmaceuticals. Students on the MChem course can spend their fourth year at York, in industry or in Europe.

• Top research universities
Bath, Birmingham, Bristol, Cambridge, Durham, East Anglia, Exeter, Leeds, Liverpool, London (Imp), Manchester, Newcastle, Nottingham, Oxford, Reading, Sheffield, Southampton, Sussex, York, Edinburgh, St Andrews.

• Colleges and Institutes of Higher Education also offering degree courses
Bradford and Ilkley (Comm. Coll), Halton (Coll), North East Wales (Inst), Salford (Univ Coll), St Mary's (Coll), Stockport (Coll).

• Other courses to be considered
Agriculture, biochemistry, botany, ceramics, chemical engineering, environmental science, pharmacology and pharmacy.

CLASSICAL STUDIES/CLASSICAL CIVILISATION/ CLASSICS

• Special subject requirements: A GCSE (grade A–C) language occasionally specified. For Classical Studies the following universities 'require' or 'prefer' a foreign language at A-level or GCSE (grade A–C) as a subject requirement: Aberdeen, Bristol, Durham, London (QMW), (RH). For AS-level subject requirements check with prospectus and admissions tutors. For Classics, Latin and/or Greek are usually required.

• Subject information: The literature, history, philosophy and archaeology of Ancient Greece and Rome are covered by these subjects. A knowledge of classical languages is not necessary for many courses. Ancient History and Archaeology may also be of interest as alternative courses.

Aberystwyth (*Classical Studies*) The course covers Greek and Roman Civilisations, Epic and Drama and a wide range of topics in Years 2 and 3. Classical Studies is offered as a joint course with over ten other subjects.

Belfast (*Classical Studies*) Literature, art, society and Ancient Greece and Rome are studied. There is an option to start Greek or Latin. Latin, Greek and Classical Studies joint courses are also offered.

Birmingham (*Classics*) In this course, students make a study of Greek and Latin language, literature, history and archaeology. A four week study tour in classical locations is part of the course. (A-level Latin required, Greek preferred). In addition Latin and Greek are offered as single Honours subjects and as joint Honours courses with a large number of other subjects. There are also courses with Greek and Roman Studies.

Bristol (*Classical Studies*) There is an emphasis on literature and philosophy in this course rather than on archaeology and history. Reading from the Latin and Greek is an integral part of the course. (GCSE (grades A–C) language required). (*Classics*) The course provides an advanced training in translating, understanding and appreciation of Greek and Roman literature. (A-level Latin required, Greek preferred). Courses in Latin and Greek are also offered. Classics and Classical Studies are also offered with study in Continental Europe. (A leading Classics department in the UK).

Cambridge (*Classics; Greek and Latin*) Part I is taken at the end of the second year and covers the literature, history, philosophy, art and architecture of classical civilisation. Classics is an appropriate subject for anyone aiming to read another Tripos in their third year, for example, Archaeology and Anthropology, English, History, Law, Philosophy or Theology and Religious Studies.

Durham (*Classics*) One of the largest departments in the UK with a wide range of courses. Classics I offers a choice of courses in literature, history and philosophy. Classics II offers a similar course except that it is open to students without Greek A-level. For Classical Studies A-levels in Latin or Greek are not required. Latin is also offered as a single Honours course whilst Greek can be combined with Philosophy or Ancient History. Latin and Greek and Roman Civilisation are also offered on the Arts Combined programme.

Edinburgh (*Classics*) A study is made of the Greek and Roman civilisations with equal amounts of Greek and Latin. Additional subjects in the first year include ancient history or other courses closely related to Greek and Latin, for example, classical archaeology. In addition a special subject is studied during one term of each year. These include classical archaeology, Greek and Roman religion and law (Latin and Greek A-levels, required). Greek and Latin Studies are also offered as single and joint Honours courses.

Essex (*Classics*) The department offers courses in Latin, Greek and Greek and Roman Studies. There is a two part examination system (Part I and II). Part I teaching is done in small groups with special subject; teaching in Part II is of an individual nature. A wide range of topics is a feature of Year 3.

Glasgow (*Classical Civilisation*) The course covers drama, poetry, history and philosophy. A-level Latin and Greek are not required. Latin, Greek and Classical Civilisation are offered on a very wide range of joint courses.

Keele (*Classical Studies*) Poetry, prose, art, architecture and drama are studied. Greek or Latin A-level is not required. Latin and Classical Studies are offered on a very large range of joint courses.

Kent Degrees are offered in Greek and Latin (requiring a previous knowledge of classical languages) Classical Studies and Classical Civilisation (requiring no such prior knowledge) although these languages may be studied from scratch. A course which explores the literary, political and intellectual aspects of the Athenian and Roman Empires. A large number of Latin and Greek courses are also available.

Lampeter (*Classical Studies*) No previous knowledge of classical languages is required, although students are advised to take Greek or Latin as a Part I subject. The subject enables students to develop individual special interests covering literature, art, history, archaeology, philosophy and religion. (*Classics*) Latin and Greek A-level are required. The main emphasis of this course lies in the study of languages and classical texts. Latin and Greek and Classical Studies are also offered as joint courses with an extensive range of other courses.

Leeds (*Classics*) Classical languages are required for this course in which schemes comprise a study of both literature and language. Modern Greek may be studied. (*Classical Civilisation*) Classical languages are not required for this broad study of the literature, language, history and art of Greece and Rome. A subsidiary subject is taken in Year 1 on both courses. Joint courses with Latin, Greek, Classical Literature, Greek and Roman Civilisation are also offered.

Liverpool (*Classics*) Classics, Latin and Greek have been amalgamated into one Classics course enabling the department to offer more closely co-ordinated teaching and greater flexibility. Classical Studies involves a study of (a) ancient history and classical archaeology (b) Greek and/or Latin language and literature - with a bias in favour of (a) or (b). Both languages are available from scratch. Classics is also available on the Arts Combined and Social Combined courses.

London (King's) (*Classics*) A course unit structure is now in operation which has less emphasis on the final examination. Single Honours courses in Classics, Latin, Greek, Ancient History and Classical Studies are offered. Classical Studies is designed for students without A-level Latin or Greek. Transfer between courses is possible except for Classical Studies.

London (RH) (*Classical Studies*) The degree is particularly suitable for those wishing to give more time to archaeological, philosophical or other less language-oriented topics. Courses in Latin and Greek at single and joint Honours levels can also be taken.

London (UC) (*Classics*) In the first year Latin and Greek (prominent in all years) are provided at three levels - beginners, intermediate and advanced. Topics for detailed study include Greek philosophy, sculpture, drama and history, Roman Britain, law and history and Latin satire, elegy and late and medieval Latin, art and architecture. It is possible to take a degree in Greek with Latin or Latin with Greek. There is also a degree course in Ancient World Studies and Ancient History courses are also available.

Manchester (*Classical Studies*) A wide range of options is offered in Years 2 and 3 with the opportunity to study Greek and Latin in all years. Joint courses with both subjects are offered.

Newcastle (*Classical Studies*) This course is varied and flexible and allows students to concentrate on areas and topics of particular interest to them such as art, archaeology, history and philosophy. No previous knowledge of Greek or Latin is required for entry. The department is noted for its expertise in teaching the languages to beginners. The courses in Classics,

Latin with Greek and Greek with Latin offer a rigorous study of two superb literatures set within a study of an entire civilisation. Language work is stressed in the first year. Later years are devoted to such topics as epic, drama and lyric with a wide range of options. Latin and Greek can also be taken as part of the Combined Studies programme.

North London Classical Civilisation is offered as part of the Combined Honours programme.

Nottingham (*Classics*) The course has an emphasis on literature and is designed for students with a good knowledge of Latin. The central concern for the Honours Latin course is the world of Rome. The course in Classical Civilisation at Honours level surveys the achievement of the Graeco-Roman world without requiring a previous knowledge of Latin or Greek which are studied in the first year. Joint courses are also offered with Latin, Greek and Classical Civilisation.

Oxford (*Classics*) The Honours School of Literae Humaniores provides a unique combination of classics, philosophy and ancient history. The course lasts four years to enable students to gain a firm knowledge of Latin and Greek. It is possible to offer literature as an alternative to history or philosophy in the second part of the course. Interests in history, philosophy, literature, philology or archaeology may be pursued throughout the course. Classics may be offered with modern languages.

Reading Courses are offered in Classics (in which a fluent reading knowledge of Greek and Latin is required), Classical Studies, Latin (Classical and Medieval). The main core of these courses lies in a series of options chosen from : epic, drama, poetry, satire, the novel, history, art and philosophy. Ample opportunity exists for students to specialise or diversify in their chosen field. Joint courses with Classical Studies and Latin are also available.

St Andrews (*Classics*) Students may specialise in Greek or Latin (language and literature), and in addition study ancient history, ancient philosophy or some other aspect of Classical Studies. There is a degree course in Classical Studies covering poetry, drama, satire, religion and art for which language study is not compulsory whilst Latin and Greek are also offered as single and joint courses.

Swansea (*Classics*) The department offers courses in Classics, Latin and Greek and Roman Studies, or the languages may be combined with Ancient History and Civilisation.

Warwick (*Classical Civilisation*) The course covers the languages, literature, history, philosophy and archaeology of ancient Greece and Rome. Courses are also offered in Egyptology (one of the few universities offering this course). There are degree courses in Classics and Classical Civilisation with Philosophy.

● **Top research universities**
(Classics and Ancient History) Bristol, Cambridge, London (King's) (UC) (RH), Oxford, St Andrews, Birmingham, Durham, Exeter, Newcastle, Nottingham, Reading, Swansea.

• **Other courses to be considered**
Archaeology, ancient history and philosophy.

COMMUNICATION STUDIES

• **Special subject requirements:** These vary between courses. Check prospectuses.

• **Subject information:** Communications Studies courses are not necessarily a training for the media (see **Media Studies**) but extend to management, international communications, design and psychology. The courses listed here are those with the title 'Communications' and the reader is strongly advised to recognise the distinction which different universities and colleges will give to this title (check the prospectuses).

Anglia (Poly Univ) Communication Studies is offered as a joint course with 24 other subjects. The course includes modules in creative writing, information, video and radio.

Bradford (*Communications*) This is part of the Interdisciplinary Human Studies course which is broadly based in Years 1 and 2. Topics under 'Communications' include mass media, popular culture and the sociology of art and literature.

Brunel (*Communication and Information Studies*) A sandwich course: Part I focuses on sociology, psychology and economics or law with courses in computing, social anthropology, information technology, video and mass communications. Options include television and the media, medical sociology, mental illness and psychiatry and soap opera symbolism. The course is not intended as a practical course leading to media production.

Cardiff (*Communications*) The course combines subjects relating to linguistics, face-to-face and mass communication. A course is also offered in Language and Communication.

Central England (*Media and Communication Studies*) This is a half course emphasising the cultural and social issues of the mass media including photography. The course is intended for students aiming for careers in the media.

Coventry (*Communication Studies*) The course provides a study of sociology, psychology and cultural studies with the opportunity to study the work of journalists, advertisers and broadcasters. The emphasis of this degree is towards visual communication by way of photography, photojournalism, video, advertising, arts administration, film and TV. Exchange programme with universities in France and Belgium. (*Technical Communication*) This course involves graphics, psychology and electronic publishing.

East London Communication Studies is offered as a joint course with over 35 combinations and covers such topics as cinema and society, Indian cinema, youth culture and the media.

Glamorgan (*Communication Studies*) The course offers a study of culture, language, media and society in Year 1 with practical work (including information technology). Options in these subject areas follow in Years 2 and 3. Communication Studies is also offered as a combined or joint Honours course or in the Combined Studies programme.

Glasgow Caledonian Communication is offered jointly with Mass Media or Marketing. Practical studies include print, design, writing and video production. Options include advertising and a European language.

Huddersfield Communication Arts is offered jointly with either English, Theatre Studies or languages. The emphasis lies in the presentation of images, writing and expressive skills and information technology.

Humberside Courses are offered in Communication Processes which involves video, sound recording and writing.

Lancaster The university offers courses in Human Communication which involves linguistics, psychology and sociology.

Leeds (*Communications*) The three elements of this course are practical, professional and academic (which includes a foreign language). There is close liaison with the BBC TV training programmes.

Leicester (*Communications and Society*) The main focus lies in mass communication with modules in sociology.

Liverpool Communication Studies is offered with English and Politics and as part of the Social Combined programme. The course is theoretical in emphasis and includes topics on TV analysis, popular music, public media and the politics of language.

London (Goldsmiths') Communication Studies is offered with Anthropology. Media production, creative writing, computer graphics, photography and journalism are included in this course of Communication Studies.

London Guildhall Communication Studies is offered as part of the Modular programme. Practical aspects include film, TV, video, photojournalism, radio and journalistic writing.

Loughborough Communications is offered with Media Studies. This course has a sociological bias with options in social psychology, sociology of cultural communications, social policy and advertising.

Manchester Metropolitan A course is offered in Applied Human Communication. The course covers sociology and psychology and a language. Specialisms include interviewing and counselling.

Middlesex Communication Studies is offered as part of the multidisciplinary programme. Writing and video workshops are included in this course which can be taken at major or minor levels.

Napier (*Communication*) Students are prepared for careers in specific areas, eg advertising, public relations, marketing. The emphasis is on personal communication skills. It is not a media studies course. Spanish, French or German are language options.

Northumbria (*Information and Communication Management*) The course covers information technology, word processing, typographic design and management.

North London A course is offered in Communication and Cultural Studies. A broad academic course covering information and society. There are options in broadcasting, book publishing, women in the media and data technology.

Nottingham Trent (*Communication Studies*) This is a multidisciplinary degree covering literature, linguistics, psychology, sociology and practical work.

Robert Gordon The Communication with Modern Language course covers advertising and public relations.

Sheffield Hallam (*Communication Studies*) The course provides a broad study of human communication with particular reference to the role of language in British society. There is a modern language option. This is not a course in media training.

Sunderland (*Communication Studies*) This is a largely academic course covering sociology, linguistics, psychology and cultural studies. All students study documentary film, television and media audience research.

Wolverhampton Media and Communication courses are offered. The course involves sociological issues relating to the media (funding, ownership, gender, national identities etc). There are some opportunities for practical work with video.

- **Colleges and Institutes of Higher Education offering degree courses**
Bangor Normal (Coll), Cheltenham and Gloucester (Coll), Colchester (Inst), Edge Hill (Coll), King Alfred's (Coll), Leeds Trinity and All Saints (Coll), Queen Margaret (Coll), Ripon and York St John (Coll), Southampton (Inst), Ravensbourne (Coll).

- **Other courses to be considered**
Art, English, Psychology, Media Studies.

COMPUTER COURSES (including **Information Technology**)
(See also under **Computer Engineering**)

- **Special subject requirements:** For some courses mathematics A-level is specified. Mathematics at GCSE (grade A–C) usually essential.

- **Subject information:** Programming languages, data processing, systems analysis, artificial intelligence, graphics, software and hardware are all aspects of these courses. Several institutions offer courses with European languages and placements.

Aberdeen (*Computing Science*) Single and joint Honours courses are available covering all aspects of programming. Topics include artificial intelligence, software engineering and robotics, business computing, microprocessors and systems analysis.

Abertay Dundee (*Computing*) Three subjects are chosen by all students during Year 1 covering science and computing subjects with specialisation leading to the chosen degree taking place in later years. Computing and Computing Science are also offered jointly with several subjects.

Aberystwyth (*Computer Science*) This is a modular course with a choice of units including artificial intelligence, software engineering, computer graphics and industrial robotics. There is an optional year in industry. Several joint courses are also offered with computer science including European languages (French, German, Italian or Spanish).

Anglia (Poly Univ) (*Computer Science; Information Systems*) These are offered at the Cambridge and Chelmsford campuses respectively, jointly with several subjects. Courses are also available in Systems Modelling and as part of the Combined Science programme.

Aston (*Computing Science*) This course has an emphasis on practice in programming languages and applications, data processing and systems analysis. Artificial intelligence, graphics and software engineering are also part of the course. Professional training is a third year option.

Bangor (*Cognitive Science*) This course provides an interface between computing, psychology, linguistics, philosophy, neuroscience and mathematics. Courses are also offered in Computer Systems.

Bath (*Computer Software Technology*) This is a computer software course with a strong mathematical foundation. All students take maths, computation and statistics and follow a common first year with final course decisions taken in Year 2. Computing is also offered with Mathematics.

Belfast (*Computer Science*) Instruction is provided in the practice of programming with fundamental aspects of computer hardware during the first and second years. A year's industrial placement precedes the final year with a choice of options. Nine joint courses with Computer Science are also available and also a course in Information Management covering computer programming, finance and business policy.

Birmingham Joint courses are offered with Artificial Intelligence (Psychology, Philosophy and linguistics), computer science and computer studies.

Bournemouth (*Information Systems Management*) This is a four year sandwich course covering software development, business and management, and software technology. Computing is also offered with psychology and microelectronics.

Bradford There are two courses: Computer Science (the design of computer systems and software) and Computing and Information Systems (use of computational tools and the processing of organisational information). Both courses share a common first year, final choice being deferred to the end of the year. A- or AS-level in a mathematical subject is essential. There is an optional year in industry.

Brighton (*Computer Science*) The course has three main themes, software engineering, computer structure and information processing systems. Topics covered with these themes include programming, program design, computer engineering, computer networks, human-machine interaction and communication skills. Student-centred learning will be a feature of the course and course work will be an important part of the assessment.

(*Computer and Information Systems*) This degree course concentrates on developing computing expertise that can be directly applied to real-life situations, to meet the needs of information users of all kinds. Major areas of study are: the information environment, systems analysis, software and information technology. The course emphasises student-centred learning, with assessment significantly dependent on course work.

Bristol (*Computer Science*) During the first year all students study three subjects including languages, allowing maximum flexibility in choosing courses both within and outside Computer Science. In Year 2 the course involves programming, file structure, design operating systems and the comparisons of programming languages. Year 3 includes a one year optional course - topics from other departments may be chosen (eg conversational French). Computer Science can also be taken with Mathematics or a Modern Language.

Bristol UWE (*Computing for Real Time Systems*) There is a strong practical emphasis on this course and a modern languages option (no A-level maths required). The four year sandwich course allows for placement in Europe or the USA. (*Systems Analysis*) A course offering a combination of technology and social and organisation issues. Several Information Systems courses are offered jointly with other subjects including languages.

Brunel (*Computer Science*) There is an emphasis on software engineering, knowledge-based systems and artificial intelligence. Language options possible and placements abroad. Other courses offered are: Computer Science/Economics, no prior Economics required, one third of the study in economics; Computers in Business with 25 per cent business management modules and final specialisation in Information Systems Development; Computing and Psychology with one third of the study in psychology; Computer Science/Maths with one third of the study in mathematics.

Buckingham Computer Science is offered as a joint course with accounting, business studies, economics, mathematics, operations management and psychology.

Cambridge (*Computer Science*) Two courses are offered: (1) a two year course for students who have spent a year studying another subject, for example, Mathematics, Natural Sciences or Engineering. (2) A one year course, the Computer Science Tripos, for those who have spent two years reading another subject.

Cardiff (*Computer Science*) This is a broad course in Parts I and II, with modules on artificial intelligence, graphics, parallel computing, object-oriented languages and software engineering. There is also a course in Computer Systems which covers systems engineering, software engineering and the practical aspects of computing.

Central England (*Business Information Systems*) This is a sandwich course of four years with industrial placement in Year 3. Specialisms in information systems management, software engineering and human/machine interaction in the final year.

Central Lancashire (*Business Computing*) The course covers communication and social skills and systems analysis. There is also a course in Computing with European Language for Business offering French, German and Spanish. (*Business Information Technology*) Placements are offered in Europe, USA or China to appropriate students. Computing is also offered in the Combined Honours programme.

City (*Business Computing Systems*) The course encompasses not only theoretical and technical subjects but also knowledge of business and industry, and human communication skills. There is also a Health Informatics course covering intensive care clinical data and medical research.

Coventry (*Business Information Technology*) A modular programme covering business organisation, human resources management, information systems and programming. In addition to several joint courses there are also degrees in Business Computing and Geographical Information Systems.

Cranfield (*Information Systems Management*) Open to beginners in computing. Does not require A-level Maths. Course offers a combination of computing and management. There is also a course in Command and Control, Communications and Information Systems which has a common first year with the above course.

De Montfort (*Computer Science*) An integrated BSc/HND course with Year 3 in industry. The course emphasises the uses and applications of the computer in commercial, industrial and scientific roles in the areas of software engineering and systems analysis and design. There are also degree courses in Information Technology and Business Information Systems. Computing is also offered on the Combined Studies programme with options to study a European language.

Derby (*Computer Studies*) Computing is offered as a single Honours degree and also on the modular programme. A speciality is Health Care Information Systems Management. There is a one year placement.

Dundee (*Computer Science*) After Years 1 and 2 students may proceed to an Honours degree in Years 3 and 4. Several joint courses are also offered.

Durham (*Computer Science*) A hardware and software course with the latter predominant. It covers aspects of computer science and its underlying principles. Specialist areas are software engineering and artificial intelligence. Computer Science is also offered as part of the Natural Sciences course.

East Anglia (*Computing*) The course aims to establish an appreciation of the theoretical foundations which underlie computing as a scientific discipline and to develop practical skills. (*Applied Computing*) This comprises a study of computing and its applications including computer graphics, commercial information systems and operational research. (*Business Information Systems*) This programme aims to give a broad understanding of information system theory and technology. In the first year courses in accountancy, mathematics, statistics and economics are followed. In Years 2 and 3 data modelling, forecasting, management theory and financial information systems are some of the subjects offered.

There are also computing courses which include studies in North America.

East London A very large number of joint courses in Information Technology are offered as two or three subject combinations.

Edinburgh (*Computer Science*) This is a four year specialist study. Four other courses taken in the first two years include a choice from maths, engineering, physics, artificial intelligence, economics and business studies. The third and fourth years are devoted entirely to computer science. The emphasis of the course is on the design of general purpose systems. Joint courses with Artificial Intelligence are also offered. A top quality rating department.

Essex (*Computer Science*) A general education in computer science in which one can specialise in both hardware and software.

Exeter (*Computer Science*) This is a broad course comprising software engineering, artificial intelligence, hardware and social aspects of computing. There is also a course in Cognitive Science and several joint courses with Computer Science are also offered.

Glamorgan (*Computer Science*) The first year course is common for all courses. Students make their choice of degree course in Year 2. Courses are available with foreign languages and business studies. There are also courses in Computer Studies at Combined Honours level.

Glasgow (*Computing Science*) Core areas of study cover the organisation and processing of data, programming and computer systems (including microcomputers). Over forty joint courses are also available with Computing. A top quality rating department.

Glasgow Caledonian (*Computer Studies*) The course includes an industrial placement. Optional languages include French, German and Spanish.

Greenwich (*Computing Science*) This is a four year sandwich course involving data systems and computer engineering or information systems. Specialisms in the final year. (*Business Systems Modelling*) Final year options include the economics of Finance and Investment, business strategy and statistical models. Geographic Information Systems is available and also several joint courses are offered including one with psychology.

Heriot-Watt (*Computer Science*) No previous computing experience is required for this course which offers a choice of options. This four year course covers language theory, graphics, data processing and various topics in artificial intelligence. Courses are also offered with an emphasis on information systems, software engineering, knowledge-based systems and human computer interaction.

Hertfordshire (*Computer Science*) Year 3 of this course is spent in industry, and in the final year a wide range of topics is covered including language design, computer architecture, software engineering, artificial intelligence and computer graphics. Over thirty combined courses are also offered whilst computing is also available on the Modular programme.

Huddersfield (*Computing in Business*) Subjects studied on this course include information systems, organisation studies, computing, quantitative analysis, economics, accounting, large and small business planning. In Computing and a Modern European Language French and German options are offered. All these are four year courses with a year of supervised professional experience.

Hull (*Computer Science*) The course structure and content varies from year to year. Typically Year 1 includes programming, data structures and software engineering, commercial data, hardware fundamentals, mathematics, graphics and artificial intelligence.

Humberside (*Computer Science*) After a broad introductory course specialisms include human-computer interaction, information systems, knowledge-based systems and software engineering. Several courses involving information systems and technology are also offered.

Keele (*Computer Science*) The course is designed to give students an understanding of the logical structure and organisation of computers and the theory and practice of computer operation and programming. Final year options include software engineering, communications, graphic and artificial intelligence. Over sixty joint Honours courses are also offered.

Kent (*European Computer Science*) A four year programme with a year in a French or German university. Over thirty joint courses are also available.

Kingston (*Computer Information Systems Design*) The course includes training in problem solving skills, backed up by knowledge of computers, communication systems, programming and up-to-date fields like expert systems. It is a sandwich course with Year 3 in business or industry and opportunities for a semester in Europe or USA. The course includes industrial relations, marketing and economics. (*Computer Science*) There is a strong bias towards software design and development. Business systems and management is included in this course with a wide range of final year specialisms including artificial intelligence, graphics and programming languages. This is also a four year sandwich course. Full-time and sandwich courses in Geographical Information Systems are also available.

Lampeter Twenty joint courses are offered with Informatics. The courses are specially designed for arts (not computer science students). Topics covered include computer-aided learning, electronic mail, software engineering and word processing.

Lancaster (*Computer Science*) Strong emphasis on practical computing with a balance between hardware and software aspects. A Combined Science course with a year in the USA is also offered with Computing.

Leeds (*Computer Science*) The course covers software, computer systems, numerical methods and theory. Specialisation is offered in artificial intelligence, operational research and software technologies. Over ten joint courses with computer science are also available.

Leeds Metropolitan (*Computing*) The course offers a broad base of information technology in the first two years, an industrial placement in Year 3, systems analysis, software engineering and a foreign language option. There is also a four-year sandwich course in Information Systems for Business which includes a knowledge of computing, opportunities to take a modern language and study abroad.

Leicester (*Computer Science*) The course provides a theoretical study of computer science and the practicalities of developing computer systems. The subject is also offered in the Arts Combined and Social Combined programmes and also with a European language.

Liverpool (*Computer Science*) In Year 1, five units of computer science are taken with three other units usually mathematics. In Year 2 six units of computer science are taken with two units of a subsidiary subject (usually maths). Special studies follow in Year 3. The Arts and Social Combined programmes also include Computer Science.

Liverpool John Moores (*Computer Studies*) There are four main themes: computer systems, software development, business information systems and systems analysis. On this four year course the third year is spent in industry and commerce. The course has a bias towards computers in business use.

London (Goldsmiths') Computer Science is offered with mathematics.

London (Imp) (*Computing*) All courses have a common two year period of study leading to third year choices in computing or information systems engineering, or four year specialist courses in artificial intelligence management and information systems or software engineering with European studies.

London (King's) (*Computer Science*) There is a common first year with Software Engineering, and thereafter the course unit system permits a large element of choice. There are also various joint Honours combinations. Several joint courses are offered.

London (QMW) (*Computer Science*) The course emphasises the role of software in computer science. Year 1 and 2 cover the theory of program construction and software engineering. Project work and options follow in the third year. Computer Science can also be taken with Business Studies and languages.

London (RH) (*Computer Science*) The flexibility of the course unit systems means that students are not committed to any particular course but may choose their course from year to year as their interests develop. Students take a range of courses covering software design, computer applications and computer hardware. Computer Science is offered as a joint subject and can also be taken as part of the Science Foundation Year.

London (UC) (*Computer Science*) All computer degrees have a common core. The first year gives a broad training (including programming) and mathematics with some optional courses. There is also a course in Statistics Computing and Operational Research and Economics (SCORE).

London Guildhall (*Computing with Human Factors*) This course covers the design of systems for the user rather than the programmer. Computing is also offered on the Module Programme and a European Business Systems course with part of Year 2 in Europe.

Loughborough (*Computing*) Three and four year courses are offered. After a broad introduction specialisation is possible in database systems, networks and artificial intelligence.

Luton (*Business Systems*) The course provides an introduction to accounting, business computing and options in operation management, personnel, marketing and finance. Computer Science is offered in a large number of joint courses.

Manchester (*Computer Science*) Eight courses are offered including one with accounting in the department which was the first of its kind in the UK. Courses are modular but a free choice of unit allows for study in other subjects, eg languages, psychology, economics. Courses are also offered in Artificial Intelligence and in Medical Informatics a rapidly emerging discipline with a blend of medical knowledge, computer science and management. A top quality rating department.

Manchester (UMIST) (*Computation*) This is a vocationally-oriented course with roughly equal emphasis on three major subdivisions: (1) information systems (data processing, databases, systems analysis); (2) software engineering; (3) systems software and hardware. The course in Computation has an emphasis on systems analysis and business computer applications.

Manchester Metropolitan (*Information Technology*) The course covers software, hardware and a foreign language option. There is also a course in I.T. in Society which charts the changes related to I.T., social, cultural and economic.

Napier (*Computing and Information Systems*) The course covers computing and information systems and includes supervised work experience.

Newcastle (*Computing Science*) In the first year this course consists of three subjects - computing science, mathematics and one other from chemistry, economics, maths, physics, psychology, statistics, surveying (depending on the timetable). This gives considerable flexibility for change of course, eg to or from joint Honours, at the end of the first year. There is a preliminary year available for students without A-level maths. Exchanges with France and Germany. (*Mapping Information Science*) Covers computing, geography and mapping. Joint courses with Computing Science are also offered in addition to the subject being offered as part of Combined Studies BA and BSc programmes.

North London (*Business Modelling*) An integrated programme looking at the role of information technology, business analysis and management. Computing is also offered as part of the Combined Honours programme.

Northumbria (*Computing*) The study covers computer-based applications within manufacturing industry. Main subjects in the final year include software and hardware engineering, systems analysis and an optional European route (France, Germany or Spain). Computing for Business is also offered.

Nottingham (*Computer Science*) The course involves software and hardware systems and an optional language and study in Europe. There is also a course in Artificial Intelligence and Psychology with work experience in psychology.

Nottingham Trent (*Computing Studies*) The emphasis is on group work and the development of personal skills. Options include modern languages and international studies. (*Computer Systems*) The course covers artificial intelligence, image processing and computer architecture. There are also several joint courses with information technology.

Oxford (*Computation*) This course provides a bridge between theory and practice, hardware and software. There is also an additional one year MSc course.

Oxford Brookes (*Computing*) A four year sandwich course, in software engineering design and programming with over thirty modules from which to choose in Year 2 of the course, the third year being spent in commerce or industry. Language options are available. There are a very large number of joint courses with computing and with intelligent systems.

Paisley (*Computer Science*) In this course, students choose their specialisms at the end of the first year. All programmes have a strong practical bias with team projects introduced from the first year.

Plymouth (*Computing and Informatics*) This is a four year sandwich course. In Years 1 and 2 students cover programming, systems analysis and design and software production. In the final year, an individual project is undertaken along with two optional courses. There are several joint courses with biology and other subjects.

Portsmouth A very flexible scheme with a common first year for all courses, after which final degree choice is made between Computer Science, Business Information Systems or Technology and I.T. in Society. There is also a joint Honours programme including computing.

Reading (*Computer Science*) A practical grounding is given in fundamental computer science but the course unit system allows great flexibility. Computer Science may be combined with Chemistry, Cybernetics, Mathematics or Psychology.

Robert Gordon (*Computer Science*) The course includes a one year work placement and an option in French language. (*Business Computing*) The course covers operations management, data communications and software engineering.

St Andrews (*Information Processing*) In the first year, two half courses are offered - computing fundamentals, which is aimed at increasing computer literacy - and information technology, which involves the study of computer systems, their design and use. The course covers graphics, desk top publishing, artificial intelligence and computer systems.

Salford (*Computer Science*) The course has a bias towards the software aspects of the subject and can be taken as a three year full-time or four year sandwich course. There are also language training courses (French, German and Japanese) with Information Technology.

Sheffield (*Computer Science*) Emphasis is placed on programming techniques and software design with a choice of advanced modules in

Year 3 including artificial intelligence and operational research techniques. (*Cognitive Science*) Elements of psychology, computer science, maths, neuroscience and linguistics. Computer Science can also be taken with accounting, mathematics or modern languages.

Sheffield Hallam (*Information Technology*) The course covers software engineering, communications engineering and electronics. There is a wide range of computer based courses available including European Information.

Southampton (*Computer Science*) The course contains elements concerned with the engineering background to the design and application of computer systems, software and hardware in industry. There are also several joint courses with Computer Science.

South Bank (*Scientific Computing*) Covers two routes (a) Physical Science including physics, chemistry and astronomy and (b) Biological Science (biochemistry and microbiology).

Staffordshire (*Computers and Applicable Maths*) Business and industry has a constant need for mathematically skilled graduates who are able to formulate and solve models of real-world problems and to communicate their solutions effectively to others. This is a degree which has been explicitly designed to meet this need. There is a very large selection of joint courses with Computer Science or Information Systems.

Stirling (*Computing Science*) Computing Science may be taken to minor, subsidiary or major level in Part I. Part II covers programming, comparative languages and a series of options. There is a wide range of joint courses on offer with Modern Languages (including Japanese).

Strathclyde (*Computer Science*) This is a four year course to Honours level or three years to a Pass degree. In the first and second years computer science is taken with maths and another subject from a long list. The third year of the Honours course covers communication, and software development with project work in Year 4.

Sunderland (*Business Computing*) This is a four year sandwich course covering computer systems analysis and design and business studies. There are also degree courses in Business Computing with a foreign language (French, German or Spanish) for those who already possess some language skills, and several joint courses with Computer Studies.

Surrey (*Computing and Information Technology*) A broad-based four year course with an emphasis on group activity. It includes contributions from other disciplines, eg management economics, mathematics, engineering, psychology and sociology.

Sussex (*Computer Science*) The course covers hardware, software and mathematical foundations in the School of Cognitive and Computing Science which offers computing and artificial intelligence in conjunction with linguistics, philosophy and psychology.

Swansea (*Computer Science*) Part I courses are divided between those for students wishing to graduate in the subject and those aiming for other courses in Part II. In Years 2 and 3 it is possible to choose from a wide range of options. It is possible to combine Computer Science with

Electronics or Topographic Science and Modern Languages. A top quality rating department.

Teesside (*Information Science*) A free choice of modules is offered from computing or mathematical sciences. A European language option is available, also in Business Computing, Information Technology and Computer Science.

Thames Valley (*Information Systems*) A computing course involving problem-solving applied to the field of information systems providing a sound background in software development techniques and an emphasis on business systems.

Ulster (*Computing/Information Systems*) This is a broad-based education in computing science with an emphasis on information systems. The third year is spent in industrial training and in the fourth year students may specialise in either data management systems or software engineering. (*Computing*) The course covers a study of both software and hardware and includes an industrial placement in Year 3. Options to specialise exist in software, hardware, business management and computing, accounting and psychology.

Warwick (*Computer Science*) The first year course covers programming, logic design and computer systems and mathematics. In the second year more advanced work in programming, languages and computer systems takes place. Third year options include artificial intelligence and psychology, robot technology and computers in business.

Westminster Several courses are offered covering computer systems, artificial intelligence, cognitive science.

Wolverhampton (*Computer Science*) A broad foundation covers hardware and software and leads to a wide range of options. Computing is also offered on the Applied Science and Modular Degree Schemes.

York (*Computer Science*) This is offered as a three year full-time or four year sandwich course. About a third of sandwich placements are outside the UK. The course provides an education in a complex and fast-growing area of study - Information Technology - which is foremost in its rate of innovation and in its forthcoming impact on society. This forms a preparation for careers ranging from research work to design and application of computer systems in industry, commerce, science and administration.

● **Top research universities**
Cambridge, London (Imp) (QMW) (RH) (UC), Manchester, Newcastle, Kent, Swansea, Oxford, Sussex, Warwick, York, Edinburgh, Glasgow, Bath, Bristol, Durham, East Anglia, Essex, Hertfordshire, Lancaster, Leeds, Loughborough, UMIST, Aberdeen, St Andrews, Aberystwyth.

● **Colleges and Institutes of Higher Education offering degree courses**
Barnsley (Coll), Bolton (Inst), Bradford and Ilkley (Comm Coll), Brunel (Univ Coll), Buckinghamshire (Coll), Canterbury (Chr. Ch. Coll), Cardiff (Inst), Cheltenham and Gloucester (Coll), Doncaster (Coll), Farnborough (Coll), Gwent (Coll), King Alfred's (Coll), Liverpool (Inst), La Sainte Union (Coll), Nene (Coll), NESCOT, North East Wales (Inst),

Norwich (City Coll), Roehampton (Inst), Salford (Univ Coll), Southampton (Inst), St Mark and St John (Coll), Suffolk (Coll), Swansea (Inst), Trinity Carmarthen (Coll), Warrington Coll Inst), West Herts (Coll), Worcester (Coll).

• **Other courses to be considered**
Business Studies, economics, electrical and electronic engineering and mathematics.

DENTISTRY

• **Special subject requirements:** 2–3 A-levels from science/mathematics subjects. Chemistry often 'required' or 'preferred'.

• **Subject information:** Work shadowing or experience of this career beyond that of the ordinary patient is important.

Belfast (*Dentistry*) The course lasts five years and science A-levels are required. Students are introduced to clinical dentistry in Year 3. Intercalated degree option.

Birmingham (*Dentistry*) The course lasts five years and requires science A-levels. Biology forms an important part of the first year. A study of oral biology, human and oral diseases continues through the course. Clinical studies begin in term 6 and specialist studies at the start of the third year. Part of this clinical studies course involves attachments in oral surgery at local hospitals. Continuous assessment is an important feature of the final examination. Intercalated courses in anatomy and physiology.

Bristol (*Dentistry*) A pre-dental course is offered (previous knowledge of chemistry and physics strongly advised). First year course leads to second BDS with academically able students encourages to intercalate two years of extra study to obtain a BSc Honours degree. Regular clinical placements from Year 1.

Dundee (*Dentistry*) A pre-dental year is offered for those without science subjects at SCE or A-level extending the length of the course to five and a half years. For students embarking on the four and a half year course the pre-clinical year (first professional year) covers anatomy, physiology and biochemistry. Practical experience in hospital commences in the second professional year. In the fourth and fifth professional years students become responsible for patients' dental health. Intercalated degrees in a range of subjects including forensic medicine are offered.

Glasgow (*Dentistry*) The course extends over five years. The first two years cover medical chemistry and biology and also an environment, behaviour and health course. In April of the third year students embark on the practical aspects of clinical dentistry with patients. Students who show a particular ability in basic science subjects may interrupt their dental course for a year and study for a BSc (Ordinary) in the Faculty of Science (an additional year is required for an Honours degree).

Leeds (*Dentistry*) The course lasts five years and is divided into two periods: the pre-clinical and the clinical. The pre-clinical period lasts one year with courses being taken in both the Medical and Dental Schools. The clinical course begins in the second year with students working in the clinical departments of the Dental Hospital during the second term, performing straightforward treatments on patients. A fortnight's residence in hospital takes place in the fourth year.

Liverpool (*Dentistry*) As elsewhere in Britain there is now a new five year course covering basic medical sciences, a human disease course and clinical studies. The first year course in health and science care is common to all dental, medical, nursing and veterinary students. The opportunity to take a one-year BSc is open to most students. There is a strong emphasis on basic medical sciences, preventive dentistry and dental clinical practice.

London (UMDS/Guy's/St Thomas's) (*Dentistry*) The first two years of the new five year BDS degree concentrate on the basic medical and dental sciences, with early patient contact. In the third and subsequent years more emphasis is placed on clinical dentistry, with supervised treatment of patients. Some students may opt to take the one year BSc degree at the end of the second year.

London (King's) SMD (*Dentistry*) The course lasts five years and begins with one year of pre-clinical studies. This is taught in the Faculty of Basic Medical Sciences on the Strand campus. The clinical course is based in the Dental Hospital at Denmark Hill. Students are encouraged to take an intercalated BSc degree of two years at the end of the second year, a wide range of science subjects being offered. A foundation course in Natural Sciences (Dentistry) is also offered for students with no science background (BCC offer).

London HMC (*Dentistry*) The BDS course is five years long and the new curriculum is organised in three phases: basic medical sciences for five terms, transitional studies for two terms and clinical studies, taught on a modular basis, for seven terms. The opportunity to intercalate a one year BSc degree is open to most students.

Manchester (*Dentistry*) This is a standard dental course with an innovative, problem-based learning approach leading to the degree of BDS. There is also a pre-dental course open to those without science subjects at A-level. The dental school is on the university campus.

Manchester Metropolitan (*Dental Technology*) This four year full-time course with industrial placements covers anatomy, physiology, business and management.

Newcastle (*Dentistry*) There is an introductory integrated five term course in basic sciences and an opportunity for an intercalated science degree course. The courses lasts five years except for students without science A-levels who follow the six year pre-dental course, for which only a few places are available. Contact with patients occupies half of every day in the final three years. Purpose-built premises adjoining the city's major teaching hospital.

Sheffield (*Dentistry*) The course lasts five years, except for students without science A-levels who take a pre-dental course. Students treat patients, under supervision, from the third year onwards. A special feature of the Sheffield course is the Transitional Training unit where final year students work in an authentic working environment. A course in Dental Technology is also offered.

Wales (College of Medicine Dental School) *(Dentistry)* Pre-clinical year (two years for students without the preferred A-level combination) is undertaken at University College Cardiff. The course offers early contact with patients, teaching based on whole patient care; newly equipped areas for children and adult dentistry and an opportunity to pursue intercalated BSc Hons degree. Clinical years at UWCM in the final year incorporate an elective period programme with research projects pursued either in the UK or overseas; also secondments to other hospitals and institutions both in and outside Wales.

● **Top research universities**
London (Hospital Medical College), (United Medical and Dental School), Manchester, Glasgow.

● **Other courses to be considered**
Anatomy, biochemistry, biological science, medicine, nursing, pharmacy, physiology and speech therapy.

DRAMA, DANCE AND PERFORMANCE ARTS

Drama

● **Special subject requirements:** Vary, but A-level English, a language and history are relevant for some courses with mathematics and a language at GCSE (grade A–C).

● **Subject information:** Your choice of course will vary depending on your preferences. For example, how much theory or practice do you want? It is worth remembering that by choosing a different degree course your interest in drama can be maintained by joining amateur drama groups. Performance arts courses should also be considered as well as courses offered by the stage schools.

Dance
● **Special subject requirements:** None.

● **Subject information:** Be prepared for a study of the theory, educational, historical and social aspects of dance as well as practical studies.

Aberystwyth *(Drama)* The department is characteristically a 'performing unit' but also offers an intellectually demanding course covering a historical perspective and a study of selected periods and playwrights. Contacts exist with theatre groups and BBC Wales. Film and TV studies, set, costume, lighting and sound, theatre administration and directing are also covered in the course. Sixteen joint courses with Drama are also offered.

Birmingham *(Drama and Theatre Arts)* This is offered as a special Honours and Combined Honours course, the department establishing an emphasis in the field of practical drama. There are also over fifteen joint courses with Drama. Dance is also offered with Theatre Arts and jointly with 18 other subjects.

Brighton *(Visual and Performing Arts)* The course links three areas of study: visual art, historical studies and performance. Students may specialise in dance, theatre or music with visual studies.

Bristol (*Drama*) The course covers the theory and history of dramatic literature and performance and has an introduction to practical aspects of dramatic art. The course includes radio, TV and film drama, playwriting and American theatre. Drama is also offered with English or a Modern Language.

Cambridge (*Drama with Education*) Drama is offered at Homerton College as part of the B.Ed course for students preparing for careers in teaching in the primary or junior age range.

Coventry (*Performing Arts*) This course is offered with Dance, Small Scale Theatre or Theatre Practice.

De Montfort (*Performing Arts*) Applicants indicate a choice of options between arts administration, dance, drama or music.

Derby Dance and Drama are offered as part of the Modular Scheme.

East Anglia (*Drama*) Drama is taught with a strong practical emphasis, supported by the theory and history of the subject. This is complemented by a close study of dramatic literature. Overall, the course has a distinctive vocational element.

Exeter (*Drama*) The course is based on a study of the medium of theatre from 'the inside' as a dramatic participant, rather than as a critic, and aims to explore and develop the physical and intellectual resources which are the basis of any serious creative acting and directing. The course also aims to develop drama-teaching skills through the Northcott Theatre and the local Theatre-in-Education.

Glamorgan (*Theatre and Media Drama*) Practical creative work and theory, options in scriptwriting, world cinema, radio and TV drama. Theatre and Media Drama is also offered on Combined Honours, Combined Studies, Humanities and Joint Honours courses.

Glasgow (*Theatre Studies*) This course covers various aspects of the arts of the theatre including production, play construction and play spaces. It also deals with the place of the theatre in contemporary society and historical approaches to a play text. It is offered in combination with 30 subjects.

Hertfordshire (*Performing Arts*) Each part of this course is linked to modules in Arts management, administration, publicity and sponsorship. Specialisms cover dance, drama or music.

Huddersfield (*Theatre Studies*) Opportunities exist to work with professional practitioners and to undertake a third year project in an area of vocational interest.

Hull (*Drama*) The course is a study of drama in all its aspects - literary, historical, aesthetic and presentational, with equal stress on formal teaching and practical work. An academic system allows concentration on the theatre of certain countries and periods. Emphasis is also placed on involvement and instruction in every aspect of the theatre process, with specialisation possible in design, directing, performing and technical theatre as well as in the media. It is possible to take additional subjects in Year 1 (not examined).

Kent (*Drama and Theatre Studies*) A course which combines theoretical and practical studies involving acting, directing, community and educational theatre and management. Over 15 joint courses with Drama are also available.

Lancaster (*Theatre Studies*) The course covers all aspects of theatre and offers courses in acting, directing, playwriting, lighting and sound, set and costume design, theatre administration and TV drama as well as historical studies.

Leeds Theatre Studies is offered with English Literature.

Liverpool John Moores (*Drama*) The course covers practical work and studies in popular theatre, TV and radio drama. Several joint courses with Dance and Theatre Studies are offered. A wide range of dance subjects are studied both contemporary and Afro-Caribbean.

London (Goldsmiths') (*Drama/Theatre Arts*) A broad study of theatre, radio, film and TV as well as drama in the community. A good balance of practical experience and theatrical study.

London (QMW) Drama is offered with English and Modern Languages.

London (RH) (*Drama and Theatre Studies*) This course balances the theory and practice of drama which is considered from different perspectives and includes a two year course on film. In the second year several options are offered including direction, TV and radio drama, scene design, music and theatre and electronics and sound.

Loughborough (*Drama*) The course begins with practice in movement, speech and the art of acting and play construction plus seminars in drama and theatre. Television technique, lighting, sound, wardrobe studies, theatre practice and historical studies follow with project work in the third year. There is an exchange programme with the USA.

Luton (*Media Performance*) The course is offered as a single Honours, major, joint Honours or minor subject. The focus lies in aiming to prepare students to communicate effectively in TV and radio but also in production skills. Over 20 joint courses are also offered with Media Performance.

Manchester (*Drama*) Drama can be taken as a single or combined Honours course with languages. It is primarily for the academic study of Drama. It is not a course offering vocational training. (*Theatre Arts*) This is mainly a practical acting course helping students to evolve a working method in acting, movement and voice development, but there are also theoretical studies in theatre arts. Continuous assessment includes performance and a written dissertation is also required.

Manchester Metropolitan (*Theatre Arts - Acting*) This course prepares students for an acting career in the professional theatre and related media. Dance and Drama are also offered in the Combined Studies programme.

Middlesex (*Performing Arts*) 50 per cent of the course has a practical emphasis. Specialisation in Dance, Drama or Music. Several courses are offered including Acting (almost entirely practical), Drama and Performing Arts, Drama and Technical Theatre Arts, Drama and Theatre Studies,

Dance Performance and Technical Theatre Arts. The Dance course covers jazz, tai chi and choreography.

North London Theatre Studies can be taken in the Combined Honours programme. There is an opportunity to work with practising theatre professionals.

Northumbria (*Performing Arts*) This course emphasises drama in the community. There are specialist routes in drama and music.

Plymouth Theatre Arts and Performance Studies is offered jointly with several subjects.

Reading Film and Drama can be combined with English, Italian, French and German. The Film and Drama course covers the history of the cinema and drama with practical work in drama, film and video.

Strathclyde (*Community Arts*) The course covers, music, art, drama, dance, media studies and marketing. Specialist modules are selected in Year 4.

Surrey (*Dance in Society*) A four year course which encompasses both practical and theoretical studies of a wide variety of dance styles: African, Indian, Western classical ballet, and contemporary dance. In the third year students gain practical professional training in one of the following career areas: dance administration/management, anthropology/community work, criticism/media education, notation and reconstruction, resources and archive work, therapy.

Ulster (*Theatre Studies*) A broad course which offers specialist options in stage management, theatre technologies and administration, press, publicity and print.

Warwick (*Theatre and Performance Studies*) the main emphasis of the course lies in a study of the modern theatre (the last 100 years). It also introduces dramatic skills in the first year leading on to the second and third years which allow students to specialise in either practical work or historical and analytical studies. Options include film studies, English, Art History and Arts Education.

Wolverhampton (*Theatre Studies*) A modular course covering technical and performance skills, dance, history of drama, TV drama and criticism, modern drama, projects and play productions.

● **Top research universities**
Exeter, Hull, London (RH), Bristol, Lancaster, London (Gold), Warwick, Manchester, Glasgow.

● **Colleges and Institutes of Higher Education offering degree courses**
Bangor Normal (Coll), Bath (Coll), Bedford (Coll), Bishop Grosseteste (Coll), Blackpool and Fylde (Coll), Bolton (Inst), Bretton Hall, Brunel (Univ Coll), Central School of Speech and Drama, Cheltenham and Gloucester (Coll), Chester (Coll), Chichester (Inst), Croydon (Coll), Dartington (Coll), Edge Hill (Coll), Kidderminster (Coll), King Alfred's (Coll), Liverpool (Inst), Liverpool (Coll Perf Arts), London (Inst), Nene (Coll), NESCOT, Queen Margaret (Coll), Ripon/York St John (Coll), Roehampton (Inst), Rose Bruford (Coll), Scarborough (Univ Coll), St

Martin's (Coll), Southampton (Inst), St Mary's (Univ Coll), Suffolk (Coll), Swansea (Inst), Trinity Carmarthen (Coll), Worcester (Coll).

● **Other courses to be considered**
English, modern languages, classical civilisation.

ECONOMICS

● **Special subject requirements:** Mathematics required in GCSE (grades A–C) and occasionally at A-level. Note that some universities do not accept Business Studies and Economics as two A-level subjects.

● **Subject information:** If you haven't taken economics at A-level be prepared for a study involving some mathematics, statistics and, depending on which course you choose, economic and social history, industrial policies, the British economy and labour history, money, banking and regional economics.

Aberdeen (*Economics*) The single Honours degree provides a wide choice of subjects including financial management, regional labour economics, public policy and natural resources. A top quality rating department. Several joint courses with Economics and Agricultural Economics are also offered.

Abertay Dundee (*Applied Economics*) There are opportunities for developing I.T. and language skills. The degree emphasises case study and modelling applications.

Aberystwyth (*Economics*) There are four degree schemes including marketing and economics options. This modular course enables students to elect for a non-economics subject in Year 1 and Law or Geography minor studies in Years 2 and 3.

Anglia (Poly Univ) (*Business Economics*) This is a three year full-time course on the Cambridge campus. The European Business Economics course has links with Germany, France, Holland and Spain. Several joint courses are offered with Economics.

Bangor (*Economics*) The course includes computing and a study of banking with language options. Lectures are backed up by tutorial sessions affording discussion in small groups. The Institute of Economic Research conducts surveys in a range of topics and is financed by the World Bank and the UN.

Bath (*Economics*) This is a three or a four year course with a one year placement in industry or commerce. There is a choice of several social science subjects in the first year with introductory courses in economics and mathematics. A subsidiary subject is taken in the second year from social and economic history, politics, sociology, psychology, philosophy or social policy or languages, continued in the third year with other options. Joint courses with Economics are also offered.

Belfast (*Economics*) A BSc (Econ) course is offered for those wishing to specialise in economics. The subject occupies one-third of the first year and two-thirds of the course in subsequent years with minors in European Economics, Labour Economics and Political Studies. The Business

Economics course covers resources, labour relations, product marketing and financial management.

Birmingham (*Economics*) This may be followed as a specialist subject or in combination with other subjects. Three compulsory courses are offered in the first and second years with two optional courses. Five options are offered in the third year. Courses are also available in mathematical economics, economics and statistics, economics and modern economic history and economic and social history and languages (French, German or Spanish). Economics may also be studied with Geography, International Studies and Political Science.

Bradford (*Economics*) In Years 2 and 3 modules can be selected entirely from within economics or up to 25 per cent of the course may consist of other social science and or language modules.

Bristol (*Economics*) Ten courses are offered (including joint courses) each having mandatory and additional subject units. For economics these include philosophy, politics, sociology and accounting. There are also language options to support the course which includes study in Continental Europe.

Bristol UWE (*Economics*) Students can choose either the Social Science route or the Social Science and Information Systems route. In both modules are taken in economics, sociology and politics, with Information Systems and Technology included in the latter. Specialisms follow in Years 2 and 3.

Brunel (*Economics*) A three year full-time or four year sandwich course with electives in labour economics, international trade and development. Emphasis is on current applications of economic theories and concepts to current issues. Several joint courses with Economics are also offered.

Buckingham (*Economics*) All students of Accountancy, Business and Economics take a preliminary course lasting two terms allowing course changes. Foundation courses are followed in the first year which cover economics, computing and statistics. These lead on to specialist options which include public finance, money and banking or economic analysis in government. A modern language is also taken. There is also a degree course in Business Economics.

Cambridge (*Economics*) Part I is taken at the end of the first year, Part II at the end of the third year. A wide range of options is offered in Part II including public economics, banking and credit, industry, labour, world depression in the inter-war years and aspects of sociology. For entry to Part II, students take a qualifying exam in elementary maths.

Cardiff (*Economics*) The Cardiff Business School offers courses in Economics. Modules can be chosen from a wide range of subjects including accounting, management and a modern language. Business Economics courses are also offered and over 20 subjects can be taken with Economics as joint degrees.

Central England (*Economics*) The course provides for a study of economics and economics-related areas which include accounting, geography, history and politics/government. A wide choice of optional subjects is offered. Major and minor courses are also offered in European Studies, Government Law and Marketing.

Central Lancashire (*Economics*) First year students take core subjects in economics, quantitative analysis for economics, economic philosophy and methodology, and one option. Thereafter the course unit structure allows for considerable flexibility in choice of degree programme including language options. Economics is also offered as part of the Combined Honours programme.

City (*Economics*) The course combines academic study and vocational training. First year students study three or four main subjects specialising in one subject (single Honours) or in two subjects (joint Honours) in subsequent years. Transfer to some other courses is possible. Joint courses with ten other subjects are also on offer.

Coventry (*Financial Economics; Industrial Economics*) After a common first year students choose Financial Economics or Industrial Economics at the beginning of the second year. Maths and statistics are taken in the first year which is common for both courses. Optional subjects are taken in Year 3, German or French possible.

De Montfort (*Economics*) The course provides a good grounding in modern economic theory and its applications. There is also a choice between French, Spanish and German in each of the three years along with a wide range of other options.

Derby Economics is offered as part of the Credit Accumulation Modular Scheme.

Dundee (*Economics*) The principles of economics are covered and its applications to current problems. The course emphasises the broad outlines of national and international economic issues. Joint courses in over 30 subjects are offered with Economics and Financial Economics which are also offered in the Combined Honours scheme.

Durham (*Economics*) Single and joint Honours course students follow the same first year in economics plus three from 11 other subjects. This allows flexibility in the choice of degree at the end of the first year. These include law, psychology, politics or a modern langauge. In the second year single Honours students take compulsory core subjects plus a number of optional courses. Joint courses in Economics can be taken with History, Politics, Sociology, Law or Maths. A course in Business Economics is also offered.

East Anglia (*Economics*) Students take a common programme of courses in the first two terms introducing economics, economic and social history, sociology, philosophy and politics. They then proceed to the Honours programme, taking 12 courses (two each term) plus a minor course in another subject which could include a modern language. In the latter part of the course students may choose specialist studies from a range of options including industrial organisation, European economy and political economy. Continuous assessment (40 per cent) forms an important part of the examination structure.

East London (*Applied Economics*) Part I (first year) offers a broad introduction, followed by Part II (second and third years) in which students can devise their own courses by choosing from 35 optional units. Continuous assessment accounts for up to 50 per cent of the marks. A large number of joint courses are also offered.

Edinburgh (*Economics*) Single and joint Honours degrees are available in this subject. In the first two years a third of the work is in economics, the other subjects depending on the degree course chosen, for example, economic history, maths and business studies. Courses in economics include the study of economic theory and institutions, the organisations of firms and the banking world, and economic policy-making.

Essex (*Economics*) The first year scheme in the School of Social Studies includes economics and mathematics, economics and computing science. The second year course includes macroeconomics and microeconomics, and one from economic history, British economic policy, statistics for econometrics or an outside option. The third year offers over 15 options including international trade, public finance, labour economics and economics in the New Europe.

Exeter (*Economics*) The first year course covers a study of economics and statistics and two other social science subjects chosen from a list of options. More advanced studies continue along similar lines in the second and third years when during the latter students choose a subject in which to specialise from a wide range of options including business techniques, management accountancy, investment and the economics of banking and financial institutions. The single Honours Economics and Statistics course combines a strong foundation in statistics with applications to economics and business.

Glasgow (*Economic Studies*) Economics may be studied in the first and second years as part of the Bachelor of Accountancy degree. Courses in Political Economy are planned to cover the principles of the economy and are developed in each of the four years leading to the Honours degree. Agricultural Economics as an Honours degree follows the pattern of Political Economy adding agricultural, food and resources topics. Over fifty joint courses are also offered.

Glasgow Caledonian (*Business Economics*) This course provides a broad introduction to business with the emphasis on economics and the international sphere.

Greenwich (*Economics*) Students may choose pathways in quantitative economics, business economics and finance, political economy, economics and politics, the European economy or science and the economy. There is also an option to take a modern European language and to spend a year in a European university.

Heriot-Watt (*Economics*) Two courses are offered, the Ordinary degree after three years and the Honours degree after four years. In the first year students take economics and three elective classes, one elective class in the second year and two in the third year. A range of options is available in the fourth year including public and international finance, the European Community, Eastern Europe and international relations.

Hertfordshire (*Applied Economics*) The course provides a firm background in computing, quantitative methods and modelling. Students may include modern languages, decision sciences or business studies in their degree schemes. Final-year specialisms include international economics, forecasting and planning, science and technology, health economics, location studies and labour economics. Over twenty joint courses are also offered with Economics also offered on the Combined Modular Scheme.

Hull (*Economics*) All students taking the BSc (Econ) degree follow a largely common course and a definitive choice of specialism need not be made until the beginning of the second year. A European language may be taken with the Honours programme. Various streams are offered including mainstream economics, business economics, finance and development, accountancy or economic history.

Humberside Economics is offered with business.

Keele Economics is offered with over seventy subjects. Final year specialisms include finance, ecological economics, labour and public economics.

Kent (*Economics*) All first year students take a course in mathematics and statistics plus three other first year courses, for example, mathematics for social scientists and economic history. The final choice of degree programme is made at the end of the first year. There is a European Economics course in which students will spend the third year in France, Germany or Spain.

Kingston (*Economics*) The course is constructed around a set of core courses in each year. This enables students to select from a number of routes throughout the course. Pathways include money and finance, public sector economics, international trade, labour studies and political economics.

Lancaster (*Economics*) The first year course comprises an introduction to economics and economic history. The second year introduces a more detailed study of economic theories and their application to present-day issues. These include quantitative methods for economists (two courses, one more maths biased than the other), the British economy, British labour history and economic principles and practice. The third year offers students a choice of a number of specialised options including international trade, public finance and business enterprise. Some exchanges can be arranged with the USA.

Leeds (*Economics*) The scheme begins with a common first year covering economic principles, industrial studies and quantitative techniques, with either accounting or economic history. A subsidiary subject can be taken in Year 1. In the second year, students can specialise in either economic studies or industrial studies, although an appropriate choice of options permits choice to be postponed if necessary until the third year. The third year, apart from a core course, consists entirely of options reflecting a wide range of interests covering economic theory, applied economics, industrial relations, economic history, accounting and quantitative economics.

Leeds Metropolitan (*Economics and Public Policy*) A three year full-time or four year sandwich course. The degree focuses on economic, political and social issues. The course is assessed by both course work and examination in Years 1 and 3. Options include human resources, the European Community, international trade and a language.

Leicester Four degrees are available. A BA/BSc in Economics and BA/BSc in Business Economics. All students share a common core of economic subjects which cover economic theory and its applications. Two other social science subjects are taken in Year 1. Business Economics students also take other subjects from Economic and Social History, Geography, Politics or Sociology.

Liverpool (*Economics*) First year courses cover micro economics, macro economics, and quantitative methods plus two options. Thereafter, optional subjects offered include mathematics, business organisation, labour economics, English law, transport economics, commercial law and international economics. Other economics courses include accounting and business economics.

Liverpool John Moores Economics is offered with nine subjects.

London (Goldsmiths') Economics is offered with Politics and also with Public Policy.

London (LSE) (*Economics*) Four papers are taken in Part I with a wide range of subjects offered covering economics, mathematics, statistics, politics, sociology and a language. Students then take Part II courses during the next two years.

London (QMW) (*Economics*) In the first year students will be expected to take courses in macro and micro economics, and for those without A-level maths a basic course in maths and statistics is followed. During the second year they will take two-thirds of their courses in economics and will select the courses depending on their interests, eg languages, biology, chemistry, geology.

London (RH) (*Economics*) Recently offered as a single subject in addition to several joint courses.

London (SOAS) (*Economics*) Single or joint courses are offered with a focus on Africa and Asia.

London (UC) (*Economics*) Degree courses with Economics are based on the course unit system, some courses can be chosen from other departments. The single Honours course provides specialisation in economics with an emphasis in economic policy, and there are courses on law and economics, environmental economics and the economics of West and Central Europe.

London Guildhall (*Economics*) The course provides a broad-based first year covering social sciences, quantitative methods and computing which is followed by a wide range of options in Years 2 and 3 when continuous assessment takes place. Transfer to and from the BA in Financial Economics possible in Years 1 and 2.

Loughborough (*Economics*) Economics may be offered as a single Honours degree, or it may be taken with a minor subject (eg geography, politics, sociology, social policy) or in combination with accountancy which is designed as a more vocational degree. The course aims to provide a balanced package of theoretical and applied studies with an exceptional range of options in the final year.

Luton Economics is offered as a single Honours subject and with over eighty other subjects.

Manchester (*Economics*) This is a broad-based social science degree. Specialisation begins in Year 2 with a choice of two subjects from 12 options. A course in Agricultural Economics is also offered.

Manchester Metropolitan (*Economics*) In addition to economics, maths, statistics, computing, economic history and accountancy are taken in the first year. Two options are then chosen in Year 2 and five options in Year 3. (*International Economic Studies*) This is a new four year sandwich course including French language study in the first two years and a year spent at the University of Caen in France.

Middlesex (*European Economics*) This is a fully integrated dual qualification - the British BA and a French or Spanish qualification. Two years are spent abroad - one on placement and one in the partner institution. Economics and Business Economics are also available.

Newcastle (*Economics*) A diverse range of courses is offered by the Faculty of Social Sciences. In the first and second year of the Economics course students also choose one other subject from a list of options including accounting, law, history or a foreign language. The foreign language can continue in the second year and a range of specialised topics is offered in the third year. There are also several joint courses including Economics and Business Management and also Combined Studies courses which include Economics.

North London Business Economics is offered with either Consumer Studies or Politics and provides a broad study of the business environment.

Northumbria (*Economics*) This is a three year course studying the modern applications of economics. Options include financial studies, urban and regional studies, industrial organisation and public policy studies.

Nottingham (*Economics*) The subject is offered at Honours level and also as a subsidiary subject. In the third year specialist topics include money, banking, marketing and agricultural economics. Language studies occupy 20 per cent of Years 1, 2 and 4. (*Industrial Economics*) A strong core of theoretical and applied micro economics focuses on modern business enterprise.

Nottingham Trent (*Economics*) A broad course in economics is provided with an introduction to politics in the first year and options in geography, politics, accounting and computing available in the third year. Economics can be studied in a European context with French, German or Spanish.

Oxford (*Philosophy, Politics and Economics*) The Economics course in the first year cover macro and micro economics and a second optional part involving elementary mathematical economics. In the second and third years the principles of economics are covered and the economic organisation of the UK (in particular) from 1960.

Oxford Brookes Economics is offered jointly with over 40 other subjects.

Paisley (*Business Economics*) A broad course which includes options to study languages (French, German or Spanish) and in Year 2 major topics covering finance, marketing and human resource management. This is a modular course covering the major aspects of the subject and offering additional modules in law, business studies, geography, transport etc. A large number of joint courses are also offered with Applied Economics.

Plymouth (*Applied Economics*) The first two years introduce and develop economic theory, methodology and techniques. The focus is on policy debates in public sector economics, industrial economics, environmental economics and the international economy. Final year studies include applied economics and five options from a list of eight.

Portsmouth (*Economics*) A foreign language (French or German) can be taken in the first two semesters followed by a choice of options in semester 3 to 6 including accountancy and finance. Pathways are offered with an emphasis on Business Economics, Natural Resource Management and Political Economy.

Reading (*Economics*) For the First University Examination the Economics course has two parts. All students take economic analysis followed by a choice between quantitative methods or the British economy. Optional subjects in the second and third years include money and banking, business economics and urban and regional economics. Courses in Business and Agricultural Economics are also available.

St Andrews (*Economics*) The subject can be studied as an MA subject singly or in combination with another subject. Economics can also be taken for the Honours BSc degree either singly or in combination. Optional papers at Honours level include financial markets, labour economics and industrial relations. A top quality rating department.

Salford (*Economics*) This degree has an applied focus. It offers the student a wide choice of optional areas including the pursuit of specialist streams in business economics, world economy and quantitative techniques. Courses are also offered in Business or Human Resource Economics.

Sheffield (*Economics*) For the foundation year students select three courses from a list of up to 17 subjects. The selection depends on the degree course chosen and provides the student with flexibility up to the end of the first year. In the single Honours course economic principles and analytical and statistical methods occupy the second year, and in the third year five courses are chosen from a list of options. Seventeen joint courses are also offered.

Southampton (*Economics*) Students take economics and quantitative methods and three options in Part I. In Part II (Years 2 and 3) single Honours students spend most of their time on economics with considerable freedom of choice in their third year options. Over twenty joint courses are also available.

Staffordshire (*Economics*) Economics, maths, statistics, politics and economic history are taken in the first year, plus sociology, international relations, accounting, geography or a language. These studies lead to a range of options in the second and third year which include managerial economics, poverty, income and wealth and the economics of sport and recreation. (*European Economics*) Languages offered - French, German or Spanish. Joint courses are also offered with Political Economy.

Stirling (*Economics*) The subject can be taken at major, subsidiary and minor level. Honours students follow a sequence of core courses covering all aspects of economics, with a choice of a number of options towards the end of the course. A degree course is also offered in Technological Economics in addition to a wide range of joint subjects. Stirling also offers a course in Politics, Philosophy and Economics. A top quality rating department.

Strathclyde (*Economics*) The course assumes no previous study of the subject and is presented in two major parts: consumers, enterprises and industries; and markets and governments. After two introductory years, third year students take welfare, trade and public economies, and international economics. In the fourth year core subjects are the world economy, economic thought and macro economics, plus a range of options.

Sunderland (*Economics*) Introductory courses are chosen from economics, politics, psychology, sociology and accounting. In the second year a choice is made between the economic and social development of the USA and EC, organisations, institutions and gender issues, information technology, French, German, Spanish or accounting and finance.

Surrey (*Economics*) Courses are highly applied and vocational. In the first and second years a study is made of economics and related subjects including computing, maths, statistics, sociology, politics and history. The third year is spent on an industrial or commercial placement and the final year devoted to specialist topics chosen by the student. Opportunities exist for an exchange scheme in the USA for the students following the four year course. There is also a course in Business Economics and Computing, whilst Economics can also be taken with a language with International Business.

Sussex (*Economics*) After the preliminary term, economics occupies roughly half the student's time. Macro and micro economics occupy terms 2–4, growth and change are studied in term 5, and applied economics in term 6. In the final year students specialise in a selection of options. Economics may be studied in the School of African and Asian Studies, the School of Social Sciences or the School of European Studies.

Swansea (*Economics*) Economics can be taken in the Faculty of Arts or Economic and Social Studies. Core subjects are the same in both facilities, but the optional subjects differ. A student's choice of faculty therefore depends on the bias he or she wishes to give to the course and a number of joint Honours courses are offered. Computational experience occupies an important aspect of the course.

Teesside (*Business Economics*) Emphasis is placed on the practical relevance of economics in business and the public sector. Modules include labour, Eastern Europe, environmental, industrial and finance.

Thames Valley (*Economics*) Core subjects are taken in each year with a number of options which include accounting, business law, marketing and politics. Economics is also offered with a language (French, German or Spanish).

Ulster (*Applied Economics*) The course offers students a study of the applications of economics to business with commercial placement in Year 3. Topics covered include urban and regional development, public sector economies, new business and financial markets.

Warwick (*Economics*) Undergraduate degree courses are based on a core of courses in economic analysis, quantitative techniques and economic and social history. There is then considerable flexibility of choice available in the optional subjects taught within the department including business studies, politics and international studies, law, accounting, industrial relations and marketing. In Years 1 and 2 French, Spanish, German, Italian and Russian are also offered.

Westminster (*Economics for Business*) A general study of economics supported by modules in European economic policy, financial markets, business forecasting and strategy. A European modern language option is also available.

Wolverhampton (*Economics*) This is a broad course with options available which include accounting, business law, public finance and French, German, Spanish, Italian or Russian. Language options include a period of residence abroad. Students may specialise and take a degree in Business Economics. Economics also forms part of the Modular Degree Scheme.

York (*Economics*) In the first year all students are required to take four subjects in Part I (economics, economic and social history, statistics and one other social science subject). Students who are undecided about their choice of course need not make the final decision until the end of the first year. During the first year there are no restrictions on transfers within the department. Part II (Years 2 and 3) also offers flexibility and a very wide choice of options. One of the largest Economics departments in the UK. York also offers a course in Philosophy, Politics and Economics.

● **Top research universities**
Bristol, Cambridge, Essex, London (LSE) (UC) (QMW), Oxford, Southampton, Warwick, York, Birmingham, East Anglia, Exeter, Liverpool, Newcastle, Nottingham, Reading, Sussex, Aberdeen, Glasgow, Stirling, Strathclyde, Swansea.
Top quality rating - Aberdeen, Abertay Dundee, St Andrews, Stirling.

● **Colleges and Institutes of Higher Education offering degree courses**
King Alfred's (Coll), Nene (Coll), Southampton (Inst), Suffolk (Coll).

● **Other courses to be considered**
Accountancy, banking, business studies, estate management and valuation surveying, and quantity surveying.

ENGINEERING/ENGINEERING SCIENCES

- **Special subject requirements:** 2–3 A level passes in mathematics/physics subjects; GCSE (grades A–C) English, chemistry or a language may be required for some courses.

- **Subject information:** These courses provide the opportunity to study two, three or four engineering specialisms and enable students to delay their choice of specialism. Mathematics and physics provide the foundation of engineering subjects. Several universities and colleges now offer one year foundation courses for applicants with non-science A-levels. Extended Engineering courses are available in institutions throughout the UK; in some cases courses are open to applicants without the normal science A-levels. After the initial foundation course they move on to the degree programme. Many sponsorships are available in engineering subjects.

Aberdeen (*Engineering*) The first two years are common to all students. Year 1 covers engineering sciences, engineering drawing, applications and materials, engineering maths and computing and engineering physics leading on to more specialised studies in Year 2. Six options are then offered in the third year across the three main disciplines - civil, including structural and municipal, mechanical or electrical/electronic engineering and micro-electronics and software engineering. Honours degrees are awarded after the fourth year.

Anglia (Poly Univ) (*Foundation Science*) An Extended Science course is offered and also pathways in Combined Technologies.

Bath (*Engineering*) A common course for the first two years leads to specialisations in aerospace/automotive, mechanical, manufacturing systems, and engineering management. There is also a three year BEng or four year MEng in Innovation and Engineering Design, a studio-based course in the creation of new products, processes and design systems.

Bournemouth (*Engineering Business Development*) This course covers technology, finance and management techniques. There is also a course in low current engineering with options in manufacturing, design and project management.

Bradford (*Technology and Management*) This is a four year sandwich course covering economics and industry with a focus on management sciences, materials technology and engineering technology.

Bristol (*Engineering Mathematics*) This is a mathematics course with a strong bias to engineering applications which includes computer technology. For those wishing to have a greater computer input there is also a course in Computational and Experimental Mathematics.

Brunel (*Special Engineering Programme*) This is a high level, broad-based engineering programme aiming to develop creative design engineers capable of managing large teams and projects which require a multi-disciplinary problem-solving approach. The SEP is an enhanced engineering Dainton course, with a higher than average number of female students. The majority of SEP students take the integrated sandwich route.

Cambridge (*Engineering*) In the first two years the course is wide-ranging with no requirement for the student to select his or her specialism. In the third and fourth year students read Part II of the Engineering Tripos or the Electrical and Information Tripos. Advanced courses are also offered applicable to aeronautical, civil and mechanical engineering and management studies. Some students switch to Manufacturing Engineering or Chemical Engineering in the third year.

Cardiff (*Integrated Engineering*) This is a broad-based programme covering all engineering fundamentals. A four year sandwich course is available embracing aspects of mechanical, manufacturing, electrical and electronic engineering with a German language option.

Central England Courses are offered covering Engineering Systems with Management and Business Studies, and Computer Aided Design.

Central Lancashire (*Design and Manufacture*) This course provides a balanced study of engineering design, manufacture and organisation.

Coventry (*Engineering*) This is a broad engineering science course with specialisation from the beginning of the second year. The course is based on modules which the student selects to make up his or her degree. The choice includes mechanical, electrical, electronic control communications, manufacturing and building services engineering, design, management and language. Those taking French or German may choose to spend a year of study abroad gaining professional qualifications in France or Germany as well as the BEng.

De Montfort (*Engineering*) This is a broad-based engineering degree for those who are not initially committed to one branch of engineering. Choice can be deferred until the second half of the course, leading to engineering design, manufacturing engineering, mechatronics and agricultural manufacture, amongst other specialisms.

Durham (*Engineering*) Engineering is studied as a unified subject. Undergraduates are not committed to any particular branch of engineering before graduation. Years 1 and 2 are common for all students. Specialist studies follow in Year 3 in integrated, civil, mechanical, electronic, electrical, information systems or manufacturing engineering.

Edinburgh (*Engineering*) A wide range of disciplines is offered in this course which has a common first year. In some cases the choice of specialisation may be delayed to the end of the second year. Exemption from Year 1 may be possible for good A-level students. Specialisms include artificial intelligence, computer science, chemical, civil, electronic and electrical and mechanical engineering.

Exeter (*Engineering*) Years 1 and 2 provide a general education in engineering, leading to specialisation in civil, electrical and electronic, mechanical operations and chemical process engineering or engineering science.

Glamorgan Energy management is offered as a joint or minor degree or can be studied as part of the Combined degree course. The title of the degree will reflect the subjects chosen.

Greenwich (*Engineering and Business Management*) This is a sandwich course which offers business studies and manufacturing systems.

Hertfordshire (*Engineering Management*) Business operations, computer literacy and manufacturing and engineering studies lead on to marketing, financial management and industrial relations.

Huddersfield Technology is offered with an environmental or business focus.

Hull (*Engineering Science*) There is a common first year of mathematics and engineering science with courses in computer programming design and manufacturing engineering and digital electronics. Specialist options follow in Years 2, 3 and 4. There is a four year course for applicants without science A-levels.

Humberside (*Engineering*) A common first year course covering electrical and mechanical engineering is followed by specialisation in one of eight engineering disciplines including avionics, control systems and manufacturing engineering. New teaching methods involve computer-aided design and manufacture, and multidisciplinary approaches to keep pace with advances in technology.

Lancaster (*Engineering*) There is a common first year for all engineering, mechatronics and physical electronics students with the choice of engineering specialisms being made mid-way through the second year. Engineering specialisms include civil, civil and environmental, electronic, physical electronic, mechanical and electronic. Engineering can also be taken with a year in USA or Canada.

Leicester (*Engineering*) Six engineering degrees are offered in the department. All students follow a common course for three semesters and specialise at the end of the third semester in electrical and electronic mechanical or general engineering.

Liverpool (*Integrated Engineering*) This well-established inter-disciplinary Engineering School offers a group of three-year BEng and four-year MEng courses, with variants: with Industrial Management, with a European Language (French, German or Spanish), with Management and Language or with Manufacturing Systems. In the first two years, all students share a common core of studies in mechanical, electrical/ electronic, materials, mathematics and computing, and management. In the final year, studies may be inter-disciplinary or bias towards mechanical or electrical. Students are encourage to take an industrial placement between their second and final years (UK or abroad). IMechE and IEE accredited. Foundation year available.

Liverpool John Moores (*Combined Engineering Studies*) There is a common first and second year covering computer applications, materials technology and manufacturing followed by a wide range of modules in engineering and technology management and electrical/electronic engineering.

London (QMW) (*Engineering/Engineering Science*) A broad basic course is offered with students making their decision to specialise in their chosen branch of engineering at the end of the first year from mechanical, aero or civil. Engineering is also offered with languages, environmental science and business studies.

London (UC) Engineering is offered with Business Finance.

Loughborough (*Engineering Science and Technology*) This degree provides an excellent foundation for a career across a wide range of industry. The first two years of the course cover a broad study programme in mechanical, electrical and electronic engineering, thus providing the basis to understand the modern techniques, now widely found in industry, which integrate computer methods and electronic and electrical systems with engineering hardware. This study then allows the student to specialise in the final year in mechanical engineering or manufacturing engineering and management or electronic and electrical engineering. There is also a four year sandwich course.

Luton (*Integrated Engineering*) This course is offered as a single, major, joint or minor course and can cover mechatronics, manufacturing engineering and materials technology.

Manchester (UMIST) (*INTENGO*) A broad introduction to engineering disciplines with the major specialism being chosen at the end of Year 1 from building, mechanical, civil, electrical, electronic or chemical engineering.

Manchester Metropolitan (*Integrated Engineering Systems*) The first year covers basic engineering, software engineering, materials, manufacturing and digital systems. In Years 2 and 3 studies include process and manufacturing engineering and electrical power and control systems design.

Napier (*Engineering with Management*) This three or four year course, involving manufacturing systems engineering, design and management has been developed to meet the needs of industry. (*Energy and Environmental Engineering*) This course promotes expertise in using existing energy sources efficiently and cleanly and developing new sources for the future. Management and Technology is also available.

Northumbria Courses offered include Engineering with Business Studies and International Business and Technology, a four year course with one year abroad.

Oxford (*Engineering Science*) This is a four year course. A common first year is followed by specialisation in civil, mechanical, electrical information or chemical engineering.

Oxford Brookes (*Engineering*) Years 1 and 2 provide a broad introduction to the principles, analytical methods and creative practice of engineering. Final year studies can be biased towards electrical and/or mechanical engineering. There is also a four year sandwich course.

Paisley (*General Engineering*) This is a broad course covering aspects of civil, electrical, mechanical and manufacturing engineering.

Portsmouth (*Engineering*) Core subjects are combined with options in electronics, computing, mechanical and manufacturing engineering, business studies and language. Engineering is also offered with Business Studies or Management.

Reading (*Integrated Engineering*) The course is tailored to achieve a balanced approach between mechanical, electrical and electronic engineering. There is a considerable emphasis on the applications of microprocessors in instrumentation, control and signal processing.

Robert Gordon Technology is offered with Business.

Salford (*Unified Engineering*) There is a common first year with specialisms in Years 2–4 in aeronautical, civil, electronic, environmental, manufacturing and mechanical engineering.

Sheffield Hallam (*Engineering with Business Studies*) This is a broad-based engineering course in mechanical and manufacturing engineering which includes some industrial and business studies. Year 3 is spent in industry. Some placements are in Europe. (*Integrated Engineering with Automotive Studies*) This course covers electrical, electronic, manufacturing, mechanical and materials engineering.

Southampton (*Engineering*) Three year (B Eng) four year (M Eng) courses are offered, the latter with a European Studies option where students take a European language and spend a year in mainland Europe.

Strathclyde Engineering with Business Management and European Studies and Technology is also offered with Business Studies. There is also a course in Prosthetics and Orthotics involving artificial limbs and supports. There are two compulsory clinical placements of six months.

Sunderland (*Engineering*) This broad based degree programme, with an optional sandwich year, builds on the traditional studies of electrical power and mechanical systems with newer disciplines such as computer-aided design and manufacturing control systems. A wide range of options, including management and languages, allows the development of specialist knowledge and skills to complement core engineering. An additional year will lead to an MEng.

Surrey (*Engineering with Business Management*) The course aims to give the student a broad understanding of the design, servicing and management of engineering systems. First and second year students taking language studies as an option may have industrial placements abroad. Multidisciplinary option subjects are available in the final year together with project management.

Sussex (*Engineering*) This is a four year course for students without A-level or equivalent qualifications, with provision for specialisation in mechanical, electrical, electronic, computer or control engineering in the final year. Altogether Sussex offers 35 single or joint Honours engineering degrees.

Ulster (*Engineering*) This is a four year course with industrial placement in the third year. Specialist studies in the final year cover manufacturing, electrical/electronic and mechanical engineering.

Warwick (*Engineering*) This course comprises a common year which then feeds into two or three year programmes in each of civil, mechanical, manufacturing systems, electrical and general engineering. A course is also offered in Engineering and Business Studies.

● **Top research universities**
Cambridge, Durham, Keele, London (Imp), Oxford, Strathclyde, Warwick, Brunel, Exeter, Leicester, Sussex.

● **Colleges and Institutes of Higher Education offering degree courses**
Askham Bryan (Coll), Barnsley (Coll), Bolton (Inst), Bradford and Ilkley (Coll), Farnborough (Coll), Halton (Coll), Nene (Coll), Norwich City (Coll), Salford (Univ Coll), Southampton (Inst), Stockport (Coll), Swansea (Inst), Trinity Carmarthen (Coll).

● **Other courses to be considered**
See under separate Engineering specialisms.

ENGINEERING (AERONAUTICAL)

● **Special subject requirements:** See **Engineering**.

● **Subject information:** Courses cover the manufacture of military and civil aircraft, theories of mechanics, thermodynamics, electronics, computing and engine design and manufacture.

Bath (*Aerospace Engineering*) This is a four year MEng sandwich course which has a common first two years with Mechanical Engineering. It is also possible to take the course with French or German.

Brighton A course is offered in Mechanical and Aeronautical Engineering.

Belfast (*Aeronautical Engineering*) The course covers the manufacture and operation of civil and military aircraft, the basis of the course being in subsonic and supersonic aerodynamics, structural designs and performance.

Bristol (*Aeronautical Engineering*) Basic principles of aeronautical engineering are studied in the first and second years, with a wide range of mathematical and engineering lectures and projects in the third year taught by senior British Aerospace staff. There is also a course combining study in Continental Europe.

Bristol UWE (*Aerospace Manufacturing Engineering*) This is a modular course with language modules and a common first year with Manufacturing Systems Engineering allowing transfer at the end of the year.

Brunel Courses are offered combining Mechanical Engineering with Aeronautics.

Cambridge (See under **Engineering Science**.)

City (*Aeronautical Engineering*) Four courses are offered: (a) Three year full-time (BSc) (b) Four year sandwich (BSc) (c) Four year full-time (M Eng) and (d) Five year sandwich course (M Eng). All courses follow a common first year which, with subsequent studies, covers the fundamentals of aeronautical science and technology. Three and four options are chosen respectively in the final years of the BSc and M Eng courses. (*Air Transport Engineering*) There is a common first year with Aeronautical and Mechanical Engineering. Sponsorship is necessary for this course which gives a sound education in air transport engineering, combined with engineering management, airline economics and administration. Students on all these courses are required to complete a course in flight testing at Cranfield Institute of Technology.

Coventry (*Aerospace Systems*) A broad spectrum of engineering science subjects is covered with management and business subjects.

Cranfield (*Aeromechanical Systems Engineering*) A comprehensive course which includes flight testing and options in trials reliability, flight control systems and systems engineering.

Glasgow (*Aeronautical Engineering*) This course shares similar subjects in the first and second year with Mechanical Engineering, Naval Architecture and Ocean Engineering. Third and fourth year courses specialised in aeronautical engineering with flight experimental work taking place at Glasgow Airport. Courses are also offered in Aerospace Engineering and in Avionics with a focus on Aeronautics or Electronics.

Hertfordshire (*Aerospace Engineering*) Emphasis on design, computer-aided engineering and engineering applications. Common first year with Mechanical and Vehicle Engineering. There is an opportunity to study French or German.

Humberside Courses are offered in Engineering with the focus on aircraft structures, avionics, control systems, communication systems, electrical engineering, electronics, manufacturing systems and mechanical engineering.

Kingston (*Aerospace Engineering*) May be studied as either a three year or a four year sandwich course. Part I (two years) includes the equivalent of 12 weeks industrial training. Part II includes nine months industrial training. The course is design-based and uses design studies as the integrating themes. There is a European placement for those taking the optional modern language.

Liverpool (*Aerospace Engineering*) Broad inter-disciplinary engineering courses (mechanical, electrical/electronic, materials, mathematics and computing) with increasing aerospace specialisms (eg aerodynamics, aerostructures, propulsion systems, avionics) are offered for MEng and BEng. Optional industrial placement between the second and final years, workshop practice in aerospace manufacturing methods and Flight Test course at Cranfield are available. Accredited by RAeS, IMechE and IEE.

London (Imp) (*Aeronautical Engineering*) Two four year MEng courses are offered. These are broadly based courses in engineering science, with a strong emphasis on design, combined with the specialist study of aerodynamics and advanced structural mechanics. Opportunities exist to gain practical experience of machine tools and to attend a flight testing course at Cranfield. Students can spend their third year at a French or German university and some may have the opportunity to do so at MIT in the USA.

London (QMW) (*Aeronautical Engineering*) The course is designed for those students intending to follow careers in the air frame or missile industries. The Avionics course covers aeronautics and the electronic side of the field, for example, automatic control systems, autopilots, navigation systems. Aerospace Materials is taught jointly with the Department of Materials.

Loughborough (*Aeronautical Engineering*) In the first year this is a joint course with Automotive Engineering. The three or four year (BEng) course covers all forms of aircraft and also provides a basic training education for those interested in careers in space and/or missile systems. The course combines modern theories of mechanics, fluids, thermo-dynamics, electronics and computing with practical experience of aircraft and engine design and manufacturing methods. Experimental facilities include wind-tunnels, engine test beds and industry standard CAE equipment.

Manchester (*Aerospace Engineering*) This is a British Aerospace designated centre of excellence in Aerospace Engineering. The choice of the three year BEng or four year MEng course can be made during the first two years.

Manchester (UMIST) (*Aerospace Engineering*) This is a semester based course run jointly with the University of Manchester Engineering Department. One semester in the final year is taken as an industrial placement.

Salford (*Aeronautical Engineering*) This is a three or four year course. The first two years cover the principles of engineering science and specialist aeronautical subjects such as aerodynamics, measurement and control systems. Experimental flight work is undertaken at Cranfield. Students on the thick sandwich course spend Year 3 in industrial training. The final year is common to both programmes and includes individual project work.

Southampton (*Aeronautics and Astronautics*) This is a three or four year course. The first year (Part I) covers basic engineering sciences. Part II covers the principal aeronautical engineering subjects. Flight testing takes place at the Cranfield Institute of Technology during the Easter vacation of the second year. In the third year there are options in languages, industrial law or management. (*Aerospace Systems Engineering*) A common first year is shared with the course in Aeronautics and Astronautics. The courses differ in Parts II and III with a study of aerospace design, aircraft, aero-engine and space system modelling.

Strathclyde A course is offered in Mechanical Engineering with Aerodynamics.

● **Colleges and Institutes of Higher Education offering degree courses**
Farnborough (Coll), North East Wales (Inst), Stockport (Coll).

● **Other courses to be considered**
Computer engineering, electrical and electronic engineering, instrument and control technology.

ENGINEERING (CHEMICAL)

● **Special subject requirements:** 2–3 A-levels from mathematics/science subjects. Chemistry is usually essential; physics and mathematics also important for some courses.

- **Subject information:** Courses are based on maths, physics and chemistry and lead on to studies in energy resources, nuclear energy, pollution, petroleum engineering, bio-process engineering and biotechnology.

Aston (*Chemical Engineering*) Easy transfer exists between Chemical Engineering or Applied Chemistry at the end of Year 1. The course involves some business studies and there is a European Studies programme.

Bath (*Chemical and Bio Process Engineering*) The course features the integration of biochemical engineering within the core curriculum with the option of specialising in this subject in the final year by way of project work. Topics covered include process safety and environmental control and modern language options French and German. There is the opportunity for a full year of integrated professional training. (*Chemical Engineering with Education*) This course also includes teaching practice leading to fully qualified teacher status.

Belfast (*Chemical Engineering*) This is a broad course which includes physical chemistry, mathematics, mechanical and electrical engineering, polymer science and microbiology. There is also a course combined with food engineering which involves the study of food science.

Birmingham (*Chemical Engineering*) Several courses are offered involving biochemical engineering, management, environmental management and minerals engineering. Languages (French, German, Spanish, Japanese, Russian) are also available.

Bradford (*Chemical Engineering*) A three year course with options in management economics, biotechnology and computer-aided design and control, management process control and environmental protection. French and German can be studied in Years 1 and 2. A thin sandwich course is also offered with European industrial placements. Transfer is possible to the MEng course after Year 3.

Cambridge (*Engineering Chemical*) The first two years are spent reading either Engineering or Natural Sciences (see also **Engineering Science**). Students interested in construction and design applications naturally tend to the former, those with a preference for chemistry and physics to the latter. Part I Chemical Engineering is taken at the end of the third year and Part II at the end of the fourth year.

Edinburgh (*Chemical Engineering*) The course includes chemistry, maths, economics, computing and management, and extends over four years. There is also a course combined with European Studies which includes a language.

Exeter (*Chemical and Process Engineering*) (See under **Engineering**.)

Glamorgan (*Chemical Engineering*) The third year is spent in industry in this four year course. A design project occupies much of the final year. This is a general course with a bias towards energy studies, biotechnology, and computer-aided process engineering.

Heriot-Watt (*Chemical Engineering*) This is a four year course with introductory studies in maths, chemistry, physics and chemical engineering in the first year. Accountancy and finance are introduced in the second year, and industrial chemistry, microbiology and biochemistry in the third year. Honours students present a design in the fourth year. There is also a course in Energy Resource Engineering with Chemical Engineering which shares a common first year.

Huddersfield Chemical Engineering is offered with Chemistry.

Hull Chemistry is offered with Quality Management.

Leeds (*Chemical Engineering*) A three year course (BEng Hons) or the extended four year (MEng) course are offered. The first two years are common and students can start on either course or transfer up to the end of the second year. Management studies, materials science, computer programming and economics all occupy part of a flexible course which also includes chemical reactor design, biotechnology and safety. (*Fuel and Energy Engineering*) This unique course covers all aspects of energy supply and conservation including the major fuels, coal, oil, gas and nuclear as well as alternative sources such as solar, biomass, wind, wave, etc. There is also a course in Fire Engineering.

London (Imp) (*Chemical Engineering*) There are two four year courses in which a study of basic sciences and maths and their engineering applications occupies the first two years. In subsequent years there is a considerable emphasis on project work together with management and business subjects, mineral engineering, bio-technology, energy fuels, combustion and pollution. The Chemical Engineering with a Year Abroad course includes language tuition and a year's study in Europe.

London (UC) (*Chemical Engineering; Biochemical Engineering*) In the first year all 8 degree courses share a common foundation. In Year 3 students concentrate on chemical or biochemical engineering. In the final year students design a complete chemical plant and take several optional courses. The four-year MEng emphasises advanced process design and management topics.

Loughborough (*Chemical Engineering*) Courses offered include a three year full-time BEng, a four year sandwich BEng, a four year MEng and a five year MEng, all with common first and second years studying core elements of chemical engineering, and transfers possible up to the end of the second year. Industrial placements in the UK and abroad occupy the third year of four year BEng and five year MEng courses; both MEng courses also include a professional development project. Final year options include plant engineering, pollution control and separation processes. Specialist courses are also offered in environmental protection and bioprocessing.

Manchester (UMIST) (*Chemical Engineering*) The second year includes detergents, polymers, pollution control, occupational safety and hygiene. 15 per cent of Year 2 and 30 per cent of Year 3 are electives which include chemical and biological reaction engineering, polymer engineering, offshore and nuclear engineering. There is an exceptionally large Pilot Plant Laboratory, and extensive computer facilities. It is also possible to take Chemical Engineering with French, German, Spanish, Biotechnology or Environmental Technology.

Newcastle (*Chemical and Process Engineering*) This three year BEng or four year MEng is accredited by the Institution of Chemical Engineers and the Institute of Energy. A foundation year is available.

Northumbria A course is offered in Chemistry with Chemical Engineering.

Nottingham (*Chemical Engineering*) There is a three year BEng course and a four year MEng course, but students do not have to choose which to follow until the end of the second year. There are language options in French or German and other options in environmental engineering, management accountancy, patents and licensing. (*Chemical Processing and Materials Engineering*) This is a new three year course which involves a study of ceramics, glasses, polymers and metals.

Oxford (*Chemical Engineering*) (See **Engineering Science**.)

Paisley (*Chemical Engineering*) This is a five year sandwich course in which students spend the whole of the fourth year in industry gaining appropriate work experience.

Sheffield (*Chemical Process Engineering with Biotechnology; Chemical Process Engineering with Fuel Technology*) The first year covers mathematics, chemistry, chemical engineering, fuel technology and biotechnology or chemical process engineering. Modern language options are available throughout.

South Bank (*Chemical Engineering*) The courses are accredited by the IChemE and allow specialisation in biochemical engineering, food process engineering, environmental protection, energy engineering and materials. The final year research project of this thick sandwich course is backed up by the departmental research strength in computer-aided process engineering, fires and explosions, and biotechnology.

Strathclyde (*Chemical Engineering*) A three or four year course is offered with foundations in maths, physics and chemistry in the first year, along with a computer programming course and an introduction to chemical engineering. This is continued in the second year and leads on to a more specialised study of chemical engineering, biochemical engineering and engineering design in the third year. There is also a languages option. Project work and research occupies the fourth year for Honours students only.

Surrey (*Chemical Engineering*) This four year BEng course integrates chemical engineering, microbiology and biochemistry with the use of extensive industrial case studies and a full year of training in industry. Language study options and placements overseas are offered. There is also an Environmental Chemical Engineering degree which covers air and water pollution, hazardous waste and legislation. French, German or Spanish are also offered.

Swansea (*Chemical Engineering*) The first year involves a basic introduction to the relevant branches of chemistry and process engineering. A study of chemical engineering develops in the second year alongside biochemical engineering. Those interested in biologically based processes can opt for a degree in this subject at the end of the second year. The course can be studied with a year in Europe.

Teesside (*Chemical Engineering*) In this four year sandwich course the third year is spent in industry. Subjects covers include biotechnology, separation processes and process and systems design. This highly rated department is one of the largest in the UK.

● **Top research universities**
Cambridge, London (Imp) (QMW) (UC), UMIST, Bath, Birmingham, Leeds (Fuel and Energy), Surrey and Edinburgh.

● **Other courses to be considered**
Chemistry, food science, fuel and energy technology, glass, rubber and polymer technology, industrial chemistry, materials science, nuclear and natural gas engineering.

ENGINEERING (CIVIL)

● **Special subject requirements:** 2–3 A-levels from mathematics/science subjects. English and chemistry important at GCSE (grade A–C) for some courses.

● **Subject information:** Specialist courses in this field may cover traffic and highway engineering, water and waste engineering, construction management, explosives and public health engineering. Essential elements in all courses, however, include surveying, design projects (eg Channel Tunnel to suspension bridges) and building technology. Aesthetic design may also play a part in the design of some structures, eg motorway bridges.

Aberdeen (*Civil Engineering*) (See **Engineering Science.**)

Abertay Dundee (*Civil Engineering*) This is a four year thin sandwich course. It combines academic studies with supervised professional training thus providing a strong applied engineering bias. This sandwich course leads to accreditation by the Institution of Civil Engineers (as in the case of all other degree courses).

Aston (*Civil Engineering*) The department offers two courses, one sandwich and one full-time. The first year is common to both so it is possible to transfer between them at any time during Year 1. The course covers structural, public health and highway engineering, construction management, water resources and language options in French or German. There is also a new MEng course with European Studies and placements abroad.

Bath (*Civil/Structural Engineering*) This is a four year BEng thin sandwich course with six month industrial placements in Years 2 and 3. Emphasis is on civil engineering related to buildings. Civil and Architectural Engineering is also offered.

Belfast (*Civil Engineering*) A broad course at level 1 and 2 leads on to any two elective subjects from traffic and highway engineering, management and economics, civil engineering construction, public health engineering, concrete and steelwork design and water supply.

Birmingham (*Civil Engineering*) A second year scheme places a greater emphasis on the application of theory and the economics of design and feasibility of civil engineering projects. Language options in French, German, Spanish, Russian and Japanese. There is an optional Year 3 in industry.

Bradford (*Civil/Structural Engineering*) The majority of students admitted to civil/structural engineering undertake the four year BEng course, which includes one year in industry and which has a strong emphasis in business communications and design. However, those students who perform well during the first and second years of the BEng course are offered the opportunity of transferring to the double-degree MEng course, which includes two three-month periods in industry. The basic subjects studied are mathematics, geology, materials, hydraulics, structures, drawing, computing, environmental science, law, economics and management studies. Although the School encourages students to pursue its sandwich courses, students may alternatively choose the 3-year BSc course, which does not include a period of industrial training. French and German can be studied as part of these courses.

Brighton (*Civil Engineering*) The BEng course is a combination of academic rigour and project-based practical application with an optional sandwich year in the UK or Europe. French and German language options.

Bristol (*Civil Engineering*) After a general first and second year course, the third stage includes 'The Engineer in Society' as one of the core subjects with a range of options which may include water resources, traffic engineering, concrete technology, coastal engineering and French. Twelve companies offer sponsorships to students studying at Bristol (not including sponsorship arranged by students prior to the course).

Cambridge (See under **Engineering Science**.)

Cardiff (*Civil Engineering*) There is a common first semester for students leading on to four degree schemes with courses of three, four and five years' duration, including sandwich courses, leading to the BEng and MEng degree. Creative design, computer techniques and economic and management aspects are all given full consideration. The course in Architectural Engineering shares much of the first year, and then focuses on design and environmental factors.

City (*Civil Engineering*) BEng and MEng courses are offered - both include placements in industry, some students spending one of two industrial periods in Europe. Transfer from BEng to MEng is possible during the first or second years. The course has a high management content giving students practical design and presentation skills.

Coventry (*Civil Engineering Construction*) This course will provide knowledge and skills related to the design, construction, management and some analytical aspects of civil engineering. The course structure enables an in-depth study of the planning, finance, organisation and operation of construction contracts and sites and may be studied over 3 years full-time, or 4 years sandwich. After obtaining at least a second class Honours degree it is possible through an additional year of study to obtain a degree accredited by the Institution of Civil Engineers. (*Environmental Engineering*) The course provides education in environmental engineering and management with an emphasis on civil engineering topics relevant to the protection of the natural environment during industrial, commercial and general urban activities. Study is over a 3 year full-time programme or a 4 year sandwich course with the third year in the environmental engineering industry.

Cranfield (Shrivenham) (*Civil Engineering*) During the first and second years, elements of the course are taken in common with electrical and mechanical engineering. Specialist aspects of civil engineering include buildings and energy, highways and transportation, explosives engineering and public health engineering.

Dundee (*Civil Engineering*) In Years 1 to 3 this BEng or MEng course covers the fundamental theory of civil engineering: design, analysis and mathematics, plus skills in teamwork, communications and IT. In Year 4 students concentrate on specialist topics including courses with an emphasis on management and building.

Durham (*Civil Engineering*) (See **Engineering Science**.)

East London (*Civil Engineering*) These courses cover transportation, construction, management computing and environmental engineering. 35 subjects are also offered with Civil Engineering in joint courses.

Edinburgh (*Civil Engineering*) Major topics on the course after the first year foundation course common to all engineering degrees include: design structures, geotechnics, environmental engineering, transportation, fire safety engineering and pollution control.

Exeter (*Civil Engineering*) (See under **Engineering Science**.)

Glamorgan (*Civil Engineering*) A three year full-time and a four year sandwich course are offered. The first two years are common to all students, the final choice of course being made at the end of the second year. Water, structural, transportation and highway engineering are included as final year topics.

Glasgow (*Civil Engineering*) The first year provides a very broad range of studies which include important skills for the civil engineer, including computing and communication skills (oral, graphic and written). Mathematics is an important subject throughout the course, but from the second year an increasing emphasis is placed on professional subjects. These are taken alongside optional topics such as traffic engineering, construction processes and construction management. There is also a course in Civil Engineering and Geology.

Glasgow Caledonian (*Civil Engineering*) A standard course with final year options in theory of structures, structural design, building services, surveying, highway engineering or water engineering.

Greenwich (*Civil Engineering*) Engineering applications form the basis of these three and four year sandwich courses, together with design and construction practice. The first two years are common to all students. A 9–15 month industrial placement period is available. Computer-aided design and four field courses are part of the programme. Public health, water resources, and earthquake-resistant designs are options.

Heriot-Watt (*Civil Engineering*) There are two courses: (1) a four year BEng course and (2) a five year MEng course. The first three years are common and transfers between courses are possible. Practical work is an important part of the course by way of projects. Fourth year options include water, transport and municipal engineering. There are also courses in Civil and Environmental Engineering, and Structural and Offshore Engineering, which involves the stability of floating structures.

Hertfordshire (*Civil Engineering*) This is a sandwich course with industrial placement in the third year. Final year students choose options from structural, transportation, water and geotechnical engineering. There are also options in surveying and civil engineering for developing countries and European languages (French or German).

Kingston (*Civil Engineering*) A sandwich course is available, with industrial placement in the third year. Core subjects follow the normal pattern for a civil engineering course and there are special topics in the final year which include civil engineering management, water and waste, water engineering, transportation engineering and public health engineering.

Lancaster (See under **Engineering Science**.)

Leeds (*Civil Engineering*) Five courses are available, including three extended four year courses. Transfer between courses is possible up to the end of the second year. An important feature of this programme is the great flexibility offered in selecting options leading to breadth or depth in what is studied. (*Civil Engineering with Architecture*) This is one of two courses which include the design of architectural and engineering structures as well as aspects of transportation and town planning. (*Architectural Engineering*) This follows similar lines except that the whole of the third year is spent at Pennsylvania State University studying American architecture and building services engineering.

Leicester (*Civil Engineering*) (See under **Engineering Science**.)

Liverpool (*Civil Engineering*) In addition to the three year course, there are four courses of four years' duration which offer fourth year specialisms in environmental, maritime and structural engineering. All courses comprise a common first two years with compulsory and optional elements in Year 3.

Liverpool John Moores (*Civil Engineering*) This three year degree, with an optional sandwich placement year, covers the principles underlying civil engineering disciplines across a broad spectrum of subject areas. A MEng is available for high performing students.

London (Imp) (*Civil Engineering*) Four year courses are offered in Civil Engineering and Civil and Environmental Engineering. There are variants of both these courses which include a year at a European university. All courses lead to the MEng degree.

London (QMW) (*Civil Engineering*) A broad course is offered in the first and second years giving the student a thorough grounding in civil engineering. Third year subjects offer considerable flexibility in the choice of subjects, and include geotechnical and water engineering, transport studies and construction management. Most of the first year is common to all students allowing transfer at the end of Year 1. There is also a Civil Engineering with Business Studies degree and a specialised degree in Geological Engineering.

London (UC) (*Civil Engineering*) A common first year is taken by students in the three year BEng and four year MEng programmes in Civil Engineering; these include core elements of Environmental and Structural Engineering. There are also BEng degrees in Civil Engineering with Environmental or Structural specialisms, and a four year BEng for those with qualifications matching the required level but missing the subjects required for the programmes.

Loughborough (*Civil Engineering*) Four year courses in Civil Engineering and Civil and Building Engineering share common studies for three years and prepare students for professional work in the design, construction and management of diverse projects. An Environmental Systems Engineering course is also available, concerned with designing systems that promote habitable environments, use miniumum energy and cause no harm to the natural environment.

Manchester (*Civil Engineering*) Four year MEng or three year BEng courses are offered with the final choice being made at the end of the second year. There is also an integrated European programme.

Manchester (UMIST) (*Civil Engineering*) This is a modular course which is based on two semesters per academic year. Language options exist in French and German. There is an option to transfer to other Civil Engineering courses in Year 1 and Year 2, leading to specialisms in Management, Structural Engineering and Environmental Management.

Middlesex (*Civil Engineering*) For sandwich course students there is a nine month placement between Years 2 and 3. Field courses in land surveying and geology are part of the course which has a wide range of specialist options in the final year. Construction management is studied in Year 2, with civil engineering management and financial planning and an integral design study in the final year.

Napier (*Transportation Engineering*) A course with an emphasis on the design of systems for transport purposes. There is also a standard Civil Engineering degree course.

Newcastle (*Civil Engineering*) Three year BEng and four year MEng degrees are available in Civil Engineering, Civil and Environmental Engineering, Environmental and Ecological Engineering and Structural Engineering. A foundation year is available.

Nottingham (*Civil Engineering*) The course leads to a BEng after three years' study, or an MEng after four years. Engineering drawing, computing, engineering surveying, water engineering and construction management occupy the first two years. In the third year students choose five options from nine topics which include a foreign language for engineers, finance and law, pavement engineering, traffic engineering and concrete technology. Students continuing on the MEng course choose four subject options from nine topics and undertake a project.

Nottingham Trent (*Civil Engineering*) The industrial placement occupies the third year in this four year sandwich course. Two field courses in surveying are included as well as a course of civil engineering practice and management. There is an emphasis in infrastructure design covering highway and drainage design in Year 2.

Oxford (*Civil Engineering*) This can be taken as an option in Part II of the four year course in Engineering Science.

Oxford Brookes (*Civil Engineering*) This course aims to provide a sound education in the fundamentals of civil engineering with an emphasis on the processes of civil engineering construction. This means that a reasonable proportion of the time is devoted to civil engineering construction and management. Options, which allow students to widen their interests, are provided in the final year of this four year sandwich course.

Paisley (*Civil Engineering*) This is a four and a half year sandwich course with three 24 week periods of industrial training. Structural, water, geotechnical and transport management are studied in depth.

Plymouth (*Civil Engineering*) This department is unique in its facilities for underwater diving as part of both the degree and HND programmes. Final year options are coastal engineering which includes underwater technology and diving, environmental engineering and structural design. Language options are also available.

Portsmouth (*Civil Engineering*) The courses are wide ranging and include significant elements of field work, site visits, design assignments and optional studies and can be either full time or sandwich. Options include environmental engineering and harbour and coastal engineering. Business aspects including finance and planning are featured in all courses and have a particular emphasis in the prestigious MEng degree course. Environmental Engineering and Engineering Management are also offered.

Salford (*Civil Engineering*) This is a three year or four year (sandwich) course. Civil engineering practices are studied alongside specific core subjects. In the final year optional subjects can be studied such as engineering hydrology, and transport planning. The programme is run on a modular basis with examination and assessment tests. (*Civil Engineering with European Studies*) For students wanting to study abroad this degree course incorporates the civil engineering programme with a language course. Placements abroad are arranged via an exchange agreement with the University of Blaise Pascal (CUST) Clermont Ferrand, in the French Auvergne.

Sheffield (*Civil and Structural Engineering*) This is a broad-based course with an emphasis on design. There is an emphasis on individual tuition and the development of personal and professional skills. Three and four year courses (BEng/MEng) are offered with a foundation year for applicants with non-traditional A-level subjects. French and German can be taken in Year 1 and there are options in water engineering, traffic management and solar and wind energy.

Sheffield Hallam (*Civil Engineering*) The degree course is a broadly based applied engineering course which provides the necessary education for entry to the whole of the profession of civil and structural engineering. Modern methods, such as computer-aided design, and new technology are included together with appropriate practical and field work. Transfer to the Construction BSc degree is possible and Civil and Environmental Engineering is also offered.

Southampton (*Civil Engineering*) The first year (Part I) contains a number of subjects common to other departments in the Faculty of Engineering and Applied Science. The remaining subjects have a strong civil engineering bias such as mechanics, engineering graphics, surveying and computing. The second year (Part II) continues with a civil engineering design emphasis, leading on to Part III in which students choose four subjects from a choice of twelve, including maritime engineering, industrial law, French and German, highway and traffic engineering and irrigation engineering.

South Bank (*Civil Engineering*) Three and four year courses are offered, with selection being made at the end of the second year. These courses include civil, structural, municipal, water and geotechnical engineering. The sandwich option occupies the third year. There is also a four year sandwich course in Environmental Engineering including building technology, engineering materials and mechanics, energy management, environmental engineering design, management and computing.

Strathclyde (*Civil Engineering*) Computer science, maths and basic engineering science are the main subjects in the first year, followed by a bias to civil engineering in the second year. The third year includes traffic and highway engineering and the fourth year, practical design projects, decision-making and communication. Most students take languages as part of the course, some studying in European universities before graduation.

Sunderland (*Civil Engineering*) A thorough treatment of basic principles is provided in this four year sandwich course. Major subject areas are structures, surveying, materials, geotechnics, mathematics and computing. Industrial placement occupies the third year. It is possible to combine this course with languages and/or management. Students can specialise in transportation, water and public health and environmental engineering.

Surrey (*Civil Engineering*) The course is a thick sandwich course with the third year spent on supervised professional/industrial training. About one third to a half of students complete their professional training overseas. This is the only course offering leadership and personal skills development as part of the curriculum, in addition to grounding in technological and management skills. Language courses (French, German and Spanish) and scholarships are available to suitable students as part of an electives programme. Transfer to the MEng course is possible at any stage up to the end of the third year.

Swansea (*Civil Engineering*) The course provides a scheme of study covering conventional subjects without undue specialisation. The department has an international reputation for its research and the development of computer software for the latest advances in engineering practice which involves students in the final year. Laboratory work is devised to give students hands-on experience. This is a full-time three year BEng or four year MEng course. Two field courses in surveying and one in Geology are assessed as part of the course.

Ulster (*Civil Engineering*) This is a four year BEng, or four and a half years MEng course. The content of both courses is the same for the first two years, initial selection for the MEng course taking place at the end of this two-year period. Industrial placement takes place during the third year, after which the final selection for the MEng course is made.

Warwick (*Civil Engineering*) (See **Engineering Science.**)

Westminster (*Civil Engineering*) This course is specially tailored for students entering without A-level mathematics. A standard civil engineering course is offered with free modules in each year. A four year sandwich course is also available with one year of industrial training after Year 2.

Wolverhampton (*Civil Engineering Management*) This course covers civil engineering, construction, contract management, law, finance and foreign language options. This is a four year sandwich course.

● **Top research universities**
Bradford, Bristol, London (Imp) (UC), Newcastle, Heriot-Watt, Cardiff, Swansea, Birmingham, City, Leeds, Liverpool, UMIST, Sheffield, Southampton, Belfast, Dundee, Edinburgh.

● **Colleges and Institutes of Higher Education offering degree courses**
Bolton (Inst), Bradford and Ilkley (Comm Coll), Cardiff (Inst), Doncaster (Coll), Nene (Coll), NESCOT, North East Wales (Inst), Stockport (Coll), Suffolk (Coll).

● **Other courses to be considered**
Architecture, building, public health inspection and surveying (building, land and hydrographic).

ENGINEERING (COMPUTER)
(See also under **Computer Science**)

● **Special subject requirements:** 2 A-levels in mathematics/physics subjects. Physics required at Hull and also GCSE (grade A–C) chemistry.

● **Subject information:** The design and application of modern computer systems is fundamental to all these courses which will also include electronic engineering, software engineering and computer-aided engineering. Several universities offer sufficient flexibility to enable final course decisions to be made in the second year.

Aberdeen (*Microelectronic Software Engineering*) (See **Engineering Science.**)

Aberystwyth (*Software Engineering*) The BEng course consists of three main themes: software quality, software design and software and system safety. It is enhanced by a study of business organisation, accounting finance, intellectual property rights, industrial relations, health and safety.

Anglia (Poly Univ) Several courses are offered with information systems including Multimedia Systems, Software Engineering and Business Information Systems, which can also be combined with Product Design.

Bangor (*Computer Systems Engineering*) This course provides graduates with a specialist knowledge in computing hardware and software focusing on applications and design methods. The course includes computer architecture and design, artificial intelligence and digital systems design.

Bath (*Computer Software Technology*) The course has a pronounced mathematical base which includes options in cryptography, graphics, data bases and programming languages.

Bradford (*Software Engineering*) There are four overlapping courses in computing. Software engineering focuses on problems in industry and commerce. Other courses which have a similar academic content are Computer Science, Computing and Management and Information Systems.

Bristol (*Computer Systems Engineering*) This course embraces both hardware (from micro-electronics to computer architectures) and software with a broad mathematical foundation. There is also a course with European Studies with foreign language studies in Years 1 and 2.

Central Lancashire (*Software Engineering*) This is a three year full-time or four year sandwich course covering systems analysis, technical aspects of computing and programming and business skills.

City (*Computer Systems Engineering*) Three year and four year courses aim to prepare the graduate for an engineering career in the fields of electronic digital systems and computers. In the final year six specialised subjects are chosen from a wide range of modules including aspects of programming, human computer interaction and engineering management.

Coventry (*Computer Hardware and Software Engineering*) This is a modular course with an optional year in industry. Final year topics include image and speech signals, expert systems and parallel computer architectures.

Cranfield (*Information Systems Engineering*) This course has a common first year with Command and Control, Communications and Information Systems, Computer Management Studies are completed with the emphasis on the latter.

De Montfort (*Software Engineering*) The course concentrates on modern approaches to the design, development and implementation of high quality software. The major emphasis throughout the course is on the development of automated tools. Communication Engineering is also offered.

Glamorgan Courses are offered in Software Engineering in the Combined and Joint Honours and Combined Studies programmes.

Glasgow (*Electronic Systems and Microcomputer Engineering*) This course is similar to the degree offered in Electronics and Electrical Engineering, but has a much stronger emphasis on digital systems and software elements of electronic systems. There is also a degree course in Electronic and

Software Engineering. All seven degree courses in this department have a common first year allowing the final choice to be deferred until Year 2.

Hull Courses are offered in Computer Science with Information Engineering.

Kent (*Computer Systems Engineering*) This course develops the skills and expertise necessary for designing and using computer systems. Electronic hardware and programming software aspects of the subject are covered. Practical work occupies an important part of the course. Specialist topics include robotics and image processing, design of integrated circuits, object-oriented programming, concurrent programming and artificial intelligence.

Lancaster (*Computer Systems Engineering*) The course covers computer science and electronic engineering, with optional routes to both at the end of Year 1, communications, signal processing, microprocessors and software engineering. There are fourth year options in accounting principles, modern languages and marketing.

Leeds (*Electronic and Computer Engineering*) This is offered as a three, four or five year course leading to BEng or MEng, the choice being made at the end of level 2.

Leicester (*Electronic and Software Engineering*) This three year full-time degree offers specialisation from the beginning of the course. The degree provides a sound grasp of engineering principles with expertise in computers and computing systems and includes hardware, software and communications.

Liverpool John Moores (*Software Engineering*) The courses provides comprehensive coverage of computer systems programming and large scale software systems. Computer Aided Engineering is also offered.

London (Imp) (*Computing*) The department offers: three year courses in Computing, Information Systems Engineering, and Mathematics and Computer Science: and four year courses in Computing, Computing (Artificial Intelligence and Knowledge Engineering), Computing (European Programme of Study), Computing (Management and Information Systems), Computing (Mathematical Foundations and Formal Methods), Computing (Software Engineering), Information Systems Engineering, and Mathematics and Computer Science.

London (QMW) (*Computer Engineering*) The emphasis on this course lies in computer systems, software and artificial intelligence.

London (UC) A course is offered in Electronic Engineering with Computer Science.

Manchester (*Computer Engineering*) The department is rated 'excellent' in teaching.

Manchester Metropolitan (*Software Engineering*) A modular course with many options. Alternatively a 'named' degree course can be followed in Software Engineering or Information Systems.

Manchester (UMIST) (*Software Engineering*) This is a member of a closely integrated family of courses (Microelectronic Systems Engineering,

Computer Systems Engineering, Software Engineering and Electronic Systems Engineering) with a common first year. Transfer between courses is possible at the end of the first year. The courses all lead to a B.Eng in three years or an M.Eng in four years. Students are advised to apply for the four year variant, as it is a simple matter to transfer to the three year course whilst at UMIST. The courses all enjoy strong support from industry and students are recommended to undertake vacation placements in industry. A full time Industrial Liaison Officer is employed to assist students in finding sponsorship or vacation placements.

Napier (*Electronic and Computer Engineering*) This four year course, concerned with the analysis of computer systems (from high-level software design and development to low-level electronic components) and how they interface with external equipment, aims to give graduates a complete understanding of the specification, design and testing of computer systems.

Newcastle Degrees are offered in Computer Science, Computer Systems Engineering and Software Engineering.

Nottingham (*Computer Systems Engineering*) A three year course taught jointly by the departments of Computer Science and Electrical and Electronic Engineering. There is an optional industrial placement in Year 3.

Oxford (*Engineering and Computing Science*) This is a four year course. The first year is common with Engineering Science and transfers may take place up to the end of the year. The second and third years cover computer hardware and programming science. In the fourth year students undertake a project and three courses from a range of options including robotics, VLSI, finite element methods and computer graphics.

Paisley (*Software Engineering*) This is a course with a strong practical bias and includes a 12 month period of industrial placement.

Portsmouth Courses are offered in Computer Engineering, Electronic and Computer Engineering, and Computer Systems Engineering.

Robert Gordon (*Electronic and Computer Engineering*) This is a four year course with common study for the first two years with other courses in the School of Electronic and Electrical Engineering, such as Electronic and Communications Engineering.

Sheffield (*Software Engineering*) The first year is common with Computer Science and Computer Science with Mathematics, and transfers are possible up to the end of that year. The second year involves the study of computer design, software engineering practice, theory of computing. In the third year students undertake a design project and four options from a wide range. Specialisms include computer graphics and artificial intelligence.

Sheffield Hallam (*Electronic Systems and Information Engineering*) This is an electronic engineering degree programme with a study of control engineering as an optional route. There is a common first year course and options in languages.

Southampton (*Computer Engineering*) Several courses are offered by the department of Electronics and Computer Science. The MEng course in Computer Engineering covers both hardware and software presented in modular form.

Sunderland (*Computer Systems Software*) This degree, with an optional sandwich year, covers digital and analogue electronics and computer hardware and software, as well as advances in robotics and communications. Students study applications involving the use of microprocessors, computer systems and very large scale integration (VLSI). Management and language options are available and an extra year leads to an MEng.

Teesside (*Information and Control Engineering*) A modular course with a common first year. The department is strong in research fields of flow measurement and optical measurements.

Ulster (*Software Engineering*) This is a four year sandwich course covering software, hardware and systems engineering.

Warwick (*Computer Systems Engineering*) A wide choice of options is available in Years 2 and 3. Modules include artificial intelligence, robotics, telecommunications and computer graphics.

Westminster (*Software Engineering*) This is a modular course which covers software production processes. It is one of 6 courses offered under Computer Science with some opportunities to transfer.

York (*Computer Systems and Software Engineering*) The computer science and engineering course schemes provide an education in a complex and fast growing area of study - Information Technology. The course forms a preparation for careers ranging from research work to the design and application of computer systems in industry, commerce, science and administration. Industrial experience is essential for part of the course. It is possible to transfer to Computer Science in the first two years.

• **Colleges and Institutes of Higher Education offering degree courses**
Barnsley (Coll), Bolton (Inst), Buckinghamshire (Coll), Doncaster (Coll), Farnborough (Coll), Swansea (Inst), West Herts (Coll).

• **Other courses to be considered**
Computer courses, electronic engineering, mathematics.

ENGINEERING (ELECTRICAL AND ELECTRONIC)

• **Special subject requirements:** 2–3 A levels in mathematics/physics subjects. GCSE (grade A–C) chemistry in come cases.

• **Subject information:** Options to specialise should be considered when choosing courses, so read the prospectuses carefully. In this field options could include opto-electronics and optical communication systems, microwave systems, radio frequency engineering and circuit technology.

Aberdeen (*Engineering (Electrical and Electronic)*) This is a four year BEng degree with a common first year for all students. Specialisation follows in Years 3 and 4 in microelectronics and software engineering included in this degree.

Abertay Dundee (*Electronic and Electrical Engineering*) The curriculum provides options in electronic power engineering, photonic engineering, product design, electronic/electrical systems, management, marketing management and consumer electronics.

Anglia (Poly Univ) (*Instrumentation Electronics*) This is offered as a combined course at the Cambridge campus. Courses are also offered in Audiotechnology and Audio and Music Technology.

Aston (*Electrical and Electronic Engineering*) Courses are offered in Communications Engineering, Electronic Engineering with Computer Science, Electromechanical Engineering and Electronic Systems Engineering (with a strong emphasis in computer science and telecommunications). Three and four year courses are offered, and industrial sponsorship is available.

Bangor (*Electronic Engineering*) This is a BEng/MEng course - one of the first MEng courses in Britain. Year 1 covers engineering, computing and business with foreign language options. The intensive academic study is combined with a planned programme of training and experience with the sponsoring company. The university assists applicants in obtaining the sponsorships and the course is highly regarded in industry. The degree in Electronic Engineering with Power Electronics pays special attention to the use of electronic materials in high power applications. It covers power distribution, energy exploitation and electrical machines. Particular emphasis is placed on transducers, instrumentation, computer control techniques and power electronics.

Bath (*Electrical and Electronic Engineering*) The aim of this BSc/MEng course is to provide a fully integrated programme of development for the electronic and electrical engineer. The curriculum emphasises not only the academic abilities but also the personal skills which will enable a graduate to operate effectively in industry. The final year options allow specialisation in electronics, communications, control engineering, electrical machines and power systems. A wide range of courses is offered in this department all with a common first year. Study abroad and foreign language tuition are also available.

Belfast (*Electrical and Electronic Engineering*) Levels 1 and 2 are common to all students who may then specialise in such subjects as electrical machines, systems control, power systems, microelectronics, microwaves, or computer and microprocessor technology or applied electronics. The course has a common first year with Electronics and Software Engineering and Computer Systems Engineering.

Birmingham (*Electronic Engineering*) Three and four year programmes leading to BEng and MEng are offered. Specialisms and degree courses include communications engineering, computer engineering and integrated circuit control engineering. Options in French, German, Spanish, Russian or Japanese.

Bournemouth (*Electronic Systems Design*) This is a three or four year full time course of study with a strong emphasis on design but which includes business and financial management and language study. Work experience takes place in Europe in Year 2.

Bradford Several courses are offered with a BEng programme which includes industrial training and MEng courses in electrical, electronic, communication and computer systems engineering. Most courses offer language options. There is also a course in Electronic Imaging and Media Communications which includes information technology, sound and visual media, music and marketing.

Brighton (*Electronic or Electrical and Electronic Engineering*) Enrolment is common to all the courses. In the first two years studies consist of engineering fundamentals, mathematics, software engineering, broadcast engineering, electrical and electronic engineering and engineering applications. In the final year students study engineering management, perform an individual project and select from ten specialist subjects. The choice between sandwich and full-time study and the selection of specialisation are delayed until the student is on the course. Selected students from the common entry are offered the opportunity to undertake a five year MEng degree. French and German can be taken at minor level.

Bristol (*Electrical and Electronic Engineering*) Three courses share a common first two years and specialism takes place in Year 3. Transfers between Electrical and Electronic, Electrical, Electronic and Communication Engineering are easily accommodated. Language studies are offered in Years 1 and 2. Third year options include communications, robotics, radio frequency and microwave designs and industrial electronics. A course in Computer Systems Engineering is also offered which embraces electronic engineering, computer science and artificial intelligence.

Bristol UWE (*Electronic Engineering*) The course covers electronics. microprocessor systems, communications and signal processing plus language options. There is also a modular course in Electrical and Electronic Engineering.

Brunel (*Electrical and Electronic Engineering*) This is a broad based sandwich course which includes application of electrical and electronic engineering to communications, control, instrumentation, power electronics and systems. In the final year students choose a mix of eight subjects from a range of subjects. Specialisation leading to a named degree (including microelectronic engineering) takes place in semesters 5 and 6.

Cambridge (See under **Engineering Science.**)

Cardiff (*Electrical and Electronic Engineering*) There is a largely common first year of study for all degree schemes. Limited transfer is possible between sandwich and full-time courses at the end of the first year. Separate courses in Electronics are also available.

Central England (*Electronic Engineering*) This is a four year sandwich course with industrial placements in the first and second years. In Years 2 and 3 options are available in software engineering, communications, control and automation and a foreign language option. Courses are also offered in Electrical Power Engineering and joint courses with languages (French and German).

Central Lancashire (*Electronic Engineering*) The BEng course is centred around a core of electronics including computer-aided design, computer and digital systems, signal analysis, microprocessors and control. There is a final year option between telecommunications, power electronics or digital image processing and other specialisms including medical electronic sound and vision recording, satellite communication and computing options.

City (*Electrical and Electronic Engineering*) Full-time and sandwich courses (BSc) are offered. There is also an MEng course involving an extra year of study. BSc students may apply for transfer to the MEng course. Because of a major joint programme of physics, electrical, electronic and control engineering, instrumentation and systems engineering, much of the first and second years is taken in common and transfers are possible at the end of the first year.

Coventry (*Electrical and Electronic Engineering*) The common first and second years establish a broad base in electrical and electronic engineering. The final year offers a wide range of options at both Honours and degree level. These include: microwave and optical transmission; analogue communication systems; data communication and signal processing; computer-aided electronic engineering; computer systems and networks; control systems; power drives. The majority of students take the sandwich route although the three year full-time route is also available in appropriate cases.

Cranfield (Shrivenham) (*Electrical Engineering*) This is a broad-based electrical/electronic/mechanical engineering course biased towards land or aerial vehicle systems in the final year.

De Montfort (*Electronic Engineering*) A broad spectrum of electronic engineering topics is covered in the first two years with later options including product design and industrial studies. This is a four year sandwich course with the third year spent on an industrial placement. Those who have taken language options (French or German) may spend this period abroad. A course in Electrical Engineering is also offered.

Derby (*Electrical/Electronic Engineering with the Environment*) The first stage of these courses covers electrical, mechanical and environmental sciences together with computing and mathematics. Pollutions, hazards, safety factors and control systems occupy the second stage of the course with legal and managerial issues in stage three.

Dundee (*Electronic and Electrical Engineering*) This is a four year BEng or MEng course with a common programme of study with degrees coupled with physics and management in the first two years. The range of topics offered in Year 4 covers virtually all branches of Electrical and Electronic Engineering, including Microcomputer Systems.

Durham (See under **Engineering**.)

East Anglia (*Electronic Engineering*) This course and the Computer Systems Engineering course follow a common core during the first year, the Honours programmes commencing in Year 2. Two further courses are now on offer covering Electronic Design and Technology and Electronics with Business Studies. There is also a new course in Electronic Engineering with a year abroad in Europe or North America.

East London (*Electrical and Electronic Engineering*) Five courses are offered covering electrical and electronic engineering, computer and control engineering, telecommunication systems design and power systems engineering.

Edinburgh (*Electronics and Electrical Engineering*) This is a four year course with the MEng extending to five years. A wide range of topics is covered with design projects involved in Year 3. The BEng degree can become specialised in Year 4 with options in microelectronics and communications engineering.

Essex (*Electronics Systems Engineering*) This course has several pathways including Computers, Telecommunications and a European scheme in Germany or France. Transfers between degrees offered in the department are possible.

Exeter (See under **Engineering Science.**)

Glamorgan (*Electrical and Electronic Engineering*) This three year full-time or four year sandwich course is recognised by the IEE and leads to Chartered Engineer status after appropriate industrial experience. Modules include mathematics, signal transmission and production methods. Specialist routes are available in the final year.

Glasgow (*Electronics and Electrical Engineering*) The department also offers seven different undergraduate courses including Avionics and Electronics with Music. The first year is common to all courses (except Electronics and Music) and the final choice of degree can be deferred to the beginning of the second year. The course in Electronics and Electrical Engineering is broadly based and aims to produce graduate engineers familiar with many aspects of the field from power engineering to digital computers.

Glasgow Caledonian (*Electronic Engineering*) The course covers control and monitoring systems and quality assurance. There are options in telecommunications, power electronics and computer networks.

Greenwich (*Electrical and Electronic Engineering*) A three year course with the option of a year in industry, which provides a good foundation in electronic engineering and computer hardware and software, with the emphasis on computer-aided analysis and design. Final year specialisms include computer hardware and software engineering, telecommunications systems or instrumentation and control systems. (*Electronic Engineering*) is also a three year or sandwich course with the emphasis and range of options in electronic subjects.

Heriot-Watt (*Electrical and Electronic Engineering*) The department offers a four year BEng or a five year MEng degree. The first three years are common to the two degree courses offered. Separate courses thereafter lead either to an Honours degree at the end of the fourth year or to an MEng degree at the end of the fifth year in automation systems, communications systems, computer systems, microwaves and electronics or power engineering.

Hertfordshire (*Electrical and Electronic Engineering*) This is a three year full-time or four year sandwich course with a strong emphasis on design and information technology. Project work is a feature of this course from

Year 1, including the design of a product through to it final marketing. Options are available in digital signal processing, languages, optoelectronics and medical electronics.

Huddersfield (*Electronic and Electrical Engineering*) This is a broad-based course covering analogue and digital electronics, microelectronics, communications engineering, software and hardware in computer systems and electrical machines. After two years academic study and a year spent in industry students choose which of the four degrees (Electronic and Electrical, Electronic, Electronic and Information or Electronic and Communications) they will study for in the final year.

Hull (*Electronic Engineering*) Four courses are offered in VLSI Systems and Computer Engineering, Electronic Communications Engineering, Electronic Control and Robot Engineering and Optoelectronic and Vision Systems Engineering. These four options have a common course for the first three out of the four years so a change of course is possible.

Humberside (*Electrical Engineering*) (see **Engineering Science**.)

Keele (*Electronics*) The fundamentals of electronics are introduced in the first two years and the final year provides a range of core and option subjects including electronic circuit designs, microprocessors, microwave electronics and computer-aided design.

Kent (*Electronic Engineering*) The first year (Part I) is taken within the Information Technology scheme made up of a number of units, and students can defer their choice of degree until the beginning of the second year. Several degree courses with different specialism are offered including Electronic Engineering with Medical Electronics and a four year European Electronic Engineering course with a period of study abroad.

Kingston Electronics is offered with Computing and Business with foreign languages and industrial placement optional.

Lancaster (See under **Engineering Science**.)

Leeds (*Electronic Engineering; Electronic and Electrical Engineering*) The course is broadly based and embraces most aspects of Electrical and Electronic Engineering but specialisation in later years is possible. The first two years are common and have a common entry requirement. Subsequently it is possible to proceed either to the final year of the enhanced three year BEng course or the third year of the extended MEng course. Both courses are fully accredited by the Institution of Electrical Engineers. Options include communication systems, microwave engineering and power electronics.

Leeds Metropolitan (*Electronic/Electrical Engineering*) Three courses are offered with a high level of common studies in the early stages. Option modules in Electronic Systems Engineering, Communication Systems Engineering and Electronic Music and Media Technology.

Leicester (See under **Engineering Science**.)

Liverpool (*Electrical and Electronic Engineering*) The department offers three and four year courses for students who wish to study either electronic or electrical engineering with a very wide choice of subjects leading to specialisation.

Liverpool John Moores (*Electrical and Electronic Engineering*) This course can be taken as a three year full-time or four year sandwich course. It covers most aspects of the subject including computer engineering and engineering design, and a very wide range of specialised electrical and electronic options. Courses in Broadcast Engineering, Electronic Systems Engineering, Combined Engineering Studies and European Engineering Studies are also offered.

London (Imp) (*Electrical and Electronic Engineering*) The department offers three year BEng courses in Electrical and Electronic Engineering and Information Systems Engineering; and four year MEng courses in Electrical and Electronic Engineering (with Management or a Year Abroad), and Information Systems Engineering.

London (King's) (*Electronic and Electrical Engineering*) All engineering courses are taught on the flexible course unit system. Degree courses are offered in Computer Systems and Electronics, Electronic Engineering and Communications and Radio Engineering. Students of high ability may transfer to the four year master's degree in Electronic Engineering Design at the end of their second year.

London (QMW) (*Electrical, Electronic, Telecommunications*) The final choice between these courses need not be made until the end of the first year. Electronic Engineering emphasises the design and application of electronic circuits. The Telecommunications Engineering course covers all aspects of communications. The Computer Engineering course emphasises computer systems and software, and the Electrical Engineering course is broad and general. Electronic Engineering is also offered with French, German and Spanish.

London (UC) (*Electronic and Electrical Engineering*) This course and Electronic Engineering with Opto-electronics EE/O and Electronic Engineering with Computer Science EE/CS all have a common first year. EEE gives a broad education, EE/O covers communications and CD players and EE/CS concentrates on digital circuits, computer design and programming. Courses are also offered with medical electronics and management.

Loughborough (*Electronic and Electrical Engineering; Electronic Computer and Systems Engineering; Electromechanical Power Engineering; Electronic Engineering and Physics; Systems Engineering*) Three, four and five year courses are offered and transfer between courses is possible during the first two years. In Electronic Engineering and Physics the first two years include a broad range of electronics and physics subjects with mathematics and computing. Experimental work is split equally. The majority of the final year is made up of electives with a project running for two terms. The Systems courses also include wider studies in management and ergonomic design whilst the Power Engineering course emphasises electrical and mechanical subjects, engineering applications, computer studies and management training.

Luton Courses are offered in Digital Systems Design and Electronic Engineering.

Manchester (*Electronic and Electrical Engineering*) There is an extensive range of programmes including European Studies and Japanese. The course leads to the BEng degree after 3 years or to the MEng after 4 years. A broad foundation leads to specialisation in Years 3 and 4. Industrial placements and overseas programmes are available.

Manchester Metropolitan (*Electrical and Electronic Engineering*) In this course, there is an emphasis on design and on practical work which begins in the first year with an electronics workshop, involving both design and construction, and with other sessions devoted to engineering practice. The course continues with a wide range of laboratory assignments and an individual technical project in the final year. A third year in industry is optional. Other routes are Communication and Electronic Engineering, Computer and Electronic Engineering and Electronic Engineering with Management.

Manchester (UMIST) (*Electronic Engineering*) This is a member of a closely integrated family of courses (Microelectronic Systems Engineering, Computer Systems Engineering, Software Engineering and Electronic Systems Engineering) with a common first year. Transfer between courses is possible at the end of the first year. The courses all lead to a B.Eng in three years or an M.Eng in four years. Students are advised to apply for the four year variant, as it is a simple matter to transfer to the three year course whilst at UMIST. The courses all enjoy strong support from industry and students are recommended to undertake vacation placements in industry. A full time Industrial Liaison Officer is employed to assist students in finding sponsorship or vacation placements.

Middlesex (*Electronic Engineering*) In this course (three years full-time or a four year sandwich), selection for the Honours and Ordinary courses takes place at the end of the second year. The final year mainstream studies cover communications, robotics, computing and microelectronics. Language options are possible in French, German and Spanish. Combined courses are also offered at major and minor levels.

Napier (*Electrical/Electronic Engineering*) This is a broad three or four year course which includes computer technology and business studies. A course in Electronic and Communication Engineering is also offered.

Newcastle (*Electrical and Electronic Engineering*) Three year BEng and four year MEng degrees are available in Electrical and Electronic Engineering, Electronic Engineering, Microelectronics and Software Engineering. A foundation year is available. Courses are fully accredited by IEE.

North London (*Electronic and Communications Engineering*) This is a three year course which emphasises design, engineering, computing and manufacturing production techniques. Electronics, communications and industrial studies are followed in all three years and acoustics is a specialised option in the final year.

Northumbria (*Electrical and Electronic Engineering*) This is a three year full-time or four year sandwich course following Foundation Studies in the first year. The second and third year studies contain increasing emphasis on electronic, information and computer systems linking academic vigour, engineering applications and business skills. Specialisation in the final year in information technology, instrumentation or power electronics leads to interesting careers in these areas. The first year is common with Communication and Electronic Engineering, and transfers are possible up to this stage. There are also separate degree courses in Optoelectronic Engineering and Microelectronic Engineering.

Nottingham (*Electrical and Electronic Engineering*) This is a three year course leading to a BEng, or four year to an MEng. The first and second years provide a largely common foundation for specialisation in the latter part of the course. The MEng course is for students who have maintained a consistently high standard throughout the first two years. Third and fourth year options include nuclear engineering, software engineering, microwaves and radiation, and French for engineers. There is also a course in Electronic Engineering with Mathematics or with languages.

Nottingham Trent (*Electrical and Electronic Engineering*) The main features of this three year full-time or four year sandwich course are design and computer case studies, project work and engineering applications. In the final year students can take electronics or power and communications options. Placements in France and Germany for some students.

Oxford Brookes (*Electronics*) Modules are offered covering electronics and computing with options in digital communications, medical instrumentation and robotics.

Paisley (*Electronic and Electrical Engineering*) A broad course is offered on a full-time or sandwich basis which includes management studies. There is also an Electronic Systems degree combined with an HND course.

Plymouth (*Electrical and Electronic Engineering*) This is a three year (full-time) or four year (sandwich) programme. Design exercises, case studies, group and individual projects are continued throughout the course. After the first two terms, students may opt for a more specialist final year in Electronic Engineering or Communications Engineering. Options available include satellite telecommunications, mobile communications, medical electronics and optoelectonics.

Portsmouth (*Electrical and Electronic Engineering*) A three year or four year sandwich course is offered. In both courses telecommunications, automation and robotics and microwave information can be taken as specialist subjects. There is a European programme and another course in Communication Systems Engineering.

Reading (*Electronic Engineering*) All Engineering students follow the same core courses in the first two terms, after which some transfers are possible. In subsequent years there is a strong emphasis on the use of computers in both the design and implementation of practical systems and with third year options in video and software engineering. Practical and project work are also emphasised throughout the course.

Robert Gordon (*Electronic and Electrical Engineering*) This is available as a broad-based three year BSc, with options in French and German, and a four year BEng with the first two years common with other electronics courses.

Salford (*Biomedical and Bioelectronic Engineering*) This course can be taken as a three year full-time or four year sandwich course. In the first two years biology, biological chemistry, electronics and human physiology are studied. The final year follows a modular programme allowing students to choose from seven subject areas. A wide range of other courses is also offered including electroacoustics and engineering with European or French Studies.

Sheffield (*Electrical and Electronic Engineering*) This is one of the largest departments in the country. A broad foundation leads to third year courses in Electrical Engineering, Electronic Engineering, and Electronic Engineering specialising in communications, computing or solid state devices. There are also degree courses in Control Engineering and Electronic Systems Engineering, which allow for considerable specialisation. A final choice between the two is made in Year 3.

Sheffield Hallam (*Electronic Systems and Control Engineering*) This sandwich course offers three main features - electronics, computer/ software engineering and instrumentation and control engineering. Language studies are also offered. Electronic Engineering and Electronic Systems and Information Engineering are also offered.

Southampton (*Electrical Engineering; Electronic Engineering*) Courses are offered in both Electrical and Electronic Engineering. Each course is divided into three parts. An emphasis on design exists in the third year of the Electrical Engineering course, whilst at the same stage the Electronic Engineering course offers options in communications, computers, control, electronic techniques or physical electronics.

South Bank (*Electrical and Electronic Engineering*) BEng (four year) and MEng (four and a half year) sandwich courses are offered, all having a common first year. These are broad-based courses which include industrial studies and computing, and allow for specialisation in the final year when students choose four options from nine subjects including languages, law and management. Electronic Engineering Management, Multimedia Engineering and Software Engineering for Real Time Systems are also offered.

Staffordshire (*Electrical Engineering; Electronic Engineering*) Both courses (which have a sandwich option) have a common first and second year, the main differences emerging in final year specialisation. Business management is studied throughout each course. A third degree course - Electrical and Electronic Engineering - has strong business management emphasis as well as a third year in industry.

Strathclyde (*Electrical and Electronic Engineering*) Courses of four and five years' duration are offered with the first three years in each case covering the fundamentals of the subject, maths and computer science. At the end of the third year candidates are selected for the appropriate course and undertake an individual project and specialisation in chosen fields.

Sunderland (*Electrical and Electronic Engineering*) This is a three year or four year sandwich course concerned with the development and operation of electrical equipment in aerospace, computer, satellite, communications and electricity generation and distribution technologies. Courses in the

School of Engineering have a common first semester (14 weeks) when the final course selection is made. Final specialism from a choice of options is made in the final year. It is also possible to take degree courses with special options in management or languages. A degree course in Communications and Electronic Engineering is also offered.

Surrey (*Electrical and Electronic Engineering*) Courses are offered at BEng and MEng levels with equal emphasis on academic study and industrial experience. Placements in France and Germany possible. A course in Information Systems Engineering is also offered to which students can transfer in Year 2 and which has a greater emphasis on computing, networks and software. All courses include Engineering Professional Studies, and enhanced four year MEng courses are also offered.

Sussex (*Electrical Engineering; Electronic Engineering; Electronics*) All engineering courses have a common first year with decisions being made to follow one of the five electrical/electronics courses in Year 2 which include Computer Systems, Business Management and Environmental Science specialisms.

Swansea (*Electronic and Electrical Engineering; Electronics with Computing Science*) Both courses share the same maths and electronic topics but the former gives emphasis to electrical power and electrical machines, and the latter emphasises computer science. There is also a degree course in Electronics with Communications and all these courses can be combined with a year in Europe or North America.

Teesside (*Electronic Engineering*) This is a three year or four year sandwich course, the first year being common to Computer Engineering and Instrumentation and Control Engineering, with transfers possible at the end of this year.

Ulster (*Electrical and Electronic Engineering*) A broad engineering course covering microprocessors, power electronics, instrumentation, communications engineering and automation.

Westminster (*Electronic Engineering*) This is an Enhanced course with an emphasis throughout on engineering applications and management and industrial studies. Years 1 and 2 are common with Control and Computer Engineering after which students choose their degree major.

York (*Electronic Engineering; Electronic Systems Engineering*) Students may transfer between courses up to the start of the third year. Part II (the second year) emphasises the design and analysis of electronic systems (including software). Years 3 and 4 have an options structure giving a wide range of choices. Electronic Engineering may also be taken as a three year course. Language options can be taken. There is also a three year course in Physical Electronics combining electronics and solid state physics.

● **Top research universities**
London (Imp) (QMW) (UC) (King's), UMIST, Southampton, Surrey, Belfast, Edinburgh, Bath, Birmingham, Bristol, Leeds, Liverpool, Loughborough, Sheffield, York, Glasgow, Strathclyde, Bangor.

- **Colleges and Institutes of Higher Education offering degree courses**
Barnsley (Coll), Bolton (Inst), Cardiff (Inst), Croydon (Coll), Gwent (Coll), Nene (Coll), New (Coll), NESCOT, North East Wales (Inst), Norwich City (Coll), Southampton (Inst), Stockport (Coll), Suffolk (Coll), Swansea (Inst).

- **Other courses to be considered**
Computer engineering, instrument and control engineering, lighting, physics, radio and television and telecommunications engineering.

ENGINEERING (MANUFACTURING)

- **Special subject requirements:** 2–3 A-levels in mathematics/science subjects; physics sometimes required at A-level and chemistry at GCSE (grade A–C).

- **Subject information:** Manufacturing Engineering is sometimes referred to as Production Engineering. It is a branch of the subject concerned with management aspects of engineering such as industrial organisation, purchasing and the planning and control of operations, and at the same time provides an overview of engineering design systems. These courses are often combined with mechanical engineering or with business/management studies.

Aberdeen A course is offered in Engineering with the focus on manufacturing systems.

Bath (*Manufacturing Systems/Engineering Management*) After a common first two years with engineering, students are involved in several management subjects including accounting, economics, industrial relations and business information systems, in addition to manufacturing systems. The course may be taken with French or German, and there is the opportunity for up to a year of integrated professional training.

Birmingham (*Manufacturing Engineering*) There is an option in Year 2 to follow the M.Eng course. Joint courses are also offered with business. A full-time industrial tutor liaises with UK and world industry.

Bradford Courses are offered in Manufacturing Systems with Management and Mechanical Engineering. The first four semesters are common with the Mechanical Engineering degree.

Bristol UWE (*Manufacturing Systems Engineering*) This is a modular course with language modules. There is a common first year with Aerospace Engineering and an opportunity to transfer at the end of the year.

Brunel (*Manufacturing Engineering*) There is a interdisipilinary design, systems integration and management emphasis on this programme. Study of technical subjects in French and German is possible. Study for a Masters degree may take place in France and Switzerland.

Cardiff Several courses are offered with Manufacturing Systems Engineering including management, mechanical engineering and Japanese Business Studies.

Central England (*Management of Manufacturing Systems*) This is a modular degree programme emphasising factors relating to manufacturing, costs and management systems. Specific subject areas cover engineering science, computer systems, design, quality and reliability.

Central Lancashire Manufacturing is offered as part of the Combined Honours programme.

Coventry (*Manufacturing Systems Engineering*) The course has a common first year with Mechanical Engineering and transfers are possible. The third year of this sandwich course may be spent in Europe, and Part II academic studies may be undertaken at a Spanish university.

De Montfort See entry in **Engineering (Mechanical)**. There is also a course in Sports Engineering concerned with the design and manufacture of sports-related equipment.

Dundee (*Manufacturing Engineering and Management*) This BEng or MEng course involves engineering science, physics and electronics in Year 1 expanding into manufacturing systems, technology and management in Years 2, 3 and 4.

East London (*Manufacturing Systems Engineering*) This is a four year sandwich course: each of the first three years consists of two academic terms followed by one spent in industry. The course is concerned with the design development, specification, procurement, installation and maintenance of equipment used in the engineering industry for the manufacture of goods. Language options in German, Spanish or French.

Glasgow Caledonian Courses are offered combining Business and Manufacturing Systems Engineering, Manufacturing Systems Engineering with Electronics and Computer Aided Engineering.

Hertfordshire (*Manufacturing Systems Engineering*) The course involves computer-aided design and robotics. French or German is studied and a three month placement in Europe is offered.

Humberside (*Manufacturing Systems*) The course covers manufacturing techniques, systems, quality assurance and reliability. An optional work placement is available in Year 3.

Kingston Manufacturing Systems is offered with Business Studies.

Lancaster Manufacturing is combined with Mechanical Engineering.

Leeds Metropolitan (*Manufacturing Systems Engineering*) This is a three year or four year sandwich course covering all aspects of production systems and manufacturing technology, and including financial and management studies. Other degree routes cover automation, design or management.

Liverpool (*Manufacturing Engineering and Management*) The course covers manufacturing technology, processes and systems, management studies and engineering and numerical studies.

Liverpool John Moores (*Manufacturing Systems Engineering*) This three year full-time or four year sandwich course covers mechanical technology, electrical technology and manufacturing systems, leading to management operations and project management. Courses in Combined Engineering Studies and European Engineering Studies are also offered.

Loughborough (*Manufacturing Engineering and Management*) Emphasis is given to the industrial application of engineering materials and manufacturing processes. Optional languages are offered at an elementary or advanced level.

Manchester Metropolitan (*Manufacturing Management*) Core units in this course include materials and manufacturing processes, design and product development, management resources and marketing.

Manchester (UMIST) (*Manufacturing Systems Engineering*) The first year course is common with Electro-Mechanical Engineering leading to Engineering Management, communications and systems analysis.

Middlesex (*Manufacturing Systems Engineering*) The course covers the technology of materials, business studies, plant operation and quality control.

Northumbria (*Manufacturing Systems Engineering*) This can be taken either as a four year sandwich course with the third year spent in industry, or as a three year course. At the end of Year 1 it is possible to transfer to Materials or Mechanical Engineering. It covers electronics, mechanics, materials, power and energy, control engineering, computer-aided engineering, process technology, and business and management.

Nottingham (*Production Operations Management*) The emphasis of this course is on the analytical techniques and methods of production and operations management. Topics include ergonomics and work designs, computer studies and management practices. There are modern language options in Years 1 and 2.

Nottingham Trent (*Manufacturing Engineering*) This is a four year sandwich course with a European language option and exchange programmes in Europe.

Paisley (*Manufacturing Systems with Management*) This is a four and a half year sandwich course with two periods of industrial training. The course covers mechanical and electrical engineering systems and computer-aided design and management operations.

Plymouth (*Manufacturing Systems Engineering*) A three or four year sandwich degree including the computing and control of the manufacturing process, the organisation and purchase of materials, planning and control of production and the use of computer technology for data handling, data acquisition and system control. After a common first year it is possible to change to Mechanical or Materials Engineering.

Portsmouth (*Manufacturing Systems Engineering*) There is a focus on manufacturing and project management with the option to transfer to other courses at the end of Year 1 including a European degree. Courses are also offered in Engineering Design and Materials and Technology Management.

Salford (*Manufacturing Management*) Two years are spent at University College Salford or North East Wales Institute followed by two years at the University. The entry point is tailored for students who don't have standard entry qualifications and who embark on a Higher National Diploma course in Years 1 and 2.

Sheffield Hallam (*Design and Manufacture with Management*) Manufacturing technology, computer applications, marketing and human resource management are all included on this three year full-time or four year sandwich course. Computer-Aided Engineering and Design is also available.

South Bank Courses are offered in Industrial Design, Integrated Engineering and Technology Management.

Staffordshire (*Manufacturing Systems Engineering*) A modular course structure enables students to choose from a wide choice of options and leads to a BEng degree. Specialist subjects include a European language.

Strathclyde (*Manufacturing Engineering and Management*) Broad-based courses are offered with a good balance between technology and management.

Sunderland (*Manufacturing Engineering*) This is one course in the Management of Technology programme which also includes Management, Operation Management, Information Technology and Product Design Management degrees. Students study the research, design, production and management of products, including technologies such as robotics and organisational issues such as Just In Time and business process engineering.

Teesside (*Manufacturing Systems with Business*) The course is an integrated combination of approximately 70 per cent engineering and manufacture and 30 per cent business studies.

Ulster (*Manufacturing Systems Management*) The course involves manufacturing techniques, processes and materials as well as accounting and marketing. European languages are also offered with a possibility of industrial placement abroad.

Warwick (*Engineering - Manufacturing Systems*) The course involves mechanical and electrical engineering, materials and design. Third year options include automation and robotics, quality techniques and reliability and design for manufacture. MEng is also offered.

Westminster (*Manufacturing Systems Engineering*) The course plan allows for the choice of three alternative pathways in Year 3 - Mechanical Engineering, Mechanical Design or Manufacturing Systems.

● **Colleges and Institutes of Higher Education offering degree courses**
Bolton (Inst), Buckinghamshire (Coll), Cardiff (Inst), Gwent (Coll), North East Wales (Inst), Swansea (Inst).

● **Other courses to be considered**
Business Studies, Mechanical Engineering.

ENGINEERING (MECHANICAL)

● **Special subject requirements:** 2–3 A-levels in mathematics/science subjects. Physics and mathematics often required at A-level. English, chemistry at GCSE (grade A–C) often specified.

• **Subject information:** All courses involve the design, installation and maintenance of equipment used in industry. Thermodynamics, computer-aided design, fluid mechanics and materials science are subjects fundamental to this branch of engineering. Many universities offer students the opportunity to transfer to other engineering courses in year two.

Aberdeen (*Mechanical Engineering*) (See **Engineering Science.**)

Abertay Dundee (*Mechanical Engineering*) There is an emphasis on design and manufacturing technology, management and mechatronics. Modern language electives are available.

Aston (*Mechanical Engineering*) There is a common first year with Electromechanical Engineering which allows students to transfer between courses. The sandwich or full-time programme provides a choice of courses in which there is an emphasis on computer-assisted design. There are final year options in materials science and production engineering. The most able students take the extra year leading to the MEng degree. MEng students can take European studies with French or German and placements abroad.

Bath (*Mechanical Engineering*) This course shares a common first two years with Aerospace, Automotive and Manufacturing MEng degrees. In years three and four students may choose from an extensive range of options such as biomedical engineering and environmental engineering. The course may be taken with either French or German, and there is the opportunity for up to a full year of integrated professional training.

Belfast (*Mechanical and Industrial Engineering*) There is a common first year with Manufacturing Engineering. The first two years introduce all students to the fundamentals of engineering at the end of which the choice is made between mechanical engineering (with or without specialisation in food industry) or industrial engineering, nuclear power or internal combustion engineering.

Birmingham (*Mechanical Engineering*) There are options in automotive engineering, modular machine systems and power engineering. There is also a course in mechanical and manufacturing engineering specifically designed for the more able student. The School of Engineering employs a full-time Industrial Training Tutor.

Bradford (*Mechanical Engineering*) The course provides a broad training in all aspects of modern mechanical engineering including a significant amount of production and manufacture and integrated EAI training provided 'in-house'. A wide range of final year topics including automotive engineering is offered. Normal entry is for an integrated thin sandwich course but a modular arrangement allows flexibility of course arrangement. For capable and well motivated students, a BEng-MEng course is available. Final selection takes place at the end of the third year of the BEng course and the selected students follow a two year course offering a further broadening and deepening of study and including an industrially related dissertation. Language options are offered.

Brighton (*Mechanical Engineering*) BEng and MEng courses are offered on a full-time or sandwich basis. Forensic engineering is offered in the final year.

Bristol (*Mechanical Engineering*) Two degree courses are offered leading to the BEng and the MEng course, both sharing a common first year. In the third year of the BEng course, a study is made of materials, applied mechanics and thermodynamics and professional engineering studies. On the MEng course the third year course covers design and manufacture, micro-electronics, dynamics and control, acoustics and process engineering followed by fourth year studies in robotics, quality control and assurance and industrial studies. There is also a course in Mechanical Engineering with Manufacturing Systems. Transfers to other engineering courses are possible up to the end of Year 2.

Bristol UWE (*Mechanical Engineering*) There are options in manufacturing systems, aerospace manufacture and languages on this three year full-time course.

Brunel (*Mechanical Engineering*) The course combines academic study and laboratory and design work over three years, with the option of industrial training for a four year package. Practical design is a feature of the course and computers are used extensively. Mode of study and choice of specialisation can be varied during the initial years of study. Courses are also offered with an emphasis on Automotive Design, Aeronautics or Building Services, or with Electronic Systems. Language studies can be followed in parallel with these courses.

Cambridge (See under **Engineering Science**.)

Cardiff There are several three or four year BEng or MEng courses, including Mechanical and Manufacturing Systems, Engineering, Manufacturing Systems and Manufacturing Management , as well as a four year Manufacturing Systems with Japanese course including three months in Japan. There is a common engineering first semester for all students and a well-established personal tutor system.

Central England (*Mechanical Engineering*) This modular course enables students to switch between degree courses at the end of the first semester.

Central Lancashire (*Mechanical Engineering*) A four year sandwich course with a period of industrial placement from April of Year 2 to December of Year 3. Language tuition is available for students who wish to complete part of their course at an institution elsewhere in the EC under the European Credit Transfer System pilot scheme.

City (*Mechanical Engineering*) Full-time and sandwich courses are offered with final two year options in computer-aided engineering, gas turbine engineering, vibration and acoustics.

Coventry (*Mechanical Engineering*) This is a four year sandwich course. There is a practical emphasis to the course with strong links with industry in UK and in Europe which includes instrumentation with microprocessors and some choice involving automotive engineering and control engineering in the final year. Foreign language options are available. (*Automotive Engineering*) This course has a common first year with other engineering courses. A design studio based course targeted to the automotive industry. A course in Manufacturing Systems Engineering is offered.

Cranfield (Shrivenham) (*Mechanical Engineering*) During the first two years, general engineering principles are studied - much of the course being taken in common with students reading for electrical and civil engineering degrees. In the final year, students can specialise in automotive or aeromechanical engineering systems, weapons systems, reliability and trials, electro-technology and land vehicle systems. The Silsoe campus has a course in Agricultural Engineering.

De Montfort (*Manufacturing Engineering*) The first half of the course in mechanical engineering and manufacture mechatronics is broadly the same as for Engineering, allowing transfers to take place. Students undertake in-depth study of stress analysis, dynamics and control, thermodynamics and fluid mechanics. This is a four year sandwich course including industrial placement. A four year integrated course in Industrial Design is also offered.

Derby (*Mechanical/Manufacture Engineering*) After a broad engineering base students specialise in some depth in three subjects chosen from a range of topics, eg thermal power, manufacturing, materials, waste systems management, finance and business management and CAD and technology.

Dundee (*Mechanical Engineering*) The first two years are common with Manufacturing Engineering, with the focus on mechanical engineering in Years 3 and 4. BEng and MEng degrees are offered.

Durham (*Mechanical Engineering*) (See **Engineering Science**.)

Edinburgh (*Mechanical Engineering*) The important basic subjects include dynamics, fluid mechanics, thermodynamics, materials science, solid mechanics and design. In addition students make an optional choice of topics such as control, nuclear engineering and heat transfer. Electronics is a compulsory subject in the second and third years.

Exeter (See under **Engineering Science**.)

Glamorgan (*Mechanical Engineering*) This is a four year sandwich course with an industrial placement in the third year. There are major options in plant, manufacturing and mechanical engineering. Considerable emphasis is placed on engineering applications.

Glasgow (*Mechanical Engineering*) A common course is taken by all students initially opting for Aeronautical and Mechanical Engineering and Naval Architecture and Ocean Engineering. Specialisation then follows in the third and fourth years.

Greenwich (*Mechanical Engineering*) Industrial training is compulsory in the third year. Final year options include thermal energy plant, fluids handling technology and automatic control systems. The degree course in Manufacturing Engineering covers mechanical principles, computer-aided design, manufacturing processes and engineering management.

Heriot-Watt (*Mechanical Engineering*) The first year is taken in common with Energy Resource and Mechanical Engineering. The four year course leads to the BEng, and the five year MEng course is offered to promising students. In the fourth year there are two streams - the conventional stream and the computer-aided engineering stream. There are also courses in Offshore Engineering.

Hertfordshire (*Mechanical Engineering*) This is a sandwich course of four years extending over eight semesters (the sixth is spent in industry). Students major in a selection of subjects from dynamics, mechanics, materials, thermodynamics, engineering design, production, science and technology or vehicle body engineering. There could be a placement in Germany for Vehicle students. A course in Manufacturing Systems Engineering is also offered with compulsory French or German.

Huddersfield (*Engineering Design: Mechanical*) A broad-based, strongly vocational sandwich course is offered with the placement in the third year. Thee is an emphasis on engineering design, science, materials and commercial enterprise. The course can also be taken with European Studies which includes a language option. A course is also offered with an energy and environmental component.

Hull (*Mechanical Design Engineering*) BEng and MEng courses are offered. An enhanced four year course includes Engineering Design and Manufacture and there is also a three year course in Computer-Aided Engineering.

Humberside (*Mechanical Engineering*) (See **Engineering Science**.)

Kingston (*Mechanical Engineering*) May be taken as a three year or as a four year sandwich course. The first year of the course is common with Aerospace and Manufacturing Engineering. The course can include topics in aeronautical or production engineering, control engineering, materials science, financial management or French. There is also a course in Manufacturing Engineering.

Lancaster (*Engineering (Mechanical)*) The first year course is common to all specialisms, with the final choice of subject being made at the end of the year. Mechanical Engineering specialisms commence in the final term of the second year and continue through the third year. A four year MEng degree in Mechanical and Electronic Engineering (Mechatronics) is an extension of the BSc course with two streams, one a bias in mechanical engineering, one in electronics.

Leeds (*Mechanical Engineering*) A common course is taken by all students who then divide between the three year BEng course with two projects and eight options from 30 subjects, and the four year MEng course in which projects and optional subjects occupy the third and fourth years. This highly regarded intensive course has a strong design component. There is a large proportion of continuous assessment.

Leicester (*Mechanical Engineering*) (See under **Engineering Science**.)

Liverpool (*Mechanical Engineering*) This is a three or four year course with options in a wide range of subjects from pipeline design to nuclear or production engineering. One of the specialist areas of the department is that of impact research. (*Mechanical Systems and Design Engineering*) This is for students who are particularly interested in design engineering and computer-aided engineering.

Liverpool John Moores (*Mechanical Engineering; Marine Engineering*) These three year full-time or four year sandwich courses cover mathematics and computation, mechanical, electrical and manufacturing technology, computer aided design, organisation and technology management, with later specialisation in mechanical or marine engineering applications. Marine and Offshore Engineering is also available.

London (Imp) (*Mechanical Engineering*) The department offers three year BEng courses in Mechanical Engineering, and Mechanical Engineering (Total Technology); and four year MEng courses in Mechanical Engineering (with Total Technology or a Year Abroad). The Total Technology courses require industrial sponsorship from firms linked with Imperial.

London (King's) (*Mechanical Engineering*) The BEng course of three years' duration covers general principles in the first two years and allows for specialisation in the third year. A study of computer programming and the use of computers occupies an important part of the course.

London (QMW) (*Mechanical Engineering*) Students take 16 recommended basic half-units including courses in maths, materials and electrical engineering, and a project is taken in the third year. Students wishing to specialise in a particular branch of mechanical engineering can take the Mechanical Engineering (Specialised) degree, and there are various combinations of joint Honours. The first eighteen months of the course is taken with Civil and Aeronautical Engineering students, allowing transfer between degree courses.

London (UC) (*Mechanical Engineering*) Four year MEng and three year BEng degree programmes are available in Mechanical Engineering, both of which provide a broad coverage of the subject across the complete range of industrial applications. Design is taught in all years, with management covered in all but the first year. Options include modern languages. Engineering with Business Finance and Mechanical Engineering with Bioengineering are also offered.

Loughborough (*Mechanical Engineering*) The modular structure of the courses offered enables students to choose from a range of options. Suitable applicants qualify for Government top flight vacancies. The course in Automotive Engineering has a common first year with Aeronautical Engineering. Courses divide in Year 2; elementary French and German are studied.

Manchester (*Mechanical Engineering*) Three year BEng and four year MEng programmes are offered, together with European and Engineering with Business programmes. The course is rated 'excellent' for teaching quality.

Manchester Metropolitan (*Mechanical Engineering*) Continually updated in line with new technology and the changing needs of industry, the mechanical engineering courses oriented towards design and analysis or manufacturing systems are broad-based and practical. Final year studies include equipment engineering, materials selection, manufacturing management and an individual industrially relevant project.

Manchester (UMIST) (*Mechanical Engineering*) In the first two years of this course it is possible to choose as an option one topic from modern languages (German or French) or history of science and technology. In the third year a study of engineering design and industrial management is compulsory. The course in Engineering Manufacture and Management is an Enhanced course leading to the BSc/BEng double degree which is run jointly by UMIST and Manchester Business School. There are also courses in Mechanical Engineering with Materials and Manufacturing Systems Engineering.

Middlesex (*Mechanical Engineering*) There are three year full-time and four year (sandwich) courses in which several options are available in Year 3 including robotics, fuels and energy, production management and materials engineering.

Newcastle (*Mechanical Engineering*) The range of accredited three year BEng and four year MEng degrees includes: Mechanical Engineering (with European option), Mechanical and Manufacturing Engineering, Marine Technology (with options in marine engineering, naval architecture, offshore engineering and small craft technology). Mechanical and Automotive Engineering is also available and a foundation year is offered for those without appropriate qualifications.

Northumbria (*Mechanical Engineering*) This is a three year full-time or four year sandwich course in which the main emphasis is on mechanics, energy studies, manufacturing electronics, business and management. Transfers to Manufacturing Systems Engineering or Materials Engineering are possible at the end of Year 1. Computer Aided Engineering is also offered.

Nottingham Trent (*Mechanical Engineering*) This is a three year or four year sandwich course with an emphasis on engineering applications. Computing and microprocessor concepts in design manufacture and the solution of engineering problems occupy an important place in the course. A course in Manufacturing Engineering is also available with the possibility of transferring to the five year MEng Manufacturing Systems Engineering.

Oxford (*Mechanical Engineering*) (See **Engineering Science**.)

Oxford Brookes (*Mechanical Engineering*) This is a three year or four year sandwich course with the option to follow an MEng degree at the end of the second year of the BEng programme. A wide range of engineering topics can be studied including quality and production management and design studies.

Paisley (*Mechanical Engineering*) Studies are design-based with the inclusion of business management studies.

Plymouth (*Mechanical Engineering*) This is a sandwich course with strong emphasis on design, manufacture and computer operation. Options include thermal power and offshore engineering.

Portsmouth (*Mechanical Engineering*) Both a full-time and a sandwich course are available. Sandwich placements last six months following the end of the first and third years. In the final year studies include engineering business systems, design technology, heat transfer and combustion, materials and control engineering. Computer-aided engineering is included in all areas of the course. There is also a course in Manufacturing Systems Engineering.

Reading (*Mechanical Engineering*) The course in Mechanical Engineering and Engineering Science starts with a common core of electronic and mechanical subjects branching out into their separate specialisms after two terms. This enables students to defer their choice since transfers are possible. Options are offered in energy and environmental topics, materials and mechanics.

Robert Gordon (*Mechanical Engineering*) A broad-based three year BSc mechanical engineering course with options in French or German. Specialised courses in Mechanical and Offshore Engineering, Engineering Technology and Energy Technology are also offered.

Salford (*Mechanical Engineering*) Full time (three year) and sandwich (four year) courses are offered, although students are encouraged to take the four year sandwich course. First year studies have a common syllabus for two terms which allows students to transfer between courses. The principles of engineering science, including computer-aided design and manufacturing technology are studied in the first two years leading to specialist topics - robotics, vibration analysis, etc - in the final year. Special emphasis is placed on the business and commercial aspects of manufacturing.

Sheffield (*Mechanical Engineering*) BEng (three year) MEng (four year) courses are offered, both having a common course for two years before final decisions are made. Computer programming is one of the many topics offered in the first year, and the engineer in society in the second. Over 20 optional subjects are offered in the final year. The subject can also be taken with a modern language and placements in Europe or Japan.

Sheffield Hallam (*Mechanical and Manufacturing Engineering*) The choice between mechanical and manufacturing specialisms comes in the final year. German is also studied in Years 1 and 2 with a one year placement in Germany. Courses are also offered in Computer-Aided Engineering and Design.

Southampton (*Mechanical Engineering*) Three and four year courses are offered leading to the BEng and MEng respectively. These courses follow the same pattern for two years after which they divide. In the three year course there are three elements in the final year - the project, core subjects (design and manufacture) and three specialised options. Fourth-year students take six additional engineering and management subjects as well as a group project. There are also degree courses in Electromechanical Engineering and Automotive Engineering.

South Bank (*Mechanical Engineering*) The course combines a study of engineering science, design, manufacture and management. An optional year of industrial placement is possible in the third year. Language options are available and students may spend the sandwich year at Mannheim Fachhochschule für Technik gaining dual qualifications. There is also a three or four year sandwich course in Engineering Systems Design with a considerable electrical and control engineering element.

Staffordshire (*Mechanical Engineering*) A sandwich course is provided with emphasis on engineering design, manufacture and computer applications. Elective subjects include vibrations and noise, environmental engineering and control and automation. Language options are available.

Strathclyde (*Mechanical Engineering*) A four year course and a five year course are offered, with a common course for the first three years. Engineering topics are studied in greater depth in the final year. Management and business studies topics are covered in the five year course. There is an essential European focus on all courses in the department. Half of all students will have studied in Europe for at least one semester - most for two semesters. There is a reciprocal agreement with five French engineering schools. Five major modern languages are offered.

Sunderland (*Mechanical Engineering*) An optional sandwich course is offered with core studies in design and realisation, engineering mathematics, computing, thermodynamics, fluid mechanics and mechatronics. The course is the same as that for Manufacturing Engineering up to the middle of the second year. Both these degree courses may be combined with a European language (usually German) and/or management. Courses in Automation and Mechatronics and Automotive Design and Manufacture are also offered.

Surrey (*Mechanical Engineering*) This is a four year sandwich course with industrial experience in the third year. First and second year students are encouraged to participate in optional elective studies outside their degree course, and language studies can lead to industrial placement abroad. In the final year students choose one of four option groups from industrial automation, power engineering, engineering mechanics, maritime and offshore engineering.

Sussex (*Mechanical Engineering*) The first three terms provide a common core of subjects for most engineering students. Specialisation in mechanical engineering starts in the second year and leads on to a series of specialised topics including robotics, computer-aided design, thermal power and microprocessors. Engineering management is studied throughout the second and third years. There is a four year MEng course for the most able students.

Swansea (*Mechanical Engineering*) Two mechanical engineering courses are offered with a year abroad in Europe or North America. Level 2 lectures cover the fundamentals of mechanical engineering, thermodynamics, fluid mechanics, materials, dynamics and statistics and engineering drawing and design. In Level 2 additional courses include engineering maths, microelectronics and control engineering. Level 3 introduces specialised topics and a group design project.

Teesside (*Mechanical Engineering*) An optional industrial placement takes place in Year 3 of the course. Four subjects are chosen as options which include dynamics, fluid mechanics, robotics, materials technology and simulation and control.

Ulster (*Mechanical Engineering*) Year 1 covers the fundamentals of both mechanical and electrical engineering and leads on to system performance, design and industrial applications and business administration.

Warwick (*Engineering (Design and Appropriate Technology)*)) This is a mechanical engineering course with a strong emphasis on design, primarily intended for those who intend to practice engineering in small organisations or in developing countries. More traditional degree courses specialising in Manufacturing Systems or Mechanical Engineering can be followed after taking the first year of the general engineering course (see **Engineering Science**).

Westminster (*Mechanical Engineering*) This is a full-time course with an emphasis on engineering applications and a focus on computer-aided engineering and information technology, engineering manufacture, energy manufacture, energy systems and design.

• **Top research universities**
Hull, Leeds, Liverpool, London (Imp), Sheffield.

•**Colleges and Institutes of Higher Education offering degree courses**
Blackpool and Fylde (Coll), Croydon (Coll), Doncaster (Coll), Gwent (Coll), Halton (Coll), North East Wales (Inst), Southampton (Inst) (Marine Engineering), Stockport (Coll), Suffolk (Coll), Swansea (Inst) (Automotive Engineering).

• **Other courses to be considered**
Agriculture, automobile, building services, heating and ventilation, marine, refrigeration, textile engineering, mathematics and physics.

ENGINEERING (MINING)
(See also **Geology**)

• **Special subject requirements:** See **Engineering**.

• **Subject information:** This subject covers geology, surveying and mineral processing with opportunities to enter careers in petroleum engineering as well as coal and metalliferous mining.

Exeter (Cambourne School of Mines) (*Mining Engineering; Minerals Engineering*) Both courses have a common first year and cover all aspects of the minerals industry and are in contact with all the major international mining companies. There is also a course in Minerals Engineering and Industrial Technology. Students normally spend a summer vacation working abroad.

Glamorgan (*Minerals Resource Development and Surveying*) There are compulsory modules in mathematics, computing, surveying, law and geology in Year 1. Surveying continues in Year 2 with engineering subjects, geology, business studies and waste technology followed in Year 3 with law, planning and minerals economics, valuation and mining technology.

Leeds (*Mining Engineering; Mineral Engineering*) On the former course first year studies include engineering topics, geology, surveying and computing. These lead on to more specialised topics such as management, economics, rock mechanics and mine ventilation, the course being completed with a project. Mineral Engineering covers chemistry and geology as applied to mineral systems and processing. The final year makes a detailed study of chemical and physical methods of processing minerals. It is possible to study languages in both courses.

London (Imp) (*Mining Engineering*) Three year (BSc) and four year (BEng) courses are offered. The first two years are common for all students when decisions are made on which students will be invited to take the four year course. Three-year course students are required to work at least 500 hours in industry during the summer vacations and this is done in the UK or abroad. It is possible to transfer between Mining and Petroleum Engineering at the end of Year 1.

Nottingham (*Minerals Engineering; Mining Engineering*) Both courses cover languages, the former including ceramics, glasses and the durability of metals, whilst the latter covers surveying, geology and mining law.

Sheffield (*Minerals Estate Management*) Stage 1 of this four year sandwich course introduces students to the principles of land management and the technological aspects of mineral extraction. Stage 2 covers mineral exploitation and extraction.

• **Top research university**
London (Imp).

• **Colleges and Institutes of Higher Education offering degree courses**
Doncaster (Coll).

• **Other courses to be considered**
Civil engineering, geology, materials science, metallurgy.

ENGLISH

• **Special subject requirements:** A-levels in English and a language often 'required' or 'preferred'; GCSE (grade A–C) in English and a language.

• **Subject information:** These courses are an extension of school studies in literature and language and may cover topics ranging from Anglo-Saxon literature to the present day. Most courses, however, will focus on certain areas such as the Medieval or Renaissance periods of literature or English language studies. Admissions Tutors will expect students to have read widely outside their A-level syllabus. (Sunday newspaper book reviews will give a useful introduction to modern literature.)

Aberdeen (*English*) The courses in English literature involve the critical and historical study of authors of all periods including Scottish and American modern literature. The English language courses are concerned with the nature and development of the English language from the earliest period to the present day. English (literature) is offered as a joint course with a choice from 14 subjects.

Aberystwyth (*English*) Part I introduces the Renaissance and modern drama, the twentieth century novel and poetry, whilst Part II (Years 2 and 3) offers specialisation in a range of subjects including Medieval to Victorian literature and 20th century British, Anglo-Welsh and American literature.

Anglia (Poly Univ) (*English*) All periods of English literature are covered on this course.

Bangor (*English*) The course covers a wide range of courses on all periods of English and American literature. In Part II of the course students are also advised to choose an accessory subject which includes drama, history or classical studies. Studies in creative writing and plays in performance are also offered. Bangor is an internationally recognised centre for work on Arthurian literature.

Belfast (*English*) Year 1 courses are offered in poetry (1850–1930), the English novel (1850–1930) and the English language and early medieval studies. In Year 2 students may proceed to single or joint Honours courses (English with one or two other subjects). There is a generous range of optional courses from which to choose or combined courses with two other subjects.

Birmingham (*English*) The first year course includes literature and critical methods in medieval English and in modern linguistics. In the second and third years there is a large range of seminar courses in literature and language from which to choose. All students study Shakespeare in the sixth term.

Bristol (*English*) English language and literature from pre-Conquest to present day. Continuous assessment plays a significant part in the exam structure which also includes conventional exams. There are some one to one tutorials with a broad study of all literature in depth prior to specialisation.

Bristol UWE (*Literary Studies*) A study of 19th and 20th century English, American and Continental writing is offered.

Buckingham (*English Literature and Modern History*) (The English language course is for overseas students only.) The two year course covers several periods of English literature and film studies. Victorian society and country house literature, British, European and American history topics are covered.

Cambridge (*English*) This is a study of English literature from Chaucer to the present day. Literature is also studied in a historical and cultural context with comparisons offered as options in Anglo-Saxon, early Norse, Welsh and Irish, and literature. Literary criticism is studied throughout the course. In addition to English, applicants for the course are reminded that classics, modern languages and history are among the most relevant A-levels.

Cardiff (*English Literature*) Part I subjects include English literature, medieval English and language. Three subjects are taken in Part I from a wide range depending on the chosen course. Despite the applicant's original UCAS choice of the English course it is possible to change during

Year 1 to another degree course within the School. There is also a course in Modern English with elements of English literature and language teaching.

Central England (*English Language and Literature*) The course has a 35 per cent language content in Years 1 and 2 with a wide range of options in Year 3 with students choosing eight modules from approximately 24 on offer.

Central Lancashire (*English Language Studies*) This is a course in the teaching and learning of English language with options in linguistics and literature.

De Montfort (*English*) The course covers English literature and literature in translation as well as literature in a social context.

Derby (*English*) Students may take English as a major or joint subject in Stages 2 and 3 of the Credit Accumulation Modular Scheme. Modules are combined from at least two of the following subjects - Literature, Experience of Writing and Theatre Studies.

Dundee (*English*) All periods of literature are studied from Chaucer to the present time. Joint Honours courses with English are available with a choice from 11 other subjects.

Durham (*English Literature*) This is a very broad-ranging course to suit all tastes from traditional literary humanism to post-structuralism, with specialisms ranging from modernism through the Victorians, Renaissance and the seventeenth century to medieval literature. Language options are available along with several other subjects, eg history, biblical studies, philosophy. (*English Language and Linguistics*) This is an in-depth study of the workings of the modern English language, with special emphasis upon the ways speakers organise their sentence structures and pronunciation: the social, occupational and gender differences reflected in the present day language; its main variations worldwide and the ways in which it has changed through time. (*English*) A study of classical and medieval literature. Options in English and American literary periods in Years 2 and 3.

East Anglia (*English Literature*) The School of English and American Studies offers flexibility to study a wide range of different, but related subjects: American and English history and literature, drama, film studies, landscape archaeology etc. Students 'build' their own course. Major studies can also combine with other humanities, eg art history or modern languages.

Edinburgh (*English Language and Literature*) This is a popular course for those wishing to teach English. English Literature begins with a broad study, then focuses on the early seventeenth century period and leads on to a study of five major authors. English Language covers pronunciation and grammar and examines the historical background to language through Anglo-Saxon English, Medieval English, Elizabethan English and older Scots.

Essex (*English Language and European Literature*) There are also degree courses in Literature (English and European) for which GCSE in a foreign language is required, and in English Language and Linguistics. All students take the first year course on the European Enlightenment.

Exeter (*English Literature*) This course provides a knowledge of the major texts, literary forms and periods of English literature and allows for considerable specialisations. The basic courses are the Renaissance, Shakespeare, the Restoration and the eighteenth century, the nineteenth and the twentieth centuries. Combined courses are also offered with English literature in seven subjects (including Medieval Studies and also American and Commonwealth Arts - which is a four year course, with the third year spent in Canada or the USA).

Glamorgan (*English Studies*) Language, literature and creative writing are included at level 1 with options in language and society, women's writing and the writing media. Options in Year 2 include language as power, Romantic poetry and journalism and in Year 3 there are eight options including English as a foreign language.

Glasgow (*English Language; English Literature*) The English Language course covers the history of the language from the earliest times to the present day. Phonetics and grammar are included and there are specialist options including dialectology and sociolinguistics. The Literature course concentrates on the Romantic period with optional subjects covering the Renaissance period and European literature in translation.

Hertfordshire (*English Literature*) The subject is offered as part of the Humanities Modular Scheme and may form a major or minor part of the degree. A degree is also offered in Modern English Literature.

Huddersfield (*English Studies*) Optional modules include language or literature, media studies, information technology, desk-top publishing, creative writing and a European language.

Hull (*English Language and Literature*) This course is a variation from that offered elsewhere. After an introductory core year students choose freely between a wide range of options, with an emphasis on language or literature and also between courses in either subject. New literature in English is also covered. Language options are offered.

Keele English is offered jointly with over seventy subjects.

Kent (*English Studies*) The first year is made up of courses in language, literature and society. Thereafter the degree course allows students to combine the study of English language and linguistics with English and American literature, or History, or Politics and Society in Britain. There is a separate degree in English and American Literature and English Language may be studied as part of a combined Honours degree.

Kingston (*English Literature*) This course is broad-based, including some unusual options such as the history of ideas, visual arts, French and women's studies. English, American, European and Commonwealth writers from Shakespeare onwards are discussed in the context of their times, with the twentieth century well represented. Critical theory is also considered but does not dominate the course.

Lampeter (*English Literature*) The degree is based on four core courses referring to historical periods and optional courses such as cinema literature, society in post war Britain, Australian literature, Jewish-American writing and creative writing. There is also a video production option. Half the course may be examined by continuous assessment.

Lancaster (*English*) In the first year literature and language (Anglo-Saxon to Shakespeare) are studied. Language and literature continue in the second and third years, with a range of topics such as Victorian, nineteenth and twentieth century literature, women writers of Britain and America, language, anthropology and psycho-linguistics. There is also a course in English Language and Literature.

Leeds (*English*) A traditional course in English language and literature is combined with an extensive range of options covering English, American and Commonwealth literature. Students have a choice from a list of over 40 options in Years 2 and 3. These courses are combined with 'core' courses which involve a study of English from the Middle Ages to the present day. The department is rated as a centre of excellence.

Leicester (*English*) A supplementary subject taken from the Combined Honours list is studied with English in the first year which includes an introduction to English language and literature. Special author courses accompany the study of literary periods in the second year which also includes communication skills. The third year includes two special subject courses chosen from a range of options.

Liverpool (*English Language and Literature*) English can be studied from its origins in the Anglo-Saxon period to the modern period covering all the major literary and linguistic developments. Optional courses are available in the second and third years.

Liverpool John Moores (*Literature, Life and Thought*) Core modules cover literary and historical material studying a range of issues such as gender and race. Specialisms include American studies, women's writing, popular writing and working class writing.

London (Goldsmiths') (*English*) There are three compulsory introductory courses, but later on students are able to choose from a wide range of courses which include Chaucer, Shakespeare, Gothic literature, the Victorians, Caribbean women writers and the English detective story. English may be combined with one of several Arts subjects and Interdisciplinary Studies.

London (King's) (*English*) The course covers all the major periods of English literature from Old English to the twentieth century. Optional courses in the second and third years allow specialisation in such fields as medieval French literature, the history of structure of the English language, and archaeology and theatrical history.

London (QMW) (*English*) The course covers the study of both English language and literature from the earliest periods to the present day, plus a wide range of options. The Combined Studies degree allows students to combine English with Drama, a language or Hispanic Studies.

London (RH) (*English*) A course common to all students occupies the first two terms comprising literature, critical ideas, lectures on aspects or periods of literature and introductory language courses. This enables students to plan the remainder of their course to suit their own particular interests.

London (UC) (*English*) A wide choice of options accompanies a central core of subjects. All first year students follow courses on set English texts and take introductory courses on medieval literature and on modern English language. In the second and third years there are core courses on Chaucer, Renaissance literature and Shakespeare. There is some emphasis on individual teaching.

London Guildhall (*English Studies*) This is a modular programme offered as a joint degree or a minor subject covering literature and language.

Loughborough (*English*) The course concentrates on modern English literature starting with the Renaissance although there is an option in medieval literature. It also includes an option in creative writing (few universities offer this topic) and drama (practical, recreational and academic). A wide range of subsidiary subjects is offered.

Luton (*English Studies*) English Language and literature are covered and also American and African literature. Media writing, journalism and creative writing are also included.

Manchester (*English Language and Literature*) In this course one other subject can be taken in Year 1 at subsidiary level.

Manchester Metropolitan (*English Studies*) English, American and African literature, creative writing, language and theory and cultural studies can be taken as specialised studies in Years 2 and 3.

Middlesex (*English*) This is part of the modular scheme and covers English and American literature. The BA degree in literature and philosophy makes a comparative study of these two subjects, and in the Humanities and Combined Studies (BA) courses English can be taken with other subjects. 'Core' courses involve a study of English from the Middle Ages to the present day. In addition there is a BEd (Qualified Teacher Status) degree leading to primary teaching and a course in contemporary writing covering 20th century studies.

Newcastle (*English Literature*) This course has a firm basis in traditional literary areas, combined with a variety of options (film, American literature, Russian novel). There is a variety of examination methods and an emphasis on small group teaching. (*English Language and Literature*) The English Language content is distinctive and occupies one-third of the student's work load in Year 1. Thereafter there is much freedom in the choice of options. (*English Language*) This course covers a wide range of approaches to the study of the English language - both historical and descriptive - and also medieval English literature. Subsidiary subjects, eg Psychology, Computer Science, can be taken.

North London (*English*) Compulsory core subjects include Shakespeare, the Renaissance, drama and modern fiction. This is followed in Year 2 with a very wide range of options which include American and West Indian literature. English can also be taken with a second subject in the Humanities (BA) course. An exchange scheme with New York State University is operated.

Northumbria (*English Studies*) A study of literature and its historical background from 1790 to 1900 in level 1 and from 1390 to 1630 in level 2. Departmental options are chosen in level 3.

Nottingham (*English Studies*) The course covers the entire range of English literature from its beginnings to the twentieth century and also medieval and modern English language. Several joint Honours courses are available.

Oxford (*English Language and Literature*) The first year is largely concerned with English literature (1832–1960) whilst the second and third years offer two alternatives (1) a general course in English language and literature or (2) a special course in English language and Early English literature. In addition there is a long list of specialised topics on offer, eg Old English literature, women's writing, American literature, prose and poetry.

Plymouth English is offered jointly with thirteen other subjects.

Portsmouth (*English*) A foundation course in poetry, narrative and drama is offered, in addition to which there are creative writing, drama workshops and photography and film writing.

Reading (*English Language and Literature*) Nine individual courses are taken under the English heading, four of which are compulsory core subjects covering literature from the Elizabethan period to the mid-nineteenth century. The remaining five courses are chosen from a long list of options, three of them medieval, the others ranging from the sixteenth to the twentieth centuries including a drama course. There are a number of joint Honours courses available.

St Andrews (*English Language and Literature*) English language and literature are studied in the first two years. Students proceeding to the single Honours degree may follow course I with a literature emphasis, or course II with a language bias. There are, however, many topics common to both courses.

Salford (*English Language and Literature*) This course offers a study of English language and also English literature with an emphasis on the modern period (post-1750) literature and its connections with society, which are central to the degree.

Sheffield (*English Language; English Literature*) The Language course covers the history of English language, medieval English language and literature, modern English and linguistics. The English Literature degree programme makes a close study of literature from the sixteenth century, with a drama option available.

Sheffield Hallam (*English*) The course covers literary studies (16th–19th centuries), linguistics and writing skills. A half unit is shared with the History of Art, Design and Film.

Southampton (*English*) The first year introduces the major genres of English literature after which students form their own course by choosing topics out of the whole range of English literature, from the medieval period to the present day. During the first year English language and an additional subject in another department are studied. Twenty seven such subjects are available including languages, the sciences and law.

South Bank Courses are offered in Psychology and Social Science with English.

Staffordshire (*Literary Studies*) Modules are selected from narrative/fiction, poetry, drama and American literature.

Stirling (*English Studies*) A study of the novel, drama and poetry occupy the first three semester of this course. Thereafter, in the next three semesters, studies focus on the poetic tradition, Shakespeare and Renaissance drama and the nineteenth century novel. During this time, and in the final year, a range of options allows the students to choose their own specialist areas to study.

Strathclyde (*English Studies*) The degree course is based on the study of English literature from the Renaissance to the present day. Overall there is a carefully planned balance between the study of literary periods and general literary topics which establishes an understanding of the development, nature and methods of literature.

Sunderland (*English Studies*) In this course a range of topics is on offer including twentieth century literature and poetry and American literature. There is also a Combined Studies (BA) course in which students take two disciplines and one area of study.

Sussex (*English*) This programme is one of considerable breadth and presents the subject in terms of intellectual, moral, religious, political, social and aesthetic contexts. The first term introduces the range of approaches to the study of English in addition to giving the student a choice of options. English literature options are introduced in the second year which allows the student to focus his or her interests in their chosen field. English is offered with four different Schools of Studies.

Swansea (*English*) All students take two other subjects in the first year of this course. In the English syllabus Chaucer, Shakespeare, practical criticism and twentieth-century texts are covered in Part I. For single Honours during the next two years there are two core courses - literature from Chaucer to the present day and criticism - plus a choice of options. A very wide range of joint Honours courses is available. The degree is awarded on the basis of course work and written examinations, 50 per cent of each.

Teesside (*English*) Course modules introduce English prose and poetry with remaining modules chosen from other humanities and social science subjects. In the second and third years, students construct their own programme which includes historical periods, women's writing, drama and children's literature.

Thames Valley (*English - Humanities*) Students choose English as a major or minor subject. The course includes a study of Shakespeare, 17th, 18th century and Victorian literature and literature in the USA.

Ulster (*English*) A wide choice of units of study is available in this literature course which particularly focuses on the nineteenth and twentieth century periods. Anglo-Irish, American and medieval literature are options in the second and third years.

Warwick (*English*) Two main degrees are offered (1) English and European Literature and (2) English and American Literature. The course in European Literature provides students with the opportunity to extend their knowledge of a foreign language and literature (French, German or Latin) but spending most of their time on the study of English. It is also possible to begin a study of Italian and Spanish. The foreign language study is maintained throughout the three years. For those taking American literature the balance between this subject and English is largely left to the student. Students are still encouraged to take a foreign language course in the first year.

Westminster (*English Studies*) A modular course covering a study of English in its historical aspects in Britain.

Wolverhampton (*English*) The subject can be taken in specialist, joint, major or minor programmes of study. The course covers Shakespeare, the novel, journalism and American literature.

York (*English*) English can be studied as a single subject or in combination with six other subjects. When in combination, English can be taken as a main, equal, or subsidiary subject. Single subject students must take at least one course involving the study of literature in a foreign language. All students follow the preliminary course for one term before choosing their subject or subjects. The single course is a specialised study of English literature. Courses are examined by continuous assessment.

● **Top research universities**
Cambridge, Leeds, London (UC) (King's) (QMW) (RH), Oxford, Sussex, Edinburgh, Cardiff, Birmingham, Durham, Essex, Lancaster, Leicester, Liverpool, Manchester, Nottingham, York.

● **Colleges and Institutes of Higher Education offering degree courses**
Bath (Coll), Bishop Grosseteste (Coll), Bolton (Inst), Bretton Hall, Brunel (Univ Coll), Buckinghamshire (Coll), Canterbury Christ Church (Coll), Cardiff (Inst), Cheltenham and Gloucester (Coll), Chester (Coll), Chichester (Inst), Doncaster (Coll), Edge Hill (Coll), Gwent (Coll), King Alfred's (Coll), Leeds (Tr/All Sts), Liverpool (Inst), La Sainte Union (Coll), Nene (Coll), Newman (Coll), Norwich City (Coll), Oxford (Westminster Coll), Ripon and York St John's (Univ Coll), Roehampton (Inst), Scarborough (Univ Coll), S Martin's (Coll), St Mark and St John (Coll), St Mary's (Univ Coll), Swansea (Inst), Trinity Carmarthen (Coll), Westhill (Coll), Worcester (Coll).

● **Other courses to be considered**
Combined arts courses, drama, journalism and librarianship.

ENVIRONMENTAL SCIENCE/STUDIES
(including **Ecology**)

● **Special subject requirements:** variable depending on the emphasis of course.

- **Subject information:** Environmental Health courses usually lead to qualification as an environmental health officer. Environmental Science, however, can cover a range of subjects with options to specialise which may include biology, geography, geology, oceanography or chemistry. Environmental Science/Studies could also involve town and country planning or environmental health options thus leading to two quite different careers.

Aberdeen (*Environmental Science*) The course covers ecology, chemistry, geography and geology in the early years with a strong physics/chemistry/biology element in Years 3 and 4.

Abertay Dundee (*Environmental Science*) Years 1 and 2 provide a strong base in chemistry and biology leading on to special topics which include biotechnology, pathology, aquatic and atmospheric chemistry and the environmental impact of materials processes and chemicals.

Aberystwyth (*Environmental Science*) This is an integrated course provided by eight departments. Parts I and II cover physical and biological processes and support studies. Final year option courses cover geography, botany and zoology. There is also an optional year out.

Anglia (Poly Univ) (*Environmental Science*) This course involves heredity, ecology, biology and physiology.

Bangor (*Environmental Science*) A modular course comprising a study of the earth, atmosphere, rocks, minerals, soils, agriculture and forest systems and oceanography.

Birmingham (*Environmental Science*) There are four main pathways - the biological, atmospheric and physical environments and water in the environment - in which practical skills are emphasised. The course is modular containing core, compulsory and optional modules.

Bournemouth (*Environmental Protection*) A course with options in river/water/waste management, health and industrial safety and coastal protection. It combines elements of material science, environmental science and monitoring technology with a study of management and legislative aspects of the protection of the environment.

Bradford (*Environmental Science*) This is an integrated course covering chemistry, ecology, physical and economic geography, applied economics and biology. The third year involves practical experience in an appropriate organisation. The final year provides three fields of specialisation in planning, environmental biology, occupational health and pollution management. Students gain some exemptions from the Institute of Landscape Architects, the Royal Town Planning Institute and Occupational Hygiene bodies.

Brighton (*Environmental Science*) The course involves a study of the human and physical environment, ecology, energy and pollution.

Bristol UWE (*Environmental Science*) Special options cover ecology, toxicology, environmental biotechnology, pollution and waste management. There are also courses in Environmental Health and Environmental Quality and Resource Management.

Central England Environmental Technology and Environmental Pollution Control are offered as part of the Modular Degree programme.

Central Lancashire (*Environmental Management*) This covers geography, ecology, law, chemistry and planning. Specialist areas include pollution and land reclamation.

Coventry (*Environmental Science*) A study of physical and biotic components of the natural environment. Transfer is possible to Applied Biology or Geography in Year 1. There is a choice of a four year sandwich course or three year full-time or four year full-time (with European Study). (*Energy Studies*) Core studies are in energy systems with supplementary studies in environmental science, physical geography and industrial and resource management.

Cranfield (*Environmental Technology*) Environmental issues, physics, chemistry and a European language are included in Year 1. Work experience takes place in Year 3 and pollution control, soil conservation and landscape engineering follow in Year 4.

De Montfort (*Science and the Environment*) First year studies cover biology, chemistry and physics, with biometry, mathematics, statistics and computing. Year 2 is spent on ecology, microbiology, analytical techniques and planning, law and administration. After the second year students may choose to spend a year on an industrial placement, returning in the final year to study environmental studies, land and water resources management, environmental toxins and applied physiology. Courses in Environmental Studies/Biology are also offered.

Derby (*Environmental Studies*) This is taken within the Credit Accumulation Modular Scheme as a major, joint or minor subject. A single Honours degree is also offered.

Dundee (*Environmental Science*) The first year covers Global Environmental Processes and Natural Environmental Systems. Second year topics include ecosystems and resource monitoring and management whilst the third year themes cover environmental geoscience, remote sensing and resource management.

Durham (*Environmental Management*) The course covers environmental management - focusing on the practical management of the environment, environmental technology and environmental development.

East Anglia (*Environmental Science*) This is one of the largest interdisciplinary developments in the country with a very strong research base. Within one department it brings together subjects such as geology, geography, ecology, oceanography, economics, politics, planning, meteorology, soil science, geophysics, resource management, risk assessment, hydrology and environmental pollution. The degree programme is made up from a choice of over 30 courses and can lead to a very specialised degree, biased in the interests of the student. (*Developmental Studies*) The subject covers natural resources as well as economics, sociology, social anthropology and politics.

East London (*Environmental Studies*) The course includes environmental biology, the ecology of animals and birds and conservation.

Edinburgh (*Ecological Science*) The course is intended for resource managers, rural planners, conservationists and ecologists, and concentrates on the integration of biology, environmental sciences and resource management. Specialisation is offered in ecology, wildlife and fisheries management, agriculture, forestry and rural economy. (*Environmental Health*) This course, within the Faculty of Medicine, focuses on hazards in the environment and the influence of housing, work and food safety on health. There are good career prospects in environmental health, pollution control, environmental consultancy and health and safety.

Glamorgan (*Environmental Pollution Science*) This new course will be taught on a modular basis and aims to develop an understanding and knowledge of pollution sources, treatment and control. There is also a course in Environmental and Social Values otherwise called 'Green Studies'.

Glasgow (*Environmental Science*) The course covers plants and animals, habitat zones, ecology and pollution.

Glasgow Caledonian (*Environmental Toxicology*) In the final year the main topics are pollution, clinical biotechnology and occupational hazard analysis.

Greenwich (*Environmental Earth Science*) This is a three year or four year sandwich course. Core subjects include geology, surface processes, mineralogy, palaeontology, map interpretation, hydrogeology and ecosystems. Final year options include engineering geology, natural hazards, waste disposal and resource management and micropalaeontology.

Hertfordshire (*Environmental Science*) This is a study of the biological, physical and social environment. In Year 2 environmental planning, landscape development and pollution issues are covered. Supervised work experience takes place in Year 3. Specialisms include conservation and recreation management, environmental protection and monitoring.

Huddersfield (*Environmental Analysis*) This course covers ecology, food and microbiology with options in water industries, food, and the chemical and agrochemical industries.

Hull (*Environment and Resource Management*) Core compulsory subjects in this course include geography, environment and society, management studies, and environmental policy and planning, and students may opt to specialise in the management of physical systems or the management of human systems.

Humberside (*Environmental Studies*) A substantial core of scientific content is supported by issues relating to human geography, economics, technology, business and management.

Keele Over fifty joint courses are offered with Environmental Management which covers geography, economics, politics, transport, environmental hazards and 'green' issues.

Kent Environmental Science is offered with Chemistry.

Kingston (*Resources and the Environment*) This course covers chemistry, geology, computing and biology.

Lancaster (*Environmental Science*) The Environmental Science (ES) department is a major centre for ES training. Specialisation is introduced in the final year when a choice is made between aquatics and atmospheric systems, applied earth science or environmental assessment and management. Final year topics include air pollution, water resources management, waste disposal and environmental radioactivity.

Leeds (*Environmental Management*) The course mainly covers geography, economics and law but each year there are optional modules some of which allow for a study in other departments, eg modern languages.

Leeds Metropolitan (*Environmental Health*) Five study areas run through the course, comprising environmental science, technology, management, the environment, methodology and practice. Topics include occupational health, food safety control and public health. Year 3 is spent in practical experience. The course leads to qualification as an environmental health officer. Other similar Environmental Health courses are offered at the following universities:- Bristol UWE, Greenwich, London (King's), Manchester Metropolitan, Middlesex, Nottingham Trent, Ulster and also at Cardiff (Inst).

Liverpool (*Environmental Physical Science*) This course involves chemistry, physics, planet Earth ecology, conservation and marine pollution.

Liverpool John Moores (*Environmental Science*) A three year full-time or four year sandwich course covering biology, chemistry and earth science supported by management and policy-making studies.

London (Imp) (*Environmental and Earth Resources*) This is an environmental engineering course overlapping with mining and petroleum engineering in the early stages, prior to specialisation.

London (King's) (*Applied Environmental Science*) The course focuses on man and the environment with topics such as population growth and natural resources. All students follow a common first year and then choose between environmental health or land and aquatic resource management. There are also degree courses in Human Environmental Science, Ecology and Environmental Health.

London (QMW) (*Environmental Science*) This is a multidisciplinary course studying the natural environment, covering physical geography, geology, environmental biology and chemistry. Some emphasis on marine aspects, eg oceanic, river and coastal environment, and marine biology. Specialisms include conservation, ecology management, chemistry or environmental quality.

London (RH) Joint degrees are offered in Environmental Studies with science subjects and social policy.

London (Wye) (*Rural Environmental Studies*) This course is centred on the interaction of people and the environment - population changes, urbanisation of the countryside, recreational impacts, ecological and resource constraints and pollution. There is also an Environmental Science course with options in crop protection, global environmental change, plants/insects and pesticides and a course in Environment and Business.

Luton A very large number of joint courses are offered with Ecotoxicology and Pollution Studies and also Environmental Science.

Manchester Metropolitan (*Environmental Management*) The course in Environmental Management focuses on the physical, social, scientific, political and economics aspects. Year 3 includes environmental planning, nature conservation and countryside studies. Options include studies in geography, geology and tourism. Environmental Studies can also be taken as part of the Combined Studies course.

Middlesex (*Environmental Science and Technology*) After foundation courses in physical sciences, earth sciences, life sciences and mathematics, students go on to study engineering geology, hydrology, environmental chemical analysis, computer techniques and instrumentation, with options in energy technology, public health engineering or pollution. This is a sandwich course with a year's industrial placement. There is also a European Environmental Engineering Science course.

North London (*Environmental Science*) This course includes units of geography, ecology, geology, archaeology, conservation and pollution.

Northumbria (*Environmental Studies*) This course focuses on environmental management and ecology with options in energy pollution, soils, natural hazards, climatology, global issues and the Third World.

Nottingham (*Environmental Engineering and Resource Management*) Options in this course include conservation, re-cycling of materials, dust control engineering, hazardous materials and industrial safety.

Nottingham Trent Environmental Conservation Management is offered jointly with five subjects. There are also Environmental Systems joint courses.

Oxford Brookes A large number of joint courses with Environmental Sciences.

Paisley (*Environmental Science and Technology*) Core subjects are in biology, chemistry, geology and physics with modern environmental problems. There is a sandwich option between Years 3 and 4.

Plymouth (*Environmental Science*) The course includes a study of environmental biology, chemistry, geology and the human environment. Environmental management, food and water resources, pollution and urban development are concentrated in Year 3. In the Combined Studies degree programme courses in meteorology and oceanography are offered.

Portsmouth (*Applied Environmental Science*) After two foundation years and a possible Year 3 placement, final year modules cover eco-audit, materials re-cycling, pollution and monitoring and energy conservation. There is also a course in Marine Environmental Science.

Reading (*Environmental Science of the Earth and Atmosphere*) The first year comprises courses in geology, meteorology and soil science, supplemented by chemistry, mathematics or physics. During the second year the focus is on sediments, processes at the surface of land and oceans, and transport processes in soils. The final year is a mixture of courses in techniques, practical and project work.

Robert Gordon (*Environmental Science and Technology*) The course covers radiation, noise control, petroleum science and pollution, clean-up technologies, environmental geochemistry and environmental management strategies. There is an optional industrial year and European language training.

Salford (*Environmental Sciences*) The course aims to provide a comprehensive understanding of environmental problems and professional practice. There is a common first year programme for all students who then opt for the environmental health or the housing option. The former is a four year course giving full exemption from the examinations of the Institute of Environmental Health Officers. The housing option (a three or four year course) gives partial exemption from the exams of the Institute of Housing.

Sheffield (*Natural Environmental Science*) The first year of this course covers geography, geology and environmental biology. A more specialised treatment of the subject follows in the second year whilst in the third year there are four compulsory subjects covering botany, geography and geology. (*Pure and Applied Ecology*) Six units are taken in Year 1 covering biological sciences or alternatively students may opt for four units of the same course plus one complementary subject from a list of 17 scientific options. Years 2 and 3 are devoted completely to ecology.

Sheffield Hallam (*Environmental Management*) This is a four year sandwich course with a European language option. The course involves environmental quality engineering, landscape management and water engineering.

Southampton (*Environmental Sciences*) The subject combines options from the Departments of Biology, Geography, Geology, Chemistry and Oceanography. Each student has the opportunity to design his or her course in groups of units. The groups cover the physical and the biological environments, chemistry and human sciences within the environment and water in the environment, hydrology and hydrobiology.

South Bank (*Environmental Policy and Science*) A study of the social, economic and political factors affecting the environment.

Staffordshire (*Environmental Science*) Geography, microbiology, ecology and chemistry lead on to options in earth hazards, weather, climate, freshwater and marine ecology and several biological and chemistry options.

Stirling (*Environmental Science*) This course focuses attention on the surface and near-surface environments of the Earth. Part I covers environmental systems, earth science and resources and the environment. Part II deals with climatology, resources, geomorphology, soils and vegetation, environmental management and computing. Final year options include countryside management, deserts, environmental hazards, rivers and tropical environments. There is a separate degree course in Ecology and a new course in Conservation Management.

Sunderland (*Environmental Studies*) Introductory courses in the relevant physical, biological, natural and social sciences lead on to options which include pollution, food, land and planning resources. Final year options include wildlife and countryside management.

Sussex (*Environmental Science*) The course establishes the link between chemistry, biology and geography. The emphasis is on scientific investigation, although social and economic aspects are also considered. (*Ecology and Conservation*) This course shares a number of topics with Biology, but also provides an opportunity to study aspects of environmental chemistry, bio-geography, systematics, animal psychology, pest control and conservation.

Ulster (*Environmental Science*) After a common first year for all students aiming for the Ordinary and the Honours degrees, Year 2 and 3 offer a choice between a study of geological aspects including natural resources and man's exploitation of them, or a course with a geographical emphasis.

Westminster (*Environmental Science*) Options in levels 1 and 2 cover biological, ecological, aquatic and genetic specialisms.

Wolverhampton (*Environmental Science*) A three year or four year sandwich course. Major themes include earth sciences, physical surface processes, and ecology. Social, political and economic aspects are also studied.

York (*Environmental Economics and Management*) This course involves both economics and biology and a study of environmental problems at both national and global levels.

• Top research universities
East Anglia, Lancaster, Reading, Southampton, London (Imp), Plymouth, Edinburgh, Bangor.

• Colleges and Institutes of Higher Education offering degree courses
Bath (Coll), Bolton (Inst), Bretton Hall, Canterbury Christ Church (Coll), Cheltenham and Gloucester (Coll), Chester (Coll), Chichester (Inst), Colchester (Inst), Edge Hill (Coll), Farnborough (Coll), Gwent (Coll), King Alfred's (Coll), Liverpool (Inst), Nene (Coll), NESCOT, North East Wales (Inst), Norwich City (Coll), Ripon and York St John's (Univ Coll), Roehampton (Inst), Scarborough (Univ Coll), Southampton (Inst), St Mary's (Univ Coll), Suffolk (Coll), Trinity Carmarthen (Coll), Warrington (Coll Inst), Westminster (Coll), Worcester (Coll).

• Other courses to be considered
Agriculture, agricultural sciences, applied natural sciences, biological sciences, countryside management, earth resources, estate management, forest resources, garden design, geography, geology, landscape architecture, maritime environmental management, meteorology, ocean sciences, soil science, underwater studies.

EUROPEAN STUDIES

- **Special subject requirements:** 2–3 A-levels, at least one in a modern language for language courses.

- **Subject information:** This is an increasingly popular subject and offers the language student the opportunity to study modern languages within the context of a European country (eg economic, political, legal, social and cultural aspects). On these courses there is usually a strong emphasis placed on the written and spoken word. There are also European Business Studies courses available.

Aberdeen (*European Studies*) First year students cover modern and contemporary European history, comparative European politics and two languages from Scottish Gaelic, French, German and Spanish. Language study continues over three years. (A fourth year may be spent abroad). Origins and institutions, Law and Economics of the EC are also covered.

Aberystwyth (*European Studies*) A choice of arts-based or social studies-based European topics - without language. The course covers politics, international relations, law, history and the economics of contemporary Europe.

Aston European Studies is offered with languages, engineering and computing.

Belfast (*European Community Studies*) The course involves the study of one European language (French or German). There are also beginners courses in Italian, Portuguese, Spanish and Russian. The course involves economics and politics with language fluency.

Bradford (*European Studies*) There are options in French, English, German and Spanish. The third year is spent in a university abroad.

Brunel (*Comparative European Studies*) This course covers European and Modern History with French or German.

Cardiff (*European Community Studies*) This is a unique course offering an integrated programme in which students can study one or two modern European languages in the context of the contemporary political, economic, legal and social structure of Western Europe. Emphasis is placed on the practical (non-literary) aspects of language (French or German). It is also possible to study Italian, Spanish, Portuguese ab initio. The third year is spent in study abroad.

Central England European Studies is offered jointly with nine other subjects.

Central Lancashire (*European Studies*) This interdisciplinary course with West and East European coverage allows students a fair amount of choice, drawing on the disciplines of politics, economics, history and languages (French or German). In the second year a full semester is spent in France, Germany, Belgium or Spain.

Coventry (*European Studies*) This is a four year programme with French, German and Spanish offered and Year 3 spent abroad.

Derby (*European Studies*) The course is offered within the Credit Accumulation Modular Scheme as a major, joint or minor subject.

Dundee (*Contemporary European Studies*) During the first two years students normally take at least two courses from English, French, geography, German, jurisprudence, modern history, philosophy and political science and social policy. A two years Honours course in French or German is compulsory for single Honours students. In the third and fourth year eight courses on Europe are chosen from 11 topics.

Durham European Studies is offered with French, German and Spanish and also as a geographical study.

East Anglia Courses are offered in Contemporary European Studies.

East London (*European Studies*) The course covers Western European society and political issues. Computing is part of the course and language study, with Year 3 being spent in France, Germany, Spain or Italy.

Edinburgh A course is available in European Community Studies and a Modern European Language.

Essex (*European Studies*) This course includes a foreign language (French, German, Spanish or Russian).

Glamorgan European Studies is offered on Combined Honours, Combined Studies and Joint Honours courses.

Greenwich Combined courses are offered with European Study.

Hertfordshire European Studies is offered jointly with several other subjects.

Hull (*European Studies/Transnational Integrated European Studies*) The degree programmes both cover Western Europe, the Iberian peninsula, Eastern Europe and Scandinavia. Students take courses in either humanities, social sciences (history, politics and literature) or economics, and core courses with a European perspective. They combine this with the study of either Dutch, French, German, Italian, Spanish or Swedish, with a period of study abroad. The four year TIES degree offers students the chance to gain an appropriate Dutch, French or German qualification as well as the BA degree by pursuing a year's study abroad.

Humberside (*European Contemporary Studies*) There is an 18-week exchange in the country of the language studied. Third year options exist in marketing, housing and health policy, tourism management etc.

Keele European Studies is offered with several other subjects. Residence abroad is part of the course.

Kent (*European Studies*) A range of degrees in European Studies is available including specialisations in French, German and Italian, combined languages and history. Other programmes look at Europe from the point of view of aspects of social sciences.

Leeds (*European Studies*) Core modules covering cultural, political and social issues with additional options in other subjects, eg law, management and sociology.

Leicester (*European Studies*) A broad and diverse approach to European Studies with half the students spending time abroad studying in East Central Europe.

Liverpool John Moores A community language is taken with a study covering history, politics, geography and economics.

London (King's) (*European Studies*) The course has a focus on politics, history, languages and culture of France and Germany. Also offered by the London School of Economics (applications through King's College).

London (QMW) (*European Studies*) The course unit system enables students to select courses in French, German, Russian or Spanish, combined with at least two courses in linguistics and/or literature, and a wide choice of other subjects such as law, politics or mathematics. A year abroad is normally undertaken.

London (RH) (*European Studies*) This is a four year course, including a year spent abroad, and involves the study of French, German or Italian. In each year students must take at least one course in geography, history, management or social sciences and may choose from a range of optional courses such as drama, classical studies or computing. There is a compulsory Year 1 course in History and a Year 2 course in Politics.

London (SSEES) (*Contemporary East European Studies*) This course, unique in Britain, focuses on a particularly exciting region of Europe. All students take a general background course in the history of Eastern Europe and may choose whether to combine this with courses in economics, politics, geography or sociology, or in one of the languages of the region.

London (UC) (*Modern European Studies*) All students study at least one foreign language and spend the third year of this four year course abroad. This is complemented by a choice of courses either in a subject (eg geography, history, linguistics, economics, planning or literature) or in several disciplines applying to a chosen region or country (eg the Low Countries or Italy) or to a central topic (eg the European Community).

Loughborough (*Modern European Studies*) This is a three or four year course combining languages and social sciences with fluency in one or more European languages (French and German). The Social Science course covers politics and economics.

Manchester European Studies is offered with modern languages (French, German, Italian, Spanish).

Manchester Metropolitan European Studies is offered as a joint course with several subjects.

Middlesex (*European Policy Studies*) The current and evolving policies of the European Union are examined from the perspectives of economics, politics and geography.

North London (*Contemporary European Studies*) This is an interdisciplinary degree comprising three core social science subjects - economics, history, and politics - and a language (French, Spanish or German). The third year of the course is spent in France, Germany or Spain.

Northumbria (*European Studies*) French or German are studied alongside a study of the EC and European integration. Specialisms include economics, geography, law, politics or sociology.

Nottingham (*Modern European Studies*) This is a new four year course with the third year being spent abroad. Taught jointly by the departments of

History and Modern Languages, it is designed to enable students to study aspects of modern European history, the contemporary societies and institutions in Eastern and Western Europe and at least two European languages. There are also several courses in the Faculty of Agricultural and Food Sciences which incorporate European Studies.

Nottingham Trent (*Modern European Studies*) The core strand of this course is 'The Idea of Europe' and the main subject areas cover history, English, geography, international relations, French and German, media and cultural studies. Students in the European Languages spend up to one year abroad.

Portsmouth (*European Studies*) A four year course providing graduates who are fluent in two European languages and who have a sound understanding of European history, culture and a specialist knowledge in chosen aspects of EU policy or a particular European country.

Reading (*European Studies*) The course covers politics, history, social and economic studies with a language (French or German).

Salford European Studies is offered with Modern Languages.

St Andrews (*European Integration Studies*) Politics and economics are taken with a modern language (or possibly two languages).

Sheffield (*Modern East European Studies*) There are two separate courses in the first year. Those with A-level Russian take an advanced Russian course and study the history, literature and society of Eastern Europe, together with two other arts subjects. Those with no Russian take a beginner's course in the language and the two arts subjects. In the second year students begin another Slavonic language and continue both language and area studies in Year 3.

Southampton (*Contemporary Europe*) This comprises a study of the history and politics of Europe, European Community institutions with options in economics, history, law or politics. Two European languages are studied from French, German or Spanish. Portuguese is also offered as a minor language.

South Bank (*European Community Studies*) Politics, Economics and Law are studied with a foreign language from scratch.

Stirling (*European Studies*) An integrated package comprising a modern European language, European history and politics.

Strathclyde (*European Studies*) This is a three year multidisciplinary course. Students take one foreign language from French, German, Italian, Russian or Spanish and combine it with geography, politics, history or literature in the first year. In the second and third years they continue the language course and choose from a range of options in historical, linguistic, philosophical, sociological, political or literary fields.

Sunderland (*European Studies*) This is part of the Combined Programmes scheme. The course covers language modules, politics, sociology, European business and trade, marketing and international relations.

Surrey European Studies is offered with French, German and Russian.

Sussex European Studies is offered jointly with over 18 subjects.

Thames Valley (*Modern European Studies*) The course covers Western, Central and Eastern Europe through the perspectives of economics, geography, history and political science. Language modules are offered in French, German and Spanish (post A-level) and Russian for beginners.

Ulster (*European Studies*) The subject can be taken as a major, joint or minor subject. The course covers Western and Eastern Europe.

Wolverhampton (*European Studies*) The main disciplines of this course are history, politics, economics, international relations, European thought and sociology, covering Eastern Europe as well as the EC. One major European language is chosen from French, German, Russian or Spanish and Year 3 of the course is spent abroad.

• **Top research universities**
Birmingham, Bradford, Loughborough, Salford, Surrey, Belfast, Edinburgh, Glasgow.

• **Colleges and Institutes of Higher Education offering degree courses**
Cardiff (Inst), Edge Hill (Coll), Gwent (Coll), Liverpool (Inst), North East Wales (Inst).

• **Other courses to be considered**
European languages, European business studies, history, international studies/relations, sociology.

FOOD SCIENCE (including **Nutrition**)

• **Special subject requirements:** usually chemistry and one or two other science or mathematics subjects at A-level.

• **Subject information:** Biochemistry, microbiology, human nutrition, food processing and technology are components of these courses. The study depends for its understanding on a secure foundation of several pure sciences - chemistry and two subjects from physics, mathematics, biology, botany or zoology. Only students offering such a combination can be considered. Food Technology covers the engineering aspects of food processing and management.

Belfast (*Food Science or Food Technology*) The first year course is common for both subjects and emphasises microbiology and the biochemistry of food composition. Students must then decide on their final degree subject. The Food Science course then covers human nutrition, food process engineering, economics and marketing, quality and safety. The Food Technology option also covers food marketing and business and also factory design and services.

Bournemouth (*Food Quality*) This is a four year sandwich course with the aim of producing graduates who can work in management and technical positions in the food industry. There are units in management, quality assurance, science and technology.

Bradford (*Nutrition and Food Policy*) A course offered within Biomedical Sciences in which the specialisms need not be chosen until the end of the second year. The course involves the study of human diet and the microbial and nutritional quality of food at national and individual level.

Brighton (*Management and Food Studies*) This course covers food studies, food and beverage, food technology and restaurant operations. There is also a course involving distribution, retail studies and marketing.

Cranfield (*Marketing and Food Management*) Work experience takes place in Year 3 of this course which has options in packaging designs, international marketing and retailing and also a European language.

Dundee (*Food and Welfare Studies*) The three themes of food, health and welfare are supported by studies in information skills, design, communication, interpersonal skills and management. The course emphasises the use of 'live' projects and industrial links.

Glasgow Caledonian (*Human Nutrition*) Year 1 includes sociology and information studies in addition to nutrition, physiology and chemistry. Community studies, management, food science and clinical dietetic studies follow. There is also a course in Food Technology.

Greenwich (*Applied Nutrition*) A study is made of cell biology, computing, genetics and human nutrition in Years 1 and 2. This is followed by an optional sandwich placement in Year 3. Project work covering nutrition in health and disease and similar topics follow in the final year.

Huddersfield (*Food and Nutrition*) Leads to technical management careers in the food and related industries. Specialisms include food processing, applied nutrition, food safety and food science. There is a foreign language option.

Humberside (*Food Science*) The course has a food quality and control emphasis with an industrial placement in Year 3. Topics covered include nutrition, food microbiology and technology. Degree courses are offered in Food Science with Environmental Studies, Food Technology, Management, Nutrition, and in International Food Technology.

Leeds (*Food Science*) Two modular courses, BSc Food Science and Food Science (European) share a common first year, formal laboratory classes and core modules in food chemistry, microbiology, organic chemistry, food biochemistry, food processing and food analysis. Options include food microbiology, nutrition, advanced food analysis and biotechnology. The European scheme includes language training and one semester on a research project in Europe.

Leeds Metropolitan (*Applied Human Nutrition*) A study of the scientific basis of nutritional science with optional placements is followed by business studies and the political economy of food. (*Dietetics*) The course shares modules with Applied Human Nutrition but includes unpaid catering training and clinical training, food science and health care modules.

Liverpool John Moores (*Food and Nutrition*) This course is offered singly or with Health or Marketing. It covers the scientific, technological, psychological and social aspects of food and nutrition.

London (King's) (*Nutrition*) The course shares the same syllabus as the degree in Nutrition and Dietetics except that the latter has a dietetic research project and 28 week placement in Years 3 and 4.

Manchester Metropolitan (*Food Manufacturing Management*) A four year sandwich course combining manufacturing, technical studies and management studies. There is a compulsory modern language option and the possibility of a German placement in Year 3.

Newcastle (*Food and Human Nutrition*) This four year BSc includes a placement in Year 3.

North London (*Food and Nutritional Science*) Course units include nutrition, food science, biochemistry, food microbiology, food analysis and quality control.

Northumbria (*Applied Consumer Sciences*) A three year full-time course focusing on the design, development, management and marketing of everyday products. There is an optional year abroad.

Nottingham (*Food Science*) The course covers food chemistry, processing, microbiology and nutrition. There is also a degree course in food microbiology.

Oxford Brookes (*Nutrition and Food Science*) Offered as a single Honours or in combination with other subjects on the modular programme, Nutrition and Food Science involves interdisciplinary study of human physiology, metabolism and health; post-harvest biochemistry of plants and animals; microbial spoilage and food poisoning; aspects of engineering and biotechnology. There is a strong practical element to most modules.

Plymouth Courses are offered in food quality and product development, food systems management and food and agriculture.

Reading (*Food Science*) Part I (two terms) deals with the agricultural and fisheries background, dairy and cereal products, physiology and biochemistry. In Part II (three terms) food processing, the chemistry, biochemistry and physics of food are covered as well as human nutrition and microbiology. Advanced work takes place in Part III. Degree courses are also offered in Food Manufacture, Management and Marketing, Food Technology and in Food Science, Economics and Marketing.

Robert Gordon (*Food Science and Management*) The course covers food processing, chemistry, food quality and safety and retailing, with an optional European language.

Sheffield Hallam (*Food Marketing Management*) Food technology and management systems are studied in depth on this course.

Southampton Nutrition is offered as a joint course with biochemistry and physiology.

South Bank (*Food Science*) Three year full-time or four year sandwich courses are offered in Food Science, Food Science with Nutrition and Food and Consumer Studies covering scientific and policy aspects of the food industry.

Strathclyde Food Science can be taken with Biochemistry.

Surrey (*Nutrition; Nutrition/Food Science*) This is a four year course, the third year being spent in a professional training placement. The first year is largely common with Biochemistry and Microbiology. In the second and final years students take nutrition, dietetics, anatomy, pathology, epidemiology and social nutrition.

Teesside (*Food Science and Nutrition*) This is a broad-based degree with a strong foundation in chemistry, biochemistry, microbiology and mathematics. There are foreign language and business studies options.

Thames Valley (*Food Services Management*) This is a business studies course with a food specialisation leading to the management of catering resources.

Ulster (*Human Nutrition*) The course includes registration in Dietetics.

● **Top research universities**
Leeds, Nottingham, Surrey.

● **Colleges and Institutes of Higher Education offering degree courses**
Bath (Coll), Birmingham (Coll of Food/Fashion), Blackpool and Fylde (Coll), Cardiff (Inst), Harper Adams (Coll), Leeds Trinity and All Saints (Coll), Queen Margaret (Coll), Scottish Agricultural (Coll), Salford (Univ Coll).

● **Other courses to be considered**
Biochemistry, biological sciences, catering management, hotel management.

FRENCH

● **Special subject requirements:** A-Levels in French and one other subject.

● **Subject information:** Courses could include an emphasis on literature and linguistics, the written or spoken word or a wider study of France and her culture as in European Studies courses. Check prospectuses before choosing courses.

Aberdeen (*French*) Emphasis is given to the written and spoken word at all levels, coupled with a study of French literature and history.

Aberystwyth (*French*) Students take two other subjects in the first year. This is a broad-based course covering French literature, culture and civilisation, in addition to imparting a good command of the written and spoken word. The third year abroad is an integral part of the course. Courses in the language of current affairs and business are also available.

Anglia (Poly Univ) French is offered in combination with over 25 other subjects including several science subjects.

Aston French is offered in combination with ten other subjects including European Studies and International Business.

Bangor (*French*) French is taken with two other subjects in the first year. The course covers French language, literature, thought, institutions and culture and offers a range of options which include French commercial language and business practice. Year 3 is wholly or partly spent abroad.

Belfast (*French*) In Year 1, two courses are offered - French language and literature and modern French studies. Second and third year courses offer increasing specialisation, with the language course being taken throughout. Options include history of the language, medieval and Renaissance literature, drama and poetry. French can be taken as a single, joint or major/minor course.

Bath French is offered with three other foreign languages (Italian, Russian or German) and also International Management.

Birmingham (*French Studies*) Study of the French language gives emphasis to this course in written and spoken forms. There are courses on the contemporary French language, literature, politics and culture. The third year is spent in France.

Bradford French is offered with German, Russian or Spanish and also International Management.

Brighton French is offered in combination with Management.

Bristol (*French*) There is a considerable flexibility in the options built into this course, ranging from a traditional literary emphasis to historical/institutional options. Computer science and language studies are also available. The third year is spent in a French-speaking country. A two year subsidiary subject must also be taken from a choice of nine alternatives.

Bristol UWE French is offered in combination with European Law, German or Spanish.

Brunel French is offered with Engineering or Mathematics.

Buckingham Law or Economics or Business Management can be taken with French.

Cambridge (*French*) The modern language course lasts four years with one year normally being spent abroad. Two languages are studied in Part I to the same level. In Part II students are free to specialise in one language.

Cardiff (*French*) The course aims to develop a command of the spoken and written word and a study of French literature and culture. The third year of this four year course is spent abroad. Options include Business French with students taking the Paris Chamber of Commerce examinations.

Central England French is offered with several Engineering courses.

Central Lancashire French can be taken as part of the Combined Honours Programme.

Coventry French is offered in combination with twelve other subjects.

De Montfort French can be taken with law or as part of an extensive Combined Arts, Humanities or Studies programme.

Derby French is offered as part of the Credit Accumulation Modular Scheme.

Dundee French is offered in combination with Physics.

Durham (*Modern Languages*) (One, two or three languages can be studied.) The first year of the French course covers the study of language, translation and history, phonetics and medieval and seventeenth century literature. The second and fourth years continue with language work and a wider study of literature. The third year is spent in France or a French-speaking country.

East Anglia (*French*) The subject is studied with an emphasis on linguistic proficiency. This is an Area Studies degree in which French language is taken with seminar courses in French literature and history and courses on contemporary France. In the Language and Linguistics degree course two term courses are available in the theory and practice of interpreting and translation.

Edinburgh (*French*) All students take a secondary subject in the first two years. A four year course with the third year spent in France.

Essex (*French (Language and Linguistics)*) The first year covers language studies, linguistics and either The Enlightenment and one Comparative Study or two Social Science options. Years 2 and 4 involve practical languages and linguistics and Year 3 is spent abroad.

Exeter (*French*) Students spend two-thirds of their time in the first two years on French, and one-third on another subject. Throughout the course a balance is achieved between literature and the written and spoken word, one term being devoted to a study of aspects of commercial, administrative and technical language. The third year is spent abroad.

Glamorgan French is offered in combination with several science subjects and also as part of a more general Combined Studies/Honours programme.

Glasgow (*French*) The course introduces French language and modern literature, leading on to the eighteenth, nineteenth and twentieth century literature translations and modern French history. Honours students spend an extended period abroad.

Greenwich The International Marketing course has a French option.

Heriot-Watt French is offered jointly with German or Russian or Spanish with the emphasis on Interpreting and Translating.

Huddersfield French is offered with Communication Arts.

Hull (*French*) There is a core course in modern French culture supported by an emphasis on communicative skills. Additional languages and several other subjects can be taken. There is an emphasis on practical language training.

Humberside (*European Administration - French*) The course is designed for students with an interest in business careers. The three main strands of the course comprise business, a language and a project. There is a twelve week work based project in Europe and an optional four week placement in the UK.

Keele Over sixty courses are offered jointly with French. There is an emphasis on written and spoken word competence.

Kent (*French*) The study of contemporary and literary language is combined with a study of one or two literature courses - an introductory survey of French literature, and a study of the 1930s and 1940s or both. A year is spent abroad and more advanced literature studies follow in Part II of the course.

Kingston (*French Studies*) Language and literature courses are offered. Other language options include German, Spanish, Italian, Russian and Japanese.

Lampeter (*French*) This is a traditional French course covering French language and literature with several options including the geography of France and the society and institutions of contemporary France. There is a wide freedom of choice on this course for students to 'build' a course to suit their own interests. The third year of this four year course is spent abroad.

Lancaster (*French*) The French course includes both language and literature and also a study of history, fine art and contemporary French society. The integrated degrees in French Studies and a management subject (accounting finance, economics or marketing) have as a main feature a course in the language of commerce.

Leeds (*French*) This course combines the study of French language and literature in all years, with one year being spent abroad. A subsidiary subject is taken with French for three years. The study of language is emphasised throughout the course and a wide range of options is available including French for business and administrative purposes, French history and institutions, and the French cinema.

Leicester (*French*) This subject is studied throughout the four years of the course, the third year being spent in a French-speaking country. A supplementary subject is studied in the first years. Language work is combined with literature and linguistics throughout the course.

Liverpool (*French*) The language component for all years includes an oral, 'communicative skills' course. First-year students are offered an introduction to literary studies course. Literature courses in the first two years are mainly genre-based (eg comic theatre, novels employing the first person narrative) and a choice of options is available from the second year. The third year is spent abroad, as an assistant or as a student at a university. Joint Honours students follow a 'linking' course, taught jointly by the two subject departments.

Liverpool John Moores Over thirty subjects are offered with French.

London (Goldsmiths') (*French Studies*) The four year course is designed to produce near-native proficiency in the French language, with complementary studies of French literature and society, and a period of study abroad is compulsory. There is a range of options within the course, including the opportunity to study another European language. A degree course in French and German Studies is also available.

London Guildhall French is offered in the Modular programme. There is a second language option. The course covers literature, politics, mass-media and French cinema.

London (King's) (*French*) This is a traditional four year course with the third year spent abroad. Students following the single subject course cover both language and literature.

London (LSE) French is offered with Management Sciences.

London (QMW) (*French*) The modular degree programme offers considerable flexibility in the composition of the degree course. French may be combined with European Studies, another language, or with linguistics and computing.

London (RH) (*French*) The course covers French language, medieval literature, Renaissance literature and literature in the seventeenth, eighteenth, nineteenth and twentieth centuries. This is a four year course including a year in Europe. A subsidiary subject is taken for the first two years.

London (SSEES) French is offered with Romanian or Russian.

London (UC) (*French*) This is a four year course with the third year spent abroad. The course covers the history of the French language and theories of language, the literature of different periods and weekly practice in the written and spoken word. Studies in depth are also possible through a range of options. All students choose two course units which include other languages.

Loughborough French is offered with Economics.

Manchester (*French Studies*) A broad French course with options to specialise in the second and final years, the third year being spent in France. The subject can be studied with several other languages or on a major/minor (75 per cent/25 per cent) basis with another subject.

Manchester Metropolitan French is offered jointly with several subjects. French Studies is offered as part of the Combined Studies, Humanities and Social Studies schemes.

Middlesex French is offered as part of the multidisciplinary programme as a major or minor subject.

Newcastle (*French*) The course gives more than average emphasis to the practical and theoretical study of the French language, while offering a wide range of options covering literature, film and socio-political history. This is a four year course including a year spent abroad. The fourth year includes interpreting and translating.

North London (*French*) This can be studied as a single or combined degree course or as part of the European Studies course.

Northumbria French is offered as part of the Combined Honours programme.

Nottingham (*French Studies*) Options include French Canada, women's writing, French cinema and media.

Nottingham Trent French is offered as part of the Humanities programme.

Oxford (*French*) During the first two terms students can study two languages - either two modern or one modern and one classical or with linguistics. A specialist course in one language or two follows.

Oxford Brookes A very large number of subjects can be taken with French Language and Contemporary Studies, French Language and Literature or Language for Business.

Plymouth French is offered with International Business.

Portsmouth (*French Studies*) This is a course with a strong bias towards modern French and modern France. Students choose three options in Year 2. The third year is spent abroad.

Reading (*French*) The course involves practical language work, French literature and thought, French history and political thought and a range of final year options. The third year is normally spent at a French university. A wide range of joint Honours courses is available.

Salford French is offered with ten other subjects.

St Andrews (*French*) French may be studied for one, two or three years or as a four year Honours subject. Competence in the written and spoken word is central to the course which is balanced by a study of literature. Students are encouraged to spend a year teaching in a French school (in addition to the four year course) or to spend the third year at a French university.

Sheffield (*French Language and Literature*) Throughout the course a balance is established between language and literature. Oral and written fluency is the aim throughout the course, with a year spent abroad in the third year. Special projects take place in the fourth year on such topics as French art, architecture or aspects of French civilisation. Two other subjects can be studied in Year 1.

Sheffield Hallam French is offered with International Business.

Southampton (*French*) A basis of language supports a study of French society, culture and literature.

Staffordshire French is offered with over thirty subjects.

Stirling (*French*) Two Part I courses are offered. The first combines the study of French language and literature (obligatory for single Honours students). The second provides French language practice for students in other disciplines. Part II of the General and Honours course covers French literature and a course on contemporary France with practical language work. Residence abroad is compulsory for a year during the course.

Strathclyde (*French*) French can be taken with German, Italian, Russian or Spanish as part of the Modern languages course. Students spend six weeks in foreign residence between Years 2 and 3.

Sunderland Over 25 subjects are offered with French.

Surrey French is offered with European Studies, International Business and Law.

Sussex (*French*) The course involves the continuous study of the French language. Students in the School of European Studies take three courses of French literature, and in addition they cover topics on politics, the economy and education. Students in the School of African and Asian Studies also study literature in the African and Caribbean context. The third year of the course is usually spent abroad in France or in the French-speaking parts of Africa or the West Indies. In the final year students work on their own special subject topic.

Swansea (*French*) Three subjects are studied in Part I. Students will be expected to reach a good level of proficiency in both written and spoken French at this stage. In Part II the subject involves literature as a core subject and minor topics covering linguistics, medieval literature and French political and social thought. A year is spent abroad and all students are required to pass an oral examination. Several joint Honours courses are available and all courses comprise intensive language work.

Teesside French is offered as part of the Humanities programme.

Thames Valley Ten courses are offered with French.

Ulster French is part of the Humanities programme.

Warwick (*French Studies*) Modern French language (written and spoken) is taken during each year of the course. Other studies cover French literature from 1470 to the present day and a number of optional studies. There is also a Cultural Studies variant which places extra emphasis on French art, cinema or music. The year in France (after Year 2) is optional.

Westminster French is offered with ten other subjects including Arabic.

Wolverhampton (*French Studies*) The course combines language learning with a study of contemporary culture, politics, economics and society in France.

York French is offered with German, Linguistics or History.

● **Top research universities**
Cambridge, Exeter, London (QMW), Nottingham, Oxford, Reading, Sussex, Warwick, Edinburgh, St Andrews, Strathclyde.

● **Colleges and Institutes of Higher Education offering degree courses**
British Institute in Paris (University of London), Buckinghamshire (Coll), Cheltenham and Gloucester (Coll), Chester (Coll), Edge Hill (Coll), Leeds, Trinity and All Saints (Coll), Liverpool (Inst), La Sainte Union (Coll), Nene (Coll), Newman (Coll), Ripon and York St John (Univ Coll), Roehampton (Inst), Scarborough (Univ Coll), Westminster (Coll).

● **Other courses to be considered**
Modern language courses and European Studies. Languages which can be combined with French. Also consider other languages not requiring the A-level language, eg Spanish, Chinese, Japanese, Russian, Italian etc.

GEOGRAPHY

- **Special subject requirements:** usually geography at A-level and mathematics at GCSE (grade A–C).

- **Subject information:** These courses cover the human, physical, economic and social aspects of the subject. Each institution offers its own particular emphasis. Check the prospectuses for all courses, with particular attention to the specialist options in years 2 & 3.

Aberdeen (*Geography*) Honours students have the opportunity to specialise in topics chosen from human, physical, regional or applied geography. A large number of combined courses are also offered.

Aberystwyth (*Geography*) Geography with the appropriate bias is offered in the Faculties of Arts or Science. In Year 1 compulsory courses take place in human and physical geography with later specialisation. In the Faculty of Science specialisation is possible in geomorphology, physical geography, mapping science and remote sensing, and climate. Over twenty joint courses are also offered.

Anglia (Poly Univ) (*Geography*) The course is taught on the modular system. Four broad areas of study are offered in Years 2 and 3: Dynamic Earth, Environmental Challenge, People and Places and Societies. Single and combined courses are offered with a language option. Geography is also available in the Combined Science programme.

Belfast (*Geography*) Human and physical geography are taken in the first year. In the second year, courses vary depending on the type of degree course chosen (Pass or Honours). Regional geography is studied in the second and third years alongside social, human or physical geography.

Birmingham (*Geography*) In the first year of this course students cover human and physical geography. In the second year single Honours students choose three from five elective courses including conservation, settlements, planning and resource management and physical geography. There is a free choice of options in Year 3. Over twenty joint courses are also offered.

Bradford Geography is offered with Environmental Science.

Brighton Geography is offered with seven other subjects.

Bristol (*Geography*) This course covers a wide range of geographical interests and related problems concerning the environment and the regions. After Stage I (first year) three different syllabuses are offered allowing concentration on aspects of the natural or social sciences or the interactions between both fields. Complementary subjects are offered as minor courses.

Bristol UWE Human and physical geography are covered with options in environmental information technology, national parks and tourism. Geography is taken with Environmental Management or as a major subject in the Teacher Training course.

Cambridge (*Geography*) Part I of this course covers physical, human and historical geography, environment and resources and geographical methods. The second year (Part II) includes economic, urban and political geography, environmental problems, cultural geography, North America and the Indian sub-continent. Specialist topics such as the geography of the EC, USSR, South Asia and Latin America are offered in the third year.

Cardiff (*Marine Geography*) This course focuses on the ocean as a maritime frontier and man's socio-economic relationship with the physical environment and the principles of maritime transport, the maritime industries and ocean and coastal management. Topics covered include geology, the ocean atmosphere, cartography, coastal hydrography and coastal zone management. The third year may be spent in industrial training.

Central Lancashire (*Geography*) Specialisms are offered in physical, human, social and industrial geography or urban planning.

Coventry (*Geography*) This BSc course is a four year sandwich course - a unique feature of this course is the third year spent in professional training in which students have placements related to geography such as hydrology, forestry, offshore surveying, marketing and transport, in the UK and abroad. Four geography modules are selected from a choice of ten in the final year. Geography is also offered as a component in the Modern Studies BA course. There is also a course in Geographical Information Systems.

Cranfield (*Geography*) A physical geography course (pending approval) covering information systems, remote sensing and environmental monitoring.

Derby (*Geography*) The course is offered within the Credit Accumulation Modular Scheme as a major, joint or minor subject. A three year single Honours degree is also available.

Dundee (*Geography*) The emphasis in the first two years on this BSc course is on population geography, urban and regional development, physical geography and the evolution of Europe's landscape. In Year 3 students select from a range of physical, human and regional courses.

Durham (*Geography*) The first year courses in the subject cover human, physical and regional geography with fieldwork in the UK and abroad and practical classes. In the second and third years a choice of specialist options from over 40 topics enables students to choose their own emphasis to the subject. One third of the degree is assessed on a 'continual' basis.

East London A course is offered in Geographical Information Systems which covers cartography, land and property law, coastal zone and management. There are some exemptions from the examinations of the Royal Institute of Chartered Surveyors.

Edinburgh (*Geography*) This subject may be studied as a natural science or a social science. The main distinction lies in the entry qualifications which must include the basic sciences for the BSc course. There is a range of options including the economic and social landscape, disease and the environment and leisure studies.

Exeter (*Geography*) The undergraduate programme extends over three years and offers nine alternative courses which lead to single or combined Honours degrees in the Faculties of Arts, Science or Social Studies. In the first two years a study is made of the natural and cultural environments and practical techniques in investigation. The third year includes a wide range of options including the geography of Eastern Europe and the Third World, urban conservation and retail location. Each student can therefore make his or her own specialist studies. Geography with European Study is a four year course involving a year abroad.

Glamorgan Geography can be taken as part of the Combined Honours or Combined Studies courses.

Glasgow (*Geography*) Physical and human geography introduce the course followed by the study of a major world area, statistics, computing and mapping. The Ordinary Class also serves as the first year of the Topographic Science Honours course. Geography may be studied in the Arts, Social Science or Science Faculties. In addition to a very large number of joint courses, a specialised course in Topographic Science can be taken.

Greenwich (*Geography*) Students elect to follow the BA or BSc courses at the end of the first year. Options include environmental or natural resources management or political and urban geography.

Hertfordshire Geography can be taken as a major in the Primary Education course and there is also a degree in Surveying and Mapping.

Huddersfield (*Geography*) This BSc course focuses on the applied aspects of geography - rural geography, commercial activities, recreation studies, transport and urban studies, and water resources. Applicants should be interested in economic, social and environmental policy issues.

Hull (*Geography*) This subject may be taken as a science (BSc) or as a social science (BA) depending on the qualifications and interests of the candidate. The course is identical in both areas and in the first two years gives a balanced picture of all the main aspects of the subject. A range of specialised courses in the third year allow for a personal choice of options. Field courses are arranged in various parts of Europe. A modular course structure has been introduced to provide greater flexibility in additional subject modules.

Keele Over fifty courses are offered. The course follows the theme of geography in a changing world and includes cartography, surveying, photo interpretation and statistics.

Kent (*Geography*) Students are required to follow a number of specialist geography topics which form the core of the degree. These are complemented by courses in economics, economic history, political science and sociology. The degree will appeal to those with interests in human geography.

Kingston (*Geography*) A foundation year provides basic training in the subject matter and techniques of the discipline. Economic and political geography, water resource management, urban geography and transport are some of the areas covered in Part II. Fieldwork and practical studies are an integral part of the course. All students complete a personal research project. There is also a course in Geographical Information Systems.

Lampeter (*Geography*) Physical and human geography are studied with one other subject in the first year. The subject is covered on a broad front ranging in options from a study of Australia, Canada, Brazil and Scandinavia, to rural and social geography. Second and third year options cover tropical rain forests, the environment and aspects of health.

Lancaster (*Geography*) All students follow courses on human and physical geography and geographical techniques, quantitative analysis and computing. Many of the courses have a strong applied theme giving a broad picture of the social, economic and environmental problems. Exchanges with the USA may be arranged.

Leeds (*Geography*) Courses in geography cover both social and natural science interests with one or two subsidiary subjects. The former offers a wide range of options with particular strength in urban and resources studies and compulsory field weeks with visits to France in Year 2. The BSc course aims to provide a broad base in geography while emphasising the scientific study of the environment. This is reflected in the training provided in field, laboratory and computing techniques. There is a wide choice of third year options including hydrology, water quality, energy resources, soils, conservation, environmental risk assessment, climatic change, geomorphological modelling, fluvial and glacial processes.

Leicester (*Geography*) A common first year is followed by both BA and BSc students. Thereafter the BA students follow a human geography course, and a bias towards physical geography exists for BSc students with a high degree of flexibility in option choice and specialisation. A supplementary subject is taken in Years 1 and 2 in both BA and BSc courses.

Liverpool (*Geography*) The subject is offered as an arts, science and social science subject. Students follow first year courses in physical and human geography and introduction to planet Earth. Options are available in the first and second years. The science bias has a strong physical geography element.

Liverpool John Moores (*Geography*) Core modules are taken from Human Geography and Earth Science with ample scope for specialisation in Years 2 and 3.

London (King's) (*Geography*) Physical and human geography and geographical techniques are covered in the first year, with half-unit courses in a range of subjects. Second year courses are optional, and in the third year students follow three optional course units and present an independent geographical study.

London (LSE) (*Geography*) This single subject BA or BSc course in the first year covers physical geography, geographical perspectives on modern society, geographical analysis. In the second and third years, eight course units are chosen from a wide range of options. A course in Population Studies is also offered covering births, deaths, marriages and migration.

London (QMW) (*Geography*) The subject is taught under the course-unit system enabling students to combine their own choice of geographical studies with a wide variety of other disciplines, for example, economics, history, politics, geology, modern language. The subject can be studied either as an arts or as a science subject. There are separate degrees in Human Geography and Physical Geography and a range of joint Honours courses.

London (RH) (*Geography*) This course avoids the traditional separation between physical and human geography and concentrates on interactions between people and their natural, economic and social environments. In Years 2 and 3, students have a free choice in the selection of specialist courses and are encouraged to acquire career-related skills.

London (SOAS) (*Geography*) This is the only geography degree course which is specific to regions of the world, namely Asia and Africa. Various joint Honours combinations are also available with ten other subjects.

London (UC) (*Geography*) Human and physical geography in the first year integrate with international topics and environmental studies. Geography may be studied as either an arts or a science subject and all students have the same wide choice of options, designing their own second and third year programmes. Geography may also be studied with Anthropology or Economics.

London Guildhall (*Geography*) Physical and human geography are studied in a course which covers environmental studies, conservation and planning. There are also options to study in the USA or Europe.

Loughborough (*Geography*) Human and physical geography are taken in the first year followed by a wide range of options in the second and third years. Language options are available.

Luton (*Geography*) This course can be taken in major/minor or joint programmes. Options are available in natural hazards, transport geography, rural planning and health and medical geography.

Manchester (*Geography*) The courses are offered in both the Faculties of Arts and Sciences with a variety of subsidiary courses in Years 2 and 3.

Manchester Metropolitan (*Geography*) After a foundation year in physical and human geography students select a programme from a very wide range of options which may include languages. Geography may be combined with Environmental Studies.

Middlesex (*Geography*) This BA/BSc course covers options emphasising a human-environment theme: ecology, countryside planning, world-development problems or applied physical geography. Geography is also offered in the Humanities and Combined Studies degree programmes.

Newcastle (*Geography*) The subject is offered in both the Faculty of Arts and Sciences. In the latter, first year students take two additional subjects from computing science, geology, maths, physics, surveying science, plant biology or zoology. Second and third year courses offer similar optional and core topics. There is also a course in Mapping Science of interest to those interested in mapping and computing.

North London (*Geography*) BA and BSc courses are offered. Both have a common first year in which one other subject is chosen from archaeology, ecology, economics, geology or philosophy. Students then choose their programme leading to BA and BSc. Regional specialisms include Europe, South Asia and the Caribbean. Geography is also offered in the BSc modular degree course.

Northumbria (*Geography*) This BA course introduces human and physical geography. In Years 1 and 2 the focus of studies is in development. A wide range of options is available in the third year, with an emphasis on applicability.

Nottingham (*Geography*) BA and BSc students follow a common first year course: human and physical geography and a course on the developing world. Specialised topics begin in the second year, including meteorology, industry and transport, environmental studies and geomorphology. Subsidiary subjects are taken as two or one year courses.

Nottingham Trent Geography is offered with a bias towards Environmental Studies and also as part of the Humanities programme.

Oxford (*Geography*) The first year course introduces human and physical geography, and offers six optional subjects (geology, ethnology, exploration and partition of Africa, political history, plant ecology and a maths subject) from which one must be selected. During the second and third year students choose four geography papers common to all students and four optional topics, depending on their geographical interests.

Oxford Brookes Geography or Cartography are offered with a very large number of subjects.

Plymouth (*Geography*) This course offers a wide range of subsidiary subjects and an extensive fieldwork programme. Geography or Hydrography are also offered with a large number of other subjects.

Portsmouth (*Geography*) This Honours degree is a single-subject, broadly-based degree programme, offering a balance between both physical and human fields of interest, and between both theory in geography and its application to the practical needs of society. After a foundation year, the course notably offers a very large range of option studies, including remote sensing, computer-assisted cartography, urban and rural studies, fluvial sensing, biogeography, medical geography, economic geography and development studies. All students complete a field course in Europe as part of a fieldwork programme at home and abroad.

Reading Geography is offered with a bias towards Human or Physical Geography or as Geography and Economics combined in the Regional Science degree course.

Salford (*Geography*) The emphasis in the first year of this course concerns environmental analysis and human ecology. In the second year, courses extend to geographical techniques including statistics and computing. Third year students have a wide choice of specialities ranging from geomorphology and climatic change to transport, tourism and regional development.

Sheffield (*Geography*) The first year BA course introduces human and physical geography followed by a choice between three streams in the second year. Two of these focus on physical geography (geomorphology, soil formation and vegetation), one on human geography (population and environmental resources). Selective specialisation takes place in the third year. The BSc course lays emphasis on physical geography throughout.

South Bank Human Geography is offered with Environmental Policy.

Southampton (*Geography*) The BA and BSc courses provide a common broad foundation until midway through the second year. Thereafter students begin to specialise and have considerable opportunity to select courses in transport geography, urban development, environmental change, remote sensing and hydrology.

St Andrews (*Geography*) This is taught in the Arts and Science Faculties, the first two years being common to all students. A system of teaching in small option groups follows for the next two years. Students may specialise in human or physical geography or may study groups of courses concerned, for example, with landscape processes, land and water resources. Some exchanges take place with European institutions.

Staffordshire (*Geography*) This BA course emphasises human aspects of the discipline. (*Modern Studies*) In this BA course human geography is introduced in the first year. Optional subjects include developmental studies, planning, resources, recreation, leisure and tourism. Geography is also offered with a large selection of other subjects.

Strathclyde Geography is offered with Planning as a three year or four year degree.

Sunderland Geography is offered with over twenty other subjects.

Sussex (*Geography*) This subject can be taken in the School of Biological Sciences in a course with a strong environmental and ecological emphasis, or in the context of Europe or Africa and Asia in the Schools of European or African and Asian Studies, or with an emphasis on social aspects in the School of Cultural and Community Studies or the School of Social Sciences. The broad study of the subject also covers social, urban, regional and historical geography, physical geography, resource development and geographical analysis.

Swansea (*Geography*) The subject is offered in the Faculties of Arts, Science and Economic and Social Studies. The first year course is common to all three Faculties and deals with human, physical, economic and social courses in the practice of geography, computing, four compulsory courses and a selection from a very wide range of options. There are various joint or combined Honours programmes.

Thames Valley Geography is offered as a Humanities subject.

Ulster (*Geography*) The first year covers human and physical geography and also short courses on information technology and computing. In the second year students may prefer to specialise in human topics such as industrial, social or rural geography or on physical geography or environmental science units.

Warwick (*Geography*) The course has an environmental base and strong links with biology.

Wolverhampton Physical or Human Geography are offered as a specialist study or as part of the Modular degree scheme. There is also a course in Geographical Information Systems.

● Top research universities
Bristol, Cambridge, Durham, London (UC), Oxford, Edinburgh, Birmingham, East Anglia, Exeter, Leeds, Liverpool, London (LSE) (RH), Newcastle, Portsmouth (teaching), Sheffield, Southampton, Strathclyde.

● Colleges and Institutes of Higher Education offering degree courses
Bath (Coll), Bishop Grosseteste (Coll), Brunel (Univ Coll), Canterbury Christ Church (Coll), Cardiff (Inst), Cheltenham and Gloucester (Coll), Chester (Coll), Chichester (Inst), Edge Hill (Coll), Gwent (Coll), King Alfred's (Coll), Leeds Trinity and All Saints (Coll), Liverpool (Inst), La Sainte Union (Coll), Nene (Coll), Newman (Coll), North East Wales (Inst), Ripon and York St John (Univ Coll), Scarborough (Univ Coll), S. Martins (Coll), St Mark and St John (Coll), St Mary's (Univ Coll), Trinity Carmarthen (Coll), Westminster (Coll).

● Other courses to be considered
Development studies, environmental studies and sciences, estate management, and town and country planning.

GEOLOGY/GEOLOGICAL SCIENCES

● Special subject requirements: 2–3 A-levels. Some courses require science and/or mathematics subjects at A-level and GCSE (A–C).

● Subject information: Topics covered include the physical and chemical constitution of the earth, exploration geophysics, oil and marine geology (oceanography) and seismic interpretation. Civil and Marine Engineering, Earth Science, Soil Science and Environmental Science could also be considered as alternative courses.

Aberdeen Geology is offered with Petroleum Geology or with Geography.

Aberystwyth (*Geology*) Single and joint Honours courses are offered, designed to give the student the widest possible background knowledge of geology and geological techniques. The modular scheme allows for breadth or specialisation in a number of fields, for example, oil geology, marine geology and mineral exploitation. A broad course in Environmental Earth Studies is offered.

Anglia (Poly Univ) (*Geology*) This is a broad programme with several options including environmental and physio-chemical studies. Single and combined Honours pathways in Applied Geology and Earth Sciences are also offered.

Bangor (*Geological Oceanography*) For all degree programmes in Ocean Sciences (the School is one of the largest in Europe) students are sought with a good scientific background. In Year 1, all oceanography students take core courses in ocean and earth science. In Years 2 and 3, the degree has a dominant oceanographic perspective. On timescales of 1,000 years it emphasies the influences on the sedimentary cycle from source to sink; on greater timescales the temporal variability of sedimentary processes is investigated.

Belfast (*Geology*) Introductory courses in geology are offered for those without previous knowledge. Depending on entry qualifications, the course will last three or four years. The broad course has a strong emphasis on earth resources and covers palaeontology, stratigraphy, petrology and structural geology.

Birmingham (*Applied and Environmental Geology; Geology*) There is a common first year for both courses followed by an emphasis in geological skills or industrial geography.

Bristol (*Geology*) This subject is aimed at those who wish to practise geology professionally and the degree is regarded as the basic foundation for further training in industry or research. Two subsidiary subjects are taken in the first year with specialism in geology in Years 2 and 3. There is a strong emphasis on field work and geological mapping projects. This is an expanding department with several new research initiatives.

Cambridge (*Geological Sciences*) This is offered as part of the National Sciences course. See **Chemistry**.

Cardiff (*Geology*) This subject is studied with two other subjects in Part I. The course is open to those with no prior knowledge of geology. There is a strong fieldwork element and up to two modules per year can be taken possibly from other departments. Topics covered include the physical and chemical constitution of the earth, exploration geophysics and seismic interpretation, geological time and earth history. Courses in Environmental Geoscience and Exploration Geology are also offered.

Derby (*Geology*) The course is offered within the Credit Accumulation Module Scheme as a major, joint or minor subject. A three year single Honours degree is also offered.

Durham (*Geological Sciences*) The first year course introduces the basic principles and methods of geology and recent advances. Single Honours students then continue through the second and third years with a study of special branches of the geological sciences, eg economic geology, lunar geology, geochemistry and geophysics.

East Anglia (*Environmental Earth Science*) A course which relates closely to Environmental Sciences but also includes applied geophysics, geodynamics, geological hazards, pollution and water supply.

Edinburgh (*Geology*) Students take geology in the first year together with two other subjects often including chemistry, physics, maths or biology. In the second year other subjects can accompany geology including oceanography and geophysics. The third and fourth years are devoted entirely to geology. In the final year the major course is the evolution of the earth. There is also a degree course in Geophysics.

Exeter (Camborne School of Mines) (*Industrial Geology*) Major emphasis is on field work. Geotechnical Engineering is a key subject in Years 2 and 3 and this has proved to be a major asset in terms of employment with many graduates finding work in this area. Languages are regarded as an important skill and students have the option of French or Spanish. This is supported by field work and industrial visits in the relevant country. Also offered is Geology with European Study, a four year applied geology degree in which the third year is spent at a university in France or Spain.

Glamorgan Geological Science is offered as a joint or major/minor degree within the Applied Sciences scheme, or can be studied as part of the Combined degree course. The title of the degree will reflect the subjects chosen.

Glasgow (*Geology and Applied Geology*) The course assumes no previous knowledge of geology. The course covers geological map-reading, the identification of common rocks, minerals and fossils. These topics lead on to broad non-specialised Honours courses.

Greenwich (*Natural Resources Management*) A course for geographers and earth scientists with particular interest in Third World Studies.

Hertfordshire (*Environmental Geology*) This course covers the relationships between environmental geology, humans and habitat.

Keele Geology is offered jointly with a large selection of subjects. The course covers rocks, minerals, fossils, geophysics and computing.

Kingston (*Geology*)The course in geology assumes no previous knowledge of the subject and is designed to provide a foundation in theoretical and practical geology. Fieldwork is an important element of the course. In the final year, students choose options from a wide range of geological subject areas which include resource exploration and evaluation, mapping and computing.

Lancaster (*Geophysical Sciences*) Geology is studied in each of the three years of this course.

Leeds (*Geological Sciences*) The first two years cover a basic training in Geology and the principles of geophysics plus a first year study of two other relevant sciences. In the final year students choose the emphasis of their course by selecting from a range of options which include environmental geochemistry, global geophysics and engineering geology. Geophysical Sciences and Environmental Geology are also offered.

Leicester (*Geology*) A supplementary subject is studied in the first year. Two parallel courses are offered in the first year, one providing a broad introduction and the other a more rigorous scientific base. The second and third years offer a range of specialised courses which include global and historical geology and geoscience. The Applied Geology course covers prospecting, mineral exploitation and mineral resources.

Liverpool (*Geology*) A range of well integrated courses in geology and geophysics can be followed in this programme. Field courses take place in Scotland, Wales, Greenland and the Alps.

Liverpool John Moores (*Earth Science*) This three year degree is available as a single subject or in combination with Countryside Management. It familiarises students with the geological, geochemical and geophysical background to resource development and environmental issues.

London (Imp) (*Geology*) The department offers a three year BSc course in Geology, and four year MSci courses in Earth Resources, Environmental

Geology, Geological Sciences, Geology and Geophysics, and Petroleum Geology.

London (QMW) Applied Geology and Environmental Geotech and Civil and Geological Engineering degree courses are offered.

London (RH) (*Geology*) This subject is offered as a specialism, as a joint course, or as an ancillary course to the main subject. The course introduces geology, earth materials and earth structure. In the second and third years a selection of optional courses allows specialisation. These include such topics as marine geology, fossil fuels, mineral deposits and engineering geology. There is also a course in Geochemistry.

London (UC) (*Geology*) This is a broad-based three or four year course covering all the major aspects of geological sciences. Introductory courses are available in maths, physics, chemistry or biology. Theoretical and practical skills are developed through the course and students are encouraged to take a computing course. There are also courses in Geophysics, Planetary Science, Earth and Space Science, Palaeobiology, Exploration Geophysics and Environmental Geoscience.

Luton (*Geology*) Geology courses focus on the dynamic earth and its products, with an emphasis on applied topics such as petroleum geology, hazards and mineral deposits.

Manchester (*Geology*) The Department of Earth Sciences offers three degree courses in Geology, Environmental and Resource Geology or Geochemistry. These have a common first year covering most aspects of geology and include a basic training in physical science. In the second year, students select which stream to follow. All students have a choice of specialist options in the third year.

Middlesex (*Applied Earth Science*) A broad science training in the first year with specialisation in geology in Year 2 and a choice of modules in the final year. 105 days of field work take place over the three years.

Oxford (*Earth Science*) The first year is designed to cater for students with a variety of A-level subjects (a good foundation being chemistry and physics with maths, geology or a biological subject). The course covers the main aspects of geology, geophysics and geochemistry.

Oxford Brookes (*Applied Geology*) The course covers mineral, water and energy resources, geological hazards, civil engineering geology, and the effects of geological activity on our environment. The course offers students with limited science an opportunity to strengthen their general sciences. Also offered are Geological Sciences, Geology (as joint or combined Honours) and International Applied Geology (with a year abroad).

Plymouth (*Applied Geology; Environmental Geology; Geological Sciences*) Students who enter the Geological Sciences modular degree programmes are expected to have an interest in geology, but no previous geological experience or qualifications are necessary. Geology can also be studied as a major or minor Honours or combined with other scientific or non-scientific subjects. The programmes have recently received an excellent HEFC teaching quality assessment.

Portsmouth (*Geology*) Fieldwork forms a major part of the course. Throughout the three years, the practical work is continually assessed and makes up 25 per cent of the total assessment in each year. There is a clear emphasis on the economic significance and practice of geology. A high proportion of graduates continue with careers in geology. There are also courses in Applied Environmental Geology, Earth Sciences, Engineering Geology and Geotechnics.

Sheffield (*Environmental Geology*) At level 1 students take modules in Geology and in other subjects including archaeology which can be taken as a dual subject. Geological hazards, economic geology, soil minerology and field projects are included at level 3.

Southampton (*Geology*) In the first year students take four units in geology. These include geochemistry, map interpretation, mineralogy and petrology and palaeontology. More advanced studies on these subjects continue in the second year plus new topics such as geotechnics and geophysics, whilst third year students choose options according to their interests. Several joint courses are also available.

St Andrews (*Environmental Geology*) Courses are also offered in Geochemistry and Geoscience.

Staffordshire (*Applied Geology*) During the first year students take one other science subject. Later years focus on engineering geology, exploration, geophysics, geochemistry and the origin of mineral deposits. Other modular Honours courses include Environmental Geology (accredited by the Chartered Institution of Water and Environmental Management) and Earth Science. Geology can also be combined with another subject.

Sunderland (*Applied Geology*) This three year course with an optional sandwich year offers studies in practical and traditional geology and its industrial applications. Subjects include earth materials, geomorphology, mineralogy, sedimentation, exploration, geophysics, energy resources and hydrogeology. The course gives progression towards accreditation as Chartered Geologist. Engineering Geology and Environmental Geology are also offered, and Geology itself is available as part of the combined programme scheme.

● **Colleges and Institutes of Higher Education offering degree courses**
Bath (Coll), Brunel (Univ Coll), Cheltenham and Gloucester (Coll).

● **Other courses to be considered**
Chemistry, civil engineering, mining engineering, earth sciences, environmental science, geography, soil science, surveying and geophysics.

GERMAN

● **Special subject requirements:** German at A-level.

● **Subject information:** Language, literature, practical language skills or a broader study of Germany and its culture (European Studies) are alternative study approaches.

Aberdeen (*German Studies*) This is a broad course covering both language and literature, but with considerable emphasis being placed on practical language skills. German may also be studied in the Faculty of Law.

Aberystwyth (*German*) A wide variety of modules in literature and linguistics and oral work are taken in Year 1. National consciousness in 18th, 19th and 20th centuries is taken as a compulsory subject along with language options, eg the language of economics and politics.

Anglia (Poly Univ) Over 25 subjects are offered with German.

Aston (*German*) The subject is offered as part of the European Studies programme and with International Business and in the Modern Languages course. The Honours German programme aims at achieving fluency and accuracy in spoken and written German and the study of the history, society, economy and politics of Germany.

Bangor (*German Language and Modern Germany*) Two subjects are studied in the first year with German or with German language and modern German. Students then opt for one of two courses (a) German Literature (b) German Language and Modern German. Single Honours students spend a year abroad in Year 3 in Germany or Austria. A high level of language proficiency is the aim of the course. Specialised translation courses are offered and also the opportunity to study Dutch.

Bath German is offered with Italian, Russian or French and also International Management.

Belfast (*German*) German language and literature is available as a major, joint or minor Honours degree. A German Studies course is also available for those with no previous knowledge of the language as a first year course.

Birmingham (*German Studies*) Over thirty subject options are offered with German in addition to German Studies. The first year of the course introduces students to written language and oral work, German history and literary studies. Students select a range of options in the second and final years, the third year being spent in Germany. There is a literature emphasis throughout the course.

Bradford German is offered with French, Russian, Spanish and International Management.

Bristol (*German*) The aim of this course is to provide students with thorough competence in modern German, together with a comprehensive knowledge of German literature and civilisation. A subsidiary subject is taken in the first two years.

Bristol UWE German is offered with European Law, French or Spanish.

Brunel German is offered with Mathematics or Engineering.

Buckingham German is offered with Economics, Law or Business.

Cardiff (*German*) The course offers a wide degree of specialisation - German language, linguistics, literature and the social, political and historical development of modern Germany. There are options in translation theory and business German. Intensive language work continues throughout the course. Over twenty joint courses are offered including German and Japanese.

Central England Several courses are offered combining German and Engineering.

Central Lancashire German with Business German is offered on the Combined Honours programme.

Coventry German can be combined with 12 other subjects.

De Montfort German is offered as part of Modern Language Studies or Combined and Joint Honours programmes.

Derby German is offered as part of the Credit Accumulation Modular Scheme.

Dundee German is offered with Physics and European Studies, and also in the Combined Arts programme.

East Anglia (*German*) Language is studied with other area studies courses covering German literature and history and courses on contemporary Germany. In the language and linguistics course a two term study is available on the theory and practice of interpreting and translating.

Edinburgh (*German*) The course is divided equally between German language and literature. The third year of this four year course is spent in a German-speaking country.

Essex (*German Language and Linguistics*) The course covers language and linguistics in Year 1 with options in the Enlightenment plus one comparative studies option or two social sciences. Years 2 and 4 continue languages and linguistics whilst Year 3 is spent abroad.

Exeter (*German*) The course is organised as a balance between language and literature. In the first two years the course provides an introduction to the most important periods of German and Austrian literature, translation, free composition and oral practice.

Glamorgan 10 subjects are offered with German, which can also be taken as part of the Combined Honours and Combined Studies programmes.

Glasgow (*German Language and Literature*) Language and literature (from 1871 to the present) lead on to a more advanced study of German language, literature and thought from the Middle Ages. Students normally spend a year abroad as part of their study prior to taking their Honours degree. A German course is also offered for beginners.

Greenwich German is offered as an option in International Marketing.

Heriot-Watt German is offered with French, Russian or Spanish with special reference to Interpreting and Translating.

Huddersfield German is offered with Communication Arts.

Hull (*German*) German may be studied for a special Honours degree, joint Honours with ten other subjects or as part of the European Studies course. Translation into and from German, comprehension and oral practice take place in each year of the special and joint courses. Elements of commercial German are offered in each year of the course. The third year is spent abroad. Aspects of modern German literature are studied throughout the course.

Humberside German is offered with European courses in Administration, Business Studies, Contemporary Studies, or Marketing.

Keele Over fifty subjects are offered with German. There is an emphasis on translation in this course.

Kent (*German*) This subject can be studied as a single or joint subject with a year spent in Germany, Austria or Switzerland. Language work is an important part of the course in each year and is balanced by a study of German literature and drama. There is an opportunity to study Dutch on this course in addition to a range of cultural, linguistic and political options.

Kingston German is offered with over ten other subjects.

Lampeter German is offered with over thirty other subjects including Islamic Studies, Swedish, Victorian Studies or Welsh. German is also offered as a beginners course.

Lancaster (*German Studies*) The course focuses on the history and culture of the German-speaking countries with stress laid on practical language work.

Leeds (*German*) Students receive a practical grounding in written and spoken German - this, however, is not regarded as a vocational language training. German literature is also covered extensively, and as a background to these studies, German history and other aspects of German civilisation will be covered. The number of options in non-literary topics has recently been increased and includes institutions, politics, economics and film. Business German has its own course.

Leicester (*German*) The subject is studied for four years, with one year spent abroad. A supplementary subject is studied for the first two years. The course aims at a comprehensive balance between language, literature and society. Finalist options include Swedish.

Liverpool (*German*) The immediate aim of the course is that students should become skilful in the written and spoken use of the German language and a broad area of German studies (literature, linguistics and history).

Liverpool John Moores German is offered with 30 other subjects including Japanese, Health Studies, Imaginative Writing, Media and Screen Studies.

London (Goldsmiths') (*German Studies*) The course covers German language (with a high level of language proficiency) and literature and introduces the student to European history, political thought, drama and music. There is a range of options, including other European languages. A period of study in a German-speaking country is compulsory, and the course lasts four years. A degree course in French and German Studies is available.

London (King's) (*German*) This is a four year course with a year spent abroad. The first year covers language, medieval and modern literature and linguistics, with considerable choice of courses in the second and final years.

London (LSE) German is offered with Management Sciences.

London (QMW) (*German*) Students following the single subject degree course also take a subsidiary subject, for example, English, French, Latin, Russian, Spanish, history, geography, economics or politics. Students may choose between the three year course and the four year course which includes a year abroad. The Combined Studies degree allows students to combine German with another subject on equal terms.

London (RH) (*German*) The syllabus covers the history of the German language, the study of modern German and German literature. This is a four year course with a year spent abroad.

London (UC) (*German*) This is a four year course with the third year spent in Germany. The main emphasis of the course lies in the study of German literature alongside German social, political and intellectual history. The advanced study of the German language constitutes a major part of the course.

London Guildhall German is offered as part of the Modular Programme.

Loughborough German is offered with Economics or Civil Engineering.

Manchester (*German Studies*) A language and literature course with the third year spent abroad. Traditional and progressive approaches to the study of the subject are applied throughout the course. Subsidiary subjects are offered for part of the course.

Manchester (UMIST) (*Applied German*) This course combines a study of the spoken and written language with linguistics, cognitive studies and multilingual information technology. This is not a literature-based course.

Manchester Metropolitan German is offered as part of the Humanities or Social Studies programmes.

Middlesex German is offered with European Business Administration and also as part of the Multidisciplinary programme. There is also a beginners course in German.

Newcastle (*German*) All the Newcastle courses place a heavy emphasis on linguistic excellence. Business translation and European film are final year options. All single Honours degrees involve a subsidiary arts or social science subject for two years.

North London German is offered as part of the Combined Honours programme and also with International Business. Language proficiency is emphasised.

Northumbria German can be taken as part of the Combined Honours programme and also with English, French, Russian or Spanish.

Nottingham (*German*) The course aims at proficiency in the German language and in providing the student with an introduction to German culture through its literature and its role in European and world history. Both single and joint Honours degrees involve a year spent abroad. The study of a second language is possible (French, Russian or Spanish).

Nottingham Trent German can be taken as part of the Humanities or the Interfaculty Combined Studies programme.

Oxford Brookes A large number of subjects are offered with combinations in German Language and Contemporary Studies, German Language and Literature, and Languages for Business.

Plymouth German is offered with International Business.

Portsmouth (*German Studies*) A broad course with options in economics, politics and culture, or politics and society. The third year is spent abroad.

Reading (*German*) The course aims to provide the student with a good command of written and spoken German and a wide experience of German civilisation, past and present. German Studies (including German art, music and politics) is the theme of the first two terms with students specialising their areas of interest in the remainder of the course. The third year is spent in a German-speaking country.

Salford German is offered with several subjects including Arabic, Information Technology with language training and Business Resources.

Sheffield (*German Studies*) The first year course introduces language and literature and leads on to the second and fourth year which involve further language work, a one year course in German history and institutions, and either ten options within the department or eight options plus a subsidiary arts subject. Special options are available in Dutch and Swedish. The third year is spent in a German-speaking country.

Sheffield Hallam German is offered as part of the International Business course.

Southampton (*German*) German can be taken as a major, equal or minor component of a combined degree or alternatively as a single Honours degree which offers a balance between the written and spoken word and literature.

St Andrews German is offered as part of the Modern Language programme and in European Integration Studies. A large number of other subjects can also be taken with German.

Staffordshire Over thirty subjects including media and film studies are offered with German.

Stirling (*German*) Students without German A-level may take an introductory German language course of intensive study to bring them up to the level of other students by the end of the first year. Written and spoken German, drama, prose and literature occupy the first three semesters in Part I. Part II of the course is divided into language work, modern German literature and medieval literature and civilisation. One semester (about two months) is spent in a German-speaking university and usually a year abroad is recommended between the second and third years.

Sunderland Over twenty five subjects are offered in combination with German.

Surrey German is offered with Economics and International Business, European Studies and Law.

Sussex (*German*) This course emphasises the study of German writers and their works in the social and intellectual setting of their times. This is a four year course with a year spent in Germany.

Swansea (*German*) Students take three subjects in Part I. The course balances a study of the written and spoken word with literature. Students with a special interest in historical and political German studies may include appropriate courses in Part II. This is a four year course including a year abroad. There are also many joint Honours combinations.

Thames Valley German is offered with French, Spanish, Russian, Law and Economics.

Ulster German is offered as part of the Humanities programme.

Warwick (*German Studies*) German language and literature is studied throughout each year of the course. Other topics include writers, media and society in contemporary Germany. It is also possible to study German with a second language (French and Italian). The third year is spent in Germany. Contemporary German culture is also studied in the German and Business Studies course.

Westminster German is offered with ten other subjects including Arabic and Chinese.

Wolverhampton German is offered as part of the Modular Degree scheme.

York Two German courses are offered with French and Linguistics.

● **Top research universities**
Birmingham, Cambridge, London (King's), Manchester, Nottingham, Oxford, Durham, Exeter, London (QMW), St Andrews, Swansea.

● **Colleges and Institutes of Higher Education offering degree courses**
Buckinghamshire (Coll), Chester (Coll), La Sainte Union (Coll), Nene (Coll), Scarborough (Univ Coll).

● **Other courses to be considered**
Languages which can be combined with German and also language courses not requiring the A-level languages such as Spanish, Chinese, Japanese, Russian, Italian etc. Modern language courses and European Studies.

HISTORY (including **Medieval Studies**)

● **Special subject requirements:** History preferred in most cases at A-level; a language usually required at GCSE (grade A–C).

● **Subject information:** This is a very broad subject with most courses covering British and European history. There is, however, a wide range of specialist topics on offer, eg American, Scottish, East European and Far Eastern history. Degree courses in International Relations, Politics, Economic and Social History could also be considered.

Aberdeen (*History*) The course aims to provide a training in critical historical thought and method, and includes coverage of European and British history, medieval history and Scottish history. In Years 3 and 4 options cover Russia, France, African history and the Commonwealth.

Aberystwyth (*History*) The subject is studied with two other subjects in Part I in which a very wide range of historical topics are included. Part II courses cover the British Isles, American history, 'the historian and the writing of history', and include aspects of change and development in various societies, eg politics and society in medieval England 1086–1399, European political institutions and magic in Europe.

Anglia (Poly Univ) (*History*) A three year course or four year when taken with a language. There are four major themes - British, European and Social History and the history of Russia and the US. Over 15 joint courses are also offered including Graphic Arts and Music.

Bangor (*History*) Part I covers Welsh history, archaeology and classical studies. In Years 2 and 3 a range of specialist history topics can be taken including medieval, modern and British political history, nautical archaeology, Renaissance art, Arthurian Britain and Celtic heritage. A degree course in Welsh History is also available.

Belfast (*Ancient History; Modern History*) Ancient history deals with Greek and Roman civilisation and its influence on the history and culture of the whole Mediterranean, the Near East and Europe. The Modern History course covers British and Irish history, short-span courses in European, American and Imperial history, in-depth studies of particular topics and special subject options. A course is also offered in Byzantine Studies (300 AD–1500 AD).

Birmingham (*Medieval Studies*) This course covers England, France, Germany, Italy and Spain in the medieval period in addition to Old Icelandic and Byzantine Studies.

Bournemouth (*Heritage Conservation*) A unique course focusing on historic buildings and monuments, landscapes and artefacts and the management of collections. There is also a course in the conservation of historic buildings.

Bradford A course is offered in Politics and History.

Brighton (*Cultural and Historical Studies*) The course covers critical traditions in western thought, nation and identity, history, narratives and gender and local history. Cultural forms include novels, newspapers, films and photographs. Modern History is also offered as part of the Humanities course.

Bristol (*History*) History I emphasises the political dimension. History II covers political, social and economic history. History III has a bias towards European history. Language options are available in the first two years. There is also a separate degree in Ancient History taught with Classics, Archaeology and the Greek and Roman world.

Bristol UWE (*History*) A broad course covering British, European, Imperial and International History.

Brunel History is offered with Politics and covers British history and government, the USA, Germany, France and Eastern Europe.

Buckingham (*History, Politics and Literature*) A common course exists for all students in the first four terms, after which students opt for their choice of course. These are History and English, History and Politics or English and Politics. English literature, Politics and Modern History can also be taken in combination.

Cambridge (*History*) One period of history from English political, constitutional, economic and social history is taken in the first year. Students choose from 13 other papers covering history in Europe, America and the Third World. It is also possible to combine one part of the Historical tripos with a part of another Tripos, for example, Law, Archaeology and Anthropology, or History of Art.

Cardiff (*History*) The history course introduces medieval history and contemporary history. Specialist topics are offered in the second and third years including medieval Britain, American and European history. There are specialist degree courses offered in Welsh History, Ancient History and Ancient and Medieval History, as well as various joint Honours combinations.

Central Lancashire (*History*) A local and national history course which covers racism, revolution and urbanism. A range of options exist from Year 2 including science and medicine and international relations.

De Montfort (*History*) A broad course covering the period from the French Revolution to the Modern World.

Derby History is offered as part of the Credit Accumulation Modular Scheme with other subjects.

Dundee (*Modern History*) After a broad first year, Year 2 of the course covers European History from 1848 to 1940. Thereafter, a choice is made to follow an Ordinary or Honours degree (single, joint or combined). Options then follow in European, Scottish and British history.

Durham (*History*) The course focuses on the history of the west from the fall of the Roman Empire. In the first year all students read early European history from the fourth to the eleventh century and later choose two courses from a selection of history topics - twentieth century Europe, the USA from the mid-nineteenth century, industrial Britain or another first year social science subject. In the second year students also choose a course from those offered by other departments in the University. (*Medieval Studies*) This course covers the emergence of Europe (300–1050) and Christendom and Islam in the period of the First Crusade and medieval literature.

East Anglia (*European History*) The course covers the period from the Renaissance to the present day across Western and Eastern Europe.

East London (*History*) The course covers: Britain and cultural imperialism; Lived histories - the past in the present; Britain in an age of revolution; Crisis 1848–1914; Modern times and Recolonisation.

Edinburgh (*History*) This is a two part course with the division coming at the end of the second year. In the first year students take a course in modern British and European history, plus two other courses from history or social science subjects. Specialised history courses are chosen by the student in the third and fourth years. Five history courses are offered.

Essex (*History*) This programme offers a comparative approach to the subject. Topics include 'The Making of Early Modern Europe 1500–1770', 'The Age of Revolution 1170–1870' and 'Europe and the World 1870 to the Present'. A wide range of optional courses is available in the second and third years.

Exeter (*History*) Students are encouraged to devise their own courses from a wide range of choices and combinations of subjects. The core of courses consists of broad outlines of English, European and world history. History can also be studied in combination with Archaeology, Politics or Modern Languages. Students have to learn word processing and there are opportunities to learn computing skills.

Glamorgan (*History*) Nineteenth and twentieth century history is studied in the context of British, American, European and Welsh history. The subject is offered as a BA (Humanities) course or in the joint, major or minor framework.

Glasgow (*History*) Two Ordinary classes are offered. Class A deals with Europe from the late eleventh to the mid-seventeenth centuries, and Class B studies Europe from 1815 to 1945. Medieval and modern Britain are studied at the Higher Ordinary level with a range of topics covering world history. Glasgow offers 77 History courses across medieval, modern and economic history. In addition a very large number of subjects are offered with Scottish History, History and Economic and Social History.

Greenwich (*History*) This is a new degree offered as part of the Humanities course in which students choose units from a number of pathways some of which will be half year or full year study periods.

Hertfordshire (*Historical Studies*) The course is part of the Humanities modular scheme and can be taken at a major or single Honours level. Year 1 covers the 17th and 20th centuries followed by specialised choices of periods in Years 2 and 3.

Huddersfield (*History and Political Studies*) Modules are offered in British, European and World History.

Hull (*History*) In the first year students take courses on the history of art and the environment, European and world history, decisive forces in modern history, and history and computing. In subsequent years students may 'track' an area of special interest through a range of options, and in the third year they must offer a special subject involving work with primary sources. As well as several joint Honours degrees there is also a separate degree course in Economic and Social History. The department is rated 'excellent' in teaching quality.

Keele There are compulsory courses in Medieval Europe, early Modern Europe and Modern Europe. Anglo Saxon is offered as a subsidiary course. A large number of subjects are offered in combination with Ancient History, History, and International History.

Kent (*History*) In the first two terms two courses are offered on medieval history and on modern British, European, African or American history. In the third term specialised topics are chosen from 12 or more interdisciplinary courses. There is a wide choice of second and third year courses. History may be studied as part of a combined Honours degree and there is a separate degree in Economic and Social History.

Kingston (*History*) There is a focus on 19th and 20th century British, European and American History. There are also several language options (French, German, Spanish, Italian, Russian and Japanese).

Lampeter (*History*) Two other subjects are taken with history in the first year. The second and third years cover British, European and American history. Courses are also offered in Victorian Studies, Ancient History and Church History. The course is strong in nineteenth and twentieth century British, European and overseas history.

Lancaster (*History*) The course covers a very wide selection of topics - medieval and modern history, British, European, African, Asian, American and Russian history. Courses such as Archaeology, Economic History, Ancient History and Politics can also be taken as part of the History degree. Some exchanges with the USA are possible.

Leeds (*History*) The size and structure of the School enables it to offer a very wide range of options over the whole of European and British History, from ancient to contemporary. Research is being undertaken on the application of computing to historical source materials, especially documentary evidence for local history. First year undergraduates are introduced to the methods and conclusions involved in this research as an introduction to historical computation. Neither A-level History nor O-level/GCSE foreign language is essential for the course. (*International History and Politics*) This course has no precise parallel in any British university at the moment; its purpose is to set the international events of the recent past firmly into their historical context. Taking the first, second and third year courses together, every student will have studied international history from 1494 to the present day.

Leicester (*History*) A supplementary subject is studied in the first year along with three history courses taken for two years in medieval, early modern and modern history. In the second and third years, options are chosen from British, European and non-European history.

Liverpool (*History*) This course concentrates on studying the ancient and medieval world through as wide a variety of sources as possible. There is scope for specialisation after the first year. There are also degrees in Economic History and Economic and Social History.

Liverpool John Moores History is offered in conjunction with over 12 other subjects.

London (Goldsmiths') (*Historical Studies*) Students take a compulsory course in concepts and methods, with a choice of two other foundation courses. In the second year they choose two history courses and two courses from other related disciplines, and in the final year concentrate on a special subject. A degree course in History and Sociology is also available.

London (Jews College) A course in Jewish History is offered.

London (King's) (*History*) Students can develop their interests in ancient, medieval or modern history in this course. An optional course in computing for historians has been introduced. A degree course in Ancient History is also offered.

London (LSE) (*History*) LSE offers one of the widest ranges of choices in historical studies of any university in the UK. Using the combined resources of all the London colleges and institutes, students choose eight papers from a range of topics in British, European and world history.

London (QMW) (*History*) Four main papers on British, European and/or extra-European history are taken, followed by a thematic paper, a special subject, and one other option. There is a separate degree course in Modern History and the Combined Studies degree allows students to combine History with several other disciplines.

London (RH) (*History*) The course is divided into two branches: (1) Ancient and Medieval History which covers the period from Ancient Greece to the Renaissance, and (2) Medieval and Modern History with the main emphasis on medieval and modern British and European history. A degree is also offered in Modern History, Economic History and Politics.

London (SOAS) (*History*) Students are offered a variety of courses in Asian and African history. Specialisms can be followed in the history of Africa, the Near and the Middle East, the Indian sub-continent, South East Asia, China and Japan and the modern Third World.

London (SSEES) (*History*) The degree course sets the study of history in a European perspective, allowing the student to specialise in the study of Central and Eastern Europe, or to use the core European courses as the basis of a broader comparative history degree. It is taught on the flexible course unit system.

London (UC) (*History*) Students may choose to specialise in Ancient and Ancient Near Eastern History, Ancient and Medieval History, Medieval and Modern History or Ancient and Modern History, but the course unit structure permits great flexibility. Students enrolling for any one of the nine degrees offered (some taught jointly) are able to select the subjects they wish to study with a very wide range of options. There is also a four year course on the History of the Americas.

London Guildhall (*History*) A subsidiary subject is taken in Year 1 which can be continued through the course as a minor subject.

Luton (*Contemporary History*) The course covers the period from 1930 in Europe and Britain. Topics include the second World War, Communism, war and social change in Britain and Europe, women's history and the Cold War. There is also a Modern History course covering the period from the French Revolution to the Present Day.

Manchester (*History*) A broad course includes a range of options covering all the major historical periods including Ancient Mediterranean, Economic Social History and Modern History. There is also a course in Modern Middle Eastern History which includes international relations covering the Balkans, the Middle East and Central Asia. A language option is also available.

Manchester Metropolitan (*Historical Studies*) The course covers historical methods and research of a number of historical periods.

Middlesex (*Historical Studies*) This is a modular degree course with a very wide choice of options such as the French Revolution, women and work in twentieth century Britain and the Renaissance.

Newcastle (*History*) In the first year a choice is made from one of two medieval European courses, one of several modern and contemporary history courses, two of four courses concerning historical method, and one course from a range of options. In the second and third years studies can cover the history of Britain, Europe, and North American history. A course in Ancient History is also offered.

North London (*History*) This subject can be studied as a single, major, joint or minor subject. Options are available covering medieval and modern history and economic and social history.

Northumbria (*Historical Studies*) A course offering a breadth of historical knowledge covering Britain, Europe and world history from the medieval period to the present day. There is an opportunity to study in the USA or Europe as part of the course.

Nottingham (*History*) First year students follow two courses in European (including British) history with an emphasis on economic, social, intellectual and institutional developments rather than political detail. At the end of the first year students then choose to graduate in either History or Economic and Social History. History students then go on to study medieval, early modern and late modern topics. Economic and Social History students are recommended to take economics as a subsidiary subject. Special subject topics are followed in the third year. A degree course in Ancient History is also offered, as well as several joint Honours combinations.

Nottingham Trent History is offered as part of the Humanities programme and also as an emphasis on the Environmental Studies course.

Oxford (*Modern History*) This course covers world history from the third century AD. In the first year students must take papers in a period of British history, but thereafter there is considerable choice at all stages. Other degree courses offered include History (Ancient and Modern), Modern History and Economics, Modern History and English and Modern History and Modern Languages.

Oxford Brookes Over 40 subjects are offered with History.

Plymouth A number of subjects are offered in combination with either Contemporary History or Maritime History.

Portsmouth (*Historical Studies*) This course has a strong emphasis on European and social history with specialist subjects in Year 3 including witchcraft, the Russian Revolution and the Labour Movement. Studies are organised around major historical problems within various periods covering 1450–1780 (in Year 1), 1780–1880 (Year 2) and 1880–1940 (Year 3).

Reading (*History*) In the first two terms students take courses in barbarians and civilisation, and the era of the two world wars. In the second year a study is made of four survey periods chosen from six (medieval, early modern and modern) in British or European history. This provides a foundation for the more specialised topics chosen in the third year. A course in Ancient History is also offered, as well as Modern History and International Relations.

Salford History is offered with English or Politics.

Sheffield (*History*) The first year provides courses in medieval and modern history. Second and third year studies comprise core courses in world civilisations, modern historical thought or political ideas, a period of British history, a topic in European history and one other choice from a range of options. The central feature of the third year is the special subject, entailing a thorough investigation of a selected historical theme. A degree in Social History is also offered.

Sheffield Hallam (*Historical Studies*) The course concentrates on modern history. Compulsory courses are taken in science in the modern world, the rise of capitalism, British political history and in historical skills, but there is a large element of choice in all years.

Southampton (*History*) A general introduction in the first year of this course covers both medieval and modern periods. Nineteen units are available in the second year, including European and British history, economic, social, political, religious, intellectual and art history, American civilisation and the history of particular countries, for example, France, the Balkans and Latin America. The third year is dominated by the study of a special subject. There is also a course in Applied Historical Studies for students wishing to specialise in the application of quantitative methods to history.

St Andrews (*History*) An integrated single Honours course is available for students who wish to take a degree course covering various types of historical subject matter. Specialist degree courses include Economic and Social History, Ancient History, Medieval History, Modern History, Scottish History, Islamic and Medieval History and Church History.

Staffordshire (*Historical Studies*) The major themes in this course are in Social and Cultural History and also International History.

Stirling (*History*) Part I of the course examines modern history and the origins of modern society in Britain and France in the late eighteenth and nineteenth centuries, and Scottish history 1707–1907. In Part II students choose a range of options which include the history of the USA, Latin America, modern Asia and Russian and Irish history. Advanced courses are taken in the last two semesters. A course in History/Scottish Studies is also available.

Strathclyde (*Modern History*) This is a four year course which does not assume any previous study of the subject. In the first year students are introduced to the history of Europe from the late eighteenth century. In the second year they study two from the history of the USA, twentieth century Europe, and the history of Scottish society. Third and fourth year courses offer a very wide choice of topics. There is a separate degree course in Economic and Social History.

Sunderland (*Historical Studies*) The course covers the modern history of Britain, Ireland, Continental Europe, Russia and North America.

Sussex (*History*) The subject can be studied in the context of five Arts Schools. Analytical techniques, historical assumptions and interpretations are covered in the preliminary 'Historical Controversy' course. This is followed by topics covering British and European history. Eleven history courses in all are offered.

Swansea (*History*) Three subjects are chosen in Part I. In History this covers two courses - medieval civilisation and war in society (the British and American experience 1854–1975). Students who speak Welsh may substitute Welsh history for the medieval course. Part II of the course involves a study of British and European history. There are also degree courses in Ancient and Medieval History, and Economic and Social History.

Teesside Joint Honours courses are offered.

Thames Valley History is offered as part of the Humanities programme.

Ulster (*History*) This subject may be taken as a major, joint or minor subject with other subjects in the Humanities course. The emphasis is on modern and contemporary history.

Warwick (*History*) All students take a basic history course in the first year, but are then able to specialise in Renaissance and Modern History, Modern European History or European and American History. History may also be combined with Politics, Sociology or French.

Wolverhampton (*History*) This is a modular course covering twentieth century Europe, Early Modern England, Women's History, British Social History from 1530, the Americas post 1860 and the West Midlands from 1600.

York (*History*) The courses in History offer study in depth and a wide range of individual choice throughout. Students study many types of history from a wide geographical and chronological range. Teaching is mainly by individual tutorial and small group seminar. Each student also undertakes an independent research project as well as a paper in historical methodology.

• Top research universities

Birmingham, Cambridge, London (King's) (LSE) (RH) (SOAS) (SSEES) (UC), Bristol, Durham, East Anglia, Lancaster, Manchester, Newcastle, Oxford, Reading, Sheffield, Southampton, Sussex, Warwick, York, Edinburgh, St Andrews, Stirling, Aberystwyth, Swansea.

● **Colleges and Institutes of Higher Education offering degree courses**
Bangor Normal (Coll), Bath (Coll), Bedford (Coll), Bishop Grosseteste
(Coll), Bolton (Inst), Brunel (Univ Coll), Canterbury Christ Church
(Coll), Cardiff (Inst), Cheltenham and Gloucester (Coll), Chester (Coll),
Colchester (Inst), Edge Hill (Coll), Gwent (Coll), King Alfred's (Coll),
Leeds Trinity and All Saints (Coll), Liverpool (Inst), La Sainte Union
(Coll), Nene (Coll), Newman (Coll), North East Wales (Inst), Norwich
City (Coll), Ripon and York St John (Coll), Roehampton (Inst),
Scarborough (Univ Coll), S. Martin's (Coll), St Mark and St John's
(Coll), St Mary's (Coll), Trinity Carmarthen (Coll), Westhill (Coll),
Westminster (Coll), Worcester (Coll).

● **Other courses to be considered**
Archaeology, economic and social history, international relations, politics
and public administration.

HOTEL AND CATERING MANAGEMENT

● **Special subject requirements:** GCSE (grade A–C) in mathematics and
science.

● **Subject information:** All courses provide a comprehensive preparation
for entry into hotel, catering, tourism and leisure industries. Alternative
courses could include Food Science, Home Economics and Dietetics.

Bournemouth There are two four year sandwich courses involving a year
in employment in the catering industry. (*Hospitality Management*) The
foundation year covers economics, information technology, accounting
and financial management, food and beverage studies, food hygiene and
behavioural studies. Organisation studies, law, marketing, tourism and
accommodation management are introduced in Year 2. The fourth year is
spent integrating the student's industrial experience with theoretical
perspectives. (*Food and Catering Management*) Students take courses in
business studies and food technology throughout the three years at
university, with a choice in the fourth year between food and product
marketing or food and culture.

Brighton (*International Hospitality Management*) All students study a
second language to certificate or diploma level in French, German, or
Spanish. Placements in all parts of the world during the third year of this
four year course.

Buckingham (*Business Studies; International Hotel Management*) This
course starts in January and lasts three years. All students study for a
period in a French Hotel School.

Cardiff (*Hospitality Management*) This professionally accredited degree
scheme includes two periods of work experience within the three years. A
range of European languages are available as options and the second
period of work experience may be spent abroad.

Central England (*Hospitality Management*) This is a broad-based course
with options in personnel, marketing, tourism and languages and
worldwide placements in Year 2.

Central Lancashire (*Hospitality Management*) A four year sandwich course taught jointly with Blackpool and the Fylde College, providing management education for those wishing to enter the hotel and leisure industries. There are two short periods of work experience in the first year, as well as the whole of the third year. Successful completion of the course, followed by submission of an industry-based project during postgraduate employment, leads to full membership at the HCIMA.

Dundee (*Hotel and Catering Management*) There is a sponsorship scheme in operation with the Gleneagles Hotel.

Glasgow Caledonian (*Hospitality Management*) The course covers food, sales, marketing, restaurant management, languages, tourism and travel.

Huddersfield (*Hotel and Catering Management*) The three main areas of study are hotel and catering studies, human behaviour and business. There is a one year period of supervised work experience following the second term of Year 2. The course also focuses in international aspects of the hotel and catering industry.

Leeds Metropolitan (*Hospitality Business Management*) A three-year full-time or four-year sandwich course which covers all aspects of the industry - food and accommodation studies, tourism, European Business, management and manpower studies, finance, law and business policy.

Manchester Metropolitan (*Hotel and Catering Management*) Operations management (catering and accommodation), management and business are the core subjects in Years 1, 2 and 4. Industrial placement occupies the third year. There is also a course in International Hotel Management with language options (French, German, Spanish).

Middlesex (*Hotel and Restaurant Management*) The course places an emphasis on the management of the commercial hotel and the restaurant business. French is studied during the first two years. Industrial placement in France and Britain occupies the third year. Core study programmes in business studies take place in the final year.

Napier (*Hospitality Management*) This is a modular course which includes options and electives. A foreign language is included. Particular emphasis is given to personal development and transferable skills. There is a strong information technology resource base.

North London (*Hospitality Management*) Food, accommodation studies and institutional management are the main core subjects of this course. The course includes a year's placement in the industry. There is also an International Hotel and catering course which includes a foreign language.

Nottingham Trent (*International Hospitality Management*) A four year sandwich course with the possibility of placements abroad. There are five main themes - management, finance, personnel, languages and hospitality activities. Language study is mandatory in French, German, Italian or Spanish.

Oxford Brookes (*Hotel and Catering Management*) There is a three year course (single field) and a four year course (double field). The double field course combines a core of catering and accommodation studies with management accounting, marketing and economics. Students normally have a year of industrial experience during Year 2. In the single field course catering is combined with one of a very wide range of other single field courses, for example, accountancy, French, food science.

Plymouth (*Hospitality Management*) A modular programme which includes hospitality, the consumer, food and beverage services, front office and accommodation services. French, German, economics and accounting modules are also included.

Portsmouth (*Hotel and Catering Management*) This is a four year sandwich course with industrial experience taking place in Year 3. The course covers catering and accommodation studies, behavioural science, personnel work, law, marketing and finance.

Robert Gordon (*Hospitality Management*) Two options are taken in each year which include tourism, leisure, nutrition, languages, interior design and planning.

Sheffield Hallam (*Hotel and Catering Management*) Supervised work experience takes place in Year 3 of this four year course, which has six main areas of study (1) financial aspects of catering (2) human aspects of catering (3) food studies (4) food production and service (5) catering systems, and (6) accommodation studies. The main focus is on business management and European studies. The early stages of the course are common with the BSc programme in Food Marketing Management to which students may transfer in Year 1 if they wish.

South Bank (*Hotel Management*) A four year sandwich course leading to exemption from the HCIMA membership examination. Language options are available.

Strathclyde (*Hotel and Hospitality Management*) Compulsory courses throughout cover hotel operations with options in tourism, food and beverage, and leisure management and planning. In the first and second years one class is normally chosen from business-related subjects such as marketing, business law, computing and accounting and finance.

Surrey (*Hotel and Catering Management*) There are four main areas of study in the first two years - management studies, quantitative studies (accounting), food and beverage management and business studies. The third year is spent in supervised practical training in selected hotel and catering organisations. In the final year all students study hotel and catering management, human resource management, financial management and marketing, and follow a course in either food and nutritional management or tourism. French and German language study available.

Thames Valley (*Hospitality Management*) The course has an international emphasis with the opportunity for modern language study and placements in Europe and the USA. The course covers the Business Environment, Operations (Food/Beverage/Wines/Spirits/Room Division) and includes, information technology and accounting.

Ulster (*Hotel and Tourism Management*) This is a four year sandwich course which covers food and accommodation studies, tourism, accounts and marketing. A foreign language is taken in Year 1 and becomes optional in Years 2 and 3.

Wolverhampton (*Hotel, Tourism and Licensed Retail Management*) A four year sandwich course with language options available. Final year students may specialise in tourism, hotel management, licensed retail management or international hospitality.

• **Colleges and Institutes of Higher Education offering degree courses**
Barnsley (Coll), Birmingham (Coll of Food), Blackpool and Fylde (Coll), Bradford and Ilkley (Coll), Cardiff (Inst), Cheltenham and Gloucester (Coll), Colchester (Inst), Farnborough (Coll), Norwich City (Coll), Queen Margaret (Coll), Salford (University Coll), Suffolk (Coll), Swansea (Inst), West Herts (Coll).

LAW

• **Special subject requirements:** English A-level and mathematics GCSE (grade A–C) very occasionally required.

• **Subject information:** Law courses are usually divided into two parts. Part 1 occupies year 1 and introduces the student to criminal and constitutional law and the legal process. Thereafter many different specialised topics can be studied in years 2 and 3. The course content is very similar for most courses.

Aberdeen (*Law*) Ordinary and Honours degrees are offered. Topics covered include jurisprudence, mercantile law, conveyancing and Scots law (in the first and second years). Options in German, French or economics are possible. ERASMUS exchanges with Italy or Germany are available. As part of the Law degree students may study up to four non-law courses.

Abertay Dundee (*Law; European Business Law*) The course covers business law of the UK and one other EC country and includes EC law, a foreign language, commercial property and employment law, international trade and dispute settlement.

Aberystwyth (*Law*) The scheme of study is divided into three parts. Part I covers criminal, constitutional and international law, the law of contract and legal method. In Part II five topics are offered from which the student must choose three, and in Part III 11 topics are available of which five must be chosen.

Anglia (Poly Univ) (*Law*) A standard law course with options in languages, business or computing. Combined courses are possible.

Bangor (*Criminology*) This is a modular scheme with sociology and social policy also offered in the same department.

Belfast (*Law*) This is a four year course commencing with a study of constitutional law, criminal law, law of torts and legal process. In the second year core subjects include the law of contract, land law, equity and European and welfare law. Compulsory and optional subjects are taken in Years 3 and 4 covering over 40 different topics.

Birmingham (*Law*) The course aims to provide a liberal education in addition to a vocational training. Core subjects taken in the first two years provide students with exemptions from certain professional examinations should they wish to practice law. EC law is a compulsory second year (Part I Finals) course. The third year offers a wide range of subjects from which students select four options. Other degree courses offered by the Faculty of Law include Law and Politics, Law with French and Law and Business Studies.

Bournemouth (*Business Law*) Although the course concentrates on the applications of law in business, it is recognised by the Law Society as a qualifying degree for the academic stage of legal training. The theme of European enterprise is taken in Year 2. A study of information technology for lawyers is also offered. A four-year course, with a year in professional practice.

Brighton Law is offered with Accounting.

Bristol (*Law*) This course is designed to give the student a thorough understanding of the basic principles of English law and a thorough training in its techniques and methodology. The first year covers an introduction to the English legal system and property law, the law of the tort and public and criminal law. In the second year land law, the law of contract and jurisprudence are the core subjects, plus one option from eight alternatives. In the third year students choose four new options from 32 topics which include politics, accounting and economics.

Bristol UWE (*Law*) This is a comprehensive law course comprising four law subjects in the first year and five in the second year, with an option to take one or two non-law subjects, eg forensic science, accountancy and modern languages. Additional law subjects are taken in the third year along with a number of options. There is a course in European Law and Languages in which two languages are studied and nine months spent in France, Germany or Spain.

Brunel (*Law*) Three and four year courses are offered. For the latter students spend three periods of approximately 20 weeks each year in law-related work placement. The study of law is placed in a wide context, and two of the four courses studied in each of the first two years are selected from those offered by other departments in the Faculty of Social Sciences with all courses in law being taken in the third and fourth years. This results in students having taken 12 law courses and four social science courses including the sociology of law and/or economics and law, by the end of the course. A course in Business and Finance Law is also offered.

Buckingham (*Law*) This is a two year course comprising courses in the English legal system, the six essential core subjects - public law, criminal law, contract, torts, land law and law of trusts - plus three other legal subjects. Students are also required to complete a two term language course and a further two supporting subjects. Law is also offered with Politics and Economics.

Cambridge (*Law*) The emphasis in this course is on principles and technique although, as in other courses, many students do not intend to practise. Part IA of the Law Tripos is taken at the end of the first year (criminal, constitutional and Roman law and law of tort). In the second year five subjects are studied leading to Part B, most students taking contract and land law among a wide range of other subjects. In the third year (Part II) there is an even wider range of options.

Cardiff (*Law*) The degree scheme is designed to give students a wide choice of subjects to suit their professional interests. The first year consists of standard core subjects, contract, tort, the legal system, constitutional and administrative law. This is then followed in the second and third years with a choice of eight courses from a list of 29 options including maritime law and international trade and finance. Students who have studied law as part of a degree scheme in the first year can be considered for direct entry into the second year course. Law is also offered with French, German, Italian, Japanese and Spanish.

Central England (*Law*) The course aims to provide a broad-based legal education sensitive to the social, economic and political contexts of modern society. Students have the opportunity to take part in simulated legal disputes by way of moots, mock trials and 'clinical' legal exercises. An emphasis is placed on the wide range of options available in the final year, which include commercial, company, consumer and EC law and also American Constitutional Law and Psychology and the Law. There is also a course in Criminal Justice and Policing.

Central Lancashire (*Law*) In this Law course it is possible to take a language option in each year of the course (French or German). There is also a 'half course' in computer studies in the second year. Students have the opportunity to go on placements with local solicitors.

City (*Business Law*) A course which emphasises all aspects of commercial and financial law. After a study of core subjects in Years 1 and 2 a range of options are offered in Year 3.

Coventry (*Business Law*) The main emphasis of this course is placed on those legal disciplines which are closely related to business in its widest sense. There are four main routes - LLB, Business Law, European Business Law and Criminal Justice.

De Montfort (*Law*) This Law course is recognised by the Law Society and the Bar. In addition to the comprehensive legal education, students take either sociology throughout Years 1 and 2, or a foreign language (French or German) throughout the three years of the course. The School of Law promotes the use of computer-assisted learning.

Derby (*Law*) An LLB course is offered with foundation areas of EC Law, Contract, Tort, Criminal, Constitutional, Land Law and Trusts. A wide range of options is offered in Years 2 and 3. Law can also be taken as part of the modular scheme.

Dundee (*Law*) Four subjects are studied in the first year, including the private law of Scotland. In the second year there are two compulsory subjects - public law and jurisprudence - and a choice of six other courses. The third and fourth years consist of optional choices from a wide range, depending on the student's interests. English Law is also taught leading to qualification in England and Wales.

Durham (*Law*) Core courses in the first year leading to the examination (Preliminary Honours) at the end of the first year cover contract, tort, law and government and civil liberties. Eight full subjects are then taken in the second and third years from 20 law topics or nine non-law subjects. There are courses on international European and French law as well as English law. Although students on the single or joint Honours degree courses can obtain exemption from CE, the courses are intended as an education rather than professional training. Apart from the four first year courses in single Honours (which provide background) all other subject courses are optional giving a wide range of choice.

East Anglia (*Law*) The preliminary programme (Year 1) covers criminal, constitutional and land law. The Honours programme (Years 2 and 3) in Part I covers a study of the laws of contract, tort, trusts and one optional subject. Part II comprises administrative law and four optional subjects . A degree in Law with German Law and Language is also offered.

East London (*Law*) Compulsory subjects are taken in Years 1 and 2, with a range of options offered in Years 2 and 3 which give the necessary exemptions from professional examinations.

Edinburgh (*Law*) In the first year compulsory subjects include the Scottish legal system, contract, family and constitutional law. It is also possible to take a course outside the Law Faculty, eg French, German, history. The decision to follow the Honours course is taken at the end of the second year when the required courses for those wishing to enter the profession will have been taken. In the third and fourth years further professional courses and options are taken.

Essex (*Law*) The course is in three parts each covering one year. The Law Qualifying Examination is taken at the end of the first year, and Parts I and II of the Final LLB at the end of the second and third years. In the second year it is possible to take a non-law subject as an option, whilst law of the European Community is a compulsory subject in the third year. A course in English and European Law is offered and also a course in English and French Law in which the third year is spent in the Law Faculty of either Strasbourg or Bordeaux Universities.

Exeter (*Law*) In the first year seven subjects are taken which include European Community law. Examinations take place at the end of each year, LLB Parts I and II being taken at the end of the second and third years. The LLB (European) is a four year course which covers French or German law. It includes French and German language and the third year is spent abroad.

Glamorgan (*Law*) A modular semesterised course. Options are available in Years 2 and 3 and include languages, environmental law, international trade, patent law and criminology and social justice.

Glasgow (*Law*) Ordinary (three year) and Honours (four year) courses are available. A wide range of courses is available which can give appropriate exemptions from professional examinations. The Scottish legal system and Scots law occupies an important place in the first year course.

Glasgow Caledonian (*Law with Administrative Studies*) Core and optional subjects are offered including some subjects suitable for those students aiming for careers in business, eg accountancy, personnel, economics. The degree is not a law degree and not recognised by the Law Society of Scotland.

Greenwich (*Law*) A standard law course with the opportunity to take study units from other degree courses, eg languages, economics.

Hertfordshire (*Law*) The course is designed to offer exemptions from the first (academic) stages of legal training for barristers or solicitors, but also provides the opportunity to study the business, economic and social contexts in which law operates for those who wish to pursue other careers. Information technology and modern languages may be studied.

Huddersfield (*Business Law*) The course covers the application of law to the activities of government, local authorities and commerce. Business finance, economics and industrial sociology are taken as additional subjects in the first and second years. Students are also introduced to aspects of information technology.

Hull (*Law*) The first two years of the course introduces legal techniques and the English legal system. A significant emphasis is placed on the law relating to the European Union. In Year 2 Jurisprudence is a compulsory module with options in Years 2 and 3 which include information technology, law, government law and international environmental law.

Humberside Law is offered with Business.

Keele Law or Criminology are offered in combination with a very large number of subjects.

Kent (*Law*) The course provides a basis for subsequent training and work in the law and also a study in its broader social context. In Part I three of the five courses are taken from other social science areas. In Part II the range of law topics enables students to gain the necessary exemptions from the Law Society examinations. Four other Law courses are offered combined with French Law, German Law, Spanish Law, History or a language. Courses are also offered in English and French/German/Italian or Spanish Law.

Kingston (*Law*) All the major aspects of law are covered in this course with a wide choice of subjects in the final year. These include revenue and family law, the law of international trade, EC, medical, and welfare law.

Lancaster (*Law*) Part I introduces the principle of law and a detailed study of constitutional and administrative law. Part II covers eight units in law and a free ninth unit course. The units cover various aspects of law and some are compulsory to comply with the examinations of the Law Society. A course in European Legal Studies is also on offer.

Leeds (*Law*) Four compulsory subjects are taken in the first year and five in Years 2 and 3, with optional subjects chosen from a wide range of topics. Unusually, law may be combined with Japanese or Chinese studies.

Leeds Metropolitan (*Law*) Core subjects give exemptions from professional legal examinations for the Bar and Law Society. A special feature of this course is the French option which enables students to continue with French studies in each of the three years of the course.

Leicester (*Law*) First year compulsory subjects cover the English legal system, contract, tort, and constitutional and administrative law. Fundamental branches of the subject continue in the second year with a compulsory course in European Community law. There are no compulsory subjects in the third year when students select their courses from a range of specialist studies including law and medicine.

Liverpool (*Law*) The first year course (Intermediate) covers the core courses of criminal, constitutional law and an introduction to English law. Final Part I covers the second year with three compulsory subjects - tort, land law and equity - plus one optional subject. The third year course (Final Part II) provides a wide range of options from which students select five subjects.

Liverpool John Moores (*Law*) This is a comprehensive law course covering all the relevant subjects to enable students to be exempted from the first examinations of the Council of Legal Education and the Law Society. The third year of the course is composed of five options chosen from a range of over 20. Courses in Criminal Justice are also offered.

London (King's) (*Law*) The course provides a grounding in the basic areas of legal knowledge, methods and technique in the first two years and permits a greater degree of specialisation in the final year. King's also offers English and French Law and Law with German Law.

London (LSE) (*Law*) Public law, the English legal system, contract and property law are studied for the Intermediate examination at the end of the first year. Parts I and II follow in the second and third years and include compulsory and optional subjects. Law with French Law or German Law are also offered and the degree in Social Anthropology and Law is unique to LSE.

London (QMW) (*Law*) The Intermediate course (Year 1) covers common, public, criminal and property law. Part I (Final) (Year 2) continues the study of common, property and public law, and Part II (Final) (Year 3) requires students to study jurisprudence and three subjects from a range of options. Law may be studied with Politics for the Combined Studies degree.

London (SOAS) (*Law*) This is a unique course in which instruction comprises English law subjects, including those required for professional purposes, aspects of law relating to a particular region in Asia or Africa, and comparative law. The second and third year involves eight courses chosen from 12 options.

London (UC) (*Law*) A large law faculty offering a standard law course. Specialist areas cover labour law, media and communications law and Japanese law. Law is also offered with French, German or Italian law.

London Guildhall (*Business Law*) This Business Law degree is recognised by the Bar and the Law Society as giving full exemption from the academic stage of professional education. Its aim is to examine law in a business context and thus includes the study of economics and those areas of the law most relevant to business.

Luton (*Law*) Core modules stipulated for the award of LLB giving maximum exemptions are followed by a choice of three compulsory modules, eg aviation, commercial, environmental, family, tax and property law, consumer protection, human rights and international trade law.

Manchester (*Law*) Students wishing to become solicitors are guaranteed a place at a branch of the College of Law to do the legal practice course. A very wide range of options can be chosen in Years 2 and 3 following a study of the basic subjects in Year 1.

Manchester Metropolitan (*Law*) The first 'qualifying' year is made up of basic legal subjects followed by a series of options which are chosen in Years 2 and 3. Degree courses in Law with French and German are also offered when students take Year 3 in Europe.

Middlesex (*Law*) Compulsory law subjects are studied which, with a wide range of options including European Law and which lead to exemption from professional examinations. Law is also offered as part of the modular degree scheme.

Napier (*Legal Studies*) A broad legal education with the opportunity to study other subjects (European languages, business and management, information management and managerial finance).

Newcastle (*Law*) This is a flexible law course with constitutional and administrative law, land law, contract and tort judicial process in the first two years. Two options in the second year are followed by five options in the third year and these include international law and European Community law. Throughout the course there is an emphasis on the relationship between law and other social sciences, with a special optional course in law and economics. Newcastle is strong in the teaching of traditional legal subjects.

Northumbria (*Law*) This is a standard law course of compulsory and optional subjects leading to exemption from professional examinations. The course combines a high degree of student choice of subjects with the requirements of the legal professional bodies.

North London (*Law*) In addition to compulsory subjects required to provide exemption from professional examinations, second year options include accounting, economics, French and politics. (30–40 per cent of applicants are from non-traditional academic backgrounds).

Nottingham (*Law*) BA and LLB courses are offered and students can defer their final choice until their arrival at the University. The LLB follows the traditional route of four compulsory courses in the first year, followed by compulsory and optional subjects in the second and third years. In the BA course, legal subjects are studied in each year along with two subsidiary non-law subjects. There is a joint Honours degree in Law and Politics.

Nottingham Trent (*Law*) Law is offered as a three year full-time and four year sandwich course. The latter six and nine months respectively are spent in practical training in a solicitor's office at the end of Year 1 and during Year 3. Both courses give exemptions from professional examinations. The course is currently under review and the optional element may be increased. There is also a course in European Law.

Oxford (*Jurisprudence*) Students take the qualifying examination of Law Moderations at the end of two terms and cover the basic concepts of Roman private law, English criminal law and the British Constitution. The remaining seven terms consist of four compulsory subjects - jurisprudence, the law of contract, tort and land - and four optional subjects.

Oxford Brookes (*Law*) A flexible degree scheme within the modular degree course. By taking a prescribed combination of modules students may obtain exemption from the first stage of Law Society professional examinations.

Plymouth (*Law*) An LLB course offering the basic course subjects required for professional practice. Options in Year 3 include maritime law.

Reading (*Law*) For the First University Examination all students study two law subjects and a third subject. Thereafter the course comprises the traditional compulsory and optional subjects leading to qualification through the Law Society or Bar Council. Law with French Law is also offered.

Robert Gordon (*Legal and Administrative Studies*) This course is a combination of law and management studies. Language options are offered in Years 2, 3 and 4.

Salford Law is offered with several science and technological subjects.

Sheffield (*Law*) In the first year students take courses in contract, property and public law and an introduction to law and the legal system. This leads to the Intermediate examination. Thereafter there is considerable freedom of choice in planning the programme of study for the final two years. For those students not aiming for a law career it is possible to transfer to the BA law course. Law is also offered with a language.

Sheffield Hallam (*Law*) Completion of the course leads to an exemption from Law Society professional examinations, but there is a considerable optional element in the course including languages. There is also a four year sandwich course in Public Sector Legal Studies.

Southampton (*Law*) The LLB course consists of a core of seven compulsory subjects studied in the first and second years, together with a wide range of optional subjects. These range from admiralty law and carriage of goods by sea to law and medicine, environmental law and EC law.

South Bank (*Law*) This course, which is recognised by the Law Society and the Council of Legal Education, abandons some of the traditional subject boundaries. It aims to develop the student's skill in the use of legal materials and their relation with the social environment. Optional units include company law, housing law, women and the law, medical law and ethics.

Staffordshire (*Law*) All students follow a common course of compulsory subjects in the first year together with criminal law or accounting and finance or a language. They may continue these options in the second year. All the final year courses are options which include the media and the law and medical ethics.

Stirling (*Business Law*) The subject is offered with accountancy, business studies, economics, financial studies, human resources management, management science or marketing.

Strathclyde (*Scottish Law*) The first year course includes law and legal processes, public law and Scottish law. Mercantile and criminal law is combined with Scottish law in the second year, with a choice of options in the second and third years which include forensic medicine, law and computers, international law and criminology. A degree course in Business Law is also offered.

Sunderland A course is offered in Business and Legal Studies.

Surrey Law is offered with French, German or Russian.

Sussex (*Law*) Students are examined in Law and also in contextual subjects taught within their Schools of Studies. The degree carries exemption from the Bar and Law Society examinations. The courses offered cover Law in European Studies, Law in English/American Studies, Law in Social Sciences and European Commercial Law.

Swansea (*Law*) All students follow a common first year with four law modules and two non-law modules. Five law and one non-law module are taken in Years 2 and 3. Law is also offered with a European language, Business or Politics.

Teesside (*Law*) As well as the core subjects of a standard law degree all students take a course in business studies running through the three years of the course. European law is also compulsory.

Thames Valley (*Law*) The LLB course provides a traditional legal education with a wide range of options in Years 2 and 3 including EC law, public international law, Medicine and the law, Civil liberties and the Government and Politics of Britain. Courses are also offered in Criminal Justice, European Law, and Law and Languages (French/German/ Spanish law).

Ulster Law is offered with Government or Economics.

Warwick (*Law*) Three and four year courses are available. Both courses allow the student to choose 'full' or 'half' courses in a wide range of legal subjects. In the four year course second, third and fourth year students may take up to a total of four non-law subjects. Law is studied in the context of wider social, political and theoretical practise - with expertise from 'all around the globe'. There is also a four year course in European Law which requires students to have a good knowledge of French or German.

Westminster (*Law*) The seven compulsory subjects required to gain necessary exemptions from professional examinations are taken in Years 1 and 2 with additional options in Years 2 and 3. There is a wide range of law options including EC and international law, and law and computers.

Wolverhampton (*Law*) This course is approved by the Law Society and the Bar Council for exemption purposes from Law Society Final examinations. It covers the required compulsory core subjects plus a wide range of options from which seven must be chosen in Years 2 and 3. In the first year students take one course from accounting, economics, politics, sociology, literature or psychology. Language options and European placements are possible. Holborn College, London also offers a course in conjunction with Wolverhampton in addition to an External London University LLB course.

- **Top research universities**
Cambridge, London (King's) (LSE) (UC) (QMW), Oxford, Edinburgh, Bristol, Manchester, Nottingham, Sheffield, Warwick, Belfast.

- **Colleges and Institutes of Higher Education offering law courses**
Croydon (Coll), Gwent (Coll), Holborn (Coll), Nene (Coll), Southampton (Inst), Suffolk (Coll), Swansea (Inst).

- **Other courses to be considered**
Government, history, international relations, politics, social sciences, social studies, sociology.

LIBRARIANSHIP

- **Special subject requirements:** GCSE Grade A–C English, mathematics and a foreign language are required for some courses. An A-level may be required depending on the subject option.

- **Subject information:** This subject area (which also includes information science) involves the study of information systems. These cover retrieval, indexing, computer and media technology, classification and cataloguing.

Aberystwyth (*Information and Library Studies*) The course combines practical and theoretical aspects of librarianship, information work and technology. There is also a degree course in Information Science which introduces a strong computer science element to information work. High employment success rate among students. This course is offered in combination with over 20 other subjects.

Brighton (*Library and Information Studies*) Core subjects focus on the library and community, knowledge and records, and library management, and heavy use is made of computing and media technologies. There is also a choice of specialist studies from media resources, bibliographical studies and computer studies. Short practical placements in this three year course take place each year.

Central England (*Information and Library Studies*) Year 1 covers management, information transmission and retrieval and computing for librarians. These studies are continued in Year 2 in which students have an opportunity to specialise in information resources and services in science, social science or the humanities. All students take 9 months paid training in Year 3 and choose options in the fourth year which include classification and cataloguing, work with children and young people, and computer-aided text processing. More than half the course is concerned with information technology.

Heriot-Watt A course in Information Management is offered with Accountancy.

Leeds Metropolitan (*Information Studies*) This course prepares students to work in information and library units in industry, central and local government. Management methods and the storing and recording of information, as well as the non-technical study of the use of computers, form an important part of the course. Students may also study science and a foreign language.

Liverpool John Moores (*Information and Library Studies*) Subjects covered include the role and management of library and information services, the use and application of the computer, development and reading of children and young adults, and community needs.

London (UC) (*Information Management*) Some 'information' subjects should not be confused with library studies. This course encompasses such topics as personnel, finance, marketing and business organisation and draws on the expertise of the Computer Science and Management Centre as well as the School of Librarianship.

Loughborough (*Information and Library Studies; Library Studies with another subject*) Three and four year courses are offered in both these programmes. The first two years of both courses are composed of Library Studies and cover information searching, practical cataloguing and classification, reference services and user studies. Options include the study of a foreign language and a minor subject from a wide range which includes music, geography, chemical engineering and human biology. Professional training of one year can be taken in the third year. In the course Library Studies with another subject, the latter is chosen in the first year and studied throughout except in the professional training year of the four year course. Subjects are chosen from English, geography, history, mathematics, physical education and sports science and social science. There is also a degree course in Information and Computing Studies.

Manchester Metropolitan (*Information and Library Management*) This modular course, which is recognised by the Library Association, offers the basic core subjects covering management, information systems, retrieval and information technology. Special studies in Year 3 provide flexibility to cover areas of special interest to students. These include working in academic, business and commercial communities. Students are required to undertake two periods of placement, each of five weeks' duration.

North London (*Information Studies*) This professional course includes a four week practical placement in a range of institutions, eg industrial, academic, public and special libraries.

Northumbria (*Information and Library Management*) The course is planned to prepare students for work in library and other information services. Compulsory areas include information, clients and communications, information services management, hardware, software and paperware. This is supported by a wide variety of third year options.

Robert Gordon (*Librarianship and Information Studies*) The course aims to produce graduates capable of working in a wide range of library and information services and reflects current practice with an appropriate emphasis on information technology.

Sheffield Information Management is offered with Accounting or Business Studies.

Strathclyde (*Information Science*) This is a four year course covering such subjects as communication theory, information retrieval, bibliometrics, thesaurus construction, indexing and the marketing of information.

Thames Valley (*Information Management*) This subject can be taken with the bias towards Library and Information Studies or Business Information Technology.

Wolverhampton (*Information Management*) This course is modular with a bias towards business and management and human factors over purely technical design.

- **Colleges of Higher Education offering degree courses**
Queen Margaret (Coll).

- **Other courses to be considered**
Information science, information systems, publishing, communication studies, technical communication, cultural studies and information management.

MATERIALS SCIENCE/METALLURGY/MATERIALS ENGINEERING (including **Textiles, Paper Science, Polymer Science, Photographic Science**)

- **Special subject requirements:** 2–3 A-levels in mathematics/science subjects. Mathematics occasionally required at A-level and with science subjects frequently at GCSE (grade A–C).

- **Subject information:** This is a subject which covers physics, chemistry and engineering at one and the same time! From its origins in metallurgy, materials science has now moved into the processing, structure and properties of materials - ceramics, polymers, composites and electrical materials. Materials science and metallurgy are perhaps the most misunderstood of all careers. Thus applications for degree courses are low and offers very reasonable. As with other careers in which there is a shortfall of applicants, graduate employment and future prospects are good.

Aberdeen New Materials Technology is offered with Chemistry.

Bath (*Materials Science*) This subject is offered as a three or four year course (with the third year in industry). The course covers topics related to physical, chemical and engineering subjects which are developed through the first and second year. In the final year, specialised courses deal with such areas as polymers, ceramics, glasses, production technology and management studies.

Birmingham (*Materials Science and Technology; Materials Engineering*) Materials Science and Technology is a three year course and the Materials Engineering course lasts four years. The decision to take the engineering course can be taken at the end of Year 2. Both courses include management subjects.

Brunel (*Materials Science and Technology; Materials Technology with Management; Metallurgy*) Three interlinked courses, with a common first year enabling students to change course after Level 1, are offered as a three year full-time course, a four year thick sandwich (with one industrial placement), or a four year thin sandwich (with two different placements). Both sandwich courses offer a fast track route to Chartered Engineer status. There is the option of a further year to obtain an MEng. Languages and training placements abroad are offered.

Cambridge (*Natural Sciences*) Materials Science and Metallurgy are offered as part of the Natural Sciences course. (See **Chemistry**). In the second year they are accompanied by two other physical sciences before a specialist third, and possibly fourth, year.

Coventry (*Materials Science*) This is a broad-based course which has a common first year with Physical Science. Professional training is arranged in the third year in the four year sandwich option. The course covers maths, engineering manufacture, the properties of materials and processing.

Cranfield Materials Science is offered with either Applied Physics or Applicable Mathematics.

De Montfort (*Textile and Apparel*) The course covers textile technology with a chosen emphasis on textile design and management, clothing design and production.

Exeter (*Minerals Surveying and Resource Management*) A modular course from 1996 along with Minerals Engineering, Mining Engineering, Industrial Geology. The course is based at the Camborne School of Mines. (See also under **Mining Engineering**.)

Greenwich (*Metallurgy and Materials Engineering*) The course focuses on structure and deformation, polymers and ceramics, engineering process and industrial management.

Heriot-Watt (*Textiles*) Textile studies, clothing studies and management are covered in all years with marketing and quality evaluation. Several textile courses are offered by the Scottish College of Textiles including degrees in Clothing, Textiles and Fashion Design and Textiles and Marketing.

Huddersfield (*Textile Manaufacture with Clothing Studies*) The course aims to prepare students for careers in production engineering involved with companies in the manufacture of textile and clothing products. There is a sandwich route with supervised work experience in Year 3.

Leeds (*Materials Science and Engineering*) Materials Science is taken with maths, physics and computing in the first year. The study continues in the second year with applied maths and statistics and engineering design. Materials science and engineering form the core of the third year subjects.

Courses are also offered in Metallurgy and Ceramics Science and Engineering.

Liverpool (*Materials Science*) Mathematics, computing, corrosion and oxidation are common core courses for this course and clinical engineering. The latter is hospital based and undertakes research in the area of dental and medical bioengineering.

London (Imp) (*Materials*) The department offers three year BEng courses in Materials Science and Engineering, Materials with Management, and Materials with Physics; and four year courses in Aerospace Materials, Materials Science and Engineering, and Materials with Management, Physics and/or a Year Abroad.

London (QMW) (*Materials Science and Engineering*) This subject shares a common first year with Polymer Science and Engineering so the choice of programme can be deferred until the beginning of the second year depending on whether the student prefers a physics or a chemistry bias.

Loughborough (*Mechanical and Materials Engineering*) This course shares the same programme as other Mechanical Engineering courses in the department in the first year. Later specialisms focus on the nature of materials and their use in industry.

Manchester (*Materials Science*) Four three year degree courses are offered by the university each of which can be taken as a four year sandwich course. Materials Science, Metallurgy and Polymer Materials are common for the first 2 years allowing specialisation in any to follow in Year 3. (*Biomedical Materials Science*) There is also a course in Biomedical Materials Science focusing on cell-structure, anatomy, tissue interactions and drug release systems.

Manchester Metropolitan (*Materials Science*) In the first year materials science is studied with one other subject from applied physics, biology, chemistry, computing, mathematics, economics, manufacturing or measurement and instrumentation. The second year gives more emphasis to materials science and the final year offers a choice of options. (*Polymer Science and Technology*) The course provides a training for a career as a technologist in the rubber and plastics industry. It can be studied as a four year sandwich course, with the third year spent in industry. Polymer science is also included in the Combined Studies degree programme as a three year full-time or four year sandwich course.

Manchester (UMIST) (*Metallurgy*) This course is run jointly with Manchester University. The first two years are common with Materials Science and Polymer Materials Science. Biomedical Materials Science is also offered, and higher degrees in Materials Science with Business and Management, and Aerospace Materials.

Napier (*Polymer Engineering*) A four year sandwich course with 12 months supervised work experience between Years 2 and 4. The course covers the most recent developments in the subject covering topics including liquid crystal polymers, flame retardant materials and recycling.

Newcastle (*Materials Engineering*) This 3 year BEng course has a common first year with the four year Materials Design Engineering MEng. A foundation year is available for those without appropriate qualifications.

North London (*Polymer Science and Technology*) After a broad foundation in materials, engineering and business, the course covers polymer structure, properties, manufacturing methods and computing. The third year may be spent in industry. The final year covers design, process analysis, advanced materials, industrial case studies, and an individual project is undertaken.

Northumbria (*Materials Engineering*) This focuses on the engineering applications of modern materials. At the end of Year 1 it is possible to transfer to Manufacturing Systems Engineering or Mechanical Engineering. There is also an extended route.

Nottingham (*Materials Design and Processing*) The course provides an understanding of the demands made on materials in the construction and operation of chemical plant and of how those demands may be met by appropriate choice of material and its method of manufacture and use. The course develops an understanding of the complex interactions between: the design of component parts and assemblies for chemical processing; the microstructure and properties of the materials used; the manufacturing methods required; the performance of the plant and its products in service. Courses are also offered in Medical Materials Science and the Chemistry of Materials.

Oxford (*Metallurgy and the Science of Materials*) The study is interdisciplinary, involving the physics and chemistry of solids and their engineering applications. The course lasts four years and the final year involves research in the department or in industry leading to a thesis. A degree course is also offered in Metallurgy, Economics and Management which has a common first year with the previous course.

Plymouth (*Composite Materials Engineering*) A three year or four year sandwich degree, the first year being common with Mechanical Engineering. Options following Mechanical Engineering or Manufacturing Systems are available in the second year. Final year studies focus on the production and properties of metal, glass, carbon and plastic materials, practical composite design and manufacture.

Sheffield (*Materials Science and Engineering*) In this course options exist in Ceramic Science. Polymer Science and Glass and Metal Science are also offered as specialist degrees.

Sheffield Hallam (*Materials Engineering with Management*) This is a four year sandwich course which is concerned with the production and processing of metals, polymers and ceramics for modern industrial use and aspects of management and business studies. A course in Mechanical and Materials Engineering is also available.

Staffordshire (*Ceramic Technology*) A comprehensive study of ceramic materials manufacture and design at a leading centre in the UK.

Strathclyde (*Metallurgy and Engineering Materials*) All students study extraction, physical and engineering metallurgy and materials science during the first two years, with specialisation in the final two years.

Surrey (*Materials Technology; Materials Science; Metallurgy*) Students take the same subjects in the first and second years which enables decisions to be delayed on their final degree until Year 4 (Year 3 is an industrial placement). Language and business studies options are possible. These are four year courses including a year's professional training.

Sussex Polymer Science is offered with Chemistry.

Swansea (*Materials Science and Engineering*) Scholarships are available in this course in which specialist topics include polymer engineering, microelectronics, materials technology and failure analysis. The course is also offered with a year in North America.

Westminster (*Photographic Sciences*) A three year full-time course unique in Britain and combining the study of science photography and electronic imaging. The course includes video production, applied photography, graphics, biomedical imaging and colour reproduction.

Wolverhampton Materials Technology is offered within the Applied Science and Modular Degree schemes. There is also a specialist route in Ceramics.

● **Top research universities**
Birmingham, Cambridge, London (Imp), UMIST, Oxford, Bath, Cranfield, Liverpool, London (QMW), Sheffield, Surrey, Swansea.

● **Colleges and Institutes of Higher Education offering degree courses**
Bolton (Inst) (Textiles), Buckinghamshire (Coll) (Forest Products Technology), Doncaster (Coll) (Minerals), Nene (Coll) (Leather), NESCOT (Biological Imaging), North East Wales (Inst) (Materials Science).
Several universities and colleges offer courses in ceramics, textiles and industrial design with an art/design focus.

● **Other courses to be considered**
Aerospace materials technology, biomedical materials science, chemistry and applied chemistry, engineering design, geology, geophysics, materials engineering, mechanical, mining and production engineering, mineral exploitation, paper science, physics and applied physics, polymer science, polymer chemistry, textiles and wood science.

MATHEMATICS

● **Special subject requirements:** usually 2 A-levels, mathematics essential, physics occasionally 'required' or 'preferred'.

● **Subject information:** This is an extension of A-level mathematics covering pure and applied mathematics, statistics, computing, mathematical analysis and mathematical applications. Alternative courses such as Operational Research, Statistics, Accountancy, Management Science and Actuarial Studies could also be considered.

Aberdeen (*Mathematics*) In the first year a little over half the time is spent on calculus and its applications, the rest of the time on complex numbers, matrices, vectors and probability theory. At level 2, Honours students continue with the applications of maths, whilst an alternative course is offered for non-specialist individual projects, and options follow in Years 3 and 4.

Abertay Dundee Mathematics is offered with computing or physics. In the Maths programme options are available in mathematical sciences or mathematics with business. There is a strong practical modelling element.

Aberystwyth (*Mathematics*) A number of mathematics courses are available. These include single and joint Honours Mathematics, Industrial Mathematics (for those who wish to work in industry), Biometry (for mathematical biologists), Pure Mathematics (with an emphasis between the various branches of maths), Applied Mathematics and Statistics.

Anglia (Poly Univ) (*Mathematics*) This is a three year or four year course (which includes a language). Mathematics is also offered with Statistics.

Aston Mathematics is offered as a joint course with some scientific and social science subjects.

Bangor (*Mathematics*) A flexible course in maths and further maths is followed in the first year. Courses in Part II are arranged so that students in their final year may choose to specialise in pure maths, in applied maths and computing or follow a broad-based course. A distinctive feature of this course is small-group teaching.

Bath (*Mathematics*) In the School of Mathematical Sciences a number of three and four year courses are offered covering maths, statistics and computing. All students take a common first year. In the second year students aiming for degrees in Computer Software Technology are fully committed but other students keep their options open, although some specialisms are possible which develop in the final year. Students have the option of a year out in industry in the third year. The four year course can be taken concurrently with a Certificate of Education.

Belfast (*Mathematics*) Three departments teach Applied Mathematics, Pure Mathematics, Statistics and Operational Research and Computer Science. There are four courses covering mathematics including pure, applied, industrial aspects and statistics. There is a common year for all courses and all students register initially for mathematics. Thereafter, depending on the student's interest and progress, transfers can take place to the other three specialisms at the end of Year 1.

Birmingham (*Mathematical Sciences*) Subjects offered include pure, applied and industrial mathematics. Joint programmes are also offered with Artificial Intelligence, Computer Science, Speech Science and Psychology. It is also possible to take Mathematics with a year abroad.

Bradford (*Mathematics*) In this course there is a strong emphasis on applied mathematics rather than the more abstract areas of pure mathematics. Subjects included in the course are statistics, numerical analysis, computer science, operational research and the technological applications. Microcomputers and main-frame computers are used throughout the course.

Brighton Mathematics is offered as a joint course with several other subjects.

Bristol (*Mathematics*) A particular feature is the flexibility of the course structure at every undergraduate stage. Students may transfer from joint Honours to single Honours, either at the end of the first year or at the end of the second year. Students may choose to spend one third of their time on subjects outside the mathematics department in either or both of their second or third years. This is particularly useful for students moving into the business world who may wish to study economics in their final year. However, in addition to the traditional accompaniments to mathematics such as physics, philosophy and astronomy, some students decide to study languages, history, music, art and even theology.

Bristol UWE (*Mathematics, Statistics and Computing*) Options are offered in a modern language or finance.

Brunel (*Mathematics*) The Department caters for all possible interests with a wide range of courses which includes Mathematics, Mathematical and Management Studies and Statistics, with options in languages and management. The diversity of these courses caters admirably for the changing needs of students combined with the unique sandwich course leading to a high proportion of successful graduate employment placements. Several joint courses are also offered which include Business Mathematics.

Buckingham Applicable Mathematics is offered with Computer Science.

Cambridge (*Mathematics*) The course covers pure and applied mathematics, theoretical physics together with extensive courses in probability, statistics, operational research and computing. Specialisation is allowed for in the latter part of the course. Some students stay on for an extra year (Year 4) to take Part III of the course or the Diploma in Mathematical Statistics or in Computer Science.

Cardiff (*Mathematics; Mathematics and Applications*) The Mathematics course allows students to specialise in pure or applied mathematics or statistics whilst the Applications course provides opportunities for specialisation in several branches of the subject including computer studies, statistics and operational research.

Central Lancashire (*Mathematical Sciences*) This is a three year or four year (sandwich) course, which includes pure or discrete mathematics and applications of mathematics using computers.

City (*Mathematical Science*) This course gives a good grounding in mathematics, statistics and computer science with options in pure and applied maths, statistics and computing in Years 2 and 3. Good opportunities exist for transfer across courses. There is an optional third year in industry.

Coventry (*Mathematics*) A four year full-time course with the third year spent in industry, commerce or a research establishment. The emphasis is on the application of mathematics, statistics and computing. Transfer to the Combined Science degree course is possible. There is also a degree course in Statistics and Operational Research.

Cranfield Applicable Mathematics is offered with either Materials Science or Physics.

De Montfort Mathematics can be taken as part of the Combined Studies programme and with Business, Computing or Statistics.

Derby Applicable Mathematics courses are offered which can include Statistics and Computing.

Dundee (*Mathematics*) Mathematics is studied with modules in Computer Science at the end of the third year. Honours degrees in Mathematics and Applied Mathematics can be taken.

Durham (*Mathematics*) This subject can be taken as part of the new BA in Combined Studies. In the Faculty of Science there is a single Honours course in Mathematics, and joint courses with Economics or Physics. A subsidiary subject is taken in Year 1. In the second year of the single Honours course students take two compulsory courses, one in pure and one in applied maths and two optional courses from pure maths, applied maths and statistics. During the third year students have a wide choice of options from pure and applied maths, theoretical physics, statistics and probability.

East Anglia (*Mathematics*) The Science course unit system gives considerable flexibility. The preliminary programme includes two compulsory units and one optional unit. By taking certain optional units students may then choose to follow one of several joint courses in Mathematics and Computer Studies or Mathematics and Physics or single Honours Mathematics. The second and third years are planned on a unit system allowing students further flexibility in the choice of options. A new four year degree programme offers a third year in Germany at the University of Freiburg (strong in statistics and pure mathematics).

East London Courses are offered in Mathematics, Statistics and Computing. 46 different subjects are offered in the UEL undergraduate degree scheme and a wide selection of elective units are available.

Edinburgh (*Mathematics*) The first two years cover pure and applied mathematics and two other courses in science, arts or social sciences. The third and fourth year specialise in mathematics with a wide range of options in the fourth year. Mathematics may also be studied as an arts degree course, where the emphasis is on pure mathematics.

Essex (*Mathematics*) In the first year students will take either mathematics and computing science or other science subjects. The course is organised on the unit system in which students choose ten courses in the second and third years from a wide choice of options.

Exeter (*Mathematics*) Students following courses in Mathematics, Mathematics and Computation, Pure and Applied Mathematics and Pure Mathematics and Mathematical Statistics have a common first year and then choose their specialisation at the beginning of the second year. The third year in all courses offers a considerable number of advanced optional courses.

Glamorgan Mathematics is offered as part of several degree programmes with other subjects. Transfer to the BSc course in Computational Mathematics is possible at the end of Year 1.

Glasgow (*Mathematics*) The Ordinary class in Mathematics is open to students in all faculties. Beyond the first year level Honours and non-Honours students take different joint courses; joint courses include Astronomy, Computing Science, Physics and Statistics.

Glasgow Caledonian Mathematics is offered with Business or Language.

Greenwich Several mathematics courses are offered covering Business Systems Modelling, Statistics and Computing.

Heriot-Watt (*Mathematics*) Pure mathematics, applied mathematics and statistics and numerical analysis form the basis of this four year course in which an additional subject such as accountancy, business studies or languages can be taken in the first year. A choice of specialisation is made in Year 3. There is a course in Actuarial Mathematics and Statistics. There are a number of degrees which involve 75 per cent Mathematics and 25 per cent of another subject.

Hertfordshire A large number of mathematics joint courses are offered in addition to modular degree schemes.

Huddersfield Mathematical Studies covers computing and business applications.

Hull (*Mathematics*) Degree courses are offered in Mathematics, Pure Mathematics and Statistics. In the first year six courses are offered in pure and applied mathematics, together with computation and statistics. After a qualifying examination at the end of the first year students then select their degree programme, which involves an increasing optional element.

Keele (*Mathematics*) This can be taken in combination with one from 28 other subjects. In the first and second years, the principal course covers pure and applied mathematics and statistics, whilst the third year offers a wide choice of topics, depending on the student's interests.

Kent (*Mathematics*) In Part I the student is introduced to the main areas of mathematical study with an option chosen from mathematics, economics, introductory computer science or physics. All Part II courses extend over two years and students choose compulsory or optional subjects from a wide range.

Kingston Several mathematics courses are offered including Mathematics Modelling and Computing.

Lancaster (*Mathematics*) There are two courses, one in Mathematics for students who are majoring in the subject, and one in Elementary Mathematics for students of other disciplines who require a mathematical background. The department boasts a particular strength in numerical analysis and there is an option to study statistics. Exchanges with the USA are possible.

Leeds (*Mathematics*) Pure mathematics is taken with applied mathematics, statistics and computing throughout the course. Both mathematics and statistics can be taken as subsidiary subjects. This is a course offering depth of study and great flexibility within the variety of 45 options on offer, including computing. A new four year Mathematics (European) degree includes a year's study abroad.

Leeds Metropolitan A four year degree in mathematics is offered as well as a two year Secondary Teaching course.

Leicester Several courses are offered including Mathematics (European Community) and Mathematics (USA).

Liverpool (*Mathematics*) This course has a very flexible structure. In the first year it is possible to take a common course in mathematics, computing and statistics, and students subsequently specialise in one or more area of study in the second and third years. There are several joint Honours degrees available.

London (Goldsmiths') (*Mathematical Studies*) The first year covers foundation work in computer science, mathematics and statistics, with additional courses in applied mathematics, astronomy and psychology. Options increase in the second and third years. There are also courses in Mathematics and Statistics, and Mathematical Studies and Psychology.

London (Imp) (*Mathematics*) During the first two years all students follow basic courses in pure and applied mathematics, statistics and numerical analysis. The third year provides the opportunity for students to take specialist options or to follow a more generalised course.

London (King's) (*Mathematics*) Degree programmes are offered for those who wish to specialise in mathematics and for those wishing to combine mathematics with that of other subjects. The curriculum is flexible and allows for a change of direction according to ability and interest. Specialist mathematicians in their third year follow courses of their own choice from a range of options in pure and applied mathematics and mathematical physics.

London (LSE) Mathematics is offered with Economics and Philosophy. A course in Business Mathematics and Statistics is also offered.

London (QMW) (*Mathematics*) The School of Mathematical Sciences provides instruction in pure and applied mathematics, while statistics is taught in the Department of Computer Science and Statistics. A course unit system is in operation which enables students to choose from a large number of UCAS codes both within mathematics itself and combining mathematics with another subject.

London (RH) (*Mathematics*) The first year course is divided into four parts - mathematical analysis, algebra, methods and modelling. The second and third year courses develop on these themes and introduce a wide range of optional subjects including language. Students specialising in mathematics may also take a few course units in statistics, computer science, physics, chemistry, music or environmental science. Over thirty subjects are also offered with mathematics.

London (UC) (*Mathematics*) Nine courses are offered and some sponsorships are possible. Students can be accepted with a single maths A-level.

London Guildhall A modular degree programme provides the opportunity to study mathematics.

Loughborough (*Mathematics; Industrial Mathematics*) The first course (which lasts three years) provides a study of pure and applied mathematics, statistics, numerical analysis and computing. The second course (of four years) is designed with particular emphasis on the solution of problems arising in industry and commerce. There is also a course in Mathematics and Computation.

Luton Quantitative methods are offered with twelve subjects.

Manchester (*Mathematics*) This is a broad course with options in statistics and operational research.

Manchester Metropolitan Applicable Mathematics and Business Mathematics are offered with a wide range of subjects.

Manchester (UMIST) (*Mathematics*) Students may specialise in pure or applied mathematics by their choice of third year options, or may continue to balance the two. There are separate degrees in Pure Mathematics and Computation and Mathematical Physics, and mathematics may be combined with several other subjects including languages.

Middlesex (*Mathematics for Business*) After a first year grounding in mathematics, statistics, operational research and computing, the course emphasises business applications. All students take two options from computer systems architecture, economics, accounting or a language. This is a sandwich course with a year in professional practice.

Napier (*Mathematics with Engineering Technology*) A four year course covering mathematics, statistics, computing, engineering topics and mathematical modelling, with a 20-week period of work experience in the UK or abroad in the second year. The course has a common first year with Mathematical Sciences and Mathematics with Finance in which transfers are possible.

Newcastle (*Mathematics*) The course structure allows students to defer their choice of final degree course until the end of the first year. There are degrees offered in Statistics, Computing Science and several joint Honours combinations. There are opportunities to take non-mathematical options. Changing between the various degrees offered by the department is a routine matter at the end of the first and second year.

Northumbria (*Mathematics*) This is a four-year course with Year 3 spent on placement in industry or commerce. Final year options include applied statistics, control theory, computation geometry and graphics, numerical mathematics, codes and ciphers, operational research and physical applied mathematics. Applied Statistics for Business and Industry is also available.

Nottingham (*Mathematics*) This is a very flexible course in which students take one other subject in the first year, in addition to Mathematics. Students specialising in Mathematics also take statistics and computing. Mathematics can also be taken as a joint Honours course with eight other subjects. The course in Mathematics with Engineering consists of applicable mathematics for two thirds of the course and engineering for the remainder.

Nottingham Trent (*Mathematical Methods for Information Technology*) This course includes mathematics, statistics, computing, electronics and business studies.

Oxford (*Mathematics*) The first year syllabus covers basic work in algebra, analysis, mechanics, potential theory and probability. In the second and third years the student's work is divided into three sections. Section 1 completes the core syllabus in the first term and leads on to Section 2 - a choice of options in the next two terms. In Section 3 (Year 3) the student studies one or two areas in depth.

Oxford Brookes Mathematics and Computing Mathematics are offered jointly with a wide range of subjects.

Paisley (*Mathematical Sciences*) A three or four year (sandwich) course covering a wide variety of mathematical topics - numerical studies, computing, statistics and operational research.

Plymouth (*Mathematical Studies*) After a broad foundation year, second and third year studies include linear mathematics, real and complex analysis, computational and mathematical methods, applied probability and statistics, and computer graphics. A wide range of options are available, including non-mathematical subjects in the first year.

Portsmouth (*Mathematics and its Applications*) The four year course includes a period of work experience. The curriculum covers a broad range of applicable topics in mathematics. Mathematical techniques used in management as well as those used in technology are considered. There is also a three year course in Mathematical Sciences.

Reading There are single subject degrees in Mathematics, Applied Mathematics and Pure Mathematics. For each degree there is a set of compulsory units and optional units. Students taking Mathematics take a third subject in the first year which could include computer science, statistics, physics or meteorology.

Robert Gordon Mathematical Sciences are offered with Computing and Education.

Salford (*Mathematics*) This is a broad-based course providing an alternative programme after the first year which offers specialisations in either computational methods or statistics and operational research.

Sheffield (*Mathematics*) The single Honours degree in Mathematics allows specialisation in applied and computational mathematics or in pure mathematics. There is a very wide range of dual Honours combinations.

Sheffield Hallam Mathematics and Computing Mathematics are offered.

Southampton (*Mathematics*) A common first year includes calculus, geometry, mechanics, statistics and computing, followed in Years 2 and 3 with a wide range of options. This enables students to build a course best suited to their interests and needs. Students may choose certain options outside the main mathematical areas including French, German, Spanish, oceanography and economics. Several joint courses with Mathematics are also offered.

South Bank Mathematics is offered with Accounting and Computing.

St Andrews (*Mathematics*) The three departments - Pure Mathematics, Applied Mathematics and Statistics - co-operate within a very flexible course structure.

Staffordshire A course in Industrial Mathematics, Statistics and Computing is offered.

Stirling (*Mathematics*) Part I covers topics in algebra, calculus and geometry in the first three semesters. In Part II these subjects continue with statistics, probability and microcomputer application. Mathematics may be combined with Computing Science and a new course, Mathematics and its Applications.

Strathclyde (*Mathematics*) Students take subsidiary subjects in the first year in addition to a broad-based mathematical course. In the second year theoretical mechanics, statistics and pure mathematics are included which lead to more advanced courses in Years 3 and 4. A number of joint Honours combinations are available.

Sunderland Over ten joint courses are offered with mathematics.

Surrey (*Mathematics*) The course covers a broad range of mathematical subjects, with all students following the same lecture course for the first two terms after which there is some degree of specialisation. The course is unusual since it offers an optional year of industrial or professional experience for all students including the option to take a PGCE course for intending teachers at Roehampton Institute. Mathematics may be studied with Statistics or Computing Science. Language options are available.

Sussex (*Mathematics*) The course provides a broad mathematical training and is divided into three main sections (a) the preliminary course lasting two terms (b) the core curriculum over four terms and (c) two terms in the final year when advanced courses are chosen from a wide range of options. In all, ten courses are offered and transfers are possible up to the end of the first year.

Swansea (*Mathematics*) There are several Part I courses in Mathematics. For non-specialists the Part I course in mathematical methods includes practical training in the use of computers. Part II courses include both single and joint Honours courses covering Mathematics, Pure or Applied Mathematics or Computing Mathematics. The degree results are based on 40 per cent of marks given to second year work and 60 per cent to third year work.

Teesside (*Mathematics*) A modular course structure with options in computing, business topics and a European language.

Ulster Courses are offered in Mathematics, Statistics and Computing.

Warwick (*Mathematics*) A number of degree courses are offered, including Applied Mathematics, Mathematics and Statistics and Mathematics, Operational Research, Statistics and Economics as well as several joint Honours combinations. The first year courses contain a core of mathematics together with other compulsory and optional courses. Because of the overlap it is possible to transfer from any one course to any other (providing certain options have been taken).

Westminster (*Mathematical Sciences*) Problem-solving, statistics and operational research feature in this course which provides an understanding of the broad applications of mathematics in industry and commerce.

Wolverhampton Mathematical Sciences can be studied by way of degree courses in Applied Sciences and Modular Degree Schemes.

York (*Mathematics*) A balanced foundation of general mathematical knowledge occupies the first year with flexibility for course transfer. The second and third years provide a wide choice of options depending on the student's interests.

● **Top research universities**
Bath, Cambridge, Durham, Leeds, Liverpool, London (Imp) (QMW) (UC), Manchester, UMIST, Newcastle, Oxford, Warwick, Aberdeen, Edinburgh, Glasgow, Cardiff, Nottingham, Bristol, Brunel, East Anglia, Exeter, Loughborough, Reading, Sheffield, Dundee, Heriot-Watt, St Andrews, Aberystwyth.

● **Colleges and Institutes of Higher Education offering degree courses**
Bangor Normal (Coll), Bath (Coll), Bishop Grosseteste (Coll), Bradford and Ilkley Community (Coll), Canterbury Christ Church (Coll), Cardiff (Inst), Cheltenham and Gloucester (Coll), Chester (Coll), Chichester (Inst), Edge Hill (Coll), Gwent (Coll), King Alfred's (Coll), Leeds Trinity and All Saints (Coll), Liverpool (Inst), La Sainte Union (Coll), Nene (Coll), Newman (Coll), Ripon and York St John (Univ Coll), Roehampton (Inst), S. Martin's (Coll), St Mark and St John's (Coll), Trinity Carmarthen (Coll), Westhill (Coll), Westminster (Coll), Worcester (Coll).

● **Other courses to be considered**
Accountancy, actuarial work, astronomy, computing engineering, meteorology, operational research, physics.

MEDIA STUDIES

● **Special subject requirements:** 2 A-levels from English, history, sociology or psychology. Some institutions will require Foundation Art course.

● **Subject information:** Check prospectuses carefully since subject content differs considerably between universities. The courses generally focus on radio, TV, journalism and the effects of the media on society.

Birmingham (*Media, Culture and Society*) This course covers linguistics, behavioural science and social psychology. There is no hands-on experience for the media industries. Media and Cultural Studies is also offered in combination with over fifteen other subjects.

Bournemouth (*Media Production*) This course involves audio and video studies and graphics plus some business studies. Bournemouth also offers a range of other media courses, eg Advertising Management, Creative Advertising Design and Multi-media Journalism. (press, broadcasting, radio and TV).

Bradford (*Media Technology and Production*) This is a multi-disciplinary course covering the mass-media audio visual systems, computer graphics, sound processing.

Brighton (*Information and Media Studies*) The major theme is media, management and media production. There is a foreign language option.

Bristol UWE (*Cultural and Media Studies*) This is not a vocational course. This university also offers courses in Science, Society and the Media, Electronic Publishing Technology and Publishing and Information Management.

Cardiff (*Journalism, Film and Broadcasting*) This is a non-vocational scheme of study aiming to provide an understanding of the role of mass communications in society.

Central England (*Visual Communication - Information Media*) Motivation is regarded more importantly than academic background. Applicants must have had some media experience. The course covers, radio, TV, photography and creative writing.

Central Lancashire (*Journalism*) The course covers both journalism, radio and TV skills. There is a foreign language option.

City Journalism is offered in combination with Economics, Philosophy, Psychology or Sociology. A four year course is offered with a School of Journalism abroad. First year students take a vocational language course (French, German or Spanish).

De Montfort (*Media Studies*) The course aims to develop an understanding of media institutions and industries in their historical and socio-cultural context through a study of film and cinema, photography, television and video. This is a flexible course in which students may choose to specialise in one of these areas, and may take up to eight practical work courses. Options include documentary and propaganda, race and the media, and the origin of modern photography.

East Anglia (*Media Studies and a language*) The course covers TV, press, radio, cinema and photography from historical and social standpoints.

East London Media Studies is offered in combination with over 30 subjects. One third of the Media Studies programme consists of taught production projects in radio, video, TV, print and graphics.

Glamorgan (*Media and Communication*) Four channels are offered - communication studies, media studies, cultural and creative and practical studies. The course involves journalism, radio, video production and publishing. Courses are also offered in Advertising Design and Media Production.

Humberside Courses are offered in Media production.

Leeds (*Broadcasting Studies*) The course is taught and examined jointly with BBC Television training and aimed at those seeking a career in broadcasting.

Leeds Metropolitan (*Media Technology*) Topics covered include electronics, microcomputer techniques, music technology, recording, video theory and skills.

Liverpool John Moores (*Media and Cultural Studies*) The course covers cinema history, TV, pop, music, journalism and photography.

London (RH) (*Media Arts*) The course is based around film, TV and video studies, and is a balance of practical and theoretical work with a study of cultural theory providing a basis of study for the history of film and TV.

Loughborough (*Communications and Media Studies*) The course examines the social, political and economic impact of communication and the media.

Luton (*Media Practice*) This course covers electronic publishing, photography, video techniques, radio, journalism, film and TV. This university also offers combinations of media production, media practice, multimedia and journalism with over 80 other subjects.

Napier (*Journalism*) A very vocational course for students totally committed to a career in this field.

Nottingham Trent (*Broadcast Journalism*) The course covers studio practice and microphone technique. Practical studies take place with Central TV Midlands, radio and BBC Midlands.

Oxford Brookes Publishing is offered in combinations with over 40 subjects.

Plymouth Media is offered in combinations with ten other subjects.

Robert Gordon (*Publishing Studies*) The course covers all aspects of publishing including editing, word processing, bookselling and distribution.

Salford (*Media Languages and Business*) Media languages relate to hands-on experience of media production in video and audio work.

Sheffield A course is offered in Journalism Studies.

Sheffield Hallam (*Media Studies*) This is a study of mass media from social, political and economic aspects. Some work in audio and video production is undertaken and also writing for the media.

South Bank (*Media and Society*) The course covers history, politics and sociology of the mass media. One quarter of the course involves practical workshop experience.

Staffordshire (*Media Studies*) Not a media production course, this is offered in combination with over 30 other subjects.

Stirling (*Film and Media Studies*) The teaching of this subject concentrates on the critical and theoretical work based on film, television, radio and the press.

Sunderland (*Media Studies*) The course covers the history of mass-media, radio, video, computing and photography with options in English sociology, psychology or art history. Specialist subjects include the American film, British cinema, radio and print journalism.

Sussex (*Media Studies*) The media are studied in their historical development as social and economic institutions and technologies.

Teesside A course in Journalism has been recently introduced.

Thames Valley Media Studies is offered as part of the Humanities course.

Ulster (*Media Studies*) The course is designed to promote a critical understanding of mass-media (film, TV, radio, photography and the press). Students spend one third of their time on practical projects.

Westminster (*Media Studies*) The course covers mass-media in society and the ways in which it is managed and financed. Practical studies cover print journalism, radio and video.

Wolverhampton (*Media and Communication*) This is a broad study of the media, its management and impact on society. Some opportunities exist for practical work.

- **Colleges and Institutes of Higher Education offering degree courses**
Barnsley (Coll) (Journalism and Media Technology), Bradford and Ilkley (Coll) (Electronic Imaging and Media Communications), Buckingham-shire (Coll) (Film, Media, Culture), Cheltenham and Gloucester (Coll) (Media Communications), Chichester (Inst) (Media Studies), Colchester (Inst) (Communications and Media Studies), Cumbria (Coll of Art) (Media), Falmouth (Coll of Art) (Advertising or Broadcasting or Journalism), Farnborough (Coll) (Media Production and Technology), Glasgow Caledonian (Communication and Mass Media), Gwent (Coll) (Cultural and Media Studies), King Alfred's (Coll) (Media, Film and Communication), Leeds Trinity and All Saints (Coll) (Media), London Institute (Media Studies or Advertising or Journalism or Fashion Journalism), North East Wales (Inst) (Media Studies), Queen Margaret (Coll) (Media and Cultural Studies), Salford (Univ Coll) (Media Production or Media Performance), Southampton (Inst) (Media Technology or Media), St Mark and St John (Coll) (Media Studies), Suffolk (Coll) (Media Studies), Surrey (Inst of Art) (Media Studies or Journalism), Swansea (Inst) (Multi-Media Technology), Trinity College, Carmarthen (Media Studies), Warrington (Coll Inst) (Media Studies), West Herts (Coll) (Advertising or Graphic Media Studies).

- **Other courses to be considered**
Advertising, Communication Studies, Politics, Public Relations, Publishing.

MEDICINE

- **Special subject requirements:** Usually three subjects with chemistry essential at A-level. Other subjects chosen from mathematics, physics, chemistry, physical science, engineering science, biology and zoology.

- **Subject information:** All courses will offer the same components leading to a career in medicine. For outstanding students without science A-levels, some pre-medical courses are available. Thereafter for all, a period of pre-clinical studies leads on to clinical studies. Intercalated courses of one year leading to a BSc are also offered and elective periods abroad in the final years can sometimes be taken. All courses are very similar in course content.

Deans of medical schools have decided unanimously to adopt a policy of 'no detriment' for applicants to Medicine who list one non-medical course on the UCAS application. However, applicants should know that if they receive four rejections for medicine and an offer for a non-medical course, they are not allowed to change their decision and attempt to reopen negotiations with medical schools if they achieve higher A-level grades than expected. When selecting applicants, admissions tutors first look for evidence of academic excellence, not just for its own sake but because a medical course is long and demanding, and the ability to apply oneself and to survive are extremely important. Secondly, a long-standing interest in medicine is always an advantage, together with evidence that the applicant has a well-rounded personality, a wide range of interests, imagination, research potential and is socially aware. A year out is also becoming an asset with some medical schools. A history of mental illness - even the mildest form - can be a bar to entry, and students' physical and mental stability is often under review. The confidential report from the applicant's school is very important. In addition to A-level applicants, most medical schools have a small annual intake (4 to 8) of graduates (usually dental or science). Early applications are advantageous and very serious consideration is given to the overall GCSE grades achieved. The fact that applicants have five choices does not mean that they will receive equal consideration from all the institutions named on their UCAS application. In Medicine this is especially so: applicants receiving one or two offers often will be rejected by other medical schools. Therefore medical applicants receiving even one offer and four rejections have little cause for concern since any other offer they might have received would have demanded the same, or a very similar, high level of attainment. Letters have been received from medical schools indicating that they continue to receive applications from candidates who are not predicted by their schools to achieve grades above DDD. They stress the futility of such applications.

Aberdeen (*Medicine*) The pre-clinical period occupies five terms. Term 6 (Paraclinical and Clinical Studies) covers bacteriology, chemical pathology, pathology and pharmacology. The clinical curriculum occupies Years 3, 4 and 5 (with an interview skills course in Year 3). After two years of the medical course academically able students may take an extra year of study. Intercalated degrees are offered in one or other of the subjects studied in the pre-clinical course leading to a BSc (Med Sci).

Belfast (*Medicine*) A one year pre-medical course is available for students without the necessary science qualifications. The pre-clinical period lasts four terms followed by the clinical stage. Students achieving high marks in the second MB examination can take a one year course leading to the BSc in Anatomy, Biochemistry, Medical Genetics, Medical Microbiology, Pathology or Physiology.

Birmingham (*Medicine*) The pre-clinical stage covers terms 1–6, with clinical instruction beginning at the start of the third year. Students who have attained an adequate standard at the pre-clinical examinations may be admitted to a final year course leading to a BSc in Anatomical Studies,

Medical Biochemical Studies, Pharmacology or Physiology. Medical students who have attained Honours or distinction standard at the end of the fourth year examination in Pathological Studies may take an extra year leading to a BSc in that subject.

Bristol (*Medicine*) In 1995 a new course was introduced with an integrated systems-based curriculum with early clinical contact. All pre-clinical departments are involved in research at national and international levels. 15–25 students each year intercalate to obtain a BSc in Anatomy, Physiology, Biochemistry or Physiology. Bristol operates a European Credit Transfer Scheme with 14 other schools in which a student may spend not less than 3 months in a participating medical school.

Cambridge (*Medicine*) The course of study falls into two periods, the two or three year pre-clinical period spent in Cambridge and the clinical course of two years and one term in the Cambridge Clinical School. Alternatively, the course may be taken at one of the London teaching hospitals or a medical school at another university (these courses last three years). Some students may devote the third year of the pre-clinical course to reading one of a variety of subjects for Part II of the Natural Sciences or Medical Sciences Tripos leading to a BA degree, before embarking on the clinical course.

Dundee (*Medical Science*) A pre-medical course is available for those students who do not have the necessary science qualifications. Thereafter there follows the two year pre-clinical course and the three year clinical course. Promising students may, after the second year, take a one year in-depth course leading to a degree in Anatomy, Biochemistry, Biomedical Engineering, Forensic Medicine, Human Genetics, Microbiology, Psychology, Pathology, Pharmacology or Physiology.

Edinburgh (*Medicine*) The five year course is divided into three phases. Phase 1 occupies the first two years and introduces anatomy, biochemistry, pharmacology, physiology and behavioural sciences. Phase 2 occupies the third year and introduces clinical subjects and is followed by Phase 3, two years of practical clinical work. There is a pre-medical year for students without the appropriate school science subjects. Students can interrupt their studies at the end of Phase 1 or 2 and take a BSc Medical Science degree of one year in Anatomy, Bacteriology, Human Genetics, Immunology, Medical Microbiology, Neuroscience, Parasitology, Pathology, Pharmacology, Physiology and Psychology.

Glasgow (*Medicine*) Two pre-clinical years are followed by three years of clinical studies. Promising students can take an additional year following the pre-clinical course. This leads to a BSc degree. Subjects offered are Anatomy, Animal Development Biology, Biochemistry, Cell Biology, Genetics, Immunology, Molecular Biology, Parasitology, Pharmacology and Physiology or Sports Science. Degrees in Bacteriology, Microbiology or Pathology are taken after the third year.

Leeds (*Medicine*) The course is divided into the two year pre-clinical period followed by the three year clinical period. Promising students may be invited to take an extra year (the third year) reading for a BSc degree in Anatomy, Biochemistry, Chemical Pathology, Genetics, Pharmacology, Medical Microbiology, Pathology or Psychology. This is the only medical school in the Yorkshire Health Region thus offering many opportunities for the newly-qualified.

Leicester (*Medicine*) Students start the course with two years of pre-clinical studies, with teaching on an interdisciplinary basis across 20 departments covering anatomy, biochemistry, genetics, microbiology, pharmacology and physiology. Years 3, 4 and 5 of clinical studies then follow with the elective period of nine weeks - based anywhere in the world - coming in the fourth year. There is an emphasis on the behavioural as well as the medical sciences.

Liverpool (*Medicine*) This is a standard two-part course, the first part (the pre-clinical course) lasting five terms and the second part (the clinical course) continuing to the end of five years. Promising students may be invited to take an additional year of study at the end of the pre-clinical period, leading to a BSc degree in Anatomy, Biochemistry, Physiology or Medical Cell Biology.

London (Imp/St Mary's/Charing Cross/Westminster MS) (*Medicine*) The course in basic medical science covers two years and leads on to the 33 months period of clinical studies. A BSc degree course of one year prior to the clinical course is available for some students. The main hospital sites at which clinical teaching takes place are linked by a fully interactive TV-based remote teaching system.

London (King's/SMD) (*Medicine*) The two year pre-clinical course is centred largely in the college on the Strand where students study the basic medical sciences and pharmacology in a multi-faculty environment. The three year clinical course is based at the Faculty of Clinical Medicine at King's College Hospital, Dulwich. Students are encouraged to take an intercalated BSc degree course of one year after the end of the pre-clinical period. Subjects offered include Anatomy, Biochemistry, Pharmacology and Physiology. A Foundation course in Natural Sciences (Medicine) is offered for candidates with no science A-level background (offer BBB). The course covers Chemistry, Biology, Physics and Maths and successful completion guarantees a place on the medical degree.

London (London Hospital MC) (*Medicine*) In 1990 the London Hospital Medical College, the Medical College of St Bartholomew's and Queen Mary and Westfield linked up to form the City and East London Confederation of the University of London (CELC). The curriculum for the five year course is based on modular teaching in three phases: Terms 1–5 on basic medical sciences; terms 6 and 7 on behavioural sciences and communication skills; and the third phase (terms 8–15) on clinical skills. At the end of term 6 students may opt to intercalate the one-year BSc degree course.

London (QMW) (*Medicine*) Students follow the CELC curriculum (see London Hospital) and should apply to that institution or to St Bartholomew's. The first phase, however, and the intercalated BSc degree, are both taught at QMW.

London (Royal Free HSM) (*Medicine*) The five year course is divided into two periods. A study of basic medical sciences occupies the first six academic terms followed by a three year course of clinical studies and related sciences. Students achieving good passes after the first two years may intercalate a further period of study of three terms leading to a BSc degree.

London (St Bartholomew's HMC) (*Medicine*) (See under London Hospital MC.) Medical and Dental students follow a similar set of modules for the first five terms based in the Faculty of Basic Medical Sciences on the Mile End campus. The course is integrated and designed around body systems. The third phase of the course is based on a series of clinical attachments with day-release teaching. About a third of students intercalate a one-year BSc degree course after their second year.

London (St George's HMS) (*Medicine*) The two year pre-clinical course is based on integrated topic teaching rather than traditional disciplines, and is followed by three years of clinical training. An elective period of study in the final year to practise medicine in other parts of the world is encouraged. Selected students have the opportunity to take an additional year's study leading to the BSc degree. This follows the pre-clinical period.

London UMDS (Guy's/St Thomas's) (*Medicine*) This is an integrated course emphasising communication skills, early contact with patients, flexibility of study and self-directed learning. Extensive experience in the community with the opportunity to take the intercalated BSc degree.

London (University College/Middlesex SM) (*Medicine*) The course consists of two pre-clinical years studying basic medical sciences followed by two years nine months on the clinical course. Promising students can take an additional year at the end of their pre-clinical course to take a BSc degree.

Manchester (*Medicine*) This is a semi-integrated course, systems-based and problem-solving in the first two years. The fourth year is spent in residence in the hospitals covering clinical specialities. Promising students may spend an extra year working for a BSc degree in optional subjects, prior to embarking on the clinical course.

Newcastle (*Medicine*) A new integrated curriculum is in operation at this medical school which has removed the traditional separation between pre-clinical and clinical teaching. Students come into contact with patients at the start of the course, being attached to a family doctor and accompanying him/her on some of his/her rounds. Clinical applications are emphasised throughout the course alongside basic sciences.

Nottingham (*Medicine*) The medical course is fully integrated and includes early patient contact. The course covers a two year study of basic medical sciences (Part I) and a special medical sciences course (Part II) lasting one year and leading to the BMedSci degree. (Courses are offered in Biochemistry, Community Health, Microbiology, Pathology and Pharmacology and Behavioural Science). This is followed by clinical practice lasting 26 months which includes the last term of the third year.

Oxford (*Medicine*) The course lasts five years and ten months. The pre-clinical course lasts three years. This is followed by the clinical course which is based in the John Radcliffe Hospital. A significant part of this course is examined by continuous assessment.

Sheffield (*Medicine*) There is a foundation science year for those who do not have the required combination of A-level subjects. The pre-clinical period lasts two years and is followed by three years of clinical training. Elective periods in which students can study in the UK or abroad for three months come at the end of the fourth year. An additional year of study after the pre-clinical period allows some students to follow a course leading to the BSc or BMedSci degree in Anatomy and Cell Biology, Physiology, Human Metabolism and Clinical Biochemistry or Pharmacology and Therapeutics.

Southampton (*Medicine*) The traditional division between pre-clinical and clinical studies is avoided on this course. The first three years of the course is planned as a single exercise with integrated teaching programmes. In addition there are courses in psychology and sociology, and patient contact in the early stages either in the hospital or the home. The first clinical attachments take place in the third year.

St Andrews (*Medical Science*) This is only a pre-clinical course and leads to the Ordinary degree of BSc in three years or to an Honours degree in four years. Graduates automatically transfer to Manchester University Medical School to follow the three year clinical course.

Wales (UWCM) (*Medicine*) In 1995 a new integrated course with patient contact throughout the five years was introduced. A pre-medical course is available for those without the required A-level subjects. There are opportunities for clinical experience throughout Wales and pre-registration posts are assured within Wales. Examinations are a mixture of continuous assessment and formal sessional examinations.

● **Top research universities**
Birmingham, Bristol, Cambridge, London (Royal Free) (King's) (St Mary's), Newcastle, Nottingham, Oxford, Southampton.

●**Other courses to be considered**
Anatomy, biochemistry, biological sciences, dentistry, nursing, pharmacy, physiotherapy and speech therapy.

MODERN LANGUAGES
(See also **European Studies**)

● **Special subject requirements:** A-level in chosen languages. GCSE (grade A–C) Latin for some courses.

● **Subject information:** These courses usually offer three main options: a single subject degree often based on literature and language; a European Studies course; or two-language subjects which can often include languages different from those available at school, eg Scandinavian Studies, Russian and the languages of Eastern Europe, the Middle and Far East.

Aberystwyth A European languages degree offers a choice of three languages. Modern languages is offered with Business Studies.

Aston (*Language Study Programme*) French and German may be studied separately, as single subjects with a subsidiary subject or together as joint subjects. French or German can also be studied with International Business and a third option is for the study of French and German with non-language subjects (two or three in the first year). There is an emphasis on practical proficiency in languages. A subsidiary study of Japanese is available, and Russian and Spanish as minor options.

Bangor Modern languages can be taken with accounting, banking or economics.

Birmingham (*Modern Languages*) Whilst the study of language is the central activity of all the departments within the School of Modern Languages, students are also introduced to the complementary courses in the history, society and cultural aspects of the country involved. The courses in Combined Honours and Modern Languages permit the study of two subjects equally. Two modern languages can be taken from French Studies, German Studies, Modern Greek, Hispanic Studies, Italian or Russian. Students spend their third year abroad.

Bournemouth (*Applied Languages*) Two languages are chosen with an option in translation and specialist writing in Year 4.

Bradford (*Modern Languages*) The Modern Languages department offers a range of courses which include French, German and (optional ab initio) Spanish or Russian. There is a possibility of studying a third language, eg Dutch, Greek, Portuguese or Italian. Extra-curricular courses offered in 20 languages including Arabic, Greek, Japanese and Polish, and Area Studies Modules in Society and Culture with main options in Economy/ Literature/Politics or France, Germany, Russia or Spain. Emphasis is on interpreting and translating.

Brighton (*Applied Language*) French or German are offered with ab initio Russian.

Bristol (*Modern Languages*) Two languages from French, German, Italian, Russian and Spanish are studied throughout the course. It is possible to take any of these languages as a minor study after Year 1. Language, literature and linguistics are the main topics and the third year is spent in residence abroad. It is possible to transfer to a single Honours degree at the end of the first year. ERASMUS exchanges involving two years in France, Germany or Spain are offered to the most gifted students.

Bristol UWE (*Modern Languages*) Two foreign languages are studied, chosen from French, German and Spanish. Equal weight is given to both languages. There is also a degree course in Modern Languages and Information Systems which includes five months in the country of the student's main foreign language.

Buckingham (*Modern Languages*) A two year course with small-group tuition. An intensive ten week language course is included from October to December at a university in France, Germany or Spain, appropriate to the students choice of language.

Cambridge (*Modern and Medieval Languages*) A very wide range of languages is available. In Part I two languages are offered at the same standard, the course lasting one or two years. Arrangements vary depending on whether the student has taken the languages to A-level.

Most of the examination papers offered in Part II are concerned with literature, history and associated topics of the related country. It is possible to spend the second or third year abroad.

Cardiff (*Three Languages*) The School of European Studies and Japanese offers several single Honours or joint Honours degrees involving French, German, Spanish, Italian, Portuguese or Japanese. The Three Languages scheme is unique in allowing students to take three languages to the same advanced level.

Durham (*Modern Languages*) It is possible to study one, two or three languages: French, German, Russian and Spanish. Post A-level ab initio Italian, Russian and Spanish are also offered. Subsidiary subjects 'from English, Japanese or Turkish to Theology, Mathematics or Music' are also offered.

East Anglia Several courses are offered. Students take one or two or three Honours languages. Five languages are offered - French, German, Danish, Norwegian and Swedish. The emphasis lies in the proficiency in a language. The ancillary language course provides a reading knowledge of a language for students taking European History, Modern European Studies and Russian Studies.

Edinburgh (*Modern European Languages*) French, German, Italian, Russian, Spanish, Gaelic, Danish, Norwegian or Swedish are offered in various combinations.

Essex (*Modern Languages*) Two languages are offered from French, German, Russian and Spanish, plus a study of linguistics. The courses have a strong vocational emphasis. All students take a course in the Enlightenment - a course covering European literature - in the first year. Optional courses are chosen in the second and third years, supporting a set syllabus in language and linguistics. The third year is spent abroad.

Exeter (*Modern Languages*) In addition to single Honours courses in languages it is also possible to study certain combinations of languages from French, German, Russian, Spanish and Italian. Part I occupies the first two years after which it is possible to transfer from a Combined Honours to a single Honours degree course and vice-versa if an appropriate subsidiary subject has been taken with the single Honours subject. The third year of the course is spent abroad.

Heriot-Watt (*Languages (Interpreting and Translating)*) Two languages are studied from French, German, Russian (ab initio or post-Higher/A-level) and Spanish. These are accompanied by a European Studies course. Year 3 involves a five month placement in the appropriate countries. One elective subject from a wide range of options is taken in Year 2.

Huddersfield (*Modern Languages*) Two languages from French, German and Spanish are taken with ab initio courses in all three.

Hull (*Combined Languages*) Sixteen joint degrees in languages are offered in which, at the end of Year 1, the languages studied may be divided equally (four units of each language) or on a major/minor basis with five units in one subject and three units in the other subject. The third year of this four year course is spent abroad.

Lampeter (*Modern Languages*) This is a single Honours course offering three languages - French, German and Swedish - in which two are chosen plus one other subject in the first year. Students can concentrate on one of their two major languages or treat both equally, emphasising literary or modern studies. Students spend a year abroad as part of the course. Beginners courses are also available in Spanish, Irish, Breton and Swedish.

Leeds (*Modern Languages*) Students combine two of French, German, Italian, Russian or Spanish, spending 75 per cent of their time on the principle language in the first year, but thereafter dividing their time equally between the two. This is a four year course with a year spent abroad.

Leeds Metropolitan (*European Languages and Business*) The course combines business studies, European Community studies (law, economics and sociology) and two languages from French, German, Italian or Spanish. There is also a degree course in European Finance and Accounting, a three year course with one year spent in Germany.

Leicester (*Modern Language Studies*) Two languages are selected from French, German and Italian and are studied throughout the three years of the course. An additional subject is studied in the first and second years. Students spend a short vacation period abroad in the countries of their chosen languages.

Liverpool John Moores (*Modern Language Studies*) Two languages are chosen from French, German, Spanish, Russian and Japanese. The last three can be studied ab initio. Business studies and international relations form part of this course. This is a four year course with the third year spent abroad.

London (King's) Various joint Honours courses are offered including Modern Greek, French, German, Spanish, Russian and Portuguese in combination with each other or with Computing, Management, History, English or area studies.

London (SOAS) (*Languages*) Languages are offered in conjunction with the cultures of Africa, the Far East, the Near and Middle East and South East Asia and The Islands.

London (SSEES) Degree courses are offered in Russian Language and Literature, Bulgarian, Czech and Slovak, Finnish, Hungarian/Polish Studies, Romanian, Serbo-Croat and various joint Honours combinations.

Manchester (*Modern Languages*) This four or five year degree scheme offers 20 courses covering five European languages. All students spend a year abroad. Additional courses in linguistics, history and literary studies are offered to support language study.

Manchester Metropolitan (*Modern Languages*) Two languages are chosen from French, German and Spanish, one of which must have been studied to A-level. German or Spanish can be studied ab initio. The course has a focus on literature and one year is spent abroad. Students have a considerable degree of flexibility in the choice of literary options.

Nottingham (*Modern Language Studies*) Two subjects are chosen from (post A-level) French, German, Russian or Spanish, or two from these options and a beginners course from Russian, Serbo-Croat, Slovene, Spanish or Portuguese.

Oxford (*Modern Languages*) Candidates must offer two languages in the preliminary examination from French, German, Spanish, Italian, Russian, Portuguese and Modern Greek. In the final Honours course candidates may offer one or two languages.

Oxford Brookes (*Languages for Business*) Students select a major language which they have studied at A-level (French, German, Italian or Spanish) and a minor language (German, Italian or Spanish). There is a period of work placement abroad during the summer of Year 2. Japanese may be studied as a final year option.

Portsmouth (*Language and Area Studies*) Sixteen language degree programmes are offered. These cover French, German, Spanish, Latin American Studies and Russian and Soviet Studies, combining languages with historical, geographical, political, literary and economic studies. Other programmes combine German and French, Hispanic Studies, Russian and French or Russian and German.

Robert Gordon Modern languages can be taken with Communication.

St Andrews (*Modern Languages*) A very flexible course structure allows students to study one, two or three languages (French, German, Arabic, Russian or Spanish). Students spend at least three months abroad.

Salford (*Modern Languages*) This is a four year degree programme in which two languages are studied from French, German, Italian and Spanish. A third foreign language can be taken from French, German, Arabic, Dutch, Italian, Portuguese, Russian, Spanish or Swedish. Alternatively, a one year course in business and industry is offered. (Places on this course and Arabic are limited). There is considerable emphasis on the spoken and written word in the course which is strongly vocational. A course is also available in Modern Languages and Marketing Studies, giving emphasis to the international business dimension.

Sheffield (*Modern Languages*) This is a four year degree course, the third year being spent abroad. Students choose three subjects from French, German, Linguistics, Russian and Spanish in the first year. (There are beginners' courses available in Russian and Spanish). Two of these subjects are followed as major studies in the second and fourth years. There are also degree courses in Spanish Studies, Russian Studies or Japanese Studies.

Southampton The School of Modern Languages offers French, German, Spanish and Portuguese, which may be read as single Honours, combined with each other or with a range of other subjects such as archaeology, music or economics. All single Honours students take another language which may additionally be Dutch, Catalan or Celtic.

South Bank (*Modern Languages with International Studies*) The course is based on two European languages combined with economics and politics. French can be studied (post A-level only) and German and Spanish are available post A-level and ab initio. Two six-month placements abroad form part of Year 3. Year 4 includes language studies plus a specialisation in either politics or economics. There is also a course in Modern Languages and International Business.

Staffordshire (*European Languages*) Two languages are taken from French, German or Spanish.

Stirling Modern languages can be taken with Business Studies or Marketing.

Surrey (*Linguistics and International Studies*) Students take one main language from French, German or Russian (the latter as post A-level or for beginners). In addition they select another of these languages or Swedish (with Norwegian or Danish) as a subsidiary language. All students must also select either economics, European Studies, international relations or law which is then studied to the same level as languages throughout the four year course. Two periods are spent abroad.

Swansea (*Modern Languages with Business Studies*) Two modern languages are taken throughout the course (French, German, Russian, Spanish, Italian and Welsh are offered) and a year is spent at a European university.

Ulster (*Applied Languages*) All students take two languages from French, German or Spanish.

Westminster (*Modern Languages*) Any two languages may be chosen from French, German, Italian, Spanish, Russian, Arabic and Chinese. Year 3 is spent abroad. Students of Chinese normally specialise in Chinese from the third year and one academic year is spent in China.

Wolverhampton (*Modern Languages*) Students choose two languages from French, German, Russian or Spanish. The last two languages are offered for beginners. These are complemented by studies in economics, politics, history, sociology and European thought in a very flexible modular degree scheme. A year is spent in study or employment abroad.

York (*Language and Linguistics*) Students reading Language and Linguistics as a single or main subject study one European language (French or German), and one African or Asian language previously unknown to them (Chinese, Hindi, Swahili, Creole).

● **Colleges and Institutes of Higher Education offering courses**
Cheltenham and Gloucester (Coll), Roehampton (Inst).

● **Other courses to be considered**
Courses in various language subjects not requiring the language at A-level, eg Chinese, Japanese, Arabic, Italian, European Studies courses and bilingual secretarial courses.

MUSIC

● **Special subject requirements:** A-level music 'required' or 'preferred' in most cases. Very occasionally English language is required at GCSE (grade A–C).

• **Subject information:** Theory and practice are combined in most of these courses to a greater or lesser extent. The menu of options is varied - choose with care!

Anglia (Poly Univ) (*Music*) Subject areas in this course include practical and historical studies, electronic music and recording techniques, jazz, pop music and arts administration, business studies, history of art and Italian studies. This course is offered at Cambridge.

Bangor (*Music*) Music and two other subjects are taken in the first year of the BA course which emphasises history/analytical and musicology study. For the BMus course one other subject is taken in Part I. The Department of Music emphasises the integration of the three main specialisations - composition, performance and scholarship. The study of twentieth century music is strongly featured with options in recording techniques, music theory and jazz. Organ and choral entrance scholarships are offered.

Belfast (*Music*) The BMus course provides a thorough grounding in western music from medieval times to the present day. Also keyboard skills, conducting, history, compositional technique and styles. There is a flexible course structure in Years 2 and 3 which enables students to choose their own options in practical work, as well as jazz and electronic music. The BA course is taken with one or more other subjects.

Birmingham (*Music*) The course provides a wide general grounding and at the same time offers each student the opportunity to develop special interests. Keyboard skills are covered in the first and second year and there is also an introductory course on electro-acoustics and studio techniques. Special Honours students are required to take tuition as performers in two studies.

Bristol (*Music*) The two main aims of the course are to give a wide understanding of the European music tradition from medieval times to the present day and to enable students to develop their own individual interests in historical, creative and practical fields. The first two years of the course are mainly concerned with basic techniques and the third year focuses on history and the student's chosen specialism (history, composition, performance or early music). There is a new electronic studio for recording technique studies. There is also a Music and Language course with Year 3 spent abroad.

Cambridge (*Music*) Performance has a place in the course as one of several aspects of study in which music is covered in a very broad syllabus, giving weight to the appreciation and history of the subject as well as practical techniques.

Cardiff (*Music*) The Department of Music aims to provide a musical education which achieves an equal balance between theoretical and practical studies and the pursuit of vocal and instrument study. The BMus degree enables students to offer another subject, eg modern languages in Part I. The BA scheme includes Music and two other subjects in Year 1.

Central England (*Music*) The course is offered at the Birmingham School of Music. After a common first year, students select one of four specialist areas for detailed study: performance, composition, conducting, thesis/project.

City (*Music*) The course is concerned with music in today's technological society and is intended to bridge the gap between music as 'art' and music as 'science'. Topics include the psychology of music, an electro-acoustic studio project, Afro-American and popular music, music therapy, performance and sound recording. It is possible to take a four year sandwich course in this subject as well as a three year full-time course.

De Montfort (*Performing Arts*) The programme embraces contemporary dance, music or theatre as single Honours subjects separately or on a joint or combined Honours course.

Derby Music is offered as part of the Credit Accumulation Modular Scheme.

Durham (*Music*) The course aims to provide a wide and critical knowledge of music and to develop the basic skills. Provision is made for students to develop their own special interests, with flexibility in the third year for specialisation. Options include electro-acoustic compositions, cthno musicology and palacography.

East Anglia (*Music*) A central programme is followed involving the study of musical style, orchestration and development of aural skills. Later options are performance, composition, conducting, history and criticism of music. Practical sessions are common and students pursuing the performance option receive private tuition.

Edinburgh (*Music*) This is a three or four year Honours course. In each year the curriculum is broadly divided between composition, history and practical studies. Options are introduced in the third year and include electronic music.

Essex Music is offered as a joint course with eight other subjects.

Exeter (*Music*) The degree courses offered lead either to the BA or BMus degrees. (Music can also be taken with other subjects in Combined and Single Honours courses). All students register for the BA course and follow the same syllabus for the first two years. Those who wish to concentrate on composition, contemporary music and performance transfer to the BMus course in the final year.

Glasgow (*Music*) This BA degree is intended for those considering careers in teaching, and the option in Music Performance for those wishing to follow a course leading on to performance. Both are practically-based courses taught at the Royal Scottish Academy of Music and Drama. The BMus course at Ordinary (three year) or Honours (four year) levels includes performance on the piano, organ, any orchestral instrument or voice (every student must have the ability to play the piano), writing from dictation and harmony. All these areas are examined before entry. The first two years of the course cover harmony, counterpoint, history and practical skills, with specialist options being followed in the third and fourth years. It is also possible to study Music with other subjects in the Arts Faculty.

Hertfordshire Electronic Music is combined with over 20 subjects.

Huddersfield (*Music*) In Year 1 equal weight is given to performance, composition and the history of music. In Year 2 students choose two of these subjects as their major areas of study, with the third subject being their minor study. In Year 3, two subjects are chosen - a major and a minor. The course encourages increasing specialisation throughout its three years.

Hull (*Music*) The first year is devoted to an intensive basic course in harmony, counterpoint, history, set works, analysis and aural work and performance. In the second year students select their special option. In the final year there is a choice between church music, passion and oratorio, and the symphonic tradition. Instrumental tuition in one instrument is provided.

Keele A large number of Music and Electronic Music joint courses are offered.

Kingston (*Music*) Two alternative syllabuses are offered. One concentrates on performance, theory and musicianship, and complementary studies such as psychology, world music and music technology. The other is more concerned with music and technology, and covers electronic music, recording technology and business studies. (The Gateway School of Music Technology is based at Kingston with recording facilities on site.)

Lancaster (*Music*) BA and BMus courses are offered. Both courses enable students to develop their artistic and intellectual potential. In Part I (Year 1) there are two courses - practical and composition, and historical studies - plus one other subject. In Part II BA students take six units in music, two units in a minor subject and a free ninth unit course. BMus students take eight units of music and a free ninth course.

Leeds (*Music*) The course is designed with topics common to all students in the first year (analysis, aural training, counterpoint, harmony, and historical studies). From the second year, it is possible to concentrate increasingly on one of four main options - performance, notation, composition, or history and criticism. Throughout the course there is a balance between theoretical and practical, academic and vocational aspects of music, irrespective of the options taken.

Liverpool (*Music*) The three year course strikes a balance between academic and practical work. Musical history is central to many of the complementary studies in style, composition, analysis, orchestration and practical musicianship. During the first year of the single Honours course all students take an additional subject of their choice.

London (Goldsmiths') (*Music*) The course aims to develop music skills and associated areas of study. There is a strong emphasis on the study of contemporary music, electronic music and advanced musical analysis.

London (King's) (*Music*) Music can be studied as a single Honours course or in combination with Applied Computing or German (a four year course with a year spent abroad). The BMus course aims to provide students with a knowledge of the history and theory of music, composition and techniques of analysis. The department does not offer instrumental or singing instruction as this is usually done through the Guildhall School of Music and Drama.

London (RH) (*Music*) Music can be offered as a single or combined course. The course offers a detailed study of the historical, theoretical and practical aspects of music with a wide range of second and final year options including practical and performance work.

London (SOAS) (*Music*) The course focuses on Asian and African music. Students following music and another subject can take a non-music subject, eg Japanese.

Manchester (*Music*) The aim of the course is to give students a thorough grounding in the theoretical, practical and historical aspects of the subject.

Manchester Metropolitan Music is offered as part of the Combined Studies programme.

Middlesex (*Performance Arts*) Students on this degree course may choose to specialise in music, with tuition on two instruments (voice or synthesiser may be included).

Newcastle (*Music*) Practical tuition takes place throughout this course which also covers the history of music, compositional techniques, acoustics, electro-acoustic music, and in the first year a subsidiary subject.

Nottingham (*Music*) The course is wide-ranging and offers the chance to specialise at an early stage. In the first two years it is possible to take another subject with music. The course covers both practical and historical studies as well as offering options in such topics as the music of the Middle and Far East, electronic music and the music of the twentieth century.

Oxford (*Music*) The purpose of this course is not to offer professional training but to produce musicians who are proficient in the technique of the art and its history and criticism.

Oxford Brookes Music is offered with over 40 subjects.

Plymouth Music is offered as part of the General Primary Teaching courses.

Reading (*Music*) The finals examination of the single Honours course is divided into two parts. Part I in the second year provides the basis of an all-round music training. Part II at the end of the third year provides a flexible syllabus which enables students to specialise. Combined courses are also offered.

Sheffield (*Music*) The course is aimed at students who wish to develop practical as well as academic interests. One non-music subject is also studied in the first year. A wide range of options provides students with the chance to specialise.

Southampton (*Music*) History, analysis and composition are integrated throughout this course. The history of Western music is studied from the Middle Ages to the present day. In Years 2 and 3, students choose two historical periods for special emphasis, beginning work on composition and orchestration in Year 2 when a course in electronic music is also offered.

Strathclyde (*Applied Music Studies*) Entry is by competitive audition. There are three specialised routes - music teaching, community music and music and business.

Surrey (*Academic and Practical Applications of Music*) Course A is taken by students who have a particular interest in performance, conducting, composition or musicology. French and German may be studied but are not part of the degree programme. Course B (Music and Sound Recording) (Tonmeister) is followed by those whose main concern is with the theory and practice of recording and the reproduction of music (a year being spent in industrial training in a studio, with a manufacturer or broadcaster).

Sussex Music is offered with Media or Cultural and Community Studies or English and American Studies.

Ulster (*Music*) The course may also be combined with American Studies, English, History, Philosophy or Politics.

Warwick (*Music*) A comprehensive music degree with a range of options. The excellent facilities for the Arts and Music in particular enable students to take part in a variety of events.

Westminster (*Commercial Music*) A unique course combines the production of commercial music based on Rock and Pop with a strong grounding of business, law and cultural studies.

Wolverhampton (*Music*) The subject may be studied as a specialist award or as a joint, major or minor programme. Practical experience is offered over a range of instruments, singing and keyboard. Modules cover multi-track recording and computers, popular or non-European music.

York (*Music*) The course is designed to enable students to explore music from various aspects and is concentrated in a series of projects, in which students are able to work at their own pace. Projects cover history and musicological topics, written techniques, analysis and composition, solo and ensemble performance, electronic and computer music.

● **Top research universities**
Cambridge, London (King's), Nottingham, Birmingham, City, Exeter, Keele, Leeds, Liverpool, London (RH), Sheffield, Southampton, Sussex, York.

● **Colleges and Institutes of Higher Education offering degree courses**
Bangor Normal (Coll), Barnsley (Coll), Bath (Coll), Bishop Grosseteste (Coll), Bretton Hall, Brunel (Univ Coll), Canterbury Christ Church (Coll), Cardiff (Inst), Chichester (Inst), Colchester (Inst), Dartington (Coll), Edge Hill (Coll), King Alfred's (Coll), Leeds (Coll/Music), Liverpool (Inst), Nene (Coll), Northern (Coll), Ripon and York St John (Coll), Salford (Univ Coll), Scarborough (Univ Coll), S. Martin's (Coll), St Andrew's (Coll), Trinity Carmarthen (Coll), Westhill (Coll), Worcester (Coll).

● **Other courses to be considered**
Music combined courses, music technology, acoustics, electronic music, drama and theatre studies courses, anthropology courses, performance

studies, band musicianship, popular music and recording courses, and music and sound recording.

NURSING

- **Special subject requirements:** varies depending on the School of Nursing. 2–3 A-levels; chemistry and biology are important for some courses and five GCSE (grade A–C) subjects, including English, maths and a science, are often required for non-degree courses.

Abertay Dundee (*Nursing*) Academic and clinical studies leading to registration in adult or mental health nursing. Foreign languages are a feature of this course.

Anglia (Poly Univ) (*Nursing Studies*) The course is based at the Essex campus and covers biological sciences, arts and humanities subjects for all, followed by specialist studies in child, adult, mental health or mental handicap (learning difficulties) options.

Bangor (*Nursing*) The same course is followed by diploma and degree students the latter having extra assignments requiring higher marks. After a common foundation programme of 18 months, branch programmes are offered in adult, child, mental health and learning disability nursing.

Birmingham (*Nursing Studies*) Biological and medical sciences are studied in Years 1 and 2 along with clinical placements. More clinical placements and specialised studies continue in Years 3 and 4. Specialist studies in adult, child or mental health nursing commence in Year 2.

Bournemouth (*Clinical Nursing; Midwifery*) These are both three year courses including five clinical placements. Clinical Nursing students decide whether to seek registration in adult nursing or mental health nursing. There is a dual qualification in clinical nursing and midwifery.

Brighton (*European Nursing Studies*) A comparative study of nursing topics takes place throughout the course leading to registration in adult or mental health nursing. Practice placements take place in the UK, Holland or Spain.

Bristol UWE (*Nursing*) This four-year integrated sandwich course covers biological and social sciences including psychology and sociology with nursing and health education. Each year is structured around a central theme: (1) Health, Growth and Development, (2) Nursing Adults, (3) Special Nursing Care of Adults, and (4) Professional Responsibilities.

Brunel (*Sociology; Sociology and Psychology*) A special course in mental health nursing can be followed as part of these two courses. The course leads to State Registration. Work placements are arranged either at the Maudsley Hospital or the Bethlem Royal Hospital.

Central England (*Nursing*) There is an 18 month foundation course followed by a similar period of specialist studies in adult, mental health and mental handicap nursing.

Central Lancashire (*Midwifery*) The course leads to full registration and involves clinical placements covering 50 per cent of the course.

City (*Nursing and Human Sciences*) This is part of a modular scheme in Social Sciences which includes psychology, sociology and philosophy in which the selection of a major study can be deferred to the end of the first year. The total period of study involved is four years, four months.

De Montfort Three nursing courses are offered with specialisms in Adult, Child Health or Mental Nursing. A degree course in Midwifery is also offered.

Edinburgh (*Nursing*) This four year course enables graduates to qualify for registration as a general nurse or a mental health nurse. Clinical practice is integrated with theoretical teaching throughout the four years and the whole of the third year is spent in hospital training. Students are also introduced to the wider social, economic and organisational issues in health care. Supporting courses can be selected from a very wide range of subjects in the Faculties of Social Sciences, Arts and Science.

Glasgow (*Nursing*) In Year 1 the main subjects are human biology, clinical physics, psychology and nursing studies. Integration of academic and clinical studies continue in Years 2 and 3 with community health studies and human disease. During the fourth and final year of the course students work full-time in hospitals and in the community.

Glasgow Caledonian (*Nursing Studies*) This is a sandwich programme which leads to professional qualification as a registered nurse (adult or mental handicap) and graduate status.

Greenwich Several nursing courses are offered with specialisms in Midwifery, Adult, Child, Mental Health and Caring for the Elderly.

Hertfordshire (*Nursing*) The Project 2000 structure is offered with adult and mental health branches.

Hull (*Nursing Sciences; Nursing Studies*) The Nursing Sciences programme is a four year course of theoretical and practical work for those who wish to qualify as nurses. During the first year complementary studies include physiology, biochemistry and some psychology. The third year is spent mainly in nursing practice. The Nursing Studies course covers adult, mental health, children's nursing and includes care of the elderly.

Leeds Metropolitan (*Nursing*) This four year course provides a foundation in nursing, natural and social sciences in Year 1. In Years 2 and 3, students develop their technical skills, including nursing in all the main clinical areas. In Year 4, advanced nursing skills are acquired and a study is made of major health care topics.

Liverpool (*Nursing*) This is a four year course leading to the degree, B. Nursing, with opportunities to specialise in District Nursing, Health Visiting or Clinical Nursing research.

Liverpool John Moores (*Nursing*) Child, adult and mental health options are available plus French or German with possible European placements. (*Midwifery*) The course is divided between theory and practice and includes options in the management of a professional practice, law, ethics and a European language.

London (King's) (*Nursing Studies*) The course is based on three main areas of study - the biological, medical and social sciences. A substantial amount of practical work forms an integral part of the course (80 weeks in total) through St George's School of Nursing. Graduates qualify as Registered General Nurses at the end of the course. Courses are also available for qualified nurses in Midwifery and Community Nursing. There is also a course in Physiotherapy.

Luton (*Midwifery*) Obstetrics, midwifery, the midwife practitioner, women's health, ethics and law are all covered on this course. There is also a Registered Nursing course.

Manchester (*Nursing*) The course provides a balance between theory and practice and lead to registration. Specialisms include health visiting, district nursing, care of the elderly and the mentally ill. Courses are also offered in Speech Pathology and Physiotherapy.

Middlesex (*Nursing*) Special features include a degree in nursing with first level nurse registration, clinical nursing experience and modules from health studies.

Newcastle (*Midwifery*) This is a three year programme covering three main themes: foundation studies, development and consolidation.

Northumbria Nursing Studies is offered with a bias towards Mental Health or Adult Nursing. There is also a Midwifery Studies course leading to registration.

Nottingham (*Nursing*) Courses are offered in adult, mental health and children's nursing. The emphasis is on research, social policy and the history of nursing. Practice placements increase throughout the course (one day per week in Year 1 to four days per week in Year 2).

Oxford Brookes Nursing is offered with specialisms in Adult, Mental Health or Paediatric nursing and also in Learning Disabilities. There is also a Midwifery course.

Reading (*Community Health Studies*) This is a nursing course leading to professional qualifications with specialist options in Community Nursing, Learning Disability, Community Psychiatric Nursing, Health Visiting, General Practice, District, School and Community Children's nursing.

Robert Gordon (*Nursing*) This four year course is based on the Project 2000 format with a common foundation programme followed by specialist studies in adult or mental health nursing.

Sheffield Hallam Nursing Studies is offered with specialisms in Adult, Child or Mental Health Care.

Southampton (*Nursing*) Branches of Adult or Child nursing are offered. There is also a midwifery course.

South Bank (*Nursing*) Three courses are offered covering Adult Health, Mental Health and Child Care. A fourth course offers specialisms in learning difficulties and social work.

Sunderland (*Nursing*) This course requires students to be registered nurses.

Surrey (*Nursing Studies*) These courses lead to Child Nursing, Mental Health and the Registered General Nurse status. There is also a midwifery course.

Swansea (*Nursing*) Candidates applying in Wales are paid by a bursary from the Welsh Office. It is non-means tested. The course covers adult, children's and mental health nursing prior to which a common foundation course is offered.

Ulster (*Nursing*) Years 1 and 2 and the final year are suitable for students undertaking the general or psychiatric nursing qualification. Thirty six units are studied, with both theory and practical placements in every year of the course. Theoretical units cover biological sciences, behavioural sciences (psychology and sociology), research and nursing. A radiography course is also offered at Ulster in addition to courses in Occupational Therapy, Speech Therapy and Physiotherapy.

Wales (UWCM) (*Nursing*) The course covers adult, children's or mental health nursing (to be stipulated on the application form). Elective periods of studies take place abroad.

• **Top research universities**
London (King's), Manchester, Surrey.

• **Colleges and Institutes of Higher Education offering a degree course**
Avon and Gloucester (Coll of Health), Buckinghamshire (Coll), Croydon (Coll), Leeds (Coll of Health), North East Wales (Inst), Queen Margaret (Coll), S. Martin's (Coll), Suffolk (Coll), West York (Coll of Health).

• **Other courses to be considered**
Anatomy, biochemistry, biological sciences, biology and applied biology, environmental health, health and community studies, occupational therapy, physiotherapy, psychology, radiography, social administration and speech therapy.

PHARMACOLOGY (including **Toxicology**)

• **Special subject requirements:** 2–3 A-levels in mathematics/science subjects. Chemistry normally 'required' or 'preferred'. GCSE (grade A–C) in mathematics/science subjects.

• **Subject information:** This is the study of drugs and medicine in which courses focus on physiology, biochemistry, toxicology, immunology, microbiology and chemotherapy. Pharmacologists are not qualified to work as pharmacists.

Aberdeen (*Pharmacology*) There are no first or second level courses in Pharmacology. Level 3 comprises four units of study covering all aspects of the subject, and Level 4 enables the student to make a study in depth of selected aspects. Pharmacology is also offered with Toxicology or Immunology.

Bath (*Pharmacology*) This is a four year sandwich course (followed by the majority of students), the third year being spent on placement possibly in continental Europe or America. In the first year the core subjects are human and cell biology, physiology, pharmacology and pathology, chemistry and computing skills. The second year develops these subjects more fully, and in the final year pharmacology is studied throughout and is combined with a project. The final year includes clinical pharmacology, drug discovery and design.

Bradford (*Pharmacology*) This is part of the Biomedical Sciences degree course. A four year sandwich course.

Bristol (*Pharmacology*) Subjects covered include chemistry, anatomy and biochemistry. In the second year pharmacology is taken with anatomical science, biochemistry or physiology and one other course, and in the final year pharmacology is studied throughout the year. There is an emphasis on neuropharmacology with training in a wide variety of modern techniques.

Bristol UWE Pharmacology is offered with Applied Physiology.

Cambridge (*Natural Sciences*) Pharmacology is offered as part of the course in Natural Sciences. See **Chemistry**. It is accompanied by two related sciences in the second year.

Cardiff (*Pharmacology*) The first year deals with chemistry, biochemistry and physiology, pharmacology, and toxicology. In Part II practical experience is combined with theory in a number of specialised areas including an insight into the philosophical implications of drugs and society.

Dundee (*Pharmacology*) This degree begins in Year 2 after a first year in allied sciences such as Biology or Chemistry, and can be taken as a single Honours or joint with Anatomical Sciences, Biochemistry or Physiological Sciences. During the third year, two courses are taken - pharmacology of systems and pharmacology of drug action. The rapidly developing area of neurosciences features strongly in Year 4.

East London (*Pharmacology*) The first year of this four year sandwich course is taken in common with Applied Biology, Medical Biotechnology, Microbiology and Plant Biotechnology and transfers are possible. Second year students take pharmacology, human physiology and biochemistry. The third year is spent in industrial training. Fourth year students take pharmacology and toxicology and undertake a research project.

Edinburgh (*Pharmacology*) Biology and physiology are taken by all students specialising in Pharmacology. Pharmacology and three other subjects are taken in Year 3 and pharmacology throughout in Year 4.

Glasgow (*Pharmacology*) Students enter the Honours course after studying chemistry and related subjects for the first two years.

Hertfordshire Pharmacology is offered as part of the course in Applied Biology.

Leeds (*Pharmacology*) This is a broad scientific course as opposed to an applied study. Pharmacology is taken with physiology and biochemistry in the first year. This is common to all students, who can delay their choice between single or combined courses until the end of Year 1. There are also two Combined Honours Pharmacology degree courses offered with Biochemistry and Physiology.

Liverpool (*Pharmacology*) This subject is studied as part of the Life Sciences scheme. A basic core of units is studied followed by a choice of other units to suit the student's interests. At Liverpool the emphasis is given to the physiological, biochemical, toxicology and clinical aspects of pharmacology.

London (King's) (*Pharmacology*) A single Honours degree is offered and also joint degrees with Biochemistry, Physiology and Toxicology. In the first two years the focus is on physiology, biochemistry and pharmacology. In the third year specialist topics include toxicology, immunology and environmental pharmacology.

London (School of Pharmacy) (*Toxicology and Pharmacology*) This is a four year course with the third year spent in an industrial, research or hospital placement. Both subjects are linked in each year of the course. Year 1 also includes chemistry, biochemistry, histology and statistics. Year 2 covers microbiology and chemotherapy and final year students concentrate on the two main degree subjects.

London (UC) (*Pharmacology*) Pharmacology is the study of how drugs work. Students take physiology, chemistry, cellular and molecular biology, and pharmacology in their first year. Physiology and biochemistry make up part of the second year, with more pharmacology. A range of advanced courses in the final year allows students to concentrate on particular aspects of the subject and undertake a research project.

Manchester (*Pharmacology*) This is a broad course with a range of options including an optional year in industry. It is also possible to take Pharmacology with a modern language. As with all other pharmacology courses students should be aware that they cannot practise as pharmacists on graduation.

Portsmouth (*Pharmacology*) The course has a common first year with Biomedical Science. This is a three year full-time course and includes a study of physiology, biochemistry and chemistry to support studies in pharmacology. Overall the course has a biochemical emphasis towards modern pharmacology. Emphasis is on pharmacology in all three years.

Sheffield (*Pharmacology*) The subject is studied in a joint department with medicine and located in the Royal Hallamshire Hospital. Thus the student is able to relate the scientific and clinical aspects of the subject.

Southampton (*Pharmacology*) The subject is offered with Physiology.

St Andrews Pharmacology is offered with Chemistry.

Strathclyde Pharmacology is offered with Biochemistry or Immunology.

Sunderland (*Pharmacology*) Physiology and chemistry are taken in the first year with biochemistry and pharmacology, followed by advanced studies in biochemistry and pharmacology in the second and third years. Final year modules include drug development, mammalian toxicology, psycho-pharmacology and immunohaematology.

• Top research universities
Liverpool, London (UC), Oxford, Birmingham, Bristol, Cambridge, Nottingham, Dundee, Edinburgh, Strathclyde.

• **Colleges and Institutes of Higher Education offering degree courses**
NESCOT.

• **Other courses to be considered**
Agricultural sciences, biochemistry, biological sciences, chemistry, dietetics, food science and pharmacy.

PHARMACY

• **Special subject requirements:** 2–3 A-levels in science/mathematics subjects. Chemistry always required. GCSE (grade A–C) mathematics, physics and biology usually required.

• **Subject information:** All courses are very similar and lead to qualification as a pharmacist who may then work in hospitals or private practice. Alternative courses include Biochemistry, Biological Sciences, Chemistry or Pharmacology.

Aston (*Pharmacy*) This is a three year full-time or four year sandwich course which covers the basic sciences including maths and computing in Year 1. In Year 2, pharmacology occupies one-third of the total time along with pharmaceutical and medicinal chemistry. There is continuous assessment in the second year with an emphasis on communication skills. In Year 3, a core course includes chemotherapy, disease mechanisms, toxicology and professional practice. A large proportion of the student's time is occupied in studying areas of his/her own choice. Introductory courses are available for students without A-levels in biology and mathematics.

Bath (*Pharmacy*) This is a three year full-time course introduced by basic studies in biology, human biology, pharmaceutical chemistry and physical pharmacy. Pharmacy practice begins in the second year along with pharmaceutical biology, chemotherapy and pharmacology. Options are offered in the third year in pharmaceutics and chemotherapy.

Belfast (*Pharmacy*) In the first year students are introduced to physical pharmacy, dispensing and aspects of microbiology. These lead on to a study of the traditional subjects (pharmaceutics, pharmacology and pharmaceutical chemistry). Topics are included which reflect the pharmacist's wider role as a member of the health care team and involve visits to hospitals and health centres.

Bradford (*Pharmacy*) This course in Pharmacy offers two six-month practical training periods in two different areas of practice as part of this four year sandwich course. This counts as one of the two years required for registration as a qualified pharmacist.

Brighton (*Pharmacy*) In Years 1 and 2 subjects studied include microbiology, clinical pharmacology, legislation, marketing management, computing and statistics. In Year 3, core subjects involve chemotherapy, pharmaceutics and an opportunity is provided to gain work experience in hospital and in community pharmacy.

Cardiff (*Pharmacy*) The Welsh School of Pharmacy is divided into four main divisions: pharmaceutical chemistry and pharmacognosy (natural products, synthetic drugs and their effects on living tissues); pharmaceutics (design, production and control of all medical preparations); and clinical pharmacy (the law and practice of pharmacy). All subjects are covered in each year of the course.

De Montfort (*Pharmacy*) General pharmaceutical science subjects are taken in Years 1 and 2. In Year 3 a number of elective topics are offered combined with pharmaceutics, pharmacy and clinical studies.

Greenwich (*Pharmaceutical Science*) The first year lays a foundation in chemistry, biology, physiology, product formulation and process technology, with mathematics and computing. Further studies include microorganisms, drug testing, pharmacokinetics and quality assurance.

Liverpool John Moores (*Pharmacy*) This accredited four year course includes study of the scientific basis of therapeutics, dosage form design, medicinal chemistry and quality control, pharmacy practice, and clinical and experimental pharmacology. Courses in Biomedical Sciences and Pharmaceutical and Chemical Science are also offered.

London (King's) (*Pharmacy*) This is a three year full-time course covering physiology, pharmaceutical chemistry, pharmacology and the law and practice of pharmacy in Years 1 and 2. In the third year options include the chemical aspects of drug action, product evaluation and clinical pharmacy.

London (School of Pharmacy) (*Pharmacy*) Pharmaceutical chemistry, pharmaceutics and pharmacology are studied in Year 1, all these subjects being developed in Year 2 with microbiology and chemotherapy. In Year 3 students take courses in drug design and testing, and clinical pharmacy, and visit hospitals; they also specialise in one elective subject.

Manchester (*Pharmacy*) This is a standard pharmacy course leading to full qualification of the MPS to work as community hospital or industrial pharmacists.

Nottingham (*Pharmacy*) The main subjects taught are pharmaceutics, pharmaceutical chemistry and pharmacology. The BPharm Part I examination is held at the end of the second year and the Honours degree at the end of the third year. In each of the two summer vacations students are encouraged to take posts in some branch of pharmacy, the department assisting students to find suitable posts. The course is biased towards careers in industry, hospital pharmacy and research.

Portsmouth (*Pharmacy*) The first year foundation courses cover pharmaceutical chemistry, physiology and biochemistry with more advanced and professional studies following in Years 2 and 3. Elective subjects are available in Year 3.

Robert Gordon (*Pharmacy*) The course develops the scientific basis of pharmacy through the study of pharmaceutics, pharmacology and pharmaceutical chemistry, and develops the application of this knowledge to practical situations and the communication skills necessary to perform competently as part of the health care team in the clinical situation.

Strathclyde (*Pharmacy*) The degree is offered by the departments of Pharmacy, Physiology and Pharmacology. In Year 1 students take chemistry, bioscience, mathematics and a foundation course in pharmacy.

In Years 2, 3 and 4 the major subjects are studied - pharmaceutical chemistry, pharmaceutics and physiology and pharmacology. The final year is largely concerned with the use and action of drugs in humans (clinical pharmacology).

Sunderland (*Pharmacy*) An overall knowledge of the action and uses of drugs is achieved by a study of pharmaceutical chemistry, pharmaceutics and associated subjects. These studies are combined with ancillary computer appreciation, maths and statistics. Specialist options include drug information handling, clinical pharmacy and toxicology.

● **Top research universities**
Bath, London (Sch. of Pharmacy), Nottingham, Aston, London (King's), Manchester, Cardiff.

● **Other courses to be considered**
Biochemistry, biological sciences, chemistry and pharmacology.

PHILOSOPHY

● **Special subject requirements:** GCSE (grade A–C) mathematics, and a language in some cases.

● **Subject information:** Contemporary philosophy covers political, educational, psychological, aesthetic and religious issues. Some reading of the works of the leading philosophers is recommended prior to applying for the courses.

Aberdeen (*Philosophy*) The course covers general and moral philosophy and the philosophy of social science. The single Honours course in Mental Philosophy provides a grounding in the history of the subject and an understanding of its contemporary development. Joint courses are offered with 14 options.

Anglia (Poly Univ) (*European Philosophy and Literature*) This is a three year or four year (with languages) course combining philosophy and literature. It can also be pursued as a Combined Honours course. The course is based on the Essex campus.

Belfast (*Philosophy*) This subject can be studied as a single Honours course or in conjunction with other subjects. In both cases a study is made of the works of leading philosophers over the last 2500 years, on debates relating to truth, proof, meaning and value. Each Honours student works with a personal supervisor on a one-to-one basis.

Birmingham (*Philosophy*) Central areas of philosophy including ethics, logic, political philosophy and the philosophy of the mind are studied in the first year. These courses provide a basis for later and more advanced studies in Kant's philosophy, analytical philosophy and ethics. Optional courses are also available in the second and third years covering such topics as Plato's philosophy and the nature of human emotion.

Bradford (*Philosophy*) The course is studied in conjunction with psychology, sociology and literature.

Brighton Philosophy is offered as part of the Humanities programme.

Bristol (*Philosophy*) The course aims to present a thorough understanding of contemporary philosophical issues (political, psychological, linguistic and aesthetic) and provides a grounding of the subject covering philosophy in antiquity and from the seventeenth century onwards. Course choices and specialised topics give students considerable freedom to select those areas of philosophy which are of particular interest to them. A range of complementary subjects is offered including languages in addition to several joint courses.

Cambridge (*Philosophy*) The Tripos is divided into three parts, each taking one year. In the first year a study is made of logic, ethics and metaphysics, followed in the second year by the philosophy of the mind, science, aesthetics, politics and empirical psychology (which includes some lab work). A range of options in Part II (third year) allows for a closer study of topics studied in the first two years.

Cardiff (*Philosophy*) No previous knowledge of philosophy is required by the student who is introduced to the practical relevance of political and moral philosophy and the theory of knowledge in Part I. In Part II the main branches of philosophy are covered with a wide range of courses available. Joint courses are also offered in Social Philosophy and Applied Ethics.

Central Lancashire Philosophy is offered as part of the Combined Honours programme.

Dundee (*Philosophy*) This is taken as part of the Arts and Social Sciences programme. Students can take a self-contained general course which provides a broadly based introduction to the subject, before majoring in another area. Single Honours students take the intermediate, advanced courses and senior Honours courses, the latter including several optional topics including the philosophy of religion (Christianity or Indian), aesthetics and the philosophy of science.

Durham (*Philosophy*) The subject can be studied as a single Honours course, a joint course or with two other subjects in Combined Honours. All students take a common first year course. The second and third years of the Honours course cover ancient and modern philosophy, metaphysics and logic. In addition students can also take specialised subjects - aesthetics, political and religious philosophy and Indian philosophy.

East Anglia (*Philosophy*) A wide range of programmes can be taken on this modular course, eg with Social Sciences, European Languages or with Politics and Economics.

Edinburgh (*Mental Philosophy*) A first year course in philosophy is taken by all students, with options in aesthetics and general philosophy, the history, logic and philosophy of science, metaphysics and moral philosophy. This continues in the second year, whilst in Years 3 and 4 philosophy may be studied either on its own (MA Mental Philosophy) or combined with another subject.

Essex (*Philosophy*) In the School of Comparative Studies the first year will include a study of both philosophy and the Enlightenment. In the second year there is a general philosophy course, two philosophy options, an outside option (or a further philosophy option) and a special subject. In the third year philosophy is taken with three further options. Philosophy is also offered in the School of Social Sciences.

Glamorgan Philosophy is offered as part of the Humanities course.

Glasgow (*Philosophy*) The subject is studied within the Social Science programme and includes general and moral philosophy and the work of the leading philosophers. A very large number of joint courses are also offered.

Greenwich Philosophical Studies is offered as part of the Humanities programme.

Hertfordshire (*Philosophy*) The subject can be taken as a minor subject in the Combined Studies programme and also as major or single Honours courses in the Humanities modular scheme.

Hull (*Philosophy*) The first two terms are devoted to an introduction to the subject - its history, methods and problems. Over the next six terms courses are taken in epistemology (theory of knowledge), moral philosophy and metaphysics. Students then choose courses to develop their own interest. Small group tutorial teaching. A range of complementary subjects can be taken including law, psychology and languages.

Keele A very large number of joint courses are offered. The course aims to develop the students analytical and critical abilities. Final year options include the philosophies of Mind, Religion and Politics.

Kent (*Philosophy*) After an introduction to the subject in Part I, core courses in Part II cover moral philosophy, theory of knowledge, logic and social philosophy, aesthetics and ancient philosophy. Options courses are also offered as specialised studies in the second and third years.

Kingston Joint courses are offered with the History of Ideas.

Lampeter (*Philosophical Studies*) Western philosophy is studied with options which include mathematical logic and foundations of mathematics. Courses are also offered in Religion, Ethics and Western Society.

Lancaster (*Philosophy*) Two philosophy options (from a choice of four) are taken in the first year. These include logic and metaphysics, the history of philosophy, philosophy, politics and society. Two other subjects are also taken in the first year. In Years 2 and 3, six philosophy courses are taken, three in each year plus two other courses in another subject (one in each year).

Leeds (*Philosophy*) In Year 1, two philosophy courses are taken (introduction to philosophy and reason and argument) plus two other subjects. In Years 2 and 3, courses include the history of ancient, medieval and modern philosophy, ethics and social philosophy and logic. Philosophy can be combined with 20 other subjects. Second year logic is taught with the assistance of computers.

Liverpool (*Philosophy*) Ethics, epistemology and logic plus another subject offered by the Faculty of Arts or other faculties are taken in the first year. The non-philosophy subject can be continued in the second year along with further compulsory philosophy courses. In the third year students choose topics of special interest to them taken from a wide range of options. Joint courses in philosophy are also available.

Liverpool John Moores Philosophy is offered as a joint course.

London (Heythrop) (*Philosophy*) Students follow courses in logic, epistemology, metaphysics, ethics and the history of philosophy, as well as two courses from a wide range of options, and produce a dissertation on a special topic. Philosophy may be combined with Theology.

London (King's) (*Philosophy*) Five compulsory subjects are taken through the course - logic and methodology, Greek philosophy, modern (seventeenth/eighteenth century) philosophy, ethics or political philosophy, epistemology and metaphysics. Students also choose two options from a wide range including aesthetics, religion, language, science and the philosophy of the mind as well as a study of the great philosophers.

London (LSE) (*Philosophy*) Philosophy is studied as the theory of knowledge especially scientific knowledge. Special attention is also given to philosophical problems arising within the social sciences (anthropology, economics, history, linguistics, politics, psychology and sociology).

London (UC) (*Philosophy*) First year students attend introductory courses in logic and methodology, epistemology and metaphysics, Greek philosophy, modern philosophy, and ethics or political philosophy. These studies continue in the second and third years with a wide range of subject options. Philosophy can also be taken as a joint subject with Economics, Greek, History of Art or Linguistics.

Manchester (*Philosophy*) This is a broad course covering the main subject topics. Joint courses in several subjects are offered.

Manchester Metropolitan Philosophy is offered as part of the Combined and Humanities programmes.

Middlesex Philosophy can be taken in the Multidisciplinary programme. There is also a course in the History of Ideas. This is an interdisciplinary course covering periods and movements in intellectual history, literature and society in European cultural history, and history of sciences.

North London (*Philosophy*) A wide coverage of topics with level 2 and 3 units covering the philosophies of language, science and technology, artificial intelligence and virtual reality, parapsychology, psychoanalysis, war, law, ethics, art and gender.

Nottingham (*Philosophy*) The first two years cover the problems, theories and arguments concerning appearance and reality - the limits of knowledge, truth, thought perception and sensation, mind and body, personal identity and the existence of God, space and time. Subsidiary subjects can also be taken from other departments and optional choices form the major part of the third year.

Oxford Philosophy is offered as part of several joint courses.

Reading (*Philosophy*) A small department in which courses are taken in logic and theory of knowledge and moral philosophy - subject-centred rather than author-centred. Thereafter, other courses follow covering a range of specialisations.

Sheffield (*Philosophy*) Year 1 is organised round six basic topics: ethics, knowledge, religious belief, free will and determination, liberty and logic. From Year 2 onwards Philosophy can be studied as a single Honours subject or in combination with one of nine other subjects by way of a dual Honours course. A generous system of option courses provides a wide choice of specialist subjects in Years 2 and 3.

Southampton (*Philosophy*) Single and combined Honours courses are offered, the latter available with Economics, English, Politics, French, German, Mathematics or Sociology. The course is planned (like most other courses in this subject) on the assumption that entrants know little about the subject. In Year 1 a study is made of historical and contemporary philosophers, which leads on in Years 2 and 3 to optional subjects taken from 14 options.

St Andrews (*Philosophy*) This is one of the very large number of courses offered in the Faculty of Arts. Several degree courses are offered with philosophy as both single and joint Honours.

Staffordshire Joint courses are offered with philosophy.

Stirling (*Philosophy*) This may be taken as a minor, subsidiary or major subject in Part I with semesters in introduction to philosophy, the justification of behaviour, and the scope and limits of knowledge. Part II involves logic and language, problems from Wittgenstein and a choice from a wide range of options. Combined Studies courses are also offered with 12 subject choices.

Sunderland Philosophy is offered with over 15 other subjects.

Sussex Philosophy is offered in conjunction with various Schools of Studies.

Swansea (*Philosophy*) Part I courses are offered in the Faculties of Arts, Science and Economic and Social Studies. In each Faculty introductory courses vary slightly (eg philosophy and literature or science and society or philosophy of the social sciences). Compulsory and optional papers follow in Years 2 and 3.

Ulster (*Philosophy*) This may be taken as a single Honours subject or combined as a major, joint or minor subject with over 12 subjects. In combined courses it is possible to take a course which is approached either thematically or historically.

Warwick (*Philosophy*) This can be offered as a single Honours or joint course with Education, Literature, Politics, Psychology, Mathematics, Computer Science or Classical Civilisation. In Year 1, students wishing to broaden the scope of their degree can take courses in other subjects, eg economics, film studies, French studies, history, history of art, mathematics, politics.

Wolverhampton (*Philosophy*) The course covers ethics, philosophy of science, political philosophy and the philosophy of the mind. Religion, feminism, ecology and history also feature.

York (*Philosophy*) A range of integrated courses is offered by the Philosophy department. In addition to the single Honours course, combined courses are also available. Advanced options are also offered in certain specialised areas (classical philosophy, modern European philosophy, political philosophy, the philosophy of science and the philosophy of religion). A Politics, Philosophy and Economics course is also offered.

- **Top research universities**
Cambridge, London (King's) (LSE), Birmingham, Bradford, Durham, Essex, Liverpool, London (UC), Sheffield, Sussex, Warwick, Edinburgh, St Andrews, Stirling.

- **Colleges and Institutes of Higher Education offering degree courses**
Bolton (Inst), King Alfred's (Coll), Ripon and York St John (Univ Coll), S. Martin's (Coll).

- **Other courses to be considered**
Religious studies, social sciences and psychology.

PHYSICS (including **Applied Physics**)

- **Special subject requirements:** 2–3 A-levels in mathematics/physics subjects.

- **Subject information:** There is a considerable shortage of applicants for this subject. Many courses have flexible arrangements to enable students to follow their own interests and specialisations, eg circuit design, microwave devices, cosmology, medical physics, solid state electronics. Possible alternative routes include Astronomy, Astrophysics, Computing, Engineering, Geophysics.

Aberdeen (*Physics*) In level 1 there are two courses, one in physics and one in mathematical physics. Courses continue through levels 2 and 3 giving flexibility in the choice of course and leading on to specialisms in level 4 including industrial physics.

Abertay Dundee Applied Physics is offered with Chemistry, Computing or Mathematics.

Aberystwyth (*Physics*) Honours courses are offered in Physics and physics-based courses with specialisation in other areas, eg Planetary and Space Physics, Atmospheric Physics, and Business Administration. Five joint courses are also offered with Physics.

Bath (*Physics*) This is a three year full-time or four year enhanced sandwich course, the latter having a placement year in industry in the third year, possibly in Geneva, Munich or Stuttgart. (Students wishing to take the Certificate of Education course spend only six months in industry.) The final year of the Physics degree course allows for a choice of specialisms between geophysics, microelectronics, computing or applied physics. Three year and four year full-time BSc and M Phys courses are also offered.

Belfast (*Physics*) Courses in Physics and Applied Physics are offered. Physics can also be offered with Geology providing for a study of geophysics, and with Maths and Computer Science. All students take a common course in level 1 after which they can choose which Physics degree course they wish to follow or proceed to a degree in another science subject.

Birmingham (*Physics*) This course emphasises mathematical concepts and the use of computers. The first year course covers basic physics and maths, after which a study of the major areas of physics continues with a wide choice of options allowing considerable flexibility for students to build their own course. Personal tutorials and small group teaching takes place throughout the three years of the course. Physics can also be taken with Astrophysics.

Brighton Physics is offered as a joint course with seven other subjects.

Bristol (*Physics*) This is a mathematically-oriented course with core subjects being taken in the first and second years. In the third year students choose from a wide range of options. The Physics first year is so arranged that by a suitable choice of first year subjects, students can transfer into or out of one of these other Honours courses. Languages are offered as an additional feature of the course and several complementary subjects can be taken including geography, psychology or philosophy.

Brunel (*Physics*) Students can choose from a flexible programme of three and four year Honours degrees in Physics, Physics with Computer Science, Physics with Management Studies and Physics with Advanced Instrumentation. The four year courses include periods of training in industry or research establishments, leading to the award of an additional Diploma. A foundation course is available for those without the BSc entry requirements. The MPhys course includes a semester-long project, usually in a national research laboratory, and a chance to specialise in one of five different research areas in the final year.

Cambridge (*Natural Sciences*) Physics is offered as part of the course in Natural Sciences. (See **Chemistry**). Mathematics is also an important component of physics in the first and second years.

Cardiff (*Physics*) First year studies include physics and another science subject (astrophysics, chemistry, computing, geology or mathematics). In Years 2 and 3 the course is physics-based with the option to specialise in solid state electronics. Courses in Medical Physics and Astrophysics are also offered.

Central Lancashire (*Physics/Applied Physics*) The first year provides a firm foundation in applied physics, mathematics, laboratory and IT skills. At the end of the year students choose from applied physics, physics/ astronomy or physics, or combine applied physics with another subject on a Combined Honours programme. In both the four year MPhys and three year BSc, students can spend part of their final year studying in Europe.

Coventry (*Applied Physics*) This is integrated into the modular degree courses in Sciences. Maths and physics are core courses in the first year with a choice from several other subjects including economics, biology, French and German. Year 2 involves atomic and nuclear physics, electronics, optics and acoustics which lead on to other applications of physics in Year 4. Year 3 is spent in industry. A wide choice of modules is offered in the final year.

Cranfield Applied Physics is offered with Mathematics or Materials Science.

De Montfort Physics is offered as part of the Combined Studies course and with Business Studies.

Dundee (*Physics*) Courses at various levels are offered, the single Honours student selecting a number of topics to be studied in the final year with a bias towards theoretical or applied physics. Students may change to other courses, eg Natural Science or Applied Physics, with options in electronics and materials at the end of the first year.

Durham (*Physics*) The course is designed to prepare people in the understanding and use of knowledge and techniques in any branch of physics. With mathematics being extensively used, expertise in that subject is also obtained. This training is wide enough to find application in many fields outside scientific research and development. In the first year the subjects studied include relativity and atomic physics, wave motion, solid state physics, electricity and magnetism. Second and third year courses develop these topics and allow for specialisation, including astrophysics and planetary physics, modern optics and nuclear physics. A change to other Physics courses is possible at the end of Year 1. A course in Applied Physics is also offered at Durham.

East Anglia A wide range of courses is offered with additional study in USA or Europe, as an interdisciplinary subject or as Chemical Physics.

Edinburgh (*Physics*) The Department of Physics offers two Honours courses. Physics students take the subject in each of the four years with options in nuclear physics, optical imaging, electronics and computing and meteorology. The second course in Mathematical Physics is aimed at students whose interests lie in the more theoretical aspects of the subject. There are also courses in Chemical Physics, Computational Physics and Astrophysics.

Essex (*Physics*) Four courses are offered: Physics, Applied Physics, Physics with Laser Technology or Theoretical Physics. All first year schemes follow a similar path, with students choosing the option between Theoretical Physics and the other three courses. The choice between the first three schemes above may be deferred until the end of the second year. There is also a four year course in Technological Physics with Business Studies, including language options.

Exeter (*Physics*) Three year and four year single Honours degrees are offered in Physics, Physics with Medical Applications, Physics with Optoelectronics and Theoretical Physics. The first year is common to all four courses, enabling students to transfer between courses up to the beginning of the second year.

Glasgow (*Physics*) Physics can be taken by students aiming for an Honours degree (Option A) and for those wishing to pursue the subject as a general study but aiming for another degree (Option B). The Honours course covers all the main branches of classical and modern physics including electronics and lasers. A wide range of options is available in the final year. Courses are also available in Chemical Physics and Physics and Astronomy.

Glasgow Caledonian Applied Physics is offered with Instrumentation or Information Technology and Electronics. The programmes aim to provide students with skills to solve a wide range of industrial and environmental measurement problems.

Greenwich Physics is offered as a joint subject with Computing or Electronics.

Heriot-Watt (*Physics*) In the first year, physics is taken with mathematics, chemistry or computer science or applied mathematics. In the second year physics and mathematics are studied with an additional subject which can include computer science, accountancy and finance, French, geography, philosophy, economics or industrial organisation. An additional subject can also be taken as an alternative to mathematics in the third year. The final year of the course involves a physics research project and a choice from experimental physics, theoretical physics and solid state electronics.

Hertfordshire (*Applied Physics*) Year 1 covers mathematics, computing and other subjects followed later with options in health physics, electronics and acoustics. Astronomy is also offered as a joint course.

Hull (*Applied Physics*) The Applied Physics courses (which include electronics and laser technology) combine a thorough training in the basic concepts of physics and the application of these to established and new areas in technology, engineering and science. A broad range of special options is available in the final year including magnetism and its application, superconductivity, laser and semiconductor technology. There is also a degree course in Physics with Medical Technology or Optoelectronics.

Keele Physics and Astrophysics are offered with a very large number of subjects.

Kent (*Physics*) The Physics course allows considerable flexibility and enables students to defer their choice between Physics and other degree programmes in the Faculty until the end of the first year. Physics can also be studied with Theoretical Physics, Astrophysics and with a year in Europe. There is also a degree course in Chemical Physics.

Kingston Several subjects are offered with Applied Physics.

Lancaster (*Physics*) The chosen degree programme in Physics will determine the first year courses to be followed. All students take a physics course and one in mathematics or physical systems. The third course is taken in another subject (those taking combined degrees must take a relevant subject). In the second and third years, subjects include electronics, wave and optical applications, nuclear and atomic physics. In Year 3 students also choose four options which can include circuit design, microwave devices, cosmology, medical physics and the physics of stars.

Leeds (*Physics*) Mathematics is taken in the first two years of the course. At the end of the first year there is the opportunity to transfer between Physics courses (Physics, Physics/Astrophysics). Core subjects include atomic and quantum physics, nuclear physics, thermodynamics and electronics. Optional subjects include low temperature, polymer and theoretical physics, astrophysics, geophysics and computing.

Leicester (*Physics*) These courses are offered: Physics, Physics with Astrophysics, Physics with Space Science and Technology. Specific core subjects are studied in all three degrees, supplemented by a wide range of optional courses.

Liverpool (*Physics*) Several Physics courses are offered in addition to the single Honours programme. These include Mathematical Physics and Radiation Physics. Students opting for Physics and Mathematics can study these subjects equally or defer a choice between the two until the end of the first or second year. There are degree courses in Physics for New Technology, Geophysics (with either a mathematics or physics bias) and Chemical Physics.

Liverpool John Moores (*Applied Physics*) After core modules in physics, mathematics, laboratory work and computing, students on this three or four year course can choose from a range of options including applied physics, modern optics, spectroscopy, acoustics and nuclear physics. There are also courses in Astrophysics and Biophysics.

London (Imp) (*Physics*) The department offers: three year BSc courses in Physics and Physics with Theoretical Physics; and four year BSc amd MSci courses in Physics, and Physics with a Year in Europe or with Studies in Musical Performance.

London (King's) (*Physics*) The course provides a thorough grounding in the concepts and techniques of physics and the essential elements of mathematics and computing. The course unit structure provides for a wide choice in the second and third years. Various joint Honours combinations are also available.

London (QMW) (*Physics*) Core courses, the flexibility of the course-unit system and the wide range of options in the final year allows for students to change their choice of course as their interests develop. In addition to Physics and Astrophysics courses there are also six joint courses.

London (RH) (*Physics*) All courses have a common first year and provide a wide range of classes from applied physics and theoretical physics topics. Further options are courses in astrophysics, microcomputer electronics, management studies or music, and a possible third year out in an industrial or government laboratory preceding a final fourth year.

London (UC) (*Physics*) Study is based on the course unit system in which students can select units appropriate to their interests. Courses offered include: Physics, Applied Physics, Astrophysics and Medical Physics.

Loughborough (*Physics*) Three and four year courses are offered, the latter being either a sandwich course with industrial training or an MPhys. Breadth of studies continues through to the final year, and there are optional courses in French or German in Years 1 and 2. Industrial placements abroad are a feature of the course. Three and four year courses are also available in Engineering Physics, Electronic Engineering and Physics, and Physics with Mathematics, Sports Science or Physical Education.

Manchester (*Physics*) There are six Physics courses including Physics with Astrophysics with a wide range of options.

Manchester Metropolitan (*Engineering Physics*) This course aims to develop knowledge and skills for todays industrial and commercial environment. It is a sandwich degree, with laboratory-based work in experimental physics and in instrumentation in all years. Applied Physics is also offered.

Manchester (UMIST) (*Physics*) After a common first year course developing theoretical and experimental skills, students choose between Physics with Astrophysics, Environmental Science, Computation, Electronics, Optoelectronics or Mathematical Physics. A major research project in Year 3 leads to further specialisation in Year 4. All courses are available as four year MPhys and most can be taken with French or German involving a period abroad.

Napier (*Applied Physics with Computing; Environmental Physical Science*) After common study for two years, these courses offer specialisms in signal processing techniques, instrumentation and microcomputer systems, or in environmental problem-solving, evaluation and management.

Newcastle (*Physics; Theoretical Physics*) Three year BSc degrees and four year MPhys degrees are offered in Astronomy and Astrophysics, Physics with Medical Applications, Theoretical Physics and Physics. A foundation year is available for those without appropriate qualifications.

North London (*Physics*) The course is part of the university's modular degree scheme giving flexibility in the choice of units particularly in Years 2 and 3. There is a modern language option.

Northumbria (*Applied Physics*) This three year full-time or four year sandwich course includes a European option in which students spend one year abroad.

Nottingham (*Physics*) This is a long established modular scheme. All single and joint Honours students take physics, maths and a third subject. This allows for flexibility for transfers between single and joint courses at the end of the first year. Most single Honours students take electronics as their third subject (other subjects are chemistry, computer science, materials science, philosophy, psychology and music). Other courses offered include Physics and Applied Physics with Electronics, Physics with a European Language and Physics with Medical Applications.

Nottingham Trent (*Applied Physics*) This is a BSc and M Phys course in which Years 1 and 2 are common whilst the third year has an industrial flavour. Possible project work in France and Germany.

Oxford (*Physics*) The first year is equally divided between maths and physics, with an introductory course in computing. It is now also possible to study related subjects such as astronomy, biophysical chemistry or earth sciences. The second year covers all the main areas of modern physics. In the final year there is a choice of two from: (1) statistical mechanics and solid state physics (2) atomic physics (3) nuclear physics (4) modern optics and laser physics (5) electronics (6) physics of the atmosphere, ocean and earth (7) astrophysics (8) mathematical physics.

Paisley (*Physics*) This is part of the science and technology degree scheme offering students maximum flexibility. Applied Physics is also offered with either language or management.

Portsmouth (*Applied Physics*) This is a four year enhanced MPhys sandwich course in which Years 1, 2 and 4 are spent in the university and Year 3 in a research establishment or in industry. Specialised options include nuclear instrumentation, microwaves and solid state electronics and communications. Physics is also offered as a three year BSc or four year MPhys.

Reading (*Physics*) Three subjects are taken in the first two terms by students intending to take Physics or Physics and Electronics or combined subject courses with Physics. The single subject course provides flexibility in the final year options which can provide considerable experience in applied physics.

Robert Gordon (*Applied Physics*) The course covers physics principles underlying new subject areas and modern applications such as space physics, semi-conductor developments and medical physics.

Salford (*Physics*) The first year covers subjects ranging from electricity and magnetism to atomic and nuclear physics. Industrial training in Year 3 is considered very important and leads on to a comprehensive study of solid state physics in the final year.

Sheffield (*Physics*) Physics and Chemical Physics are offered. In Year 1 students take either physics, pure maths and applied computational maths or physics, joint maths and one other complementary subject (eg astronomy, electronics). Year 2 is mainly physics with some maths and Year 3 is entirely devoted to physics. Chemistry, physics and maths are the core subjects of the chemical physics course.

Sheffield Hallam (*Engineering Physics*) A focus on the physics of materials, measurement and modelling with a one year industrial placement at the end of Year 2.

Southampton (*Physics*) Contemporary and classical physics subjects are taught from the beginning of the course. Most of the core course material occupies the first two years, leaving the final year for a selection of advanced topics. These include lasers, cosmology, solid state and advanced quantum mechanics. Options in other scientific subjects can also be taken (chemistry, biology, electronics, geology and computation). Courses in Astronomy and Space Science are also available.

St Andrews (*Physics*) Physics may be taken as a single Honours subject or as part of a joint Honours course with one of Astronomy and Astrophysics, Chemistry or Electronics. There are separate degree courses in Theoretical Physics and Laser Physics and Optoelectronics.

Staffordshire (*Physics; Applied Physics*) After a common first year the applied route concentrates more on industrially relevant areas of the subject such as digital electronics, computational physics and materials. An MPhys year includes substantial project work and professional development modules as well as advanced physics. Extended routes allow entry for those with non-standard qualifications and physics can be taken as a Joint Honours.

Strathclyde (*Physics*) This is a modular course with flexibility in curriculum choice. Three courses are offered - the single Honours Physics, Applied Physics and Laser Physics and Optoelectronics. The first two years are common to all courses and provide a foundation in physics, mathematics, electronics, computational physics and experimental measurement. At this stage students also take elective classes in subjects such as languages, accountancy, geography, or management. They may then take a further two years to complete one of the Honours degree courses or transfer to the Pass degree and obtain a BSc award after one year.

Surrey (*Physics*) In addition to the BSc and MSci Physics single Honours course, Physics can be taken with acoustics, medical physics, management studies or nuclear astrophysics. All BSc programmes can be taken as a three year course or a four year course including a period of professional training at a research laboratory or in industry in the UK, Europe or North America. Students have access to excellent computing facilities and well-resourced teaching laboratories. Option modules in a broad range of topics are available in all academic years.

Sussex (*Physics*) The physics core is taken by all Physics students irrespective of their choice of degree. The core is fixed for the first two years. Students have a choice of options they wish to follow in terms 7 and 8. Students follow additional courses according to their choice of degree. A minor study of Astrophysics is also offered as a degree course.

Swansea (*Physics*) Courses are offered in Physics, Physics with Laser Physics, Physics with Microelectronic and Computing Physics, Physics with Medical Physics and Physics with Particle Physics and the Foundations of Cosmology. In the core course common to each degree there is an intensive study of the main branches of both classical and modern physics which is continued beyond Level I. This is supplemented by one of the specialised courses appropriate to the chosen degree.

Warwick (*Physics*) A central core of physics and mathematics is taken by all students, ensuring flexibility and freedom of choice in the option courses which follow in the second and third years. Mathematics and Physics, Physics with Computing and Physics and Business Studies courses are also available.

York (*Physics*) A common first year course includes physics, mathematics and electronics for students taking the single Honours degree. Optional courses are also offered in astrophysics, mathematics, languages and philosophy and single Honours students are encouraged to take a non-science-based course in Year 1. For those not fully committed to a particular course, some degree of flexibility exists enabling students to leave their final choice of course until the end of the first year. Other courses involve Theoretical Physics, Physics with Astrophysics, Physics with a Foundation Year (for those without the normal entry requirements) and Computational Physics which highlights the mathematical modelling of complex problems and their solution by computational techniques. ERASMUS exchanges are possible.

● **Top research universities**
Belfast, Birmingham, Bristol, Cambridge, Durham, Edinburgh, Essex, Exeter, Glasgow, Heriot-Watt, Leeds, Leicester, Liverpool, London (Imp), (QMW), (UC), Manchester, Nottingham, Oxford, Southampton, Stirling, Strathclyde, Surrey, Warwick.

● **Colleges and Institutes of Higher Education offering degree courses**
Bradford and Ilkley Community (Coll), Canterbury Christ Church (Coll), North East Wales (Inst).

● **Other courses to be considered**
Astronomy, astrophysics, computing, electronics and geophysics.

POLITICS (including Government and Peace Studies)

● **Special subject requirements:** 2–3 A-levels; GCSE (grade A–C) mathematics.

● **Subject information:** These courses have become increasingly popular in recent years and usually cover the politics and government of the major powers. Through the degree courses on offer it is possible to study the politics of almost any country in the world.

Aberdeen (*Political Studies*) This course gives special attention to Britain, France the former Soviet Union and the USA. In levels 1 and 2 courses are offered in Politics and International Relations which can be combined for a degree in Political Studies, but either subject can be read as part of a joint degree with one of ten other subjects.

Aberystwyth (*International Politics*) International Politics covers aspects of sovereignty, nationalism, power and diplomacy. International Politics and Strategic Studies covers the military aspects of politics and the foreign policies of the UK, the former Soviet Union, China and the USA. Political Studies and International Relations courses are also offered whilst the Politics course explores democracy in Britain, France and the European Community. In Part II, six themes are studied with opportunities to specialise.

Anglia (Poly Univ) Politics is available with over 20 other subjects.

Bath Politics is offered with Economics or Russian.

Belfast (*Political Science*) This subject can be studied in the Faculty of Arts or the Faculty of Economics and Social Science, although each course is broadly the same. The difference lies in the choice of other subjects which can be studied with Politics. All students take three basic courses - foreign governments, history of politics, and comparative politics. Single subject students also take government of Ireland, political ideologies and three optional subjects.

Birmingham (*Political Science*) The first year consists of two social science courses (a political option must be chosen). In the second and third years students take either political theory or political analysis, with a choice of options from British, European, American, Latin American, Soviet, or

African politics. A course in International Studies is also available. Several subjects can be taken with Political Science as joint courses.

Bradford (*Peace Studies*) This is an interdisciplinary course (a joint course in politics and sociology) with opportunities to specialise in conflict resolution, international relations and defence and security studies.

Bristol (*Politics*) The first year course involves a study of politics (UK, USA and the former Soviet Union) and two other subjects. In the second year a choice of four from five major areas of the subject is made; these include world, Western Europe and communist politics. More specialist studies are taken in the third year. The department is developing considerable strength in international politics.

Bristol UWE (*Politics*) This is part of the Social Science Undergraduate Modular Programme in which Politics can be studied with economics, history or sociology or as a single Honours course. The course covers West European, British and World Politics, political philosophy and justice.

Brunel Politics is offered with Modern History and Government is offered with Economics. Options to specialise exist in 'Politics and Policy', 'European Politics' or 'Politics and Philosophy'.

Buckinghamshire Politics can be taken with Economics or Law or History or in combination with these subjects under Politics, Economics and Law.

Cambridge (*Social and Political Sciences*) Part I covers politics, social psychology, social anthropology and sociology tracing the development of modern societies. Options in Part II include Russia, Western Europe, and North America. There is an option to change to another subject in Part II.

Cardiff (*Politics*) Part I covers the foundation of Western political theory, electoral systems, party systems, internal and international war. Part II offers a number of optional subjects including European Community policy and the comparative systems of Britain, France and USA.

Central England (*Government*) In Year 1 students take two compulsory courses in political institutions and social and political theory. Three other subjects are also taken from economics, statistics, law, social psychology and history. In Part II (Years 2 and 3) options include foreign governments, local government, and British central administration.

Central Lancashire (*Politics and Government*) This is a study of the politics and government in Britain and Europe and the principles of public administration.

Coventry Political Science can be taken with Geography.

De Montfort (*Politics*) The course covers British, European, American and Third World politics.

Dundee Political Science is offered as a joint course with over 12 separate subjects or in the Arts and Social Sciences or Combined Honours programmes.

Durham (*Politics*) All first year students take an introduction to politics course followed by a further eight courses, two of which may be taken from other subject areas usually within the Faculty of Social Sciences.

Optional subjects include political activity in the USA, the former Soviet Union and Eastern Europe, Western Europe, the Middle East and Southern Africa, as well as British government, local government and public administration.

East Anglia (*Politics*) The course examines such issues as conflict in society, political parties and public opinion, and international relations in Europe, America and Russia.

East London (*Politics*) The course includes a study of politics in its social and economic settings, political theory and historical ideas, government in Britain and other European countries, the law, human and civic rights and local government.

Edinburgh (*Politics*) The degree course offers an introduction to political theory, British government and administration. In the third and fourth years options are offered in Scottish government, political parties and the politics of the former Soviet Union, Eastern Europe, the USA and Africa.

Essex (*Politics*) In the School of Social Studies the course includes politics and Britain in the modern world, whilst in the School of Comparative Studies the Enlightenment is also studied. The choice of syllabus depends on GCSE/O-level language qualifications, on the subjects and bias preferred - arts or social sciences - and in turn the preferred approach to the study of political science in breadth or in the social science context.

Exeter (*Politics*) Single Honours students take courses in all branches of the subject. In the first year, three courses are followed - contemporary British politics, world politics and political thought from the Greeks to Machiavelli. The subject is widened in Years 2 and 3 with both compulsory and optional courses which include the politics of Western Europe and the Middle East, Canada, local politics and international relations. Exeter is a national centre for the study of the politics of the Middle East at postgraduate level. An interdepartmental course in Economic and Political Development is offered.

Glasgow (*Politics*) The course is distinctive in concentrating on ideas and ideologies, liberalism and socialism while looking at political institutions, parties and pressure groups. Political organisations' behaviour in the UK and the USA is studied as well as the former Soviet Union, Spain, Nigeria and Mexico.

Greenwich (*Politics*) The course is part of the Humanities programme. Options taken in Year 2 cover modern political thought, international politics and political systems in America, Russia and China. Year 3 options include political philosophy, urban politics, gender and society, policing and British political parties.

Huddersfield (*Politics*) The course involves British government and politics, European politics, international relations, Third World politics and American politics. In Year 1, four modules from other subjects can be taken, eg economics, business studies, history and modern languages.

Hull (*Politics*) Students taking the Special Honours programme take five wide-ranging courses in first year and two core and two optional courses in the second year. In the final year four courses are taken from a choice of over 30 options. There is also a course in International Relations and Politics, a four year course in Politics and Legislative Studies, and there are a number of joint Honours courses.

Humberside Politics is offered with European Policy.

Keele Politics and International Politics are offered with a large number of subjects.

Kent (*Politics and Government*) In the first year of the course (Part I) students take the study of politics course which introduces contemporary theories and analyses the three main political systems - Britain, USA and the former Soviet Union. In the second and third years (Part II) students have a wide choice of degree programmes - Politics and Government, Politics and International Relations, and American Studies (Politics and Government) (some students from this course spend a year in the USA). A number of Combined Honours degree courses are also offered.

Kingston (*Politics*) The course is offered as part of the modular scheme which offers a choice from 16 subjects.

Lancaster (*Politics*) In the first year students take politics (including British and American government and international relations) and two other subjects, for example law, religious studies, history, economics. In Years 2 and 3 a wide range of political topics is covered including political thought, government, comparative politics, international relations and strategic studies (of which there is a degree course). Two other courses are taken in Year 2 and one in Year 3.

Leeds (*Political Studies*) First year compulsory subjects cover the introduction to politics and British government and explanation in political science. Second year subjects cover foreign governments and comparative government in the USA, USSR, France, China, India and Pakistan; modern political doctrines; and political and social history. A wide range of final year optional subjects is available. There is also a unique Politics and Parliamentary Studies course involving five months working as an intern in a Congress member's or senator's office in Washington DC, and a similar period in the House of Commons.

Leicester (*Politics*) The first year covers three aspects of the subject: government and politics, political philosophy and international relations. In Year 2 four courses are taken: government (Britain, US, France and Germany); political ideas; international relations; comparative politics (Britain, the former Soviet Union and a Third World country). In Year 3, the compulsory courses cover twentieth century political movements and political theory. In addition students choose two subjects from a wide range of options.

Liverpool (*Politics*) The course covers British politics in Year 1 and later, Western Europe, Russian, American, Latin American and South American politics.

Liverpool John Moores Politics is offered with over 10 subjects including Japanese. The course includes politics and the media, Third World, and European Community politics.

London (Goldsmiths') Politics is offered with Economics.

London (LSE) (*Government*) The first year covers an introduction to the study of politics and political theory. Years 2 and 3 offer courses in the politics and government of another country and options in political thought and processes plus four options in Government.

London (RH) Politics is offered jointly with nine other subjects.

London (QMW) (*Politics*) The course is for students wishing to specialise in modern Western political institutions, theory and ideas. There are also several joint Honours programmes.

London (SOAS) (*Politics*) Single subject and joint degree students all take the courses introduction to political study and comparative politics. Students then follow a programme with an increasing optional element. Courses taught at SOAS stress the materials and problems more specific to the non-European world, but the opportunity exists to choose courses at other colleges within the University of London.

London Guildhall (*Politics and Government*) Britain is used as the main field of study in Year 1, followed by core subjects covering France, USA, the former Soviet Union and China in Year 2. Options covering public policy, mass media, law and political economy are offered in the final year.

Loughborough (*Politics with a minor subject*) Three and four year courses are offered with Economics, Social Administration, French, German, Sociology, Social Psychology or English as a minor subject. The course provides a thorough grounding in political science with particular reference to Western and Eastern European states, the European Community, the USA and the former Soviet states. Language students may opt to spend the third year in France or Germany. Politics may also be studied in the context of European Studies courses.

Luton (*Politics*) The course covers Britain and European politics, American and South East Asian politics, and political ideas, eg communism, fascism, anarchism and political economy and history.

Manchester (*Politics*) The Department of Government is one of the largest in Britain, enabling students to build a well-rounded foundation in the study of Politics and then, in their final year, either to specialise in depth or to develop their interests across a broad front. Students also are able in their first two years to maintain links with other disciplines, including a foreign language. The Department is a participant in eight different degree programmes.

Manchester Metropolitan Politics is offered as part of the Humanities and Social Studies programme.

Middlesex Political Studies is offered in the Multidisciplinary Programme.

Newcastle (*Politics*) In Year 1 four courses are taken, two or three from: British politics, world politics, introduction to democratic politics and political ideas; and one or two from a range of other subjects which include languages, history, law and psychology. In Years 2 and 3, the focus is on political studies which cover Western Europe, Africa, East Asia, the USA and China. Politics can also be studied with History, East Asian Studies (includes a year in the Far East) or Social Policy. There is also a degree in Government and European Community Studies which includes language study as part of the course (French, German or Spanish) and involves a year abroad.

North London (*Politics*) The course provides a strong core curriculum in political institutions and processes, political philosophy, theory and systems.

Northumbria Government is offered as part of the joint Honours or Combined Honours programmes.

Nottingham (*Politics*) Part I occupies Year 1, and Part II Years 2 and 3. The first year covers an introduction to politics (theories and institutions) and two courses taken from outside the department. These include economics, sociology, law, psychology, history and American studies. Part II courses are chosen from a range of options, for example local government, the media, the politics of France, Germany, the former Soviet countries and Eastern Europe. The department has a recognised strength in comparative politics, especially of Eastern and Western Europe.

Nottingham Trent Government is offered with Public Policy.

Oxford Politics is offered with Philosophy and Economics.

Oxford Brookes Politics is offered with 40 separate subjects.

Plymouth (*Politics*) The course can be taken as a single Honours, major or minor subject. It largely covers British and European politics but provides options in the politics of Eastern Europe and Third World issues. The subject is often combined with Social Policy, Sociology, Psychology, Law and Languages.

Portsmouth (*Politics*) In the first year politics is studied alongside economics, modern history, political thought and current politics. In Years 2 and 3, core courses are accompanied by options including British political parties, the politics of the Third World, Central Europe and the Middle East, computer literacy and personnel management.

Reading (*Politics and International Relations*) After the First University Examinations in term 4, students take four courses, two in the government sector and one each in theory and international relations. Five options are then available from 17 topics. The study covers the politics of the UK, USA, former Soviet states, Africa and Northern, Southern and Western Europe.

Salford Politics can be taken with either Sociology or Contemporary History.

Sheffield (*Politics*) In Year 1, two other first year subjects are taken with Politics. These can include Japanese, a modern foreign language, law, and a wide range of other subjects. Years 2 and 3 offer several political topics and cover European, Middle Eastern and Far Eastern politics in addition to studies of the USA and the former Soviet Union countries.

Southampton (*Politics*) All students in the Social Sciences Faculty take an introductory first year course in politics and may also take a course in international studies. In Years 2 and 3 students become more progressively specialised and may opt for such topics as arms control, foreign policy analysis, British government, imperialism, Third World in international relations and Latin American politics.

South Bank (*Politics*) The course provides a sound understanding of contemporary political issues covering a wide range of social science subjects and political issues in Europe, the USA and the Third World.

Staffordshire (*International Relations*) In Years 1 and 2 a language can be taken from French, German or Spanish. The programme covers all aspects of international affairs, with a wide range of options in the third year. It is also possible to study Politics or International Relations as part of the Modern Studies degree.

Stirling (*Political Studies*) The first three semesters (Part I) will introduce the practical and theoretical aspects of the subject and survey different political systems. Part II is designed to develop analytical skills and there will be courses in nationalism, political philosophy and environmentalism.

Strathclyde Politics is offered as part of the Arts and Social Studies programme.

Sunderland Politics can be taken jointly with 20 separate subjects.

Sussex Politics is offered in five programmes: African/Asian or English/American or European or North American Social Sciences.

Swansea (*Politics*) All students take two courses in Politics in Part I: (a) the modern state (b) modern ideologies. Single Honours students may then take a number of courses which vary depending on whether the subject is offered in the Faculty of Arts or the Faculty of Economic and Social Studies. The Politics course at Swansea is philosophical and historical rather than statistical in character. There is also a degree course in Social Philosophy.

Teesside Politics is offered in the Joint Honours programme.

Ulster Politics is offered with International Studies.

Warwick (*Politics*) The courses in Politics have been designed to cater for a wide range of interests. As well as the single Honours degree, Politics may be combined with Sociology, French, History, German, Economics or International Studies.

Wolverhampton Politics can be taken as part of the Modular Degree Programme.

York (*Politics*) A wide spectrum of subjects is covered in this course. These include the major governmental systems of Britain, Western Europe, America, China, Japan and the former Soviet Union. Subject strengths include Third World and British politics and political philosophy. Thirty-seven Part II courses are offered, none of which are compulsory.

• Top research universities
Essex, Hull, London (King's) (LSE), Manchester, Glasgow, Strathclyde, Bradford, Exeter, Keele, London (SSEES), Newcastle, Oxford, Sheffield, Southampton, Warwick, York, Aberystwyth, Swansea.

• Colleges and Institutes of Higher Education offering degree courses
Edge Hill (Coll), La Sainte Union (Coll), Southampton (Inst).

● **Other courses to be considered**
Economics, economic history, international relations, history, public administration, government, public and social policy, social administration, sociology, social sciences and social studies.

PSYCHOLOGY

● **Special subject requirements:** 2–3 A-levels; GCSE (grade A–C) mathematics.

● **Subject information:** This is an ever popular course covering studies in development, perception, learning, personality as well as social and abnormal psychology. (It is not a training to enable you to psycho-analyse your friends!) All courses approved for future training as psychologists are listed in the publications of the British Psychological Society, St Andrews, 48 Princess Road East, Leicester LE1 7DR.

Aberdeen (*Psychology*) Level 1 covers social and child psychology followed by more detailed studies of developmental and biological psychology on Level 2.

Abertay Dundee (*Behavioural Science*) This course integrates the study of psychology and sociology with specialised options which include health, sociology and psychology, organisations and work.

Aston (*Human Psychology*) This is an applied course with three and four year programmes. Students following the latter course spend a year on work experience. The emphasis of the course lies in the study of human behaviour and the underlying mental processes with options in child, clinical, occupational and social psychology. There are eight joint courses with psychology; most are offered on a three year full-time or four year sandwich basis, the decision as to which course to follow being taken at the start of Year 2.

Bangor (*Psychology*) In Part II of the course topics include perception, learning, remembering, language and thinking, developmental psychology and personality. These lead on in Year 3 to studies in social and clinical psychology. In an expanding department, a unique feature is the presence of several clinical specialists who are also Health Service practitioners, providing special opportunities for those students interested in applied mental health studies covering such topics as child abuse, schizophrenia, AIDS and addictive behaviour. There is a new course in Psychology with Health Psychology. Twelve joint courses are also available.

Bath A course is offered in Sociology and Psychology.

Belfast (*Psychology*) The flexibility of the course structure enables students to make the final decision on the choice of subject at the end of the first year. Emphasis is laid on practical and experimental work throughout the course. Final year options include sport psychology and women and psychology.

Birmingham (*Psychology*) The scientific study of behaviour in all its aspects is followed related to developmental and child psychology, perception, learning, social and abnormal psychology. In the final year students choose from a number of options in contemporary psychology. Continuous assessment occupies a major part of the course.

Bournemouth Applied Psychology is offered with Computing.

Bradford (*Psychology*) Psychology is taught as a science, with an emphasis on physiology and psychopharmacology and behavioural neuroscience. There is also an emphasis on clinical psychology which leads to clinical training courses.

Bristol (*Psychology*) The emphasis is on both human and animal behaviour (no practical work on animals). Courses in the first two years provide a basis for specialisation in the third year and cover perception, learning, motivation, personality, social and physiological psychology. Two additional subjects are taken in the first year and one additional subject in the second year. There is an emphasis on experimental and empirical approaches to individual and social psychology. Languages at a minor level can be taken.

Bristol UWE Psychology is offered in the Combined Sciences programme.

Brunel (*Psychology*) A broad coverage of the subject takes place during the first and second years, in which nine courses are taken including human science, social and psychological processes and psychological structures and development. In addition students choose three courses in other disciplines from within and outside the Faculty of Social Sciences. Students follow two separate programmes - 'Human Sciences' or 'Intelligent Systems'. Brunel offers an integrated sandwich course with three placements. Language options and placements abroad are possible. In Years 3 and 4, students can specialise in clinical, developmental and social psychology.

Buckingham Psychology is offered as a joint course with Biology or Business Studies or Computer Science.

Cambridge (*Psychology*) Experimental Psychology is taken in Part B of the Natural Sciences course with two other subjects. Students concentrate on a single subject in Year 3.

Cardiff (*Psychology*) Three aspects are covered in the first year - 'Machinery of the Mind', 'Psychology in Action' and 'Understanding People'. In Part II (second and third years) core courses and options are taken, including social and occupational psychology, abnormal psychology and applied biology. A course is also offered in Applied Psychology in which a year of occupational training takes place in the third year. Final year options lead to vocational and professional areas of work.

Central Lancashire (*Applied Psychology/Psychology*) The first and much of the second year content is common to both courses. In the third year Applied Psychology students take organisational psychology and a techniques course, as well as six options and a project in an applied field. Psychology students take nine courses from a wide range of options and also complete a project. The decision as to which course to follow is taken at the end of Year 1.

City (*Psychology*) This is taken as part of the Social Sciences programme and can be taken singly or with Economics, Philosophy or Sociology. The course involves cognitive and social psychology, learning, clinical and abnormal psychology. Emphasis on health psychology or organisational psychology.

De Montfort (*Human Psychology*) A comprehensive psychology course covering human communication, language development, developmental, social, education, clinical psychology and counselling. Psychology is also offered as part of the Credit Accumulation Modular Scheme.

Derby (*Psychology*) The course leads to registration as a Chartered Psychologist. Child, Cognitive and Social Psychology are studied in Year 1. Options in Year 3 include the psychology of mental illness, counselling, personal relationships, racism and gender. The Psychology of Human Communication is also offered as part of the Combined Sciences programme.

Dundee (*Psychology*) This is offered as a First, Second and Third Science course which can lead on to the Honours course in the fourth year. Basic topics and special options across the whole field of the subject are offered leading to a final year independent research project.

Durham (*Psychology*) The BA and BSc courses follow the same topics, the difference being in the subsidiary subjects offered. The course features three main aspects - Biological (physiological and behaviour), Cognitive (memory, language and thinking) and Social (group and interpersonal relationships). Psychology is also offered as part of the Natural Sciences and Social Sciences Combined programmes.

East London Over sixty combined courses are offered involving psychology and psychosocial studies. Some three subject degree schemes are also available.

Edinburgh (*Psychology*) A general introduction to the subject in Year 1 is followed by a mainly experimental and biological programme in Year 2. Compulsory core subjects in Year 3 combine with a range of options such as social psychology or animal behaviour. A wide range of options continues in Year 4. Research methods, analysis and the use of computers are included in the first three years.

Essex (*Psychology*) Year 1 is common for both BA and BSc courses. Options taken in Year 2 dictate the final degree. The course has an emphasis in cognitive science, linguistics and the social sciences.

Exeter (*Psychology*) Single Honours courses are available in the Faculties of both Science and Social Studies although the syllabus is much the same in both, only ancillary subjects being different. The course covers the whole field of psychology - comparative, physiological, social and abnormal - with students being introduced to the clinical and other applications of the subject. There is a relatively high practical component to the course and considerable freedom in the choice of options. There are also courses with European Study, including a foreign language and a year spent abroad.

Glamorgan Psychology is available in the Combined Honours, Combined Studies and Joint Honours programmes. The course in Behavioural Science combines psychology with sociology.

Glasgow Over fifty joint courses are available with Psychology which is also offered as a single Honours course or as part of the Social Sciences programme. Computation techniques, abnormal and developmental psychology and cognitive science are included on the course.

Glasgow Caledonian (*Psychology*) There is a wide range of options in this course which has an emphasis on small-group teaching.

Greenwich (*Psychology*) The course draws together the biological and social bases of mental processes and human behaviour. Information technology and computing are fully integrated into the curriculum.

Hertfordshire (*Psychology*) The course focuses on the experimental study of basic human and animal behaviour. Students also take courses in statistics, mathematics and the use of the computer, and can choose subsidiary courses from psychology, sociology, philosophy or human genetics. Attention is given to computer applications and artificial intelligence. Language options (French, German, Spanish) can be taken at minor levels.

Huddersfield (*Behavioural Science*) The course offers a firm grounding in psychology and sociology with an applied focus. Third year options include health and illness, organisational behaviour, decision processes, culture and illness.

Hull (*Psychology*) Three special Honours degrees in Psychology are offered, two of them having an emphasis in either occupational psychology or clinical psychology. The course in Psychology includes both biological and social science subjects. The course combined with Occupational Psychology runs for four years and offers students a professional qualification and includes studies in selection and career development, training and applied psychology. The course with Clinical Psychology is a six year integrated programme. Four years lead to the BSc degree and a further two years of part-time study lead to an MSc award.

Humberside (*Psychology*) Final year units are offered in health and illness, environmental psychology, the psychology of communication and child psychology.

Keele Over sixty joint courses are offered with Psychology. Specialist areas include clinical and occupational psychology, special education and personal relationships.

Kent (*Psychology*) Psychology students take introductory courses in biological, general and social psychology, a psychology practical and statistics course, plus one option for their Part I. In Part II there is an emphasis on practical work and the opportunity to specialise in one of a number of alternative topics including clinical psychology, psychology and law, or occupational psychology. There is a separate degree in Applied Social Psychology and several other degree courses with educational, clinical or computing emphases.

Kingston Psychology is offered as a joint course.

Lancaster (*Psychology*) Developmental, cognitive and social psychology are taken in the first year plus two other subjects. Second and third year studies include cognitive, social and neuro-psychology. Two other courses are also taken, one in each year. Some exchanges with USA are possible.

Leeds (*Psychology*) Four major areas are covered - applied sociology and psychology, biological psychology, cognitive psychology and developmental and clinical psychology.

Leicester (*Psychology*) Courses are taken covering the biological bases of behaviour, cognitive psychology - learning, language, thinking - and in abnormal, social and developmental psychology. In the third year students are able to choose subjects to suit their own academic or vocational interests.

Liverpool (*Psychology*) In Year 1 psychology is introduced, along with psychological statistics and methods and practical work. In Year 2 psychological themes include biological, abnormal, developmental and cognitive psychology. In Year 3 five courses are taken from about 12 options including forensic psychology, artificial intelligence, drugs and behaviour.

Liverpool John Moores (*Applied Psychology*) Modules include social problems and client rehabilitation and care; there is also an elective module in counselling.

London (Goldsmiths') (*Psychology*) The degree is studied through course units which allows considerable flexibility in what can be studied. In addition one or two courses are taken from other science subjects. Final year options include occupational psychology and the psychology of language. Psychology with Computer Science is also available.

London (LSE) (*Social Psychology*) This is a study of the behaviour of individuals and groups in society, dealing with decision-making, language, and interpersonal relations. A study is made of the basic psychological processes of perceiving, learning and thinking. The emphasis throughout the course lies in the role of society and its institutions.

London (RH) (*Psychology*) The syllabus covers both theoretical and experimental work on a whole range of topics. These include psychometrics, psychopathology, social and developmental psychology and animal behaviour. Individual differences, occupational psychology and clinical psychology are among 13 options in the third year.

London (UC) (*Psychology*) This is taken as part of the BSc programme in which students make up their course by combining any prescribed subjects with elective subjects chosen according to their interests. Those wishing to enter careers as psychologists are recommended to take the single Honours course.

London Guildhall (*Psychology*) The course offers a broad psychological programme including up to 26 options in Years 2 and 3. Projects undertaken in Year 3 include marketing, social psychology, child psychology and ergonomics.

Loughborough (*Psychology*) Two courses are offered (with no animal work). One has an emphasis on human science - Human Psychology (aspects of biology and behaviour, health and illness, and clinical psychology). The other course has a focus on social science - Social

Psychology (aspects of class, race, crime sociology and industrial conflict). ERASMUS contacts.

Luton Over eighty subjects are offered with Psychology or Organisational Behaviour.

Manchester (*Psychology*) A wide range of options can be taken in Year 3 of this comprehensive course. Subsidiary subjects are also offered with psychology.

Manchester Metropolitan (*Psychology*) Various aspects of the study of psychology are covered in this course which has two major units - social and individual psychology and cognitive psychology. Optional subjects include communications, criminology, educational psychology, personal relationships, psychology and work, and the psychology of women. The Combined Studies course also includes psychology.

Middlesex (*Psychology*) This is a three year full-time or four year sandwich course which includes educational, occupational and health psychology.

Newcastle (*Psychology*) In Years 1 and 2 students receive a broad foundation in the major areas of experimental psychology - abnormal, developmental, social and psychological as well as animal behaviour, learning and language. Two other subjects which can include languages are taken in the first year, and three major and three minor subjects from a range of psychology options are taken in Year 3. It is possible to take a BSc degree which differs slightly in putting more emphasis on intelligence, perception and cognition and quantitative methods.

Northumbria (*Psychology*) A general introduction to the subject takes place in the first year, followed by more specialised areas. These include social psychology, artificial intelligence, behaviour, health and illness, and dyslexia and word recognition. (No animal experiments.)

Nottingham (*Psychology*) Central topics include social and developmental psychology, biological and cognitive psychology. In Year 3 there is a wide range of options which include clinical and occupational psychology, child development and computer applications. There is a considerable emphasis in applied psychology in this course in which there is an optional year of work experience. There is also a course in Behavioural Science covering animal and human behaviour - a mix between zoology and psychology.

Nottingham Trent (*Psychology*) A broad psychology course with specialist options in health psychology, criminology, black psychology and applied psychology.

Oxford (*Experimental Psychology; PPP*) The former is a study of the subject as an experimental science and covers the whole range of research - human experimental psychology, animal and physiological, development, behaviour and linguistics. The latter course in Psychology, Philosophy and Physiology allows candidates to combine sciences with humanities subjects.

Oxford Brookes Psychology is offered as jointly with over forty other subjects.

Plymouth (*Psychology*) This broad-based course introduces students to a range of topics including cognition, learning, motivation, psychopathology and social development and applied psychology. There are special facilities for work in clinical psychology, and psychological and social psychology. This is a three year course with an optional sandwich year.

Portsmouth (*Psychology*) Introductory courses in the first year lead on to a range of specialist topics including developmental psychology of childhood and adolescence, social and physiological psychology, the psychology of hypnosis, language, criminology, clinical psychology and social problems and politics. The course emphasises human behaviour, and the final year contains options in applied psychology and counselling.

Reading (*Psychology*) The basic subject matter of modern psychology is studied during the first four terms. This is followed by a choice of two special options in the final year, covering a wide range of topics including speech and language, clinical and neuropsychology.

Sheffield (*Psychology*) In Year 1 lectures fall into four groups (a) psychobiology (b) personality, social psychology and psychological disorders (c) cognition and (d) developmental psychology. Two other subjects may be taken in Year 1. In Years 2 and 3 these topics are covered at greater depth, supported by optional courses. There is also a degree course in Cognitive Science for which A-level Mathematics is required.

Sheffield Hallam (*Psychology*) Specialisms are offered in social, occupational and developmental psychology including communication disorders and mental health. Psychology can also be taken with the Combined Studies programme.

Southampton (*Psychology*) Students follow three course in psychology in Year 1 - introduction to psychology, the biological bases of behaviour and motivation, emotion and abnormal psychology. Practical work is an important component of the course. Four half-units or two whole units must also be followed from those offered by other departments in science and social science subjects. Specialisation takes place in Years 2 and 3 covering such topics as language, perception, criminal behaviour, education, amnesia and pain.

South Bank Psychology can be taken with English or Health Science.

St Andrews (*Psychology*) This can be offered in the Faculties of Arts and Sciences. Single and joint Honours are available in both Faculties. Joint courses and 'with' degrees are also offered, those degrees with other subjects having two thirds of the time spent with psychology and one third with the second subject.

Staffordshire (*Psychology*) This broad course provides options in health, neuro-psychology, crime and counselling. There are over thirty subjects which are also offered with Psychology.

Stirling (*Psychology*) This subject can be taken to minor, subsidiary or major level in Part I. Psychology is introduced as a biological and social science. Other studies include psychological psychology, learning, clinical and abnormal psychology, and the social cognitive development in infants and young children. Part II covers psychological methods, animal behaviour, social psychology, perception and performance, clinical and counselling psychology, and occupational psychology.

Strathclyde (*Psychology*) The first year offers a broad introduction to the subject, dealing with the biological bases of behaviour, the major themes of cognitive psychology, and differences in abilities and personalities. The second and third year emphasis is on developmental and social psychology, with clinical and educational psychology in the fourth year.

Sunderland (*Psychology*) The first year is part of the Combined Studies (Arts) scheme, offering a broad introduction to the subject, together with other social sciences, English or a foreign language. Later years emphasise experimental methodological aspects, but there is a wide choice of options which may include a language. There are also a large number of joint courses.

Surrey (*Psychology*) This is a four year sandwich course in which the third year is spent in professional placement. These placements take place in hospitals and clinic schools, social survey companies, personnel and occupational guidance services, industry and commerce. Surrey also offers a sandwich course in Applied Psychology and Sociology which covers most areas of human behaviour, both individual and social. No animal experimentation takes place on these courses.

Sussex (*Psychology*) The School of Cultural and Community Studies offers degree courses in Applied Psychology and Developmental Psychology. The School of Cognitive and Computing Sciences offers Psychology, Developmental Psychology or Psychology and Computer Models. The School of Biological Sciences offers a BSc in Experimental Psychology. The School of African and Asian Studies and the School of Social Sciences both offer a degree in Social Psychology.

Swansea (*Psychology*) Psychology is offered by the Faculties of Arts, Science and Economic and Social Studies. In all faculties in Part I there is a range of lecture courses, including the biological bases of behaviour for arts and science students. In Part II students take, and have the choice of, a very wide range of topics. Some options are provided by the Departments of Philosophy and Computer Science. There is an opportunity to specialise in biological, social or applied aspects of the subject.

Teesside (*Psychology*) Although the course provides a broad theoretical and practical base, together with computer skills, it is taught on the flexible modular system. Options include sports psychology, neuropsychology and the psychology of race.

Thames Valley Psychology is offered in the Humanities programme.

Ulster Courses are offered in Applied, Occupational and Social Psychology.

Warwick (*Psychology*) In Year 1 students are introduced to the foundations of psychology and take an optional subject from a range of possibilities in science, mathematics, social sciences or humanities subjects. Core courses in Year 2 covering personality, psychopathology, perception, action, memory and language are followed by a choice of four courses from ten choices in the final year.

Westminster (*Psychology*) The new course covers cognitive, social developmental and abnormal psychology as well as units in statistics and computing and options in management and health care. It is also possible to specialise in Psychology in the modular Life Sciences degree scheme.

Wolverhampton (*Psychology*) After a broad introductory first year students choose seven out of ten option modules such as social psychology, personality and abnormal psychology, human-computer interaction or counselling and group work. They also complete an individual project.

York (*Psychology*) This course places particular emphasis on psychology as an experimental science and academic discipline. It attempts to avoid any strong bias in favour of - or against - any specific field or approach within psychology.

• **Top research universities**
Birmingham, Cambridge, Durham, Exeter, Kent, Leeds, London (RH) (UC), Nottingham, Oxford, Reading, Sheffield, Surrey, York, St Andrews, Stirling, Bangor, Cardiff.

• **Colleges and Institutes of Higher Education offering degree courses**
Bath (Coll), Bolton (Inst), Buckinghamshire (Coll), Cardiff (Inst), Cheltenham and Gloucester (Coll), Chester (Coll), Edge Hill (Coll), King Alfred's (Coll), Leeds (Trinity and All Saints) (Coll), Liverpool (Inst), La Sainte Union (Coll), Nene (Coll), North East Wales (Inst), Norwich City (Coll), Queen Margaret (Coll), Roehampton (Inst), S. Martin's (Coll), Southampton (Inst), Worcester (Coll).

• **Other courses to be considered**
Advertising, business studies (personnel work), computer science and artificial intelligence, education and teacher training, social administration and social studies/science.

RELIGIOUS STUDIES (including **Biblical Studies, Theology** and **Divinity**)

• **Special subject requirements:** GCSE (grade A–C) language in some cases.

• **Subject information:** Religious Studies courses cover four degree subjects, namely Religious Studies, Divinity, Theology and Biblical Studies. The subject content of these courses varies and students should check prospectuses carefully. They are not intended as training courses for the church ministry; an adherence to a particular religious persuasion is not a necessary qualification for entry. (A-level religious studies is an acceptable second or third A-level for any non-scientific degree course).

Aberdeen (*Divinity/Theology/Biblical Studies*) Areas of study cover Church history, New Testament, Hebrew and semitic languages. Honours courses are available in several specialised subjects.

Aberystwyth (*Divinity (BD)*) Part I of the BD degree covers the Old and New Testaments, Church history and philosophy. In Part II students choose eight topics from a wide range of subjects.

Bangor (*Biblical Studies; Theology; Religious Studies*) In the Biblical Studies course optional subjects cover the Old and the New Testaments, the history of Christian thought, the philosophy and sociology of religion, and biblical archaeology. In Part I of the Theology course there are introductory courses in the Old and New Testaments, Church history and doctrine, and the history and philosophy of religion. These topics continue in Part II, in addition to which students take four other courses from the list prescribed for the Biblical Studies degree programme. The Religious Studies course combines biblical studies with studies in twentieth century Christianity, theological ethics and Judaism.

Belfast (*Divinity; Biblical Studies*) A study is made of the Old Testament, Church history, Greek, a philosophical subject and an arts or social science subject. The second year includes Old and New Testament, philosophy of religion, Christian ethics and Church history. Pastoral studies, modern Church history and theology and biblical studies are taken in the third year.

Birmingham (*Theology*) All students study the history of religions, Israelite religion, the life and teaching of Jesus, New Testament Greek and theological thinking. Second and third year options are taken from early Christian doctrine, Church history and modern theological thought, and students also take a special subject.

Bristol (*Theology and Religious Studies*) The course in Theology and Religious Studies commences with biblical studies, Christian history and theology, Hellenistic Greek or another language and Indian civilisation. (First year students opt to specialise in traditional Theology (Course A) or Religious Studies (Course B).) In the second year students choose five courses and in the third year a further five courses from a total of 26 options. There is also a course in Religion with Literature with some opportunity to transfer to Theology and Religious Studies at the end of Year 1.

Cambridge (*Theology and Religious Studies*) The Tripos is taken in two parts. Part I is taken after one year and Part II after a further two years. The Part I course provides for a wide variety of interests - biblical, historical, philosophical and comparative - students choosing four out of 14 papers. Hebrew, Greek or Sanskrit is studied by all who spend more than one year in the Faculty. Part II builds on the foundation laid by the Part I course and includes modern theology, the philosophy of religion, the history of Christian life and thought, and comparative religion (chiefly Indian religions and Judaism). Homerton College offers Religious Studies as part of their B.Ed course.

Cardiff (*Religious Studies; Theology*) The Religious Studies course comprises a study of world religions, language and text theology and optional topics which include the history of the early Church, the Crusades and Welsh history and religious literature. Theology students cover the Holy Scriptures, the Old and the New Testaments, Christian doctrine, ethics and Church history.

Derby Religious Studies is offered as part of the Credit Accumulation and Transfer Scheme.

Durham (*Theology*) The first year includes a study of the Old Testament, one of the Gospels and the history of the Church. Beginners' classes in Greek and Hebrew are offered. In the second and third years students choose between three options. Option A has an emphasis on biblical studies. Option B covers systematic theology, philosophy and the Christian religion. Option C provides a special study of selected parts of the history of Christian tradition. New Testament Greek is compulsory and taught with the aid of computers.

Edinburgh (*Religious Studies*) Subjects covered include Hebrew and Old Testament studies, the New Testament, Church history, systematic theology, Christian ethics and practical theology. Degrees in Religious Studies offer comparative religion and religious studies (which are also offered as options in Arts and Social Sciences). These courses lead on to the phenomenology and history of religion exploring a wide range of issues across different religions. In addition MA students specialise in one religion - from Christianity, Judaism, Islam, Hinduism, Buddhism, Chinese or Ancient Near Eastern religions - and either a second world religion or sociology, psychology, anthropology or philosophy.

Exeter (*Theological Studies*) The course provides an introduction to theology by way of Old Testament studies (history and literature), the theologies of Paul and John and the development of Christian doctrine. Other areas of study include New Testament, Greek, Hebrew, biblical texts, the synoptic gospels, modern theology, Christian ethics, Islam and Church history.

Glamorgan Religious Studies can be taken in Combined Humanities or joint courses.

Glasgow (*Divinity*) This is a four year course. The first two years involve two divinity courses and two courses from a wide range in the Faculties of Social Science, Arts and Science. In the last two years students choose from a wide range of subjects including Old and the New Testament theology, various aspects of Church history, sacraments, ministry, Church and culture. Religious Studies (in the Faculty of Arts) covers world religions, including Christianity and Hinduism, studied as living faiths and in the light of the philosophical issues emerging from them.

Greenwich (*Theological Studies*) This is offered as part of the Humanities programme. There is an emphasis on Christian Theology, theological themes in history, contemporary studies, Biblical Studies and the philosophy of religion.

Hertfordshire Religious Studies is offered as part of the Primary Teaching Programme.

Hull (*Theology*) All first years begin by taking a two-term course in certain areas of Christianity and other religions. Second and third year studies comprise free options which allow students to plan their own course. During the first year special Honours students take one option in another department. Indian religions is a departmental speciality.

Kent (*Theology*) Introductory courses in Part I and II have no compulsory elements, allowing students to select from a range of courses in theology and religious studies. The interdisciplinary nature of the subject covers literary, historical, philosophical and sociological methods of enquiry.

Lampeter (*Divinity; Theology; Religious Studies*) A modular course with single and joint Honours courses in both Theology and Religious Studies. There is also a course in Religion, Ethics and Western Society, a degree programme in Church History and a Bachelor of Divinity degree (a three year course) which includes a study of Hebrew and Greek. A wide range of options is on offer including Greek and Roman religions and new religious movements.

Lancaster (*Religious Studies*) In Year 1, the course covers western and Indian religions, the Bible, the Koran, Judaism and the philosophy of religion. In Years 2 and 3, the main studies include Judaism, Christianity, Islam, Hinduism, Buddhism and philosophy. Two courses in related subjects (one in each year) are also taken. Exchanges with the USA are possible.

Leeds (*Theology and Religious Studies*) In Year 1, there is an introduction to Christian theological tradition, ancient Middle Eastern religion, New Testament Greek, early Indian religions or another subsidiary course. In the second and third years students take eight courses from a range of options. The course tends to stress the contemporary and 'lived' aspects of religions rather than their classical and theoretical aspects.

London (Heythrop) Degree courses are offered in Divinity, Biblical Studies and Philosophy and Theology at this small college, yet one of the largest schools of theology in the UK.

London (King's) (*Religious Studies; Theology; Biblical Studies*) These degree courses follow the course unit system. After a common first term students decide on which core units they will take, which determines the degree course they will follow. There is considerable choice of options in the second and third years. Various joint Honours combinations are also possible.

London (SOAS) (*Comparative Religions*) The course specialises in the religions of Asia and Africa.

Manchester (*Theology and Religious Studies*) A flexible course structure is offered covering a wide range of topics. Degree courses in Biblical Studies and Comparative Religion are also available.

Manchester Metropolitan Religious Studies can be taken in both the Combined and Humanities programmes.

Middlesex Religious Studies, Christian Studies and Pastoral Studies can be taken as options on the modular course.

Newcastle (*Religious Studies*) In Year 1 an introduction to the subject is combined with the study of two topics from introduction to the study of the Bible, religion in contemporary society and another subject. In Years 2 and 3 options are taken from biblical studies, history of religious thought, Hinduism, Judaism, Islam, Buddhism, philosophy, sociology and archaeology. Optional languages in Greek, Hebrew or Sanskrit.

Nottingham (*Theology*) The course has three main themes - Christian Theology, Religious Studies and Biblical Studies. In Part II (Years 2 and 3) the three compulsory courses concern the social anthropology of religion, biblical theology and systematic theology. The remaining two subjects are chosen from a very wide variety.

Oxford (*Theology*) The course provides an informed and critical understanding of the Old and New Testaments, of the historical development of the role of the Church and the contemporary meaning of the Christian faith. A large range of options include the philosophy of religion, ancient and modern Church history, Christian ethics, textual criticism and biblical Hebrew. Theology may also be studied with Philosophy.

St Andrews (*Biblical Studies; Theology; Divinity*) Biblical Studies and Theology can be taken as Arts or Divinity subjects. Within the Bachelor of Divinity (BD) course an Honours subject or group may be chosen from among Old or New Testament language and literature, ecclesiastical history, divinity and practical theology. There are also separate degree courses in Old Testament Language and Literature, New Testament Language and Literature, Church History and Practical Theology.

Sheffield (*Biblical Studies*) In Year 1 Biblical Studies is combined with a wide ranging survey of biblical history and literature and a detailed study of the book of Hebrews. Years 2 and 3 cover Old and New Testament texts, broader areas of biblical history, literature and theology. Students also take a special option course.

Stirling (*Religious Studies*) Religion, myth and meaning, ethics and society, and Indian religions are taken in Part I (the first three semesters). In semesters 4–6 all students take one course in biblical studies and one in historical and philosophical studies. There are also options in Part II, along with Eastern religions.

Sunderland Religious Studies can be taken as a joint subject.

Warwick (*Religious Studies*) This is placed within a programme of initial teacher training education.

Wolverhampton There is a specialist route in this subject in addition to combined and joint course options.

● **Top research universities**
Birmingham, Cambridge, Durham, Lancaster, Leeds, London (King's), Oxford, Sheffield, Bristol, Manchester, London (Gold), Edinburgh, Glasgow, St Andrews.

● **Colleges and Institutes of Higher Education offering degree courses**
Bangor Normal (Coll), Bath (Coll), Bishop Grosseteste (Coll), Brunel (Univ Coll), Canterbury Christ Church (Coll), Cardiff (Inst), Cheltenham and Gloucester (Coll), Chester (Coll), Chichester (Inst), Edge Hill (Coll), Gwent (Coll), King Alfred's (Coll), Leeds Trinity and All Saints (Coll), Liverpool (Inst), La Sainte Union, Newman (Coll), Ripon and York St John (Coll), Roehampton (Inst), Scarborough (Univ Coll), S. Martin's (Coll), St Andrews (Coll), St Mark and St John's (Coll), St Mary's (Univ Coll), Trinity Carmarthen (Coll), Westhill (Coll), Westminster (Coll).

• **Other courses to be considered**
History, philosophy, psychology and social studies.

SOCIAL ADMINISTRATION/APPLIED SOCIAL STUDIES/SCIENCES/SOCIAL POLICY
(See also under **Sociology**)

• **Special subject requirements:** GCSE Grades A–C in mathematics usually necessary with 2–3 A-levels.

• **Subject information:** These courses are a good vocational preparation for careers in the Social Services. A wide range of topics are covered, eg housing policy, health services, mental illness, the family and prisons. See also under **Sociology**.

Anglia (Poly Univ) Social Policy is offered with over 20 separate subjects.

Bangor (*Social Policy*) Primary modules on this course include the National Health Service, poverty, housing and health care. Optional modules cover family and the law, welfare agencies, health care and health policy and housing management.

Bath (*Social Policy and Administration*) The course covers health, social services, income maintenance, education and housing.

Birmingham (*Social Policy*) The course covers health care, housing, social work and criminology.

Bradford (*Applied Social Studies*) This is a four year course in which academic work and practical experience are combined in the third and fourth years. Basic social sciences (economics and sociology) are studied in the first year along with a choice of other subjects such as politics or social psychology. In the second year, social policy, the sociology of social problems and the training of social workers is introduced. This degree course also leads to the Certificate of Qualification in Social Work. There is also a degree course in the Social Sciences. This has a common first year which leads to a choice from Economics or History/Politics or Sociology/ Social Psychology.

Brighton (*Social Policy and Administration*) Core studies include social policy and administration and studies in context with the health services, housing and social services. Sociology, economics and law are studied throughout Years 1 and 2. Students select specialist studies at the end of the second year from housing, health or personal social services which includes a five week placement.

Bristol Social Policy is offered with Planning or Politics or Sociology. A wide range of options can be taken. The course is drawn from perspectives of history, law, philosophy, economics and sociology.

Bristol UWE (*Women's Studies*) The course covers history, literature studies, cultural and media studies, women in film, literature and the city.

Cardiff (*Social Policy*) Students must take six first year courses: social welfare and social change, social welfare in modern Britain, and four options in the social sciences. Later studies cover poverty, housing, crime, the care of the elderly, health and welfare agencies.

Central Lancashire (*Applied Social Studies*) During the first year students decide whether to take the social policy and administration branch or the social work branch. The first two years are common to both, with specialisation taking place in the final year. Those choosing social work are awarded the Diploma in Social Work (DipSW) on graduation. There are exchange programmes in Germany and Portugal. A course in Women's Studies is also offered.

City (*Social Sciences*) This is a modular BA degree in which students select 3 or 4 subjects from economics, philosophy, psychology, sociology, accountancy and computing.

Coventry (*Applied Social Science*) The foundation year introduces sociology, social policy and administration, psychology and a choice between government and politics, social history and economics. The course has a health visiting option, a social work option, and Combined Honours programmes in Sociology, Psychology, Sociology, Social Policy and Administration, and Psychology.

Dundee Social Policy is offered as a joint course or in the Combined Honours or Arts and Social Sciences programmes.

Durham (*Social Science*) Three or four subjects are chosen from a range of subjects, eg anthropology, archaeology, economics, geography, history, management studies, Middle Eastern Studies, philosophy, psychology, sociology and social policy.

East London (*Social Science*) The course comprises study units from economics, law and sociology. It is offered jointly with a large number of separate subjects. The course in Women's Studies includes media workshops, history, literature, anthropology and sociology. There is also a special focus on New Technology.

Edinburgh (*Social Policy*) Students take core courses in the principles of social policy and research methods, and choose from more than 20 options including health, social security, moral perspectives or a specialist area.

Exeter (*Society, Economy and Social Policy*) Courses are taken in sociology and economics with options in law, politics and history.

Glasgow Social Policy is offered with a large number of separate subjects.

Hull Social Policy can be taken with six separate subjects.

Humberside (*Applied Social Science*) The course covers the core subjects in Social Sciences and also includes health, employment, welfare, youth, community work, crime and law.

Keele Applied Social Studies can be taken jointly with a very large number of separate subjects.

Kent (*Social Policy and Administration*) Students take social problems and social policy in Part I plus four other social science courses. In Part II a variety of courses are offered thus allowing the student to build his or her own degree package. The course also places an emphasis on related subjects such as economics and law. There is also a degree course in Public Administration and Management.

Kingston (*Applied Social Science*) Subjects offered in Part I are economics, sociology, politics, modern British history and social psychology. Options include development, labour, social welfare, European industry or urban studies.

Lancaster (*Social Administration*) In Year 1 social administration is taken with two other courses, for example English law, philosophy, psychology. In Years 2 and 3 compulsory and optional courses are taken in the main subject including welfare and urban environment, education, understanding youth, social policy and social work for young people, criminology and the psychology of sex and gender.

Leeds (*Social Policy and Administration*) In Year 1 a study is made of the foundations of social policy, general economics, politics and British government. In the second year students continue to study social policy making in Britain, together with research methods and computing, and the organisation and management of social policy. In the third year they study welfare institutions and the public service, plus three optional courses.

Leeds Metropolitan (*Social Policy and Administration*) In addition to these two main studies, other topics cover British government and politics, work and welfare, health and health care, housing, stress and mental health in modern society and sexual divisions and social policy.

Liverpool Social Policy is offered with Sociology.

London (Goldsmiths') (*Social Policy*) (See also **Nursing**) The foundation course covers politics and government, economics, British social history, social statistics and research design, and British society. In the second and third years there are compulsory courses in the development and administration of social welfare, but there is also the opportunity to choose from a range of options, possibly including courses offered by other departments. There is also a degree course in Social Science Investigation which shares a common first year.

London (LSE) (*Social Policy and Administration*) The history of social policy, sociology, social economics and one optional course are studied in the first year. In the second and third years there are five core courses, an extended essay on a topic chosen by the student, and two courses chosen from a range including women in society, psychology and social policy, and housing and urban structure.

London (RH) (*Social Policy*) This degree is taught on the course-unit system. The first year's work provides a grounding in the major social sciences. The second year provides for specialisation in one or more of these, and in the third year there is a wide choice of courses. Social Policy may be studied with Sociology or Economics.

London Guildhall (*Social Policy and Management*) Equal opportunities, human resource management, and sociology are studied. There is also an opportunity to take a European language.

Loughborough (*Social Administration*) This course of three years also includes volunteering or block placements for practical experience. The course involves social psychology, sociology, social economics and history. In the third year electives are offered in family and social policy, work and social policy, personal social services, health care and health services, and law, probation and penal policy.

Luton (*Social Policy*) A study of social issues, eg industrial relations, crime, the inner cities, public health and community medicine.

Manchester (*Social Policy*) A study of contemporary social needs and problems and society responses. Topics covered include child abuse, unemployment, the National Health Service, education, anti-racism and feminism. See also under **Sociology**.

Middlesex (*Social Policy*) An unusual course because of its sandwich placement. The subject can be studied with a range of relevant subjects, eg politics and industrial relations. A popular course with mature students.

Newcastle (*Social Policy*) This unique course combines the study of sociology, social administration, psychology, statistics and social work. Social Policy can be studied as part of the Combined Studies BA course. (*Social Studies*) The first year includes a study of anthropology, sociology and options from world politics, economics and psychology. In Years 2 and 3, social issues can be studied including housing and planning, marriage and parenthood, population studies, criminology, industrial relations, mental health, and social security law. Social Studies can also be taken as part of the Combined Honours degree.

North London (*Applied Social Science*) The course covers community and cultural studies, health studies, policy studies and social work.

Nottingham (*Social Policy and Administration*) In Year 1, a study is made of society and institutions seeking to deal with social problems. Two other optional subjects are also taken, for example psychology, law, politics, economics and philosophy. In Year 2, one subsidiary subject is taken and in the third year three optional subjects are taken from options covering social work, criminology, childhood and society, social change and manpower planning. Fieldwork takes place at the end of the first and second years.

Paisley (*Applied Social Studies*) A broad-based first year followed by options in either Social Policy, Behavioural Science, Social Work or Technology and Society. There is also a European language option.

Plymouth (*Social Policy and Administration*) This course focuses on the relationship between social problems, social policies and social welfare institutions. A second course of the same name is of four years' duration and includes practical placements which lead to Certificate of Qualification in Social Work (CQSW) - recognition for those wishing to enter social work. A further course provides training for the Diploma in Community Work.

Portsmouth (*Social Policy and Administration*) Core papers include welfare, sociology, politics, economics and social statistics. Topics covered in Years 2 and 3 include criminology and criminal justice, race and society, gender and society, housing policy and management in the public sector. There is also a European language option.

Sheffield (*Social Policy and Sociology*) First year students take an introductory course in sociology and social policy, a course in quantitative techniques and two other courses in a range of arts, sciences and social sciences. A wide range of options is available in the second and third years, and the emphasis of the Department is on the processes by which sociological knowledge is acquired. There are also degree courses in Social History and Social and Political Studies.

Sheffield Hallam (*Applied Social Studies*) Years 1 and 2 include studies in sociology, psychology, economics, law in society and methods of social research. In Year 3 students choose one option from work and society, socio-legal studies or the social problem of inequality. A four year course leads to professional qualification in social work.

Southampton (*Social Policy and Administration*) Degrees are offered in Social Policy and Sociology with students following a common first year programme. Courses are then chosen by the student leading to their chosen degree.

Stirling (*Social Policy*) This course is closely related to sociology and there is an emphasis in the relationships between the two which can both be studied with a range of other subjects.

Strathclyde (*Social Science*) Five subjects are taken in Year 1 followed by two in Year 2 followed by specialisation in Years 3 and 4.

Sussex Social Policy is offered in Cultural and Community Studies or in Social Sciences.

Swansea Social Policy is offered as a joint course.

Teesside (*Social Policy*) Politics, government, economics and a European language are offered in Year 1. In Years 2 and 3, community care, education, housing, health and personal social services are covered in a series of option modules.

Ulster (*Social Administration and Policy*) The course involves a detailed study of the operation of the social services covering health, housing, education and social security.

Warwick Social Policy is offered with Sociology.

Wolverhampton Social Policy is offered as part of the Modular Degree Scheme.

York (*Social Policy*) The single subject course provides for a study of the historical, sociological and political foundations of social policy. Year 2 includes social policy, analysis, economics and methods of social research. Options include social work (as a career), social and political theory or options in the Education department. Optional courses occupy Year 3. These include crime and the penal system, mental handicap services and housing policy.

- **Top research universities**
Bath, Cambridge, Kent, London (LSE), York, Birmingham, Brunel, Manchester, Sheffield, Ulster, Cardiff, East Anglia, Stirling, Hull, Lancaster.

- **Colleges and Institutes of Higher Education offering degree courses**
Bangor Normal (Coll), Queen Margaret (Coll).

- **Other courses to be considered**
Anthropology, economics, government, law, politics, psychology and sociology.

SOCIOLOGY

- **Special subject requirements:** GCSE (grade A–C) mathematics usually required.

- **Subject information:** This is the study of societies in general, both in Britain and abroad. Elective subjects offered will include industrial behaviour, crime and deviance, health and illness.

Aberdeen (*Sociology*) Level 1 includes social institutions in Western Europe and the Third World followed in level 2 by relationships between self and society.

Anglia (Poly Univ) (*Sociology*) Twenty nine modules are offered ranging from capitalist societies, science and technology, politics, popular cultures and class inequality to educational problems, race, deviance, health and illness and understanding crime.

Bangor (*Sociology*) Sociology is taken with two other Part I subjects in Year 1 and with an accessory course in Year 2. Year 3 is devoted exclusively to sociology. A course is also offered in Sociology with Social Administration. A separate degree scheme in Welsh is offered.

Bath (*Sociology*) In each year of the three year course elective subjects are stipulated, and in Years 2 and 3 subsidiary subjects (psychology, history, politics, philosophy, and economics) are offered. Elective subjects cover a very wide range of topics including industrial behaviour, the sociology of science, of health and illness, of crime and deviance and of education. Degrees in Sociology are also offered with Psychology, Social Policy, Social Work and Industrial Relations. The four year sandwich course is taken by most students. There is considerable flexibility between degree schemes in Sociology and options to choose courses.

Belfast (*Sociology*) A broad course (single, joint, combined or major/minor Honours) with options in the society of Modern Ireland and class and class conflict.

Birmingham Sociology is offered as a joint course.

Bradford (*Sociology*) This is offered as part of the Social Sciences programme. Core subjects are taken by all students in Year 1; thereafter a choice is made to take Sociology/Social Psychology with options in minorities in Britain and social problems.

Bristol (*Sociology*) The first year introduces the subject and covers the principal issues of contemporary society with topics on the family, world of work, media, social inequalities, race relations and education. The second year emphasises the work of the 'founding fathers' of sociology - Marx, Weber and Durkheim - and allows students to choose topics of special interest which continue in the third year with an examination of contemporary sociological thinking.

Bristol UWE (*Sociology*) This is part of the Social Science Undergraduate Modular Programme in which Sociology can be taken with economics, history or politics or as a single Honours subject.

Brunel (*Sociology*) The course covers psychology and social anthropology as well as sociology, and a wide range of topics related to theory, methods and specialisation in aspects of British and international societies. There are also programmes in science and technology studies and environmental technology. During the four year course students spend three long periods of work experience outside the university. Options exist in medical anthropology. There is an exchange programme with University of New Mexico on the Social Anthropology joint course.

Cardiff (*Sociology*) Sociology and the social structure of modern Britain are covered in Part I, with studies in social change and development research methods, communist regimes, the mass media, women and the welfare state and the sociology of Wales as Part II options.

Central England (*Sociology*) This is a rigorous four year academic sandwich vocational course, with sociology and methodology as core subjects and elective subjects chosen from social psychology, social economics, social history and politics in the first year. Electives in Part II (Years 2 and 3) include deviance, race, values and beliefs and the sociology of art and literature. There is an opportunity either to study abroad or to take a placement in the second semester of Year 2.

City (*Sociology*) This subject can be taken as a major within the Social Sciences and Humanities programme. The course includes applied sociology, race and society, mass communications, the sociology of work and industrial relations.

Durham (*Sociology*) The subject can be taken as a single Honours subject, or within the Combined Honours degree, or with Social Policy, Anthropology, Economics, History, Law, Politics or Psychology.

East Anglia (*Sociology*) Optional units in this course include, art, media studies and social politics.

East London (*Sociology with Professional Studies*) All students in the department follow a common first year during which they decide whether to complete the three year Honours degree in Sociology, or to follow a vocational pathway combining Sociology with European Studies, Psycho-social Studies, Social Policy Research or Social Work, which involves a further three years including professional placements. There is an emphasis placed on ethnicity and gender.

Edinburgh (*Sociology*) In the first two terms three broad topics are covered - social inequality, social order and deviant behaviour and socialisation.

The second part of the course relates sociology to social and intellectual issues, and the Honours course to social theory and methods of social research.

Essex (*Sociology*) Students in the School of Comparative Studies take a course in the Enlightenment and sociology whilst those in the School of Social Studies will include sociology and at least one subject from economics, linguistics, philosophy or politics. In Social Studies courses will cover social structure and social policy, social psychology, British social history and gender and social structure. In Comparative Studies optional courses include industrialisation and development, peasant societies (Latin America, the Third World and Europe), the city in Europe and America and racism and social structure.

Exeter (*Sociology*) This can be studied on its own or in combination with another subject. Single Honours students take two compulsory courses - modern society and social analysis - along with a wide choice of more specialised subjects including criminology, the Third World and the sociology of politics, education and welfare, and women in society.

Glamorgan Sociology is offered as part of the Humanities Combined Honours, joint Honours or Combined Studies programmes.

Glasgow (*Sociology*) Sociology is studied within the Faculty of Arts and Social Sciences. The study covers issues arising from the social relations of work, family, community and market, and from the distribution of wealth and power.

Greenwich (*Sociology*) Sociological debates, comparative sociology, sociological skills and reasoning, and science in society are covered in Year 1. Options are available in Year 2 covering Britain in Europe and political economy. In Year 3 students choose three options from eight alternatives ranging from human attributes and deviance to media in society and racialism.

Hull (*Sociology*) In their first year students take one course in social anthropology and then decide whether to take further courses in the subject. A wide range of joint Honours courses is offered.

Keele Sociology is offered with a large number of subjects in the joint Honours programme.

Kent (*Sociology*) In Part I students are recommended to take courses in sociology and social anthropology along with other Part I courses, for example politics, law, economics. In Part II core courses are taken including social analysis of industrial societies and research practices in sociology, as well as optional third year courses such as the sociology of politics, education, knowledge, sex, gender and the family.

Kingston (*Sociology*) The course is organised around three themes: sociological research, theory and the comparative analysis of societies.

Lancaster (*Sociology*) In Year 1, the introductory course includes two options from the sociology of class and gender, criminal law, culture and the media. In Years 2 and 3, these subjects can be continued with additional topics such as deviance and social control, education and society, health and illness, the sociology of sport, popular culture and race.

Two other courses are also taken, one in each year. Some exchanges with the USA are possible.

Leeds (*Sociology*) In the first year social, intellectual and cultural trends in the nineteenth and twentieth centuries are studied with one other subject from economics, politics, philosophy or psychology. Social processes and institutions form the core subjects in Year 2, and in Year 3 seventeen aspects of sociology from Canadian society to medicine, religion, education and race relations are offered to students who are asked to choose two for further research.

Leicester (*Sociology*) In Year 1 students take the course in 'Understanding Societies' plus two subjects taken from economic and social history, economics, geography or politics. In Year 2 studies cover the sociology of individual behaviour and capitalist and socialist societies, and in Year 3 with a study of European societies, three optional subjects are taken. Students who are particularly interested in social work can take the BA or BSc course in Applied Sociology.

Liverpool (*Sociology*) The sociology of modern Britain and social theory and social change plus two other subjects are taken in Year 1. In Year 2, five subjects are taken from a range which includes British society, sociology of race, social anthropology and social administration. In Year 3 students choose from a wide range of options including the Third World, industrial relations and medical sociology.

Liverpool John Moores Sociology can be taken jointly with a wide range of subjects.

London (Goldsmiths') (*Sociology*) Core courses cover theory, methods of research and social structure. In addition optional courses are offered in the sociology of art and literature, health and race. Sociology is offered with Anthropology (work divided equally in Years 1 and 2, with options in Year 3) or Communication Studies (language, experience and behaviour) or with History.

London (LSE) (*Sociology*) One of the largest departments of Sociology, LSE offers a course planned on a unit system with core courses in sociology, social structures, statistical analysis and sociological theory. In addition there is a choice of 86 topics from which students must select five.

London (RH) Sociology is offered with a large number of separate subjects. There are three main disciplines within the department - social policy, sociology and public administration.

London Guildhall Sociology is offered as part of the Modular programme. The emphasis lies in contemporary debates in Sociology.

Loughborough Sociology is offered with a minor subject.

Manchester (*Sociology*) The department of Economic and Social Studies offers a wide variety of subjects (260 modular units are offered). Students choose their own combination of subjects and can take a specialist degree in Sociology, Politics, Social Policy, Social Anthropology, Economics and Accounting.

Manchester Metropolitan Sociology can be taken as part of the Humanities or Social Studies programmes.

Northumbria (*Sociology*) This is a broad-based course emphasising sociological aspects but including the related disciplines of economics, history, psychology and philosophy. Optional topics are available in Years 2 and 3 which enable students to qualify in social work or social research.

Nottingham (*Sociology*) The course aims to develop an awareness of the workings of social groups and organisations and to understand the theories and evidence about social and political problems. In addition to core courses students select two options, one in each year from a range of subjects including the sociology of religion, education, industry and politics, race and minority groups and ideologies and social movements. There is an emphasis on the empirical aspects of research. There is also a degree course in Social and Cultural Studies.

Oxford Sociology is taken as part of the Human Sciences programme.

Oxford Brookes Sociology is offered with a wide range of second subjects.

Plymouth (*Sociology*) The course can be taken in single Honours, major or minor programmes. It offers a range of specialised studies covering feminist thought, the Third World, the media, education, health and illness, religion, management and work.

Portsmouth (*Sociology*) Social theory, analysis and statistics, politics and economics are included in the first year. Options including psychology, criminology and criminal justice, race and society, social work and society are offered in Years 2 and 3.

Reading (*Sociology*) After the first four terms students follow three compulsory courses and six or seven optional subjects. Among these options, one theme covers historical and comparative aspects of the subject (the sociology of religion, politics or morality). Other courses concern people - decision-making, criminology, education and industrial sociology.

Salford (*Sociology*) Sociology, anthropology and psychology are studied in Year 1 with methodology. A fifth social science course is also studied. In Years 2 and 3 core subjects continue along with a choice of subjects, some of which deal with European and African societies.

Sheffield (*Sociology*) The level 1 modules cover Sociology and Social Policy with specialisms appearing in levels 2 and 3. The department has an 'excellent' rating for teaching.

Sheffield Hallam (*Sociology*) The subject is offered within the Applied Social Studies degree programme. Applied Social Studies, Sociology and Social Policy having a common first year with the opportunity to transfer between routes at the end of the year.

Southampton (*Sociology and Social Policy*) There are 12 courses offered in this subject area including six combined courses. All students follow the Part I programme and choose their final course at the end of the first year. There is also a four year degree in Social Work Studies.

Staffordshire (*Sociology*) The course offers a combination of specialist aspects of sociology and related sciences including social psychology. Human geography, economics, law and international relations are options in Years 1 and 2, and a wide range of options is offered in Year 3.

Stirling (*Sociology*) A common first year course is offered for the degree course in Sociology and for Social Policy and Social Administration. Students make their choice of degree programme including combined courses at the end of Year 1. The Sociology programme is built around core courses in theory and methods with options to suit the student's field of interest.

Strathclyde (*Sociology*) This is a four year course with an introductory first year covering social class, the family, education, work, sexual division, the media and deviance. In the next two years there is a range of options such as women and work or modern sociological theory. The final year is spent on a research seminar, a dissertation and two classes from a range of options.

Sunderland (*Sociology*) Options in Year 1 include politics, history, media studies, cultural studies and modern languages and in levels 2 and 3 in health factors and promotion, race, work, leisure and criminology.

Surrey (*Applied Sociology*) This is a four year course with a year spent in professional training in industry, commerce or the public sector. Sociology is offered with Applied Psychology. There is also a course in Economics and Sociology which provides an adequate base for a career in either area.

Sussex (*Sociology*) The main emphasis of this course is in sociological theory, independent critical work, the opportunity for specialist studies in contextual courses and the practical approach to planning and conducting research. Sociology can be offered with one of six different languages.

Swansea (*Sociology*) Sociology can be taken as a single or joint Honours course. The Sociology and the Social Anthropology courses follow a common course in Part I. Specialist courses in Years 2 and 3 include industrial sociology, labour markets, deviance, race relations, peasants and peasant societies, witchcraft and heresy.

Teesside Sociology is offered in a joint Honours programme.

Ulster (*Sociology*) A common first year with Psychology enables students to transfer at the end of Year 1. The emphasis in the second year covers contemporary industrial societies with Third World themes and a variety of options following in Year 3.

Warwick (*Sociology*) The aim of the course is to provide students with an insight into theoretical sociology, methods of social research and the problems of the society in which we live. In Year 1, in addition to sociology courses, students choose an option from a course in applied social studies, economics, education, history, languages or psychology. Thirty one different options are available in Years 2 and 3.

Wolverhampton Sociology is offered as part of the Modular Degree Scheme.

York (*Sociology*) The course provides a wide structural choice of subjects and perspectives. It may be taken as a single subject or in combination with Economics, Economic and Social History, Politics, Philosophy, Education or History. There are no compulsory courses in Years 2 and 3 and no examinations - only essays.

● **Top research universities**
Cambridge, Essex, Lancaster, Loughborough, Warwick, Edinburgh, City, Kent, Leeds, London (LSE), Manchester, Oxford, Salford, Sheffield (excellent teaching rating), Surrey, Sussex, Belfast, Glasgow.

● **Colleges and Institutes of Higher Education offering degree courses**
Bath (Coll), Bolton (Inst), Buckinghamshire (Coll), Colchester (Inst), King Alfred's (Coll), Leeds Trinity and All Saints (Coll), Liverpool (Inst), La Sainte Union (Coll), Nene (Coll), Norwich City (Coll), Roehampton (Inst), Southampton (Inst), St Mark and St John's (Coll), St Mary's (Univ Coll), Worcester (Coll).

● **Other courses to be considered**
Anthropology, history, social studies/science, social administration, social policy, social work, government, politics.

SPEECH PATHOLOGY/SCIENCES/THERAPY

● **Special subject requirements:** 2–3 A-levels, chemistry or biology preferred; GCSE (grade A–C) in mathematics and science subjects (biology preferred) and a language.

● **Subject information:** This is the study of speech defects which may be caused by accident, disease or psychological trauma. Courses lead to qualification as a speech therapist.

Central England (*Speech and Language Pathology and Therapeutics*) The course covers communication disorders, clinical phonetics and linguistics and psychological and social disorders.

City (*Clinical Communication Studies*) A four year course leading to membership of the College of Speech Therapists.

De Montfort (*Human Communication*) Eight modules in speech therapy are taken each year supplemented by modules in psychology, linguistics, medical science and information technology. A clinical practice programme is also followed.

Leeds Metropolitan (*Clinical Language Sciences*) The course covers clinical practice, communication skills, counselling and psychotherapy.

London (UC) (*Speech Sciences*) This is a clinical four year course sharing the first year with Speech Communication (non-clinical). Second and third year courses include the acoustics of speech and hearing and speech perception. Transfer between the degrees is possible at the end of Year 1.

Manchester (*Speech Pathology*) A vocational course with academic and clinical components leading to registration as practising speech therapists.

Manchester Metropolitan A three year full-time course with clinical practice. There is a clinic on the premises for demonstration and practice and a well-equipped speech laboratory.

Newcastle (*Speech*) This is a speech therapy training course with clinical practice. There are two courses, Speech and Speech and Psychology, students making a choice at the end of Year 2.

Reading (*Linguistics and Language Pathology*) This is a preparation for a career as a speech therapist and involves a study of physiology, phonetics, audiology and psychology.

Sheffield (*Speech Science*) The course covers linguistics, psychology, anatomy, audiology and clinical practice leading to a career as a speech therapist. There is also a course in Human Communication and its disorders.

Strathclyde (*Speech Pathology*) In addition to academic studies practical studies in sport are included.

Ulster (*Speech and Language Therapy*) The course, which involves supervised clinical placements, studies language disorders. Included in the course are modules on linguistics and phonetics, psychology, anatomy and medical specialisms.

• **Colleges and Institutes of Higher Education offering degree courses**
Cardiff (Inst), Central School (Speech & Drama), Queen Margaret (Coll), St Mark and St John (Coll).

• **Other courses to be considered**
Nursing, Occupational Therapy, Physiotherapy and Radiography.

SPORTS SCIENCE and LEISURE STUDIES

• **Special subject requirements:** GCSE (grade A–C) English and mathematics for some courses. Some Sports Science courses require a science subject at A-level.

• **Subject information:** These are very popular courses and unfortunately restricted in number. Ability in gymnastics and involvement in sport are obviously important factors.

Bangor (*Sport, Health and PE*) The SHAPE course includes sport psychology, health promotion, information technology and counselling. It is a 'theory' and 'practice' course.

Birmingham (*Sport and Recreation Studies*) The course covers detailed studies of physical performance and the role of physical education and sport in society. Practical studies give experience in team and racket games, swimming, athletics, dance and outdoor pursuits. Students select from a comprehensive range of activities in the second and third years, All students study one subsidiary subject for two years, or two subjects for one year each. The degree is non-vocational although many graduates proceed to teacher training.

Bournemouth (*Leisure Marketing*) A general course covering economics, accountancy and management studies with a focus in arts, entertainment, sport, recreation and tourism. There is an international option with 2 years in France, Germany, Holland or Spain.

Brighton (*Sports Science*) The course has five main components - biological studies, sports psychology, social perspectives of sport, applied sports studies and quantitative methods. Physical activities include games, athletics, outdoor pursuits, gymnastics, dance and water-based activities.

Coventry (*Leisure Management*) A three year full-time course designed to examine the leisure industry. The course includes modules which cover business and finance, sport, physical education, exercise and fitness, sport psychology and sport coaching.

Exeter (*Exercise and Sport Science*) This degree has replaced the four year BA(Ed) in Education Studies and PE. The course covers anatomy, biomechanics, physiology, psychology and sociology, teaching, learning, leadership, communication skills, coaching sport and exercise. Opportunities for some specialisation in Years 2 and 3.

Glamorgan Sport Studies combined courses are offered.

Glasgow Physiology is offered with Sport Science.

Glasgow Caledonian (*Leisure Management*) This course of three or four years duration provides a comprehensive study of the leisure industries and environment. Marketing, planning, finance and administration are included and there is an optional European language.

Greenwich (*Sport Science*) The course covers human movement, the sociology of sport, sport physiology and psychology, computing, nutrition and performance.

Leeds Physiology is offered with Sport Science.

Leeds Metropolitan (*Sport and Exercise Science*) A modular course taken within the School of Leisure and Sports Studies sharing Year 1 with Physical Education and Sport and Recreation Development.

Liverpool John Moores (*Sport Science*) Studies cover research methods (including statistics) and coaching and applied sports science. Topics include physiology, health science, psychology and recreational management.

Loughborough A range of courses in Physical Education and Sport Science are offered.

Luton (*Sport and Fitness Science*) The course covers general health, coaching, sports psychology and leisure management.

Manchester (*Leisure Management*) The course is offered within the Department of Educational Studies. The Centre for Physical Education and Leisure Studies has an international reputation in these areas. The course covers management science, marketing, law, planning, countryside recreation and sport.

Manchester Metropolitan (*Sport and Exercise Science*) This is a multi-disciplinary course with opportunities to specialise in Exercise and Health or Performance Excellence.

Newcastle Physical Education is offered with Sport Studies.

North London Several courses are offered in Sport and Management including a course in Sport Science and Nutrition.

Northumbria (*Sport Studies*) Two main fields are explored (a) Sports performance (human structure and function, psychological studies and sports experience), which includes practical courses (b) Sport in the social context (management and organisation). One month is spent in work experience in sport, leisure and recreation.

Nottingham Trent A range of sport courses are offered including combinations in Coaching and Administration.

Oxford Brookes Exercise and Health is offered with several other subjects.

Portsmouth (*Sport Science*) The course offers students the opportunity to participate in sport and obtain a variety of coaching awards.

Sheffield Hallam (*Recreation Management*) Management studies with specialist areas in countryside, the arts, sport, facility management and tourism.

Staffordshire (*Sport and Recreation Studies*) Years 1 and 2 cover the theory and practice of sport and recreation, and individual performance. Financial information and control, fieldwork and projects occupy Year 2, and advanced theory and practice of selected sports and recreative activities with academic options occupy Year 3.

Stirling Several joint courses with Sport Studies are offered.

Strathclyde (*Sport in the Community*) The course involves management, psychology, finance, community education. The three main specialist areas cover Community Arts, Sport in the Community and Outdoor Education in the Community.

Sunderland (*Sport Studies*) The course includes physiology, sport performance, psychology, business management, sport medicine and leisure management.

Teesside (*Sport Science*) In addition to involvement in one's chosen sport the course involves anatomy, physiology, psychology, biomechanics and performance development.

Ulster (*Sport and Leisure Studies*) During the first two years students undertake an analysis of sport and leisure from both theoretical and practical perspectives. These include individual performance, interpersonal relations, issues in sport and vocational studies. At the end of Year 2, students can apply for a degree with Certificate in Education or a degree with a Diploma in Industrial Studies.

Wolverhampton (*Sport Studies*) This can be taken as a specialist award, joint, major or minor subject and covers a wide range of topics from community recreation and games performance to coaching, dance and European leisure policy.

• **Top research universities**
Birmingham, Loughborough.

• **Colleges and Institutes of Higher Education offering degree courses**
Barnsley (Coll), Bangor Normal (Coll), Birmingham (Coll/Food/Tourism), Bolton (Inst), Bradford and Ilkley (Coll), Brunel (Univ Coll), Buckingham (Coll), Cardiff (Inst), Cheltenham and Gloucester (Coll), Chester (Coll), Chichester (Inst), Colchester (Inst), Edge Hill (Coll), Farnborough (Coll), King Alfred's (Coll), Leeds Trinity and All Saints (Coll), Liverpool (Inst), La Sainte Union (Coll), Moray House (Inst), Newman (Coll), NESCOT, Ripon and York St John (Coll), Roehampton (Inst), Scottish Agricultural (Coll), Salford (Univ Coll), Scarborough (Univ Coll), St Mark and St John's (Coll), St Mary's (Univ Coll), Southampton (Inst), Suffolk (Coll), Swansea (Inst), Warrington (Coll Inst), West Herts (Coll), Westhill (Coll), Writtle (Coll).

• **Other courses to be considered**
Anatomy, biology, human movement studies, leisure studies, physiology, recreation management and sport studies.

SURVEYING/ESTATE MANAGEMENT
Surveying (Building)

• **Special subject requirements:** 2–3 A-levels from mathematics/physics/chemistry.

• **Subject information:** This field involves the preparation of land for building.

Surveying (Land)

• **Special subject requirements:** 2 A-levels; English and mathematics at GCSE Grades A–C.

• **Subject information:** This branch of surveying focuses on the mapping and surveying of large areas of land and water.

Surveying (Quantity)

• **Special subject requirements:** 2 A-levels from mathematics/physics subjects. GCSE Grades A–C in English and mathematics.

• **Subject information:** This is a specialised field of surveying which centres on the costs involved in the construction of buildings.

Surveying (General Practice/Valuation)

• **Special subject requirements:** 2 A-levels (mathematics required at Heriot-Watt). English and mathematics at GCSE Grades A–C.

• **Subject information:** This branch of surveying largely involves the valuation and purchasing of all types of land and property.

Aberdeen (*Land Economy*) The theory and principles of land tenure, land use and management, investment planning, development and conservation.

Abertay Dundee (*Quantity Surveying*) The course leads to an Honours degree and professional recognition. There is optional supervised work experience. Courses in Building Surveying and Building Engineering and Management are also offered.

Anglia (Poly Univ) (*Surveying*) The course, based in Chelmsford, allows students to choose their own specialism. The range of programmes includes Building Economics and Design, Estate Management and Countryside Management.

Brighton (*Building Surveying*) The first and second years will cover building performance, built environment, building surveying practice and the professional environment. The third year is spent on supervised professional experience and the final year will cover building design, rehabilitation, asset management and two options, including a dissertation.

Bristol UWE (*Quantity Surveying*) This is a four year sandwich course with professional placement in the third year. Topics include construction technology and measurement, contract and legal studies. Final year studies cover construction services, building construction and civil engineering. Maximum exemptions are afforded graduates from RICS examinations. (*Real Estate; Valuation and Estate Management*) The course covers valuation, taxation, law, planning, construction technology, estate management, economics, business studies and finance. It gives maximum exemptions from RICS examinations.

Cambridge (*Land Economy*) This course is concerned with the use of land and property and with the protection of the environment. Students take courses in law and economics relating to the ownership, exploitation, planning and protection of land, and explore the issues raised. The degree gives exemptions from RICS examinations.

Central England (*Estate Management*) Land valuation, business studies, economics, quantitative methods and law are covered in Stages 1 and 2. Much of Stage 3 involves property development, management and taxation. The main emphasis of the course is property valuation in a legal context, and property development and management. (*Quantity Surveying*) This is a four year sandwich course which includes professional experience. Course topics include construction studies, measurement and cost studies, economics, quantitative methods and law. The major strength is the application of information technology throughout the course as a tool to problem solving and information management.

Central Lancashire (*Quantity Surveying*) A four year sandwich course covering economic, technological and legal studies. The first stage of the course introduces the concepts of measurement, value, conflict and modelling. The third year is spent on a professional placement, possibly in Europe. Final year students are involved in project simulation exercises.

Cirencester (Royal Agricultual Coll) (*Rural Land Management*) The course gives exemptions from examinations of RICS and the Incorporated Society of Valuers and Auctioneers.

City (*Property Valuation and Finance*) The course is designed to meet the needs of qualified specialists in the field of property, finance and investment, law and taxation. Valuation is studied throughout the course along with building design and construction, company structure and planning. The course is recognised by the RICS for their General Practice Division.

Coventry (*Building Surveying*) This is a three year or four year (sandwich) course in the built environment. There is a language option with possible placements in France, Germany and Spain.

De Montfort (*Land Management*) Valuation and law are studied in each of the three years of the course. Other subjects include economics, the history of planning and the development of property, town and country planning, estate agency and land use planning. Courses are also offered in Building Surveying, Property and Business and Property Development and Management.

East London (*Surveying and Mapping Sciences*) Years 1 and 2 provide a grounding in the basic principles and procedures in surveying and mapping the land and sea. In Year 2, students can specialise in a wide range of option topics including cartography, geodesy and hydrography. There is also a course in Land Administration giving exemptions from the RICS examinations in the General Practice Division.

Glamorgan (*Quantity Surveying*) This is a four year sandwich course covering measurement, construction technology, economics, law, administration and computer applications. Year 3 is spent in work experience in an approved office which, with the degree, gives theoretical and practical experience exemptions from RICS examinations.

Glasgow Caledonian (*Building Surveying; Quantity Surveying*) The course includes six-month periods of supervised work placement with private offices, contractors and local authorities. Property Management and Development is also offered.

Greenwich (*Building Surveying*) This course can be studied on a three year full-time or four year sandwich basis. The main subjects cover construction technology, design, economics of land and building, law and management. The RICS recognises the degree for maximum exemption from their examinations. (*Quantity Surveying*) A three year full-time, four year sandwich or five year part-time course with topics focusing on construction technology measurement, law and economics. Professional practice on the sandwich course comes in Year 3. The RICS recognise the degree for exemptions from their examinations.

Heriot-Watt (*Building Surveying*) This four year course covers building technology, building economics, building appraisal and surveying, and gives exemptions from several professional institutes' examinations. (*Building Economics and Quantity Surveying*) In the first two years building technology, mathematics, economics and legal and business studies are included. Quantity surveying studies begin in the second year and continue to the end of the final (fourth) year. Professional and industrial practice are also included. (*Estate Management*) In the first two years the course involves a study of building technology, economics, urban appraisal and legal and business studies. In the third year legal and planning studies and urban sociology are introduced and continued in the fourth year with building maintenance and a research design project.

Kingston (*Quantity Surveying*) Year 3 of this four year sandwich course is spent in professional placement. Basic economy theory and the principles of law lead on to applications in building work in Years 1 and 2. Other studies cover construction technology and measurement. Exemptions from RICS examinations are gained on graduation. Similarly with the course in Urban Estate Management.

Leeds Metropolitan (*Quantity Surveying*) The course provides a thorough understanding of all aspects of quantity surveying and building economics. Distinct themes include measurement and contractual procedures, cost price, and various supporting studies. Year 3 is spent in professional practice. RICS exemption is gained on graduation.

Liverpool (*Building Surveying*) Years 1 and 2 provide a foundation course which is followed by a year in professional practice. Year 4 develops the theme of 'Building Life Cycle Management' (building maintenance, design and production). The degree affords RICS exemptions.

Liverpool John Moores (*Quantity Surveying*) This is a three-year full-time or four-year sandwich course. Industrial training takes place in the third year of this course which includes economic, quantitative and legal studies and construction management. The course exempts from RICS examinations. There is also a course in Building Surveying.

Loughborough (*Commercial Management and Quantity Surveying*) This programme, sponsored by fifteen major contractors, covers construction technology, law, economics, management and professional practice.

Luton (*Building Surveying*) The course covers construction methods and techniques and management. Quantity Surveying is available as a part time programme focusing on financial management, measurement and estimating. There is also an ISVA-accredited course in Estate Management.

Napier (*Building Surveying; Quantity Surveying*) These courses have a common first year with Architectural Technology, Building Engineering and Management, Building Control, Estate Management, Planning and Development Surveying. Building Surveying follows the same course as architectural technology, building engineering and management and control until the end of Year 2.

Newcastle (*Surveying and Mapping Sciences; Mapping Information Science*) The degrees cover land surveying and are accredited by the RICS.

Northumbria (*Quantity Surveying*) This is a four year sandwich course with professional placement in Year 3. Core subjects follow the set pattern prescribed by the RICS for exemptions from their examinations. Courses are also offered in Building Surveying, Housing Development, Planning and Development Surveying, and Urban Property Surveying.

Nottingham Trent (*Estate Surveying*) This is a three year full-time or four year sandwich course with professional placement in Year 3. The course involves the core subjects of land economics, law, land use planning, property management and valuation, communication and building technology. This course has full exemption from RICS examinations. Courses are also offered in Building and Quantity Surveying, Facilities Management, and Planning and Development Surveying.

Oxford Brookes (*Estate Management*) This course is designed primarily for those students aiming to become chartered surveyors in the general practice division. The curriculum focuses on subjects based on valuation, building technology, town planning, economics and law.

Reading (*Building Surveying*) The course concentrates on the technological and management aspects of the construction process. The first two years' studies are common with those of the courses in Building Construction and Management and Quantity Surveying. In the third year courses are taken in building technology, law, management, economics and town and country planning. (*Land Management*) The course is in three parts. Part I and II comprise six separate subjects which cover valuation, law, land use and planning, economics and building construction. Part III comprises a main specialisation, two common subjects which include recreational land management, European law and property, and residential development. There is also a degree course in Rural Land Management.

Portsmouth (*Construction Management-Quantity Surveying*) The three year course covers in depth all the aspects of quantity surveying practice under the three main themes - economics, technology and the environment. The course also introduces new themes for future development in the field such as computer use, cost planning and design management. RICS exemptions are gained on graduation. Financial management is an important feature of the course. (*Land Management*) Inter-related studies cover economics, property management, valuation, law, construction and management studies. The degree carries exemptions from RICS General Practice Division. There are also courses in Leisure Resource Management and Facilities Management.

Salford (*Building Surveying*) This is a four year sandwich course and incorporates elements common to the degree course in Quantity Surveying. There are three main study areas: professional, management and construction studies leading to project work in the final year. (*Quantity Surveying*) This is a four year sandwich course, the third year being spent in approved professional experience. Construction technology is taken throughout Years 1, 2 and 4 with other aspects of science and design. Other subjects include management, finance and applied economics and mathematics and computing.

Sheffield Hallam (*Building Surveying*) Much of the first year is studied in common with Construction, Quantity Surveying and Civil Engineering, with transfers being possible at this stage. Years 2 and 4 will cover construction technology, building services, law, economics, building surveying, design and refurbishment. The third year is spent in professional placement. (*Mineral Estate Management*) This degree exempts the holder from the examinations of the RICS (Minerals Division). Year 3 of this four year course is spent in industry. It is the only course giving full exemption from the written examinations of the Minerals Division of the RICS (it is not a Geology degree). (*Urban Land Economics*) The main subjects covered are land administration, economics, valuations, planning and building. This is a four year course in which the third year is spent in professional training.

South Bank (*Building Surveying*) This is a four year sandwich course with Year 3 being spent in supervised professional attachment. Subject areas cover construction, quantitative, economic, legal and management studies. RICS exemptions are gained on graduation. (*Quantity Surveying*) This is a four year sandwich course with Year 3 being spent in professional placement. The course is based on three main areas: (a) technological studies (b) economic studies and (c) legal studies. The degree gives RICS exemptions. (*Estate Management*) This is a four year sandwich course in which the third year is spent in an approved professional office - this counts as one of the two years of professional practice required by the RICS after completion of their examinations. The course follows the prescribed pattern leading to RICS exemptions and includes valuation, economics, law, building technology and town planning. There are also options in conservation, housing, management and leisure and recreation development.

Staffordshire (*Quantity Surveying*) After a common first year with the rest of the Property and Construction Management programme, specialist studies cover the analysis, construction and documentation techniques needed by the quantity surveyor. Business studies, law, planning and management are also studied. Courses in Building and Valuation Surveying and Property and Construction with a strong business management theme are also offered.

Ulster (*Quantity Surveying*) This is a four year vocational course leading to qualification as a quantity surveyor. The three main areas of study cover economic studies, professional studies and technological studies. Year 3 is spent in commercial or industrial placement. A course in Estate Management is also offered.

Westminster Degree courses in Building and Quantity Surveying are offered and also Estate Management, giving exemptions from the examinations of the Royal Institute of Chartered Surveyors.

Wolverhampton (*Quantity Surveying*) Studies include construction technology and economics, contract procedures, measurement and costing, law, the use of computers and foreign language options.

● **Colleges and Institutes of Higher Education offering degree courses**
Bolton (Inst), Harper Adams (Coll), Nene (Coll), North East Wales (Inst), Seale Hayne (Coll), Southampton (Inst), Swansea (Inst).

● **Other courses to be considered**
Accountancy, architecture, building, civil engineering, structural engineering, housing, town planning and urban studies.

TOWN PLANNING/URBAN STUDIES

- **Special subject requirements:** 2–3 A-levels; mathematics GCSE Grades A–C.

- **Subject information:** These courses, which are all very similar, lead to qualification as a member of the Royal Town Planning Institute. Courses usually include a year out. This is an ideal course for the geographer. The change in employment prospects for graduate planners has undergone a remarkable transformation in recent years. There is now a considerable shortage of planners in view of the increased demand by the local authorities and private sector. Increasingly consultants, developers and other property-related organisations such as major retailers, are employing qualified planning graduates and the net result is that demand is far outstripping supply. In response, the planning schools have increased their intakes but there would appear to be a significant shortage for the foreseeable future.

It also may be worth mentioning that the new 3 + 1 format of courses provides an opportunity for students who are well trained in environmental matters to leave such courses after three years with an honours degree, but without the necessity of completing the BTP for professional qualification. There are also increasing job opportunities for such students.

Belfast (*Environmental Planning*) Year 1 combines studies with architecture students.

Birmingham Several joint courses with Planning are offered.

Bristol UWE (*Town and Country Planning*) A three year degree course plus a further two years of practical experience leads to membership of the Royal Town Planning Institute. There is also a course in Urban Development covering housing, valuation, transport and surveying.

Cardiff (*City and Regional Planning*) This is a five year sandwich course providing a comprehensive study of all aspects of town planning, including environmental design, economics, industrial development, social structure, urban land use and transportation planning. It includes a two year sandwich course leading to the Diploma in Town Planning which gives the necessary exemptions from the examinations of the Royal Town Planning Institute (RTPI) and the Chartered Institute of Transport. Compared to other courses, Cardiff puts particular stress on social science approaches to planning and upon analytical and computing skills.

Central England Several courses are offered in Environmental Planning each offering a bias, eg European Planning, Transport, Urban Design and Regeneration.

Coventry Planning is offered with either Geography, Recreation or Local Economic Development.

Dundee (*Town and Regional Planning*) This is a four year course divided into three components - the planning process, administration and the physical environment. Final year options include housing policy, minerals, planning employment, agriculture and forestry, countryside planning and urban design. ERASMUS contacts with the Netherlands.

East London (*Urban Studies*) The course covers urban sociology, land property law, information technology and property valuation.

Greenwich (*Urban Environmental Studies*) Three pathways are offered (one to be chosen) from planning, housing or humanities. Some units give exemption from the Institute of Housing and the Royal Town Planning Institute.

Heriot-Watt (*Town Planning*) This is a five year course with a sandwich year spent in practice between the second and third years. All aspects of planning are covered in this course which leads to a BSc degree leading to full exemption from the final professional examinations of the RTPI. Students may graduate after three years' full-time study with a BSc in Planning Studies.

Kent (*Urban Studies*) The course reviews the problems of towns and cities and the various processes (political, economic, geographic and social) which affect their planning.

Leeds Metropolitan (*Urban Development*) This is a three year full-time course. The first two years provide a broad foundation of town planning studies leading on to options in employment policy, urban planning and social welfare, leisure, recreation and tourism, and transportation. There are links with Dortmund in Germany which provides the opportunity to establish comparisons.

Liverpool Urban Studies is offered as part of a Combined programme.

Liverpool John Moores (*Urban Studies*) The course includes studies of transport, urban design, urban processes and problems, the urban countryside, the pre-capitalist city, the city in Europe, urban philosophical issues and Britain's urban crisis.

London (UC) (*Town and Country Planning*) This subject is taken within the Faculty of Environmental Studies. It is based on the course-unit system and comprises studies involving architectural design, building production, environmental building technology, the history and theory of architecture, economics and management.

Luton Town Planning and Housing are offered with a wide range of subjects.

Manchester (*Town and Country Planning*) This four year BA course includes a one year course leading to the degree of Bachelor of Planning. The latter is recognised by the Royal Town Planning Institute, giving exemptions from their examinations.

Middlesex (*Urban and Commercial Development*) This broad course covers geography, sociology, politics and history.

Napier (*Planning and Development*) The course has a common first year with all other building subjects and, in Year 2, with Estate Management, offering the chance to transfer courses.

Newcastle (*Town Planning*) This is a five year course with one year of professional experience between the third and the fifth years. The course carries full exemption from the examinations of the Royal Town Planning Institute. This includes the 'year out' which counts towards professional practice.

North London (*Urban Studies*) This is an inter-faculty degree scheme, the majority of the programme being drawn from Environmental Science, Geography and Social Sciences. Urban Studies may be combined with other subjects in the modular degree scheme.

Nottingham (*Urban Planning and Management*) Design, economics and management form the basis of this course supported by studies in financial and management accountancy, planning, law and transport economics.

Oxford Brookes (*Planning Studies*) This is a three year full-time course followed by a one year Diploma in Planning course. The first five terms cover foundation studies in planning theory, history, site planning, transport, economics and law. In the last four terms students choose one major and one minor option from rural, regional, policy development, transport and design aspects of planning. The degree exempts from the final examinations of the RTPI, and partial exemptions are possible from RICS examinations.

Sheffield (*Urban Studies*) The three major subjects studied in Year 1 are urban studies, the design of urban areas and one of economics, social history, geography, politics or sociology and social policy. In the second and third years ten compulsory subjects are studied, and four options from within the Faculty of Architectural Studies, such as housing or comparative studies of urbanisation.

Sheffield Hallam (*Urban Studies*) The first year is partially in common with Urban Land Economics and Housing Studies, covering urban growth and change, economic, legal and social issues. Final year studies are in property and planning, urban housing issues, urban economic development and two options from a choice of fourteen.

South Bank (*Town Planning*) The four year course includes seminars, project work and field courses. Options in Year 4 include computing, transport, housing, urban design, rural land management, planning in the Third World and social planning. The course exempts from all RTPI and RICS and some Institute of Housing examinations.

Strathclyde (*Planning*) The first two years form a foundation course in social science, the environment and planning, and training is given in communication skills. There is a wide choice of options in the third and fourth years which make up the advanced course. In each year there is at least one week of field work. After graduation and two years' professional experience, chartered membership of the RTPI may be applied for.

Westminster (*Town Planning*) A preparation for a career in Town Planning, but also a wide ranging subject of general interest. The course covers planning, environmental design, social and economic policies and community studies.

- **Top research universities**
Sheffield, Glasgow, Cardiff, Bristol, Cambridge, Liverpool, Newcastle, Oxford Brookes, Sheffield Hallam, Aberdeen.

- **Colleges and Institutes of Higher Education offering degree courses**
Doncaster (Coll), Worcester (Coll).

- **Other courses to be considered**
Development studies, architecture, geography, housing, landscape architecture, sociology, politics, social administration and transport management.

VETERINARY SCIENCE

- **Special subject requirements:** 3 A-levels in mathematics/science subjects. Chemistry or physical science required.

- **Subject information:** These are very popular and academically demanding courses for which some work experience prior to application is obligatory. Every course has much the same content, but check with prospectuses for all courses.

Bristol (*Veterinary Medicine*) The first three years cover the pre-clinical stage and include the basic sciences (anatomy, biochemistry and physiology) with animal management, breeding and genetics. Years 4 and 5 are the clinical years and include veterinary medicine and surgery, pathology, public health and animal husbandry.

Cambridge (*Veterinary Medicine*) In the first and second years students read for Part IA and Part IB of the Medical Sciences Tripos with both parts including veterinary anatomy and veterinary physiology, pathology and pharmacology. Part II enables students to make a study of a single subject in depth such as applied biology, biochemistry, genetics, psychology and zoology. The three years which follow the pre-clinical course include 26 weeks' practical experience with a vet in practice.

Edinburgh (*Veterinary Medicine*) The curriculum falls into three inter-related main parts. The first (pre-clinical) covers the biology and chemistry of the animal body, the second (para-clinical studies) deals with the nature of disease, diagnosis and treatment. Students can interrupt their studies for a year to take an intercalated degree in Anatomy, Animal Nutrition, Biochemistry, Neuroscience, Pathological Sciences, Physiology or Physiological Sciences.

Glasgow (*Veterinary Science*) In the first two years (the pre-clinical period) studies cover anatomy, biochemistry, physiology and animal management. The third year (para-clinical subjects) studies cover pathology, bacteriology, virology, parasitology, animal husbandry and nutrition. The fourth and fifth years initially include lectures but are largely clinical with practical lessons in medicine, surgery and pathology. Applicants are expected to have spent time working on a dairy farm and working in a veterinary practice.

Liverpool (*Veterinary Science*) In Year 1 of the five year course the structure and development of the animal body is studied. Animal husbandry, management, disease processes and disease-producing organisms are studied in Years 2 and 3. In Years 4 and 5 subjects include drugs, their actions and uses, clinical pathology, food hygiene, preventive and clinical medicine, surgery and reproductive studies.

London (RVC) (*Veterinary Science*) Years 1 and 2 are the pre-clinical years which introduce such subjects as anatomy, physiology, animal management and husbandry. Years 3 to 5 (para-clinical) studies involve pathology, toxicology, animal husbandry and hygiene, and veterinary medicine. Twenty six weeks of vacation study takes place in a veterinary practice.

• **Top research universities**
Glasgow, Bristol, Edinburgh, London (RVC).

• **Other courses to be considered**
Agricultural sciences, animal sciences, biological sciences, medicine, pharmacology.

ZOOLOGY

• **Special subject requirements:** 2–3 A-levels in mathematics/science subjects at A and/or GCSE Grades A–C.

• **Subject information:** These courses have a biological science foundation and could cover animal ecology, marine and fisheries biology, animal population development and behaviour and on some courses wildlife management and fisheries. There is a shortage of applicants. Refer also to **Biological Sciences**.

Aberdeen (*Zoology*) Students may pursue a broad-based curriculum or specialise in selected areas over the four years of this course. Seven named specialist degrees within this subject area are also offered - animal ecology, environmental physiology, marine and fisheries biology, and parasitology.

Aberystwyth (*Zoology*) This course has a biological foundation. In Year 2, all students take a number of core units including freshwater biology, genetics, immunology, marine biology, and animal development and behaviour. In Year 3 students specialise in an area of their choice.

Bangor (*Applied Animal Biology*) Three courses are offered - Animal Biology, Applied Zoology and Zoology with Marine Zoology. All courses start with biology, biochemistry and soil science or chemistry. Year 2 includes animal biology, plus an appropriate accessory course, and Year 3 is devoted to the degree subject.

Belfast (*Zoology*) Courses begin at level 1 with the animal biology course which provides a broad introduction to all aspects of the subject. Students also usually take a course in environmental biology, plus other courses including biochemistry, geography and psychology. In level 2 other subjects are studied including marine biology, animal physiology and population biology.

Bristol (*Zoology*) In the first year students take zoology, botany and one other course. In Year 2 more zoology is studied with a further course, whilst in Year 3 zoology is studied throughout the year. The course offers considerable flexibility and opportunities to specialise in various aspects of zoology (physiological, ecological or behavioural). Transfers to Botany, Biology or joint courses at the end of Year 1.

Cambridge (*Natural Sciences*) Zoology can be studied as a component of Part II of the Natural Sciences course. (See **Chemistry**). Students can study animal biology, molecular cell biology, ecology, experimental psychology and physiology in the second year before specialising in zoology.

Cardiff (*Zoology*) After a foundation course in common with other biological sciences for Part I, students may take single, joint or general Honours degrees in Part II. For single Honours students the theme of the course is 'The animal in its environment' and studies the behaviour, physiology and ecology of animals and special topics on cell and marine biology.

Dundee (*Zoology*) See **Biology** for the course structure. A zoology emphasis begins in Year 3.

Durham (*Zoology*) The first year course includes genetics and molecular biology, vertebrate origins, evolution, locomotion and behaviour. At the end of the first year students may either continue with an Honours degree in Zoology (or joint Honours) or may take a degree in Biology, Molecular Biology and Biochemistry.

East Anglia (*Zoology*) Students wishing to delay a decision about subject specialisation - or take a broader course - apply in the first instance for Biological Science. Those taking Zoology choose topics selected from animal behaviour, fisheries biology and parasitology.

East London A course in Animal Biology is offered.

Edinburgh (*Zoology*) From the second year the department provides a course reviewing animal groups, their behaviour and their physiology. This is followed in Year 3 with four half-courses. The final year includes a series of four-week workshops on specialist topics.

Glasgow (*Zoology*) There is no Ordinary class in Zoology, an introduction to the subject being by way of the Ordinary Class in Biology. The Higher Ordinary course provides a survey of the animal kingdom followed by the third year course covering histology, insect, marine, and developmental biology, immunology and ecology. Special options are chosen by students in the final year. The Faculty of Science also offers named degrees in Animal Developmental Biology and Aquatic Bioscience.

Leeds (*Zoology*) In Year 1 zoology is concerned with invertebrates including population and evolutionary ecology. Most students also take a course in biochemistry and/or biophysics. In addition a wide choice of subsidiary subjects is also on offer. There are also degree courses in Applied Zoology and Biology, and several combined Honours courses.

Leicester Zoology is offered as part of the Biological Sciences programme.

Liverpool (*Zoology*) Zoology is one of the courses offered within the Life Sciences scheme. This is an integrated scheme providing flexibility and enabling students to cross disciplinary boundaries. Zoology courses include animal diversity, ecology, freshwater biology and animal behaviour.

Liverpool John Moores (*Applied Zoology*) The course explores the principles and applications of modern zoology and provides the options of specialising within a subject area, or taking a more general route.

London (Imp) (*Zoology*) See **Biology**.

London (QMW) (*Zoology*) All first year students in the School of Biological Sciences take a similar first year programme including genetics, biochemistry, animal physiology, ecology, microbiology, zoology and plant biology, plus two other science courses. They may then choose a broad-based biology degree course or specialise in one or two biological disciplines.

London (RH) (*Zoology*) This subject is offered along with biochemistry, botany, psychology and physiology as part of the Life Sciences programme. Teaching is divided into course units and at the end of the first year students may be allowed to revise their choices. Zoology may also be offered with Geology or Physiology.

London (UC) (*Zoology*) This provides for the study of animal biology. The first year is largely common with other life science programmes, students studying genes to organisms, cellular and molecular biology, microbiology and chemistry. In Years 2 and 3 it is possible to choose themes which emphasize either the whole organism approach or cell and molecular aspects. The degree includes practical classes and some field work.

Manchester (*Zoology*) This programme has a modular course structure which gives flexibility and easy transfer within the School of Biological Sciences. Final year modules can be chosen to reflect interests and career aspirations. Three year full-time and four year sandwich courses are offered. It is also possible to take zoology with a modern language.

Newcastle (*Zoology*) See **Biology** for details.

Nottingham (*Zoology*) In the first year students take courses in behaviour, ecology, parasitology, animal design and evolution. They also take another subject selected from biochemistry, chemistry, genetics, geology or psychology. Years 2 and 3 cover a wide range of optional subjects leading to the student's particular interests.

Oxford (*Zoology*) This is a modern and flexible course in which students take preliminary courses in biology, biological chemistry, genetics and ancillary subjects such as applied maths and environmental science. In Years 2 and 3 all aspects of the animal kingdom are covered, with optional courses in animal behaviour, neurobiology, ecology, entomology and genetics.

Reading (*Zoology*) Options in the first four terms include zoology, botany and chemistry, geology, microbiology, statistics, geography and psychology. (A study of these subjects also leads to other degree courses.) In Year 2 ecology, behaviour, genetics, statistics and computing are introduced. Applied Zoology is based on the application of the principles of population biology to the control of pests, wildlife management and fisheries. The Zoology course provides a flexible final year allowing students to specialise in a variety of options. There is a separate degree course in Animal Sciences.

St Andrews A course is offered in Animal Biology.

Sheffield (*Zoology*) In Year 1 students take either six units of the Biological Sciences course (including plant and animal biology and ecology), or biology plus two complementary subjects. Second year studies are divided between zoology (two thirds) and a subsidiary subject (one third) usually chosen from biochemistry, botany, genetics, geology, physiology or psychology. Zoology only is taken in Year 3.

Southampton (*Zoology*) Four degrees (Biology, Applied Biology, Botany and Zoology) all start from a common foundation of first year units. Half-unit courses in a range of biology, plant science and zoology topics occupy Year 2, and specialisation and options occupy Year 3.

Swansea (*Zoology*) This modular course allows for flexibility of study for students who are able to specialise in one or more areas of interest. For example, the student of zoology can take some units in genetics, microbiology and marine biology.

● **Other courses to be considered**
Animal sciences, biological sciences and biology.

BOOKLIST

Standard Reference Books

Compendium of Higher Education Butterworth-Heinemann Ltd, Linacre House, Jordan Hill, Oxford OX2 8DP. Published annually.

Handbook of Degree and Advanced Courses in Institutes of Higher Education Linneys ESL, 121 Newgate Lane, Mansfield, Notts NG18 2PA. A list of courses. Published annually.

The UCAS Handbook The Universities and Colleges Admissions System (UCAS), PO Box 28, Cheltenham, Glos GL50 3SA. Published annually.

University and College Entrance – The Official Guide Available from Sheed and Ward Ltd, 14 Coopers Row, London EC3N 2BH. The official list of all degree and diploma courses, giving details of average offers. Published annually.

The Scottish Universities Entrance Guide (for courses in the Scottish universities, obtainable from the Scottish Universities Council on Entrance, Kinnessburn, Kennedy Gardens, St Andrews, Fife).

Entrance Guide to Higher Education in Scotland COSHEP, St Andrews House, 141 West Nile Street, Glasgow G1 2RN.

Further Education Colleges in Scotland SFEU, University of Strathclyde, Jordanhill Campus, 76 South Brae Drive, Glasgow G13 1PP.

Other Books

Access to Higher Education – Courses Directory ECCTIS, Fulton House, Jessop Avenue, Cheltenham, Glos GL50 3SH.

Careers Encyclopaedia Cassell & Co Ltd, Villiers House, 41–47 Strand, London WC2N 5JE.

The Complete Degree Course Offers Brian Heap. Trotman and Company Ltd, 12 Hill Rise, Richmond, Surrey TW10 6UA.

Degree Course Vacancies (June/July 1996) Higher Education & Planning Service. 2 John Rushout Court, Northwick Park, Moreton-in-Marsh, GL56 9RJ. £6.95.

Discretionary Awards Survey and *Welfare Manual* (Both are published by the National Union of Students and can be consulted in Student Union offices in universities and colleges.)

Grants to Students DFEE, Sanctuary Buildings, Great Smith Street, London SW1P 5BT.

How to Complete Your UCAS Form Tony Higgins. Trotman and Company Ltd, 12 Hill Rise, Richmond, Surrey TW10 6UA.

Taking a Year Off Val Butcher. Trotman and Company Ltd, 12 Hill Rise, Richmond, Surrey TW10 6UA.

INDEX OF COURSES

GET IN WITH A GUIDE

Getting into higher education may be the toughest challenge you've yet faced. *MPW Guides* can help.

Written by experts with a wealth of experience, *MPW Guides* are set out in straightforward language. They give clear, practical advice to help you win a place on the course of your choice. You'll find *MPW Guides* in all good bookshops.

To get your *Guides* fast, phone 0181-332 2132 or send the coupon below.

MPW is the UK's leading group of independent sixth form colleges. We have over twenty years experience of guiding students through the application procedures for higher education and helping them gain the high grades they need. We cover a wide range of A-level and GCSE subjects in courses lasting from ten weeks (retakes) to two years. At our colleges in London, Birmingham, Bristol and Cambridge, we teach in small groups or individually.

MPW offers a unique blend of expert tuition, close supervision, study skills and exam technique. *If you would like more information about MPW, telephone us on 0171-584 8555.*

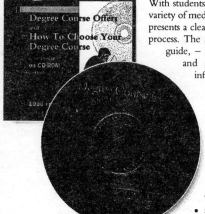